LUTHER COLLEGE · 1861–1961

LUTHER COLLEGE

1861–1961

by

DAVID T. NELSON

DECORAH, IOWA

LUTHER COLLEGE PRESS

1961

DEDICATION

*To the host of unnamed men and women
whose devotion to Luther College made possible
its past and assures its future*

LUTHER COLLEGE

*gratefully acknowledges the generous assistance of
Lutheran Brotherhood Life Insurance Society
toward the preparation and publishing
of this volume*

Foreword

The story of Luther College has been told, but never more completely or more objectively than in this volume. On the hundredth
anniversary of the college we are pleased to present what we
consider a definitive, an accurate, and a human chronicle: David
T. Nelson's history of our first century.

In a sense this history has been a long while in preparation.
On the occasion of the ninetieth anniversary a committee was
appointed to begin preparations for the centennial. The committee's first concern was to publish a history of the college's one
hundred years. Its second concern was to name the historian.
When Professor Nelson was designated, the project was on its
way. Besides being a Luther graduate, he is a distinguished
member of the faculty of forty years' standing and is head of
the Department of English. In the estimation of the committee
he was a logical choice.

Actually the history has been a century in preparation. Every
event and every character has had a part in developing the story.
Other histories have preceded this one. The first after twenty-
five years, the second after thirty-five years, the third after sixty
years all had writers who were contemporaries of the history
makers. This is also true of the writer of this book. He has been
closely identified with the college, as student and teacher, for
more than half the span of the history he has written, has had
personal acquaintance with early leaders, and has known all five
presidents.

He has succeeded in combining his first-hand information and
his research materials into a warm and living story. He has not
hesitated to tell of the dark as well as the bright side, of mis-

takes as well as successes. He has made the story very human. He writes about people, about a migration to a new land, about the beginning and growth of a church, with the result that this account of a church college moves with the events of history and with the people who had a part in them. The selection of material, the appreciation of significant events, and the author's sense of humor make this a readable book with a charm all its own. The history shows how a Christian college can bear witness to the relevance of the gospel of Christ to higher education in every age, and how the college has moved from pioneer days to our modern era without losing direction and without abandoning the principles for which it has stood.

Professor Nelson was appointed a Rhodes scholar immediately before World War I, but interrupted his studies at Oxford to work with the Commission for Relief in Belgium, to drive an ambulance in France, to function with the United States Army military intelligence, and, after the armistice, to serve with the American Mission to Negotiate Peace. He is a charter member of the Norwegian-American Historical Association and has been a vice president of it since October 1942.

David T. Nelson's publications include *The Diary of Elisabeth Koren* (1955), which he edited and translated, and an English version of Peer Strømme's *Halvor* (1960), in which the late Mrs. Inga Norstog was his collaborator.

It is hoped that *Luther College 1861–1961* will captivate the reader as completely as it has those of Professor Nelson's colleagues whose privilege it has been to be associated with him at the college and in this present project

J. W. YLVISAKER

LUTHER COLLEGE
DECORAH, IOWA

Preface

This history has been written primarily for students, former students, and friends of the college.

To many, especially those who have Norwegian blood in their veins, some of the introductory pages may seem superfluous. So also may some of the pages summarizing church movements among Norwegian Lutherans in this country. But one cannot escape the fact that the subject of this volume was established by Norwegian Lutherans who had migrated to this country and that without them no Norwegian Luther College would have been founded. This college is one of their great achievements. A little taste of the past of these men and women, perhaps enough to whet the appetite of the curious, may be forgiven.

The story of the origin of the college is today locked up in the Norwegian language, which for many years was the tongue used by the founding fathers. Except for those few in the present generation who study Norwegian seriously, the language is a closed book. Therefore the beginnings of the school have been treated at more length than would otherwise have been done. Some of that early history is a little tedious. But now, at any rate, it is told in English in some detail; perhaps in the future it will not need repeating.

There have been three earlier histories of the institution:

1. *Luther College* by Johan Th. Ylvisaker in both an English and a Norwegian version (Decorah, 1890), a charming account of many of the early aspects of the college.
2. *Det norske Luther College, 1861–1897* by Gisle C. J. Bothne (Decorah, 1897), a 472-page account in Norwegian, which he began in 1886. About one third of Bothne's history first ap-

peared as a series of articles in *Norden* (Chicago). The book contains a wealth of information concerning the early days of the college, the faculty, the courses of study, the students, student activities, the college's corporate form, its income and expenditures.

3. *Luther College through Sixty Years, 1861–1921* by the Luther College faculty under an editorial committee consisting of Olaf M. Norlie, Oscar A. Tingelstad, and Karl T. Jacobsen (Minneapolis, 1922). This is a 512-page volume with an almost appallingly large amount of statistical information—perhaps a bit tiring for the average reader, but a welcome mine of data for the student

It is hardly necessary to say that these three histories have been invaluable. Nevertheless, in the present volume the plan of telling the story in chronological order has made many demands and created many problems which the earlier historians did not face. Whether this method has advantages over theirs is another matter; it is at least different.

In the three earlier histories there has been a strange reticence, if not complete silence, about certain events in the college's history. Apparently these events were sacred cows that no one wanted to touch, much less discuss. Yet these same matters were discussed freely, and sometimes not too charitably, by those who disagreed with the founding fathers. It is time to drag the family skeletons out of the closet. Every family has them. They may as well be faced. They are far enough removed to permit some objectivity in discussing them. A chapter has been devoted to the first rebellion (what a high-sounding word!) at Luther College and to the far more difficult and tantalizing slavery controversy. These are now both skeletons of respectable antiquity. After rattling such bones around for a time, one feels that they are not horrendous enough to shake one's faith in one's ancestry. The family is still normal and sound.

What should one do with the slavery controversy—pretend it was not there, look the other way, and ignore it? That was one possible course. The only other was to tell the story in enough detail for the reader to form his own judgment. This is what has been attempted. The controversy is there; the documents are there; the official acts are there. They are all part of history. The men who had a part in it have all gone to their reward. No longer is there an emotional disturbance as they appear before the bar of history. We study; we reflect; we trust we may garner wisdom for the problems that inevitably will call for answers in our time or in the future. And we hope that eventually charity will spread its mantle over all.

One who spends any considerable time on the college's history is sure to form definite convictions about many aspects of it. There is always the temptation to voice such convictions. Nor is such a temptation easy to escape. But it has been my purpose to let people and events speak for themselves. The picture is one I have not felt called on to retouch or pretty up.

Nor does the college need any glossing over of its past. One is impressed by the high seriousness of those who planned and established it and by the devotion of all who rallied to its cause. Through all these years it has relied on the voluntary loyalty of its friends; only the compulsion of love has kept them faithful. And faithful they have been in evil days and good. If, after a century, the college appears to have surmounted its most difficult years, it owes a debt to the host of men and women who have not wavered in their loyalty. The memory of their devotion will always be warm to those who love the school.

The tasks that loom for a college "like this," as Laur. Larsen used to say of Luther, are still unfinished. They are vast and formidable. They confront each new generation. They challenge the best youth can offer. Luther College must be equal to the challenge. It must continue to confront its students with the problems of modern, different frontiers. "Youth should be awed," says Wordsworth. It should be awed with the greatness and goodness of God, before which all trivial matters sink into proper perspective. With *Soli Deo Gloria* its motto, Luther College can courageously and confidently explore and cultivate the new areas which beckon it forward to its second century.

* * *

I am well aware that I have not exhausted the sources for the history of the college. For example, the mass of archival material in Koren Library is largely unexplored. I dipped into it and found interesting items; but I soon decided that I would have to leave the evaluation of these materials to others, if I were to get out this volume in the time at my disposal.

I am deeply indebted to many individuals. I am grateful to President J. W. Ylvisaker for his patience, understanding, encouragement, and valuable suggestions during the preparation of the book, and to the other members of the Centennial Committee for their confidence in me. Without the encouragement of Theodore C. Blegen and Kenneth O. Bjork I might not have undertaken the task. A grant from the Lutheran Brotherhood Life Insurance Society enabled me to devote more time to the project than I could have otherwise.

The staff of Koren Library has been unfailingly helpful. My thanks go to Oivind M. Hovde, Vivian A. Peterson, Angeline Jacobson, Leona Alsaker, and Ingrid Julsrud, as well as their assistants. Karl T. Jacobsen aided me on many occasions. I called on Sigurd S. Reque innumerable times; his memory is a capacious storehouse of college lore. He read several of the chapters. N. Astrup Larsen and Karen Larsen read portions of the text and offered valuable suggestions. J. C. K. Preus and Walter A. Olson likewise read chapters of the text and gave me excellent criticism. The Minnesota Historical Society furnished a copy of the A. A. Veblen account of early days at Luther College. I have had the benefit of discussions with Marie Koren, J. A. O. Preus, Carl F. Granrud, E. Clifford Nelson, and Eugene L. Fevold. Sidney A. Rand made available to me the minutes of the Board of Education of the American Lutheran Church. Richard Beck of the University of North Dakota and Agnes M. Larson of St. Olaf College kindly responded to inquiries. Ernest W. Sihler of Luther Theological Seminary library furnished a copy of B. Hovde's letter of 1861 to Gullik Erdahl. The offices of the dean, registrar, and public services, and Mrs. Ralph M. Olson of the Norwegian-American Historical Museum were alert to every inquiry.

I have had the benefit of items of information and helpful comment from more individuals than I can name. Gerhard L. Belgum read the manuscript (likewise the proofs) and made many valuable suggestions. Orville M. Running furnished the basic design for the jacket. He also designed the college seal which graces the cover. Norlin E. Rober provided the map of Decorah. Augsburg Publishing House permitted me to use the map inside the front cover. John C. Bale, Oivind M. Hovde, Robert W. Jenson, David C. Johnson, and Leslie G. Rude kindly read proofs. Constance Dahl assisted in many little-known ways. Helen Thane Katz rendered valuable editorial services. My daughter, Elizabeth Seegmiller, typed the manuscript. My wife made a very considerable contribution to the undertaking. To all my sincere thanks. *Et haec olim meminisse juvabit.*

DAVID T. NELSON

LUTHER COLLEGE
JUNE 1, 1961

Contents

		PAGE
FOREWORD		vii
PREFACE		ix
I.	THE BACKGROUND	1
II.	TEN YEARS OF DISCUSSION	20
III.	GETTING STARTED	34
IV.	HALFWAY CREEK TO DECORAH	45
V.	THE FIRST MAIN BUILDING	61
VI.	REBELLION AND SLAVERY	75
VII.	THE EMERGING AMERICAN COLLEGE	89
VIII.	EARLY STUDENT LIFE	113
IX.	CRISIS AND RECOVERY	130
X.	CLOSE OF AN ERA	148
XI.	EXPANSION AND GROWTH	166
XII.	THE PIONEER PASSES	189
XIII.	MODERNIZING THE COLLEGE	210
XIV.	THE GATHERING STORM	231
XV.	STRUGGLE FOR SURVIVAL	251
XVI.	THE TRIUMPH OF COEDUCATION	270
XVII.	POSTWAR ADJUSTMENTS	286
XVIII.	PLANNING FOR GROWTH	303
XIX.	RAISING STANDARDS	318
XX.	A LAST WORD	342
APPENDIX		349
BIBLIOGRAPHICAL NOTES		373
FOOTNOTES		375
INDEX		403

Look to the rock from which
you were hewn, and to the quarry
from which you were digged.
—Isaiah 51:1

1

The Background

The story of the origin and development of Luther College can be understood only against the background of those forces which led thousands of Norwegians to leave Norway to establish homes in the American Midwest. Whatever changes one hundred years have wrought in the constituency of a now thoroughly Americanized educational institution, the pastors and laymen who founded Luther College a century ago were almost exclusively of Norwegian blood and ancestry. Most of the leading principles animating these founders have their roots in the heritage which the Norwegian brought with him. Therefore, a glance at the history of Norwegian immigration to the United States, and at the religious organizations formed among Norwegians in this country, is necessary.

One cannot claim as part of the story the discovery of North America by Leif Erikson, son of Erik the Red, in the year 1000. Nor the expedition under Captain Jens Munk which, searching for the Northwest Passage to Asia, entered Hudson Bay and wintered at the mouth of the Churchill River in 1619–20. Nor the fact that 57 Norwegians entered New York in the period 1630–74 and that possibly one fourth of the early immigration to the Dutch colony of New Amsterdam consisted of Norwegians. Nor the claim that a Norwegian child, John Vinje, who saw the light of day in 1614, was the first white child born in New York. Nor the fact

1

that Norwegians and Swedes settled here and there in this country in such numbers that prior to the Revolution a Scandinavian Society was organized, of which George Washington became a member in 1783. These are part of the history of Norwegians in the United States, but not of the Norwegian groups which settled so extensively in the Middle West during the nineteenth century.

The modern migration began in 1821 with the exploratory work of Cleng Peerson and Knud Olsen Eide of Tysvær parish north of Stavanger, Norway; their favorable reports led to the sailing of the sloop "Restoration" from Stavanger in 1825 with 52 persons aboard. (A child born during the voyage made the number 53.) These first immigrants have since been called the Sloopers. Upon arriving in New York, they proceeded westward to Orleans County, about 35 miles north of Rochester, where they formed the Kendall settlement. Later, most of those in Kendall moved to La Salle County, Illinois, about 70 miles southwest of Chicago, where they founded a second Norwegian colony, the Fox River settlement, in 1834.[1]

During the ten years following the voyage of the "Restoration," a number of individuals, singly or in very small parties, left Norway. In 1836 two large groups emigrated, and most of their 200 members went to the Fox River settlement in La Salle County, Illinois. The next year brought 170 immigrants, including Ole Rynning of Trondhjem, who led his people to the ill-fated Beaver Creek settlement in Iroquois County, Illinois. From this time the stream of immigration was fairly constant and, over the years, grew to large proportions.

In 1838 the first Norwegian, Ole Nattestad, entered Wisconsin Territory from the Fox River settlement. In 1839 the famous Muskego colony was founded about 20 miles southwest of Milwaukee. In the same year Nattestad induced others to follow him to Wisconsin, where settlements on Jefferson Prairie (south of Clinton) and Rock Prairie (west of Beloit and later known as Luther Valley) grew up. In 1840 the famous Koshkonong settlement was founded in southeastern Dane County, Wisconsin, about 25 miles from Madison.

These four well-known Midwestern settlements — Fox River, Muskego, Jefferson Prairie and Rock Prairie, and Koshkonong—became the immediate goal of several thousand Norwegian immigrants who poured into them, mainly through Chicago and Milwaukee, in the 1840's. Chicago, where Norwegians had settled as early as 1836, also gradually attracted a large Norwegian colony. The immigrants tended to spread out and spill over into lands adjacent to the original nuclei of the settlements so that by the end of the decade there were strong Norwegian groups in northern Illinois and southern Wisconsin. "Practically all the immigrants of the forties settled in either Wisconsin or Illinois."[2]

These early centers soon took on the character of mother settlements for scores of later ones in western Wisconsin, Iowa, Minnesota, and points beyond. Scouts usually went out in advance to explore the lands on the more remote frontier. When they had found areas that appealed to them, they returned to report, and usually in the following year a group would set out to pioneer a new colony farther west and north. Later the continuing flow of immigrants from the mother country would follow. This pattern was repeated again and again as Norwegians pushed into western Wisconsin, Iowa, Minnesota, and the Dakotas.

By 1850 there were about 2,500 persons of Norwegian stock in Illinois, 9,500 in Wisconsin, and 330 in Iowa. By 1860 there were 6,000 in Illinois, 29,500 in Wisconsin, 8,000 in Iowa, almost 12,000 in Minnesota, 300 in Texas, and almost 400 in Michigan. In succeeding decades the pace of migration to this country from Norway greatly accelerated; the Norwegians fanned out in a general northwesterly direction from the early settlements; and Minnesota, not Wisconsin, became the center of the heaviest Norwegian population. A surprisingly large number found their way to the Pacific coast, particularly the Pacific Northwest. The 1930 census found more than 1,100,000 persons of Norwegian birth or of Norwegian and mixed parentage in the United States. To this could be added at least 1,000,000 American-born persons of Norwegian ancestry.[3] Today there must be more than 5,000,000 people of Norwegian ancestry in the United States.

A document placed in the cornerstone of the first Main Building of Luther College stated that it was "emigrated Norwegians, Lutheran Christians, living in Wisconsin, Iowa, Minnesota and Illinois" who united in establishing Luther College.[4] The college was nurtured and sustained by these early immigrants, by many other Norwegians of the same faith who came later, and by their descendants. But in the course of years, as the Norwegians became a part of the blending of nationalities that makes up America, the constituency of the college has insensibly changed; today folk of many different origins are represented in its student body, among its alumni, and within its supporting church. Nevertheless, even after one hundred years, its strongest ties are to its Norwegian heritage.

The motives which animated those who emigrated to this country were mixed. They wanted greater religious and political freedom, a better economic status, and an improved position in society. The strong urge toward one or more of these goals led them to sever connections with their native land and set out to a new and strange world. In the later years of the great migratory movement, and perhaps to a very great extent earlier, the dominant motive was economic,

4

because by winning an improved economic status the immigrant won many other freedoms also. But of the specific factors affecting the establishment of Norwegian settlements in this country, "the common denominator was land-hunger; all the other factors were usually secondary to this all-pervading desire."[5]

Most of the Norwegians brought with them a heritage of Lutheranism, for in Norway the established church was Lutheran; even today approximately 96 per cent of the population belongs to it.[6] "In the nineteenth century the Church of Norway was an episcopally-organized Lutheran state church, enjoying virtually a monopolistic position, in which control was exercised by officialdom and in whose affairs the layman had little voice."[7] But Lutheranism is not static and in Norway during the first half of the nineteenth century tendencies were appearing which were to have their repercussions in America. One of the most important of these was the revival associated with the name of Hans Nielsen Hauge. His movement was not originally a separatist or dissenting one, and his followers were generally among the most faithful churchgoers. But because he was a layman and had not been ordained, he was harassed by state officials, including some of the clergy of the state church.[8] He was arrested, was adjudged guilty on several counts, was heavily fined and thrown into prison; released ten years later, he was an impoverished man, broken in health and unable to resume his great and unselfish religious work. He died in 1824.

Hauge's influence reached into every part of Norway. He stirred large numbers of the laity to deep religious fervor. Because Hauge was persecuted by the official classes, including some of the clergy of the state church, the laity in many localities developed a distrust, if not an open antipathy, to the pastors of the state church. Moreover, since in the first half of the century the state clergy were generally

5

aligned with the city population and the government officials in culture, language, and political outlook, they were
regarded with some distrust by landed proprietors and by
the rural folk who were seeking better economic and social
conditions. In general, Norwegian immigrants, up to 1840
and even later, brought with them a memory of a social
struggle in which they sided with the Haugeans against the
state church.

Yet within the ranks of the state church there were many
who had been touched by Hauge (including some of the
founders of Luther College), who recognized his sincerity
and piety, who resented the injustice of his treatment, and
who were led by his example to a re-examination of their
own faith and to a new understanding of evangelical Christianity. But they were a minority.

The Sloopers, who pioneered migration to the United
States in 1825, included not only several Haugeans, but a
leader who was a Quaker, and in all probability several
others of his sect.[9] Quakers and Haugeans had much in
common. But Quaker influence in the Fox River settlement
did not grow to great proportions. It was overshadowed by
the work of Elling Eielsen, the Lutheran lay preacher, and
by the steady influx of other Norwegian immigrants who
had been brought up in the Lutheran faith. Quakerism therefore touches the story of the development of Luther College
only in a peripheral way.

Very early there emerged two Lutheran church groups
among the immigrated Norwegians, one with a low-church
and one with a traditional church tendency: those who represented primarily the Haugean influence and those who
represented that of the established church of Norway. The
former stressed the role of the layman and favored a loose
synodical organization; the latter emphasized the role of
the trained orthodox clergyman and favored a strong, well-

6

defined synodical organization. It was the latter group, organized as the Norwegian Evangelical Lutheran Church in America (later known as the Norwegian Synod, or the Synod), which founded Luther College. Both had internal difficulties that caused certain elements to break away from them, although some of these cleavages were later healed. It may be helpful first to sketch the progress of the low-church element and then to consider the group which founded Luther College.

The strongest Lutheran leader in the Fox River settlement was Elling Eielsen. Deeply stirred by the Haugean movement in Norway, he immigrated in 1839, built a large log cabin (the second floor of which served as a meetinghouse), rallied the settlers to their old doctrines and brought most of the Fox River settlers within the Lutheran fold. In 1841 he traveled to New York to have *Luther's Small Catechism* printed; in 1842 he made a second trip, this time to obtain Pontoppidan's *Sandhed til gudfrygtighed* (Truth unto Godliness) and the Augsburg Confession, both in Norwegian. Because winter had set in and navigation on canals, lakes, and rivers had ceased, he trudged on foot from New York back to Fox River, a heavy knapsack, filled with books, strapped to his back. He was an earnest and uncompromising man, stubborn in his prejudices against the outward forms and practices of the state church, such as the use of clerical dress; more successful in his attacks upon the evils of society and in his calls to repentance than in his efforts to establish an organized church to carry forward the Christian message. He put "an almost indelible stamp of low-churchism upon the settlement," a stamp which was marked by an emphasis on the layman's role in the church, a strong leaning to the Haugean point of view, and a distrust of the Norwegian state church and its clergy, hence of the Norwegian Synod.[10]

7

Eielsen was ordained October 3, 1843, the first Norwegian Lutheran pastor ordained in the United States. In 1846, with pastors Ole Andrewson, Paul Anderson, and others, he organized the Evangelical Lutheran Church of America, commonly called the Eielsen Synod. In 1855–56 this synod conducted the Lisbon Seminary at Lisbon, Illinois, with Reverend Peter A. Rasmussen as teacher of its three students. Later, 1865–68, it operated the Eielsen Seminary at Cambridge, Wisconsin. Both these early schools are indicative of the need and demand for Christian schools in which prospective teachers of the Word might be trained.

As early as 1848 the Eielsen Synod experienced the first split in its ranks, when Paul Anderson and Ole Andrewson withdrew. In 1876 a second division occurred, the majority continuing the low-church Haugean tradition under the name of Hauge's Norwegian Evangelical Lutheran Synod (Hauge's Synod) until, in 1917, it became a part of the Norwegian Lutheran Church of America. What remains of the Eielsen Synod, its membership now a sparse one, continues an independent existence to this day.

When Paul Anderson and his associates withdrew from the Eielsen Synod in 1848, they passed a resolution to affiliate with the Franckean Synod of the Evangelical Lutheran Church in the State of New York. Although Anderson had been ordained by the latter, he and his associates later withdrew because of its loose confessionalism. Thereupon in September 1851 he and Reverend Lars P. Esbjörn, the first Swedish Lutheran pastor in the Middle West, joined with English-speaking Lutherans in the Evangelical Lutheran Synod of Northern Illinois, an affiliate of the General Synod of the Evangelical Lutheran Church in the United States of America. Only two Norwegian pastors were members of the Synod of Northern Illinois when it was formed in 1851, but later there were ten.[11]

In the 1840's and early 1850's there was an attempt to bring about closer relations, if not actual union, between Lutheran and Reformed groups. The movement was strongest among the older Lutheran groups of the eastern parts of the country; it met with vehement opposition from the Missouri Synod and the Buffalo Synod, both of which had left Germany only a decade or so earlier to escape a forced union with the Reformed church.[12] For a time Esbjörn and Anderson appear to have been attracted to the union idea as they found it in the Synod of Northern Illinois. By 1860, however, doctrinal differences between Esbjörn and the more liberal elements of that synod brought about an open breach, and Esbjörn led the Swedes and Norwegians, including Anderson, out of it.[13]

In June 1860 in Rock County, Wisconsin (the birthplace also of both the Eielsen Synod and the Norwegian Synod), Esbjörn and his associates met at Jefferson Prairie and formed the Scandinavian Evangelical Lutheran Augustana Synod of North America, which included both Swedes and Norwegians. This group established Augustana Seminary in Chicago that same year, with Esbjörn and Abraham Jacobson as teachers and 21 young men in attendance. The school was moved to Paxton, Illinois, 100 miles south of Chicago, in 1863, and was then called Augustana College and Seminary. It continued in Paxton until 1875.

In 1869 the Swedes and Norwegians decided to separate. The Swedes formed the Augustana Evangelical Lutheran Church, which supports Augustana College and Seminary, Rock Island, Illinois. The Norwegians formed the Norwegian-Danish Evangelical Lutheran Augustana Synod; they made arrangements to purchase the Marshall Academy buildings in Marshall, Wisconsin, and there in 1869 established Augsburg Seminary, the first Norwegian Lutheran theological seminary in this country, meanwhile agreeing

9

to maintain the academy. August Weenaas (who had come to America in 1868 and had taught at Paxton) and three assistant instructors had charge of 21 students, 11 in the seminary and 10 in the preparatory department.[14]

In 1868 Claus Lauritz Clausen withdrew from the Norwegian Synod over the slavery controversy. In 1870 he and several others met with members of the Norwegian-Danish Augustana Synod and adopted a constitution for a new church body. But in a matter of weeks a split occurred within its ranks. Two church organizations resulted: 1. The Conference for the Norwegian Danish Evangelical Lutheran Church in America (commonly referred to as the Conference, of which Clausen was a leading member) and 2. A smaller group later known as the Norwegian Augustana Synod. The former took over Augsburg Seminary and the latter Marshall Academy. The academy, which in 1869–70 had been largely non-Lutheran in character, continued a precarious existence until it was moved to Beloit, Iowa, in 1881. In 1884 it was moved to Canton, South Dakota, and in 1918 to Sioux Falls, South Dakota, where, after amalgamating with Lutheran Normal School, it has continued as Augustana College. Augsburg Seminary, which served the Conference, was moved to Minneapolis in 1872 and has remained there since.

The Eielsen and Augustana church groups in their early years did not have strong synodical organizations. But they represented low-church and "Americanizing" tendencies among the immigrated Norwegians and, as events shaped themselves, came to play an important part in the evolution of a unified Norwegian Lutheran church body.

The group that adhered most strongly to the tradition of the established church in Norway and that founded Luther College took form in Wisconsin. The second Lutheran pastor to be ordained among Norwegians in this country was

Claus Lauritz Clausen, mentioned above, a Dane who had gone to Norway as a young man and was to spend the remainder of his life in the service of immigrated Norwegians. From Norway he went directly to Muskego. There the prevailing religious sentiment was Haugean—the three leading settlers, Søren Bache, Johannes Johanneson, and Even Heg all being warm admirers of Hauge. In this country they had come into early contact with Eielsen. But apparently he had not appealed to them as a religious leader—very likely because of his intransigence even in minor religious matters. So they had turned to Norway for help. There Tollef Bache, Søren's father, was instrumental in inducing Clausen, who had come within the Haugean circle in Drammen, to migrate to Muskego as a teacher of religion. He arrived in 1843, was asked to become the pastor of the Muskego group of settlers, and was ordained October 18, 1843.

The following year he came under the influence of J. W. C. Dietrichson, the third pastor among Norwegian Lutherans in this country and the first to come from Norway. Dietrichson was a firm supporter of the principles and practices of the established church in Norway. He also demanded the respect due his authority in a way that could not fail to stir up opposition among hardy frontier spirits. Clausen, following Dietrichson's promptings, attempted to make a more formal organization of his congregation, but stirred up discord more than he promoted unity. Although a modified proposal was eventually accepted by many, dissension remained and some abstained from joining the congregation. A few years later, when an effort was made to form a synodical organization, the Muskego congregation took part in the deliberations but did not join. Suspicion and hostility toward what was feared to be an attempt to establish a state-church body in this country made the Muskego congregation maintain an independent existence for many years, even though it was served by several Norwegian Synod pastors.

To the west of Muskego were the two areas that became the most influential among the Norwegian groups in Wisconsin—the large colonies centering in Rock County and the even larger Koshkonong and other settlements in Dane County. These centers came to be the cradle of the Norwegian Synod and thus closely allied to Luther College. It was Koshkonong that Dietrichson chose as his headquarters during his work in this country. He stated that he came "to investigate the religious and church conditions among Norwegians resident there [America] and, by striving to organize congregations among them, possibly to lay the foundation for a permanent church establishment there."[15] Despite the normal prejudices of Dietrichson's class, a Grundtvigian influence opened his mind to the needs of the people, says one historian, and a Grundtvigian layman, Sørenson, a dyer in Christiania, provided funds for the mission.[16]

Dietrichson was the first of the "university men" (theological graduates of the university in Christiania) to come to this country. He migrated in 1844, preached his first sermon September 1 in Amund Anderson's barn in East Koshkonong, visited on horseback nearly all the other existing Norwegian communities, and on his return to Koshkonong proceeded to organize congregations. From Koshkonong he went to the Rock County settlements and with equal vigor established congregations there. He returned to Norway in 1845 to claim his bride, was back in Koshkonong in 1846, and continued his impressive organizational work despite the controversies in which he became involved. He returned to Norway for good in 1850. "He gives us," says one writer, "an almost perfect picture of the tradition of meticulous service and authoritarianism that possessed the office-holding class of Norway before its power was broken in the late nineteenth century."[17] His ecclesiastical career was a stormy one. Yet, for the most part, he was successful in establishing among Norwegian immigrants a pattern for congregational polity and in sketching the outline of a framework under which the scattered congregations might be united in a synod.[18] He represented state-church traditions and consequently was highly suspect to those of the laity who had Haugean backgrounds (such as those in Muskego); and he clashed head on with Elling Eielsen.

Dietrichson was followed by other university-trained men, none of them, fortunately, so authoritarian. The second was Hans A. Stub, who arrived in 1848 to serve the Muskego congregation. He, too, had been influenced by Grundtvig's championship of the common people, as well as by certain of his theological doctrines; he had felt the force of H. P. S. Schreuder's appeal to the Norwegian Missionary Society in 1842 and had thought of going out to Africa as a missionary. He passed his theological examinations in 1846, and in 1847 accepted a call to America to serve the Muskego congregation.

He was followed in 1850 by Adolph C. Preus, who was distantly related to J. W. C. Dietrichson by marriage, and in 1851 by Gustav F. Dietrichson (a brother-in-law of Preus), Herman Amberg Preus (cousin of A. C. Preus), and Nils O. Brandt, the latter two having been strongly influenced by J. W. C. Dietrichson in their decision to migrate. In 1852 their number was augmented by Jakob Aall Ottesen, likewise a university man, who became one of the formidable dialecticians of the Synod.

In 1851 a synodical organization was formed, with Clausen as superintendent; but because unacceptable Grundtvigian doctrine was incorporated in the constitution, the organization was declared in 1852 to be merely provisional. In October 1853, at Luther Valley, Wisconsin, after two preliminary meetings at which a constitution had been drafted and discussed point by point, the Norwegian Evangelical Lutheran Church in America was founded, with A. C. Preus as president. This is the church body which later came to be known as the Norwegian Synod or, the Synod, and which, a few years later, founded Luther College.

The university group in the Norwegian Synod was again augmented by the arrival of Ulrik Vilhelm Koren in December 1853, Olaus F. Duus in 1854, Johan Storm Munch in 1855, Peter M. Brodahl in 1856, and Fredrik C. Claussen and Peter Laurentius (Laur.) Larsen, who was later to become the president of Luther College, in 1857. To these should be added Nils E. S. Jensen, Claus F. Magelssen, and Bernt J. I. Muus, who migrated in 1859. These men had all been trained at the university in Christiania; thus the Norwegian Synod was almost wholly in the hands of university graduates. Of the 17 pastors who made up the group through 1859 (if J. W. C. Dietrichson is included) only one, Clausen, had not attended the university. They formed a homogeneous group, they had been rigorously trained in the mother country, they had broad cultural interests, they had enjoyed the standing and prestige which was the privilege of members of a university in Europe, and they belonged to, or had come to be associated with, the privileged class of officialdom in Norway, which for centuries had exercised authority. In this country they were inclined to look askance at the raw democracy of the frontier.

While the Norwegian Synod was formed and was gathering strength, however, there had also been 16 Norwegian Lutheran pastors laboring in other synodical organizations in this country. One of these died in 1853 and one left the ministry in 1856. Of the other 14, four were in the Eielsen Synod in 1859, eight were in the Synod of Northern Illinois and two had no synodical affiliation. Only one of them was

14

a university man from Norway. That there should be differences between the homogeneous group in the Synod and the more heterogeneous group of pastors outside the Synod was only to be expected.

The Norwegian Synod soon grew to be the largest and strongest of the Norwegian Lutheran church groups in the United States. It was a closely knit, well-organized and well-disciplined body. The first serious defection from its ranks occurred in 1868 when, as related earlier, Clausen and others withdrew. The next and by far more serious breach in what has been called the "monolithic" structure of the Norwegian Synod occurred in 1887 because of the election or predestination controversy. At that time about one third of the Synod's pastors and congregations broke away and formed the Anti-Missourian Brotherhood—a protest against the influence of the Missouri Synod upon the Norwegian Synod.

In 1890 the Anti-Missourian Brotherhood, the Norwegian Augustana Synod, and the Conference succeeded in reaching doctrinal unity and formed the United Norwegian Lutheran Church in America. But the peace of this new body was marred by a dispute over Augsburg College and Seminary. This led in 1893 to the withdrawal of a group which became the Lutheran Free Church and under that name still maintains a separate existence.

From very early days efforts were made to compose the differences which troubled Norwegian Lutherans in this country. But the divisive forces seemed greater than the unifying ones. In 1880, at a meeting of the Norwegian Synod, Peter A. Rasmussen made a temperate and moving appeal for peace and unity among Norwegian Lutherans. In 1887 Gjermund Hoyme made a powerful plea for the removal of obstacles to unity and peace. Although the latter appeal failed to bring peace to the Norwegian Synod, it opened the way for the formation of the United Norwegian Lutheran Church, mentioned above.

A subsequent series of efforts toward union was successful when in 1917 Hauge's Synod, the Norwegian Synod, and the United Norwegian Lutheran Church, having composed their doctrinal differences, formed the Norwegian Lutheran Church of America, thus bringing the majority of Norwegian Lutherans in this country together for a common church purpose. Luther College, which throughout the years from 1861 to 1917 had been the major college of the Norwegian Synod, now became one of the colleges of the new united church.

In 1946 the Norwegian Lutheran Church of America, in recognition of the changes taking place in its membership—the gradual Americanization of the original Norwegian stock and the intermingling with other national groups—and of the greater outreach of the church to all sectors of American society, dropped the designation that pointed to its national origin and changed its name to the Evangelical Lutheran Church. There is hope that at some future date other Lutheran groups of Norwegian origin may cast their lot with the larger body. They are: the Lutheran Free Church, mentioned above; the Norwegian Synod of the American Evangelical Lutheran Church (the "Little Synod"), organized in 1918 by a minority group of the Norwegian Synod that abstained from the merger of 1917; the Lutheran Brethren, a smaller group organized in 1900; and the Eielsen Synod.

In 1960 the Evangelical Lutheran Church merged with the American Lutheran Church (of German background) and the United Evangelical Lutheran Church (of Danish background) to form the American Lutheran Church. Luther College is now one of the nine four-year colleges affiliated with this church body.[19]

The picture today is vastly different from that of one

16

hundred years ago. Most of the problems which then faced the fledgling church have been solved. If the Synod, in the first three decades of its existence, grew to be the largest, strongest, and best organized of the Norwegian Lutheran church groups in this country, it owed its strength and growth mainly to an intelligent treatment of its problems. This chapter is not the place for a detailed discussion of them. But a glance at them has its value for understanding the role of Luther College.

A first major problem facing the church of the 1850's was that of devising a system of organization, government, and support for a "free" church. The pastors who founded the Norwegian Synod, with the sole exception of Clausen, had been brought up within the framework of the state church of Norway. There the church operated as a branch of the government, and revenues to maintain it were raised through taxation. Pastors and higher church officials were appointed by the state-church department. In this country no such arrangement of appointments could prevail. The church here was "free"; and being free, it had, furthermore, to be self-supporting.

The problem was not easy. The church organization became essentially democratic, with the congregation as the basic unit, with clerical and lay representation equally balanced in the synodical organization, with carefully kept records at both congregational and synodical levels.

To raise the funds needed to support pastors and to defray the costs of a church organization, there was an early tendency to assess individual congregational members in a legalistic manner, as taxes are levied by a government. It took time before transplanted emigrants could work out a system of freewill offerings suited to a "free" church.

Of great importance to the new church was the preservation of orthodox Lutheran doctrine. In adjusting a church

17

with a Norwegian Lutheran background to the American scene, there were unexpected difficulties because of pressures from varying religious beliefs, traditions, and customs in the communities where the immigrants settled. How far could the church go in adjusting to American conditions? At what point would it be necessary to draw a line in order to preserve the Lutheran heritage?

Very closely connected with this question was that of language. Should the church make a quick transition to English and attempt to indoctrinate its members in English? Or would it be necessary, because of the onrushing stream of Norwegian immigration, because of the heritage from the mother country, and because of the great cultural values bound up with the mother tongue, to preserve the idiom which for the immigrant was a "heart language" and to attempt to provide a gradual transition from his native tongue to English? For this knotty question there was no easy answer; in fact, national sentiment played so strong a role that the language question troubled the church for almost a century.

Last, but by no means least, was the problem of finding pastors to serve the new church. The church leaders soon discovered that they could not expect sufficient help from the mother country. Like the pioneers on the farms, they would have to depend on their own resources, and train pastors from among the youth of this land. The Norwegian Synod pastors, themselves equipped with excellent university theological preparation from Norway, were firmly convinced that the new church in this country should also have a thoroughly trained ministry. Even though the process of finding suitable young men, carrying them through the preparatory work necessary to fit them for advanced study, putting them through college, and then adding a three-year seminary course seemed intolerably long in the face of the urgent need, the Synod leaders did not waver. They made a few concessions to expediency, but never at the expense of their main objective—that of providing well-trained pastors and teachers for the transplanted church. The laymen supported their clerical leaders in striving toward this goal, but it is clear from the very start that the laymen felt strongly that attention should also be given to the need for a well-educated laity in the church. With this dual objective before them, then—a well-educated clergy and a well-educated laity—the early leaders of the Norwegian Synod proceeded to the establishment of Luther College.

When schools flourish, then things
go well and the church is secure.
—Martin Luther

2

Ten Years of Discussion

Increasing immigration from Norway made the problem of getting pastors and teachers for the settlers constantly more acute. As early as 1847 J. W. C. Dietrichson and C. L. Clausen considered the possibility of launching a Lutheran theological seminary. Clausen offered to guarantee a salary of $200 a year and provide an acreage for a trained man from Norway willing to undertake the task of organizing such an institution and giving instruction.[1]

During 1851–53, when the Norwegian Synod was taking form, a discussion was opened in *Maanedstidende* about the advisability of collaborating with the Joint Synod of Ohio and sending students to Capital University in Columbus, Ohio. Capital University, whose seminary opened in 1830, had established a college department in 1850, when William M. Reynolds was elected president. On November 4 and 5, 1851, Jenny Lind, the famous Swedish singer, gave two concerts in Columbus and was persuaded by Reynolds to contribute $1,500 toward the endowment of a Scandinavian theological professorship in the seminary. Until the professorship was established, the interest on the principal was to be used for the benefit of needy Scandinavian students.[2]

Reynolds reported this proposal to the group of pastors and congregations that eventually formed the Norwegian Synod. He suggested in his letter that the Norwegian group enter into closer relations with the Ohio Synod and support the Jenny Lind proposal. At the church meeting held in Muskego April 2, 1852, a committee was chosen to consider this matter. It recommended that a decision be delayed because the church group itself had as yet no formal authority, and because adequate information about the ecclesiastical polity of the Ohio Synod was lacking. It also suggested that funds be gathered to send two delegates to the next meeting of the Ohio Synod; this last measure was lost.[3]

The matter did not end there. Clausen was then editor of *Emigranten*. In June he referred editorially to the Jenny Lind gift and endorsed the proposal for a Scandinavian professorship.[4] He estimated that $7,000 to $8,000 would be needed to endow it, suggested that Norwegians might help raise the additional sums, and asked interested individuals to make subscriptions. An article contributed to *Emigranten* in August replied to Clausen, criticizing him for discussing the proposal without having adequate information about the Ohio Synod.[5]

In October a more detailed article in *Maanedstidende* voiced vigorous objection to the whole plan of co-operation with the Joint Synod of Ohio. The writer questioned whether the Ohio Synod had fully freed itself from unionistic influences and indicated that its system of licensing preachers was contrary to Article V of the Augsburg Confession. As to a Scandinavian professorship, the writer in *Maanedstidende* asked how one professor could accomplish all that was expected of him—at least four men were needed in the University of Christiania to do what one was expected to do here; he pointed out that Capital University trustees were not required to be Lutherans, and argued that the instruction was not clearly Lutheran. On this last point he quoted a criticism of the work at Capital made by Reverend J. A. A. Grabau of the Buffalo Synod, whose concluding words were, "Alas, how can the blessing of the Lord Jesus rest upon a

21

school where they give instruction in nineteen subjects but do not even include the catechism as the twentieth and last subject, and instead hold a 'literary entertainment'?" After this clinching argument, the writer went on to say that the training of pastors at Capital would lead to union with the Ohio group, and that the Norwegian Synod was still too weak for union with another body. The Synod would do better to come to an agreement on doctrine and then unite and support the university.[6]

In December A. C. Preus, president of the provisional synod, published in *Maanedstidende* a letter from "A Friend" which pointed out that the Ohio Synod recognized the same confessional writings as the Norwegian Synod; that union with the German Reformed church had been disposed of long ago and was no longer an issue; that, on licensing of preachers, Ohio did not share the Norwegian Synod's view— it held that its practice did not violate either Article V or Article XXIV of the Augsburg Confession (this point involved only church practice and not an article of faith); and that Grabau had not been fully informed concerning Capital University, its seminary and college, and their relation to its board of trustees. Preus then declared himself satisfied about Capital University, but he still did not agree with Ohio's policy of licensing pastors, especially with respect to the right of administering the Lord's Supper.[7]

In January 1853 Clausen again endorsed his earlier support of the professorship, urging that it was highly desirable, if not absolutely necessary, to get something done as promptly as possible so that "those of our youth who have the desire and ability can obtain the higher education needed for both civil and spiritual callings—in their mother tongue as well as in the English language." Everyone, he said, now agreed that provisions for advanced schooling for the young people were not ideal. What could and should be done to remedy the situation? He admitted that he had moved too fast in urging subscriptions for the Scandinavian professorship at Capital University; he upheld the Ohio Synod's orthodoxy and rejected Grabau's strictures as unfounded. He saw no danger in the project, but stated that he would now await action by the synod in the matter.[8]

In February 1853, at the synodical meeting in Koshkonong, Wisconsin, Clausen moved that two delegates be sent to the meeting of the Ohio Synod in Columbus, Ohio, and that they use the opportunity to make a closer study of Capital University. H. A. Preus countered with a motion that the Church Council make complete investigations and preparations for the possible establishment of a Scandinavian theological school in Wisconsin, with particular attention to an association with the state university there. A committee, elected to consider the two motions, was unanimously in favor of a Scandinavian theological institution; then it divided, four to two, in favor of considering an affiliation with the University of Wisconsin. The dual recommendation was thereupon put to vote and carried.[9] Thus Clausen's proposal was stranded.

The Norwegian Evangelical Church in America, generally known as the Norwegian Synod, was definitely established at Luther Valley, Wisconsin, October 3–7, 1853, by the formal adoption of a constitution which had been carefully worked out and revised at the two church meetings of 1852 and 1853. To this church body the temporary Church Council, which had been elected at the February 1853 meeting to deal with synodical matters until formal ratification took place, reported as follows:

"The Church Council elected at the last meeting was specially charged with the duty of making preliminary investigations of the most feasible and advantageous means of furthering the establishment of a higher school for Norwe-

gians in America—in particular, the establishment of a professorship in Norwegian language and literature; and in its
resolution the synod pointed to the university in Madison
as a suitable institution to which such a higher school might
be attached. In the almost eight months which have elapsed
since the synod met, this important matter has been the object of the Church Council's careful consideration. The council in this period has met three times—in May at Koshkonong, in June at Madison, and in September at Muskego. It
has conferred with the chancellor of the university concerning the attainment of our goal and has given him a proposal
for arranging the matter to serve the best interests of both
parties, the university and the Norwegian population; but,
we are sorry to say, it has not been possible in advance of
this meeting of the synod to have this plan brought before
the regents of the university for a decision. For, when the
latter met last September, their meeting was so short and
the items of business so many that it was impossible for
them to consider our proposal. The regents will not meet
again before January; our Church Council has therefore
withdrawn its proposal in order to bring it before the synod
now assembled and get its views in the matter before placing it again before the university board. The chancellor has
expressed his satisfaction with this procedure. Meanwhile,
since it appears that the realization of the plan first proposed will take some time, the Church Council will lay before the synod another plan by which the need for a higher
school for our people can be temporarily relieved."[10]

At a meeting of the Church Council June 4–5, 1855, in the
Spring Prairie parsonage, it was decided that, since hope of
co-operation with the University of Wisconsin seemed futile,
the council should confer before the next Synod meeting
to prepare concrete proposals.[11]

When the Synod met October 1–3, 1855, in the Spring Prairie church, Pastors Clausen, Brandt, and Koren, and laymen Erik Ellefsen of Big Canoe and Gunder Mandt of West Koshkonong were appointed to deal with the school question. Their report was as follows:

"Because the committee recognizes that for the moment it is beyond our church's resources to establish its own theological school, and regards it as inadvisable to establish such an institution in connection with a non-Lutheran university or college, and because of the urgent need of taking definite steps for the training of pastors for our church in this country, it unanimously presents the following proposal for action by the Synod:

"Three of the Synod's pastors shall be elected to go as delegates from our church to St. Louis, Missouri, and Columbus, Ohio, there to investigate conditions at the existing Lutheran universities, particularly with a view to the desirability of establishing a Scandinavian (theological) professorship in connection with one of them. It shall be the duty of these delegates to determine as soon as possible at what time such a journey can most profitably be undertaken; and, in that connection, to take into consideration, if possible, the time when such universities conduct their annual examinations; likewise, after the completion of their journey, to make a report to the Church Council, which the latter will then bring to the attention of the congregations."

In the discussion which followed, Gustav F. Dietrichson thought that the possibility of the Synod's erecting its own institution should be further investigated; in his own congregations, for example, about $1,600 had already been subscribed toward such a school. His were the influential Luther Valley congregations, where *Maanedstidende* and *Emigranten* were published, and where there was probably an underlying prejudice against anything German because of resentment over the Prussian treatment of Schleswig-Holstein in Denmark. But his suggestion was passed by.

H. A. Preus was ready to support the committee's proposal, provided it was amended to include the original plan for establishment by the church of an independent institution. Gustav F. Dietrichson, who had an eye for economy, moved that only two delegates be sent, not three. Knud J. Fleischer of Luther Valley, editor of *Emigranten,* urged that the delegates visit Buffalo, New York, too. With these three suggestions incorporated, the committee's recommendation was adopted.

H. A. Preus then made the following motion:

"In the event the chosen delegates should present a report indicating that it seems inadvisable to establish relations with any of the above German Lutheran universities, then the Church Council shall immediately make estimates of the funds needed for the establishment of a Norwegian Evangelical Lutheran school, present to the congregations a plan for founding such a school, and appeal for contributions toward a fund for that purpose." The motion was passed unanimously.[12] Nils O. Brandt and J. A. Ottesen were elected delegates to make the trip and report.

The Church Council met at the Koshkonong parsonage January 9, 1856, fixed upon the sum of $400 for expenses of two delegates, and directed that an appeal be made to all pastors and congregations for these funds; this was formally issued by A. C. Preus on January 31.[13]

There was not, however, unalloyed enthusiasm for the project, and *Emigranten* furnished a vehicle for opposition. The resistance was regarded so seriously that H. A. Preus felt called upon to reply. He issued a six-page defense of the Church Council's proposal to send two delegates. He stated that *Emigranten's* editors apparently believed that insufficient information about the matter had been made available to the laity. He defended the Synod's action, pleaded for unity, held out the advantages of the projected investigation, showed that the delegates could not take action binding the Synod, urged the advantages of better acquaintanceship with other Lutheran brethren, and asked for support of the plan.[14]

At a meeting of the Church Council May 20, 1856, in the Koshkonong parsonage, Brandt and Ottesen were requested to send in a plan for their journey as soon as possible; and all pastors and congregations were asked to gather contributions to defray the expenses.

On February 11, 1857, the Church Council met at the Koshkonong parsonage and approved the plan of the two delegates for their journey, but asked that they also get information about each institution concerning the number of teachers at the theological seminary; student expenses; stipends for students and student aid; whether teachers in the university were teachers in the theological seminary and vice versa; what funds had been required to establish the institutions and how these had been procured; and how the various institutions were governed and what were their reciprocal relations. The council then gave assurances to the Luther Valley, Jefferson Prairie, and Long Prairie congregations that final decisions about the proposed educational institution would be taken at the next Synod meeting, and urged them, on this basis, to contribute to the cost of the investigative journey.[15]

The money came in slowly and not too generously. The delegates went on their quest in the early summer of 1857. As of August 1857, A. C. Preus reported that expenses had amounted to $300 and that there was a deficit of $88.30, of which he had advanced $33.30 and Pastor Brandt $55.00.[16]

Brandt and Ottesen made their inspection trip in June 1857 and their report, dated August 1857, was presented to

27

the Church Council. Nine pages were devoted to St. Louis and the Missouri Synod, two pages to Columbus and the Joint Synod of Ohio, and not quite two pages to Buffalo and the Buffalo Synod.

In the Missouri Synod the two pastors found a church body which based its doctrine and church practices on "old-Lutheran principles" and was devoted to "pure and genuine Lutheranism." There were no divergent theological tendencies among its pastors and teachers; all were animated by a "burning zeal" to follow established doctrine. The delegates were impressed by the warmth and fervor of the Missourians. A new building for Concordia Seminary in St. Louis had cost $25,000. There were three professors and two instructors, paid by voluntary contributions from the congregations. Instruction was thorough, old-Lutheran theology was stressed, and the original languages of the Scriptures were studied. The Missouri Synod had upwards of 200 pastors and twice as many schoolteachers. It met every third year, the four districts once a year; within the districts there were smaller meetings at frequent intervals. The delegates also visited Fort Wayne Seminary, where pastors were trained without the same stress on languages, and where teachers, too, were trained. Students intending to study theology paid no tuition. Among the Missourians the delegates noted the use of old Lutheran hymns, the chanting at the altar, the lighted candles at communion, the intercession for the sick, the proclamation of marriage banns in church, and the use of formal ministerial garb. They dwelt at length upon church discipline among the Missourians.[17]

They thought a certain vagueness and indecision characterized the Joint Synod of Ohio but felt that this synod was approaching a sound Lutheranism. At Capital University a couple of teachers had resigned and no replacements had yet been found, although Professor Adolph F. T. Biewend of Concordia Seminary had been called to become president. In college classes English was generally used, English and German in the seminary. The university had a large and imposing building. Classes were given in Latin, Greek, German, world history, Bible history, the sciences (such as chemistry, astronomy, physics, and anatomy), and in philosophy and mathematics. The Ohio Synod was in process of transition to the English language. The Jenny Lind proposal was passed over in one sentence.[18]

In Buffalo the pastors visited Martin Luther College of the Buffalo Synod. Grabau, who had led his people to this country, was president, and also the local pastor; he taught five to six hours a week at the school. Two other teachers assisted him. The studies were the usual classical ones; future pastors and teachers were instructed here. The synod exercised strong church discipline. The delegates deplored the Buffalo Synod's conflict with the Missouri Synod and its unwillingness or inability to unite with the latter. They regarded some of its tenets as not strictly orthodox and concluded that the Buffalo Synod's organization was more hierarchal than the democratic regime of Missouri.[19]

When the Church Council met on September 30, 1857, it thanked the two delegates but deplored the fact that they had not given more information concerning the costs of establishing these German schools. Upon a motion by H. A. Preus, the Church Council proposed that the following resolution be adopted by the Synod: 1. That the Synod send its young men to Concordia at St. Louis; 2. That efforts be made to establish a Norwegian professorship at St. Louis, the expense to be paid from interest on funds to be gathered immediately for founding a Norwegian Lutheran institution; 3. That as soon as adequate funds were available, a Norwegian Lutheran institution be founded and the Norwegian Lutheran professorship transferred to it.[20]

29

The report of the two delegates had left no doubt as to which course they favored. H. A. Preus's motion put the matter into concrete form. The Missouri Synod was flourishing, whereas both the Joint Ohio and the Buffalo synods were suffering from internal struggles. Concordia Seminary in St. Louis and Fort Wayne Seminary were both aggressive and growing institutions. Martin Luther College at Buffalo, on the other hand, could hardly be said to be prospering, and Capital University was going through a crisis.[21]

The meeting of the Synod at which the report of the delegates and the proposal of the Church Council were to be acted upon was held in October 1857 in the Washington Prairie Church, six miles southeast of Decorah (Iowa), Ulrik Vilhelm Koren's pastorate since Christmas, 1853. Previous meetings of the young church body had been held in established areas in Wisconsin—at Muskego, Luther Valley (near Beloit), Koshkonong, and Spring Prairie in Dane County. But new settlements had been springing up west and north of the older ones in Wisconsin, and large Norwegian colonies had by this time been formed west of the Mississippi. Now a meeting was to be held west of the Mississippi. In a way that could not fail to be noticed, the church was giving recognition to the newer areas, and this gesture called attention to its major problem. The synodical body was growing; vast mission fields were opening up; yet the man power of the Synod was increasing at only a snail's pace. It was clear to the young and energetic men who were planning the expansion of the church in the New World that the time had come for measures suitable to the magnitude of the task.

The proposal of the Church Council was made the primary business of the convention. The committee considering it stated that adoption of the plan by the church would gain the triple advantage of assuring ministers in the immediate future; of acquiring insight and experience for the establishment of its own school; and of growing and increasing in both Christian and churchly understanding and power through association with a synod tried in church conflicts and grounded upon a genuine Lutheran foundation. It therefore moved the adoption of the following resolution:

"The Synod resolves to establish its own Norwegian Lutheran institution of learning and calls upon the congregations and their pastors to make an all-out effort for the attainment of this objective by immediately gathering the needed funds. Pending further decision by the Synod, a suitable portion of the interest on the fund so gathered shall be used to establish a Norwegian theological professorship at the St. Louis university, with the understanding that the professor appointed shall be a member of our synod, shall participate in the synodical meetings and pastoral conferences of our church body, and during school vacations shall, so far as possible, visit our Norwegian Lutheran congregations. Likewise, from the interest on that fund, an amount, the size of which the Church Council shall determine, shall be used, after the appointment to the professorship has been assured, to aid young men desiring to prepare themselves at the university for the ministry of our church. The Synod shall elect a treasurer whose duty it shall be, under the supervision of the Church Council, to account for the funds and give security therefor. When an adequate fund has been gathered and the church's need requires it, the professorship shall be transferred to the new Norwegian Lutheran educational institution which is to be established among us.[22]

"Meanwhile, if before that time circumstances should so change that it might seem preferable to promote a union with the Missouri Synod and not to establish our own institution, the fund gathered shall be used for the extension of the selected German Lutheran institution. In either event, whether our own institution is established or a union with

31

the Missouri Synod is preferred, those in the minority may ask to have their contributions returned to them."[23]

After relatively brief discussion and debate the recommendation was unanimously adopted. Ottesen, secretary of the convention, then wrote, "To the joy of all, this matter was thus brought to a conclusion, and our one wish and prayer to God was simply this, that by his grace he would guide us all to a right loyalty and zeal toward this undertaking, which for us and for our children must surely be called the most significant one that our young church has had to deal with."[24]

The meeting at which this historic decision was taken was attended by 7 pastors and 29 lay delegates, representing 18 congregations. The 7 pastors, with their ages, were: A. C. Preus (43), H. A. Preus (32), H. A. Stub (35), G. F. Dietrichson (44), J. A. Ottesen (32), U. V. Koren (31), and Johan Storm Munch (30). N. Brandt (33) and Olaus F. Duus (33) had sent their excuses.

In the course of the discussions Knud Langeland, Norwegian-American newspaper editor, who was a lay delegate, offered to subscribe $100 toward the University Fund if 500 others would do likewise. Later Johannes Evenson of the Little Iowa congregation, perhaps thinking it might be difficult to find 500 to give $100 each, offered to give $100 if 250 others would do likewise.[25]

Although the convention threw cold water on a suggestion to train parochial school teachers for ordination as a means of coping with the great shortage of ministers, it gave qualified, but hardly enthusiastic, approval to part of the proposal. It was likewise lukewarm to an offer from the Scandinavian Press Association, then publishing *Emigranten*, for the use of its building at Inmansville, Wisconsin, as a seminary. *Emigranten* had been moved from Inmansville to Madison, and Knud J. Fleischer was succeeded as editor by Carl F. Solberg. A committee stated that an attempt at that time to establish a seminary for training schoolteachers for the ministry might well jeopardize the university project. Therefore, by unanimous vote, the offer was turned down with thanks.

Ottesen was designated to attend the Missouri Synod meeting at Fort Wayne, Indiana, to inform it of the Synod's decisions and to request the necessary steps for implementing the decisions. Koren was to accompany him. Other details of the general resolution were made the responsibility of the Church Council.[26]

Thus it was finally decided to establish an institution of learning by and among the Norwegian people in America. The action was taken Saturday, October 10, 1857, and this date may well be considered the founding date of Luther College. It was on this day, too, that it was resolved to use, temporarily, the facilities of the Missouri Synod at Concordia Seminary in St. Louis, and to appoint a professor to the staff there.[27]

*We can take magistrates and
princes as we find them, but not
schools, for schools rule the world.*
—Martin Luther

3

Getting Started

A sentence in the Synod resolution of 1857 hinted of future union with Missouri and joint support of Concordia College rather than the establishment of a separate institution by the Norwegians. This statement evidenced the enthusiasm of the pastors themselves for the Missouri brethren; the sentiment of the lay rank and file was sturdily independent. It was strong, if not vocal; and the pastors defensively, perhaps grudgingly, recognized it by the provision that if the proposed Norwegian institution did not materialize, subscribers to the fund could request the return of their donations.

Later developments have raised many questions as to the wisdom of the alliance with the Missouri Synod and of its effects on the development of Luther College. In the light of conditions in 1857 the decision seems a logical one. At that time the Joint Ohio Synod struck the orthodox Norwegian Synod as too liberal. The Buffalo Synod and its college were too much dominated by Grabau and were hardly making great progress. Moreover, Buffalo, the seat of the college, was too far from the Midwest. The Joint Synod of Ohio was having internal difficulties, but presented no real doctrinal problems; in fact, it was moving toward, rather than away from, the Missouri Synod and the Norwegian Synod, and later, in 1870, it gave an initial impulse to the formation of the Synodical Conference.[1] But at that time its school, Capital University, was going through a severe crisis.

President Reynolds left in 1854. President Spielmann resigned in 1857. Enrollment had dropped to less than 40 in all
departments. Professor Lehmann, who as president, 1857–80,
rescued the university and established it on a firm basis, was
not elected until July 1857, shortly after the visit of the
Norwegian Synod delegates.[2] The Missouri Synod, by contrast, was strongly unified and free from internal strife, its
early difficulties had been overcome, its Lutheranism was
conservative, its educational institutions at St. Louis and
Fort Wayne were expanding, it had embarked on a dynamic
growth that continues to this day. Led by a number of able
men, headed by C. F. W. Walther, it appealed strongly to
the university men who made up the pastorate of the Norwegian Synod.[3]

The Church Council, carrying out instructions of the convention of October 1857, sent a call to Norway to Oluf
Andreas Aabel (1825–95) to become the Synod's professor
at Concordia Seminary, but he twice declined. These negotiations resulted in a year's delay in filling the post. Although
Aabel did not accept, his background gives a clue to the
views of the founders. His father, Peter Pavels Aabel (1795–
1869), was educated under Lyder Sagen and became a
strong champion of popular education, an interest shared
by Hartvig Nissen of Nissen's Latin and Science School. The
elder Aabel wanted an awakening in the church and "was a
bitter opponent of the prevailing legalistic-formalistic administration of the state church and a warm supporter of
the new movement for the emancipation of the church." His
son, nurtured in this atmosphere, completed the theological
course at the university in Christiania and in 1848 became
headmaster of the public school founded by his father at
Land. In 1852 he became a teacher at Nissen's Latin and
Science School in Christiania; from 1851–54 he was a lecturer
in theology at the university. In 1852 he published a transla-

tion into Norwegian of G. B. Winer's "New Testament Grammar" and in 1855 prepared for advanced students at Nissen's School an "Outline of What a Christian Believes."[4] His health may have been a factor in his rejection of the post in St. Louis. Clearly, in background, training, and teaching, he was in touch with the progressive educational and religious movements in Norway. The founding fathers of Luther College evidently wanted the leader of their school to be abreast of the times.

A later report from Pastor Bruun in Christiania informed the Church Council that there appeared to be no hope of getting a man in Norway for the professorship. Meanwhile, Laur. Larsen had arrived from Norway in 1857 soon after the historic Synod meeting at Washington Prairie. He went to Rush River, Pierce County, Wisconsin, not far from Baldwin. Born in 1833, he was from seven to eleven years younger than his associate pastors in the Norwegian Synod. His father was Herman Larsen, an army officer; his mother, Ellen Else Marie Oftedahl, was the daughter of a member of the Eidsvold National Assembly of 1814. At the age of nine he entered the Kristiansand Cathedral School, where he had a high scholastic ranking. The eight-year course included, besides his mother tongue, Greek, Latin, German, French, Hebrew, religion, history, geography, arithmetic, penmanship, and geometry. He later said: "At school we studied, and in our free time we played. By concentrating our strength on our studies, and not scattering our efforts in too many branches, we acquired a thorough knowledge in the subjects we studied." There was no natural science course in the curriculum, a defect common enough in the schools of the day, although a newer tendency was making itself felt. An abiding influence during Larsen's school days was that of Christian Thistedahl, one of Norway's foremost Hebrew scholars, who later was among those engaged to translate the Old Testament. He was a thorough, up-to-date and pious teacher who for two and a half years guided Larsen's studies and turned his mind to the ministry. In 1850, after Larsen had been at the university in Christiania for five months, his health broke down and he spent the next six months as a tutor in Dean Peter Frederik Bassøe's home in Raade near Moss. There he encountered a warm evangelical Christian influence similar to that of Thistedahl.[5]

In 1851 Larsen resumed his studies at the university, supporting himself in part by tutoring and teaching. The two teachers who most influenced him when he began his theological studies in 1852 were Professors Gisle Johnson and Carl Paul Caspari—notably the latter, who joined the theological faculty in the late forties. "Through their influence, the last remnant of rationalism disappeared, and a new interest in theological matters was awakened in university circles. Both men were striking personalities and bold, original thinkers. Both were scholarly theologians, orthodox Lutherans in their confession, and at the same time very simple in their faith."[6] There was also an element of Puritanism about Gisle Johnson, and he had a manner of ascribing to those who did not conform to his views a lack of awareness of their Christian duty. This tendency, if not prominently present in Larsen and in others trained under Johnson, nevertheless cropped out among the Synod leaders in this country in a way that irritated their opponents. When this specific attitude was later reinforced by the Missouri "pure doctrine" motif, the reaction from theological antagonists was sometimes violent—a response almost incomprehensible to the Synod men.

Larsen taught for a year (1853–54) in Bergen, then returned to Christiania, and passed his final examinations in 1855. On July 23, 1855, he was married to Karen Neuberg.

37

During the two years the couple lived in Christiania, Larsen supported the family by teaching and tutoring. In 1857 he decided to accept a call to America and in September set sail for his new home. He took up his pastoral work in November. In addition to building up a pioneer congregation in Rush River, he made long missionary journeys into neighboring parts of Wisconsin and into Minnesota, visiting the Norwegian settlements that were springing up to the north, south, and west of St. Paul.

In October 1858 he took part in the pastoral conference at Rock Prairie, Wisconsin. To the March–April 1859 issue of *Kirkelig maanedstidende* he contributed a nine-page article on "Scandinavian-Lutheran Congregations" which could hardly have failed to attract the attention of the Synod leaders. Disappointed in their efforts to get a man from Norway for the Concordia post, they decided they had one of the right timber among their own number. It was not surprising, therefore, that on March 28, 1859, the Church Council issued a call to Larsen to take over the Norwegian Lutheran professorship at Concordia Seminary, St. Louis.[7] After a pastoral conference had unanimously urged him to take the post and matters had been satisfactorily arranged with his congregation at Rush River, Larsen accepted the call, stating that he would begin his new duties January 1, 1860. He was to have a salary of $1,000 a year plus $150 travel pay.

At the urging of the pastoral conference, however, Larsen hastened his departure from Rush River, attended the Synod meeting in Coon Prairie, Wisconsin, October 14–19, 1859, proceeded from there to St. Louis, and entered upon his duties November 14, 1859. In March 1860 the Church Council decided that his pay should date from October 14, 1859, on which day he had relinquished his call in Pierce County. October 14 was thus the official date of the beginning of his work at St. Louis; in the course of years it came to be regarded as the anniversary date of the beginning of Luther College and is now known as Founders Day.[8]

In accord with the developments that followed the resolution of October 1857, three Norwegian students found their way to Concordia College and Seminary in August 1858: Torger A. Torgerson of Waupaca, Wisconsin; Jacob D. Jacobsen (Ballestad) of Pine Lake, Wisconsin; and Lars Samsonsen (Fosse) of Spring Prairie, Wisconsin.[9] In 1859–60, five additional students joined the original three at Concordia. The eight students present that year ranged in age from 14 to 22 and were classified as members of Sexta (junior year in high school), Quinta (senior year in high school), and Quarta (freshman year in college). Larsen, in a careful and detailed report, pointed out that with one exception the Norwegian students were older than other students at the institution and that, although they were working earnestly, they were beyond the best stage for learning the subjects stressed at Concordia, especially the languages. He urged that younger students be sent. He stressed the difficulties of coping with German and urged all prospective students to acquire some familiarity with that language before entering.[10]

In the school year 1860–61, twelve Norwegian students were enrolled at Concordia College and Seminary (St. Louis) and three at Concordia College and Seminary (Fort Wayne). When the college in St. Louis closed in 1861 because of the outbreak of the Civil War, the work of the college division was moved to Fort Wayne, Indiana, although the "theoretical" seminary (stressing the ancient languages) remained in St. Louis. At the same time the "practical" seminary, which had been conducted at Fort Wayne, was transferred to St. Louis.[11]

Although Larsen's work in St. Louis and the growing number of students promised eventually to provide additional pastors to carry on the work of the Synod (the first three were ordained in 1863), it was only too clear that the young church was facing a crisis. There were only 12 pastors in the Synod at the 1859 meeting at Coon Prairie, Wisconsin, but there were 48 congregations. Moreover, immigration was continuing at a rapid pace and large new settlements, which needed pastors, were growing up. The clergymen in the Synod were almost overwhelmed by the urgency of the situation. They felt they must have aid from the mother country.

At a pastoral conference in Black Earth, Dane County, Wisconsin, July 5–11, 1860, it was unanimously resolved to send a representative to Norway to plead for help, and it was also decided to ask Larsen to go. This action was confirmed by the Church Council. At the same conference all pastors present signed an appeal "To Our Brothers in the Evangelical Lutheran Church in Norway, Particularly to Its Pastors and Theological Candidates," calling attention to the great spiritual need of the emigrated Norwegians, announcing the impending visit of Professor Larsen, and asking that he be given a hearing. The appeal was not in all respects felicitously worded; it contained several strictures more likely to deter than to attract.[12]

Larsen, in obedience to this duty laid upon him, interrupted his work at Concordia and sailed for Norway September 15, 1860. There he delivered a number of lectures, held many conferences, and wrote several articles for the newspapers, including one which summarized the contents of his lectures. He made an uncompromising demand, in the name of duty, that theological candidates go to America because of the great need for pastors among the emigrated Norwegians. In 1857, he said, there had been about 300 candidates in Norway without clerical appointments, many of whom would have to wait 40 to 50 years for offices. Could such candidates with good conscience turn a deaf ear to the call from America? Was it proper for them, for example, to

EARLY NORWEGIAN SYNOD STUDENTS AT MISSOURI SYNOD INSTITUTIONS

Name	Home Address	Conc. Coll. St. Louis	Conc. Sem. St. Louis	Conc. Sem. Fort Wayne	Conc. Coll. Fort Wayne	Luther College
1. Knut W. Aslaksen	Koshkonong, Wis.	1860–61				1861–63
2. Knut E. Bergh	Big Canoe, Iowa	1860–61				1861, 1864
3. Nils J. Eide	Big Canoe, Iowa	1860–61				1861
4. Jacob F. Fleischer	Madison, Wis.	1859–61				
5. John A. Fleischer	Madison, Wis.	1860–61				
6. Lars E. Folkestad	Bonnet Prairie, Wis.	1859–61				1861
7. Ole J. K. Hagestad*	Koshkonong, Wis.	1859–60	1861–63	1860–61		
8. Brynjolf Hovde*	Spring Prairie, Wis.	1860–61	1865–68		1862–65	1861–62
9. Jacob D. Jacobsen*	Pine Lake, Wis.	1858–61	1867–70		1861–62 1865–67	1864–65
10. Thomas Johnson*	Spring Grove, Minn.	1859–60	1861–63	1860–61		
11. Ole Juul*	Koshkonong, Wis.	1860–61	1861–64			
12. Iver Larsen	Big Canoe, Iowa	1859–61				1861–62
13. Amund Mikkelsen*	Rock River, Wis.	1860–61	1861–63	1860–61		
14. Styrk S. Reque*	Deerfield, Wis.	1858–60	1862–65			
15. Lars Samsonsen	Norway Grove, Wis.	1858–60				
16. Torger A. Torgerson*	Waupaca, Wis.	1858–61	1862–65		1861–62	

*Later ordained as pastor in the Norwegian Synod.

teach school when there was so great a need for pastors in the New World? Would they not be able to save more souls by going to America than by remaining at home in Norway?[13]

Larsen's blunt challenge created an issue and stirred up controversy. Upon his return to this country he reported that the pastors' "Appeal" had been called "improper" by *Morgenbladet* (Christiania), which stated that it did not devolve on the Synod to define the "duty" of Norwegian theological candidates. Larsen also said that in Norway "they feared that all was not quite well with our doctrine." Later, in a sharply argumentative article dated at St. Louis, April 10, 1861, which he sent to *Norsk kirketidende* (Christiania), Larsen defended his own and the Synod's doctrine, denied that the Synod men were dominated by the Missouri theologians, and argued that in this country they had gone back to Luther and the Bible as a foundation for their position. There was no mention in Larsen's articles of his stand on the theological aspects of slavery, but another source stated that he had expounded his views privately in Norway and that these had given rise to considerable serious questioning.[14]

No great immediate results followed the "Appeal" and Larsen's efforts. Larsen himself was bitterly disappointed. Nor did later visits abroad by Stub, Koren, Muus, and Ottesen "bring more obvious results." Nevertheless, over the years a larger number than might have been expected came to this country to enter the service of the church.[15]

Failure to obtain help from the mother country was not unique. Other national groups had the same experience. For at least three centuries Europe was inclined, on the whole, to look down its nose at its kinsmen in America. The Puritans and Harvard College met with somewhat similar disappointments.[16]

Nor was the controversy that Larsen stirred merely the result of a few lectures; rather, these were the sparks that ignited the tinder lying around. Just as in the United States the Synod was the object of attack from the day of its founding, so in Norway forces were at work which created disturbances for the established church there.

In Norway, as in England, there was criticism of the state church. Originally, the strongest critical elements were found in the Haugean movement, but other dissenting voices later made themselves heard. There was a questioning of long-established customs and usages, a tendency to look for deeper sanctions for church polity than were found in the state-church relationship, and hence a ferment of ideas which gradually revivified church life in Norway. The "free congregation" is an outgrowth of this movement. "Prayer houses" were built, Inner Mission associations were founded, the "emergency principle" to justify lay preaching was developed by Gisle Johnson, the low-church and high-church wings of the state church became clearly discernible and established their own periodicals, lay preachers invaded the congregations of the state-church clergy, the "low-church wing scored victory after victory," and finally, 1888–89, the lay movement was accepted both popularly and in the law-books.[17] Menighedsfakultetet (The Congregations' Faculty), a free theological group not controlled by the state, began its work in 1908, and in 1913 was granted the right to examine theological candidates.

The Synod founders, in attempting to organize in America a conservative, orthodox Lutheran body that was not an established church supported by the government, but a free church growing out of frontier American conditions, faced a steady stream of problems that often were akin to those troubling the mother country. How far Larsen and his associates were from comprehending the deep forces at work may be seen by Larsen's impatient remark about "the hackneyed question of laymen's activity" in the article referred to above. Yet this same "hackneyed" question persisted in Norway until 1913 and was not settled until lay

43

preaching had been recognized and laymen were permitted to speak in churches from the pulpit.[18] The stormy religious atmosphere was not confined to America.

By the time of Larsen's return to this country in the middle of January 1861 he was convinced that the Synod should increase its own efforts in training teachers and leaders for the church. To this end he buckled down to his work in St. Louis. But external events soon took charge of the situation. The Civil War broke out. St. Louis was a strategic point in a slave state. Its arsenal was a critical target. Disturbances took place, and at the end of April the faculty decided to close Concordia College and Seminary early and await a clarification of the situation.[19] The Norwegian students, and Larsen and his family, returned to their homes.

Aim that the instruction here be
thorough; that there be no show
or humbug; that everything be
pure gold; that it be all wool
and a yard wide.

—Laur. Larsen

4

Halfway Creek to Decorah

With the outbreak of the Civil War it was clear to all in the Synod that the time had indeed come to erect their own institution of learning. Events had more than vindicated those members, especially of the laity, who from the start had advocated such a course. The resolution of October 10, 1857, which authorized the professorship at St. Louis, began by providing for the establishment of a college and arranging for the collection of a "University Fund." At a meeting in Coon Prairie, Wisconsin, in 1859, the Synod passed a resolution that it should endeavor to establish its own "Norwegian university within three years' time." La Crosse, Decorah, and Janesville were discussed in committee as possible sites. A contributor to *Maanedstidende* stated in October 1860 that "we have decided at the Synod meeting next year to introduce a motion to establish immediately our own educational institution. . . . We see clearly what an exceedingly great advantage it would be, for all our people, to found a school where every parent anxious about the Christian training of his children could send them to receive a thorough education."[1]

Meanwhile the University Fund had been growing. As early as August 1858 Pastor Koren reported subscriptions of $3,125 from his congregations and Pastor H. A. Preus, $827 from one of his. The subscriptions announced later had risen to $6,402 in November 1858; to $9,276 in June 1859; to

45

$13,542 in June 1860; and to $19,322 in October 1861. The last-named sum was probably the grand total reported to the Synod meeting in June 1861.[2] Koren and H. A. Preus had been especially successful; later Bernt J. I. Muus made an outstanding record in fund raising. Although the goal of $50,000 was still far off, the progress so far had been encouraging.

At the meeting of June 1861 at Luther Valley, Wisconsin, the Synod took decisive action. It resolved to proceed at once to establish a college. Koren had already procured an option on a 32-acre site in Decorah. His congregations had subscribed more than $6,000. Supporters of the Decorah location argued that it was situated among flourishing congregations; building materials were readily available there; the city had a pleasant and healthful situation; it was west of the Mississippi and would be almost a central point amidst the growing Norwegian population; lastly, with the coming of the railroad, it would be easily accessible. So, over the rival claims of La Crosse, Madison, and Janesville, Decorah was selected, with only ten dissenting votes.

Some thought ten acres of land would have been sufficient; on the other hand, one individual had suggested the purchase of a large farm so that students, by working there, could become fitted for "practical life"; others thought the students could get enough exercise by chopping wood, doing some gardening, and looking after the cattle and horses which would be required; beyond that they would need their time for studying. Finally, however, Koren was authorized to purchase the 32 acres.[3]

A building committee was elected consisting of U. V. Koren of Decorah, C. L. Clausen of St. Ansgar, Iowa, Gulbrand O. Rustad of Decorah, Jørgen Brunsvold of Big Canoe, Iowa, and Jens J. Naeset of Koshkonong, Wisconsin.

A proposal, sponsored chiefly by the pastors, that instruction of Norwegian students be continued at Concordia College until a building was ready in Decorah was defeated. It was then decided that the Synod's educational institution should begin operations at once with the means and the teaching staff then available. If suitable space could be found, it should be initiated in Decorah; if not, in the vacant parsonage in Halfway Creek, Wisconsin.

The meeting authorized the calling of Reverend Friedrich A. Schmidt, who was favored partly because of his proficiency in the English language, to be Larsen's colleague. Schmidt was then pastor of St. Peter's Lutheran Church in Baltimore, the first congregation in the Missouri Synod to use English exclusively. At the Missouri Synod meeting in 1860 Schmidt had maintained the right of members of the church to form congregations in which all worship was in English; as a response to this, the older members expressed their wonder that "such a spirit" would venture to speak on that floor.[4]

Finally, the sum of $100 a year for two years was appropriated for a college library. (The intent was excellent, but Larsen's subsequent reports show that the money was not provided until two years later.)

It is interesting to note that the word "college" was used for the first time in the official minutes of the 1861 Synod meeting. The Norwegian *læreanstalt* (educational institution) had been used earlier, and *universitet* (university), and *skole* (school). The term *gymnasiet* (gymnasium) appeared only after the Synod men had become acquainted with Concordia College at St. Louis. In Norway the corresponding institutions had been the cathedral school and the Latin school, but "Latin school" was not used of Luther College until later. "College" had not been in favor with the university men, perhaps because it had a "Yankee" flavor, perhaps because they had not reacted favorably to such American colleges as they knew. But the language of the land they had come to serve was proving stronger than their

47

preconceived notions and prejudices.[5] More such changes were to come later.

Since "university" had been used to designate the new institution, the money being gathered for it was known for more than a decade as the "University Fund." The Synod pastors, in using these terms, undoubtedly had in mind their own alma mater, the Royal Fredrik University in Christiania, which had been founded 50 years earlier and had taken a new set of buildings into use in 1852.[6] Moreover, the Synod leaders intended that the institution should have at least preparatory and college departments, a normal or teachers' training department, and, finally, a seminary department.[7]

A teachers' training department was established in 1865 and dropped in 1886; a preparatory department flourished from the beginning of the school until 1928, when it was discontinued; and, when the time came, the Synod established its seminary—not in Decorah but in Madison, Wisconsin, in 1876. So the institution at Decorah gradually developed not into a university but into an American liberal arts college.

Following the Synod meeting at Luther Valley in 1861, some investigation was made of the possibility of initiating instruction in Decorah. "Reed's Castle" (the present home of the Winneshiek County Farm Bureau, just south of the post office in Decorah) was considered, and $8.63 was spent for minor repairs on it.[8] But the difficulty of finding suitable accommodations for teachers in Decorah presented an insuperable obstacle.[9] For two years a parsonage at Halfway Creek, about two miles east of Holmen, Wisconsin (13 from La Crosse), had stood vacant, waiting for the pastor whom the Synod, for lack of man power, could not supply. If a school were to be located there, the teachers could serve the congregations which had hopefully built the parsonage. So on August 16, 1861, the Church Council decided that the college should begin its operations in the vacant parsonage. Larsen at once prepared an announcement, dated that same day, at Koshkonong, stating that on September 1 the "Norwegian Lutheran School for the Education of Ministers" was to begin its work in the Halfway Creek parsonage.[10]

On August 17 Larsen left Koshkonong and went to Madison, where he had the announcement inserted in *Emigranten*. On August 20 he arrived at the parsonage at Halfway Creek to arrange for the opening of the school. On August 26 he engaged Christian Nilsen and his wife to serve as stewards from September 1 to April 1, 1862, for $14 per month. On August 31 "two of the older students, who previously had been at Concordia College in St. Louis," arrived: Lars Folkestad of Bonnet Prairie and Brynjolf Hovde of Spring Prairie, Wisconsin. On September 1, Knut Aslaksen of Liberty Prairie, Wisconsin, "who previously had been at Concordia College," arrived, and "the new students," Olaus A. Normann of Liberty Prairie and Niels Ottun from Holden, Minnesota. On September 4 Larsen began instruction.[11] On September 6 Professor Schmidt arrived and "at once began to assist" with the instruction. On September 10 "the older students," Nils Eide and Iver Larsen of Big Canoe, Iowa, and a "new" student, Johannes E. Bergh of Big Canoe, arrived. It is clear that Larsen in distinguishing between "old" and "new" students thought of those who had been at Concordia College as old students. On September 12 the timetable for classes which had been worked out by the two teachers was put into effect. So the new college was under way, however modest its beginnings.

Three new students arrived September 19. On September 26 Knut E. Bergh of Big Canoe enrolled and with his arrival there were six old students. The other six were new ones. Four more enrolled for the second half year. September 26 was declared a holiday because of President Lincoln's proclamation of a day of prayer and repentance. A cultural note was sounded when on November 30 Professor Schmidt's piano was brought from La Crosse.[12]

49

Larsen has given a picture of the year at Halfway Creek, which, although trying in many ways because of the cramped quarters, was nevertheless a happy one in retrospect. Several of those who were there, he states, have later spoken of these days as some of the happiest in their lives.

"The year that the school was in Halfway Creek we had only the one building, the parsonage, without other buildings of any kind. And how many people were crowded together in this building? There were two teachers and their families. Professor Schmidt had one child and Professor Larsen two, one of whom died in October. The school had sixteen students, but not more than eleven at one time. Christian Nilsen and his wife were employed as steward and stewardess for the joint household, as separate housekeeping for each family could not be established. As Nilsen was a carpenter, he made all the simple furniture we had. He also performed such manual labor as the students were unable to do. The housekeepers had one child, and Mrs. Nilsen's mother was also staying with them. Professor Larsen had one room for himself and family, a small adjoining room being used as office, spare room, and hospital. The meals were served in the kitchen, where all ate at the same table. The students were divided into two classes, each of which had one room. These rooms were furnished in the following manner: Our steward made some narrow beds with rope bottoms, which were placed along the walls. Down the middle of the floor stood long home-made tables, as narrow as possible to save room. Between the beds and the tables stood long wooden benches. When the boys rose in the morning, they had only to step across the benches to seat themselves at the tables, where they were to study their lessons."[13] "And when instruction was to begin, the teacher came in and seated himself at the end of the table on what was perhaps the only chair in the room, while the boys stayed in their places on the benches. Of course they had left them long enough to wash and dress and eat breakfast. Breakfast was served to the assembled household in the kitchen, where morning devotions were also held. But the morning washing took place, of necessity, outside under the open sky. . . . The parsonage had a pleasing location, and there were opportunities for charming walks on the surrounding heights and in the valleys between. But above all, those gathered there were healthy, normal youths. The teachers, too, were young men and had children with whom the boys could play at times. In the winter there were hills for skiing and coasting. One had to find amusements outdoors, indeed, for there was no room within. And yet this now old headmaster can still smile as in memory he sees the youngest of the boys, Olaus Normann, who had been given the honorable assignment of being bell ringer, dancing about in the hallway in his short jacket and swinging the small table bell which was then all we needed to gather our little band of students."

The students were from 16 to 26 years old and averaged 20 years. The old students formed *Quarta* (or the freshman year in college), the new students a combined *Quinta* and *Sexta* (the last two years of high school). These designations were adopted from those in use at Concordia College, where the highest, or senior, or first class was called *Prima* and the other classes ranged downward to *Sexta,* just the reverse of the usage in Norway, where Norwegian terms rather than Latin were used.[14] Five students comprised the upper class, six the lower. Schmidt taught 27 hours a week and Larsen, who was also serving four congregations, taught 17 hours a week. The subjects were Latin, Greek, German, Norwegian, English, history, religion, algebra, penmanship, singing, arithmetic, and geography.

The daily schedule was as follows:

5:30 A.M.	Students rise and dress.
6:00 A.M.	Morning devotions.
6:30 A.M.– 8:30 A.M.	Breakfast, followed by study.

51

8:30 A.M.– 9:00 A.M. Recess.

9:00 A.M.–12:00 A.M. Classes and study, with 15-minute recess at 11:00 A.M.

12:00 A.M.– 2:00 P.M. Dinner and recess.

2:00 P.M.– 5:00 P.M. Classes and study, with recess at 4:00 P.M.

5:00 P.M.– 7:00 P.M. Recess, with supper at 6:00 P.M.

7:00 P.M.– 8:45 P.M. Study period.

8:45 P.M.–10:00 P.M. Evening devotions and recess.

10:00 P.M. Bedtime for all.

As for the many minor regulations which naturally were needed, the students were governed for the time being by those in force at St. Louis, with which the "older" students were familiar.[15]

The schedule was substantially the same as that in use at Concordia College in St. Louis, except that at Concordia the day began half an hour earlier and the duties for each period were, with German thoroughness, spelled out in more detail. Approximately the same program was in force in the early 1860's at Augustana College and Seminary in Paxton, Illinois. There the day started at 5 A.M. Apparently the leaders in most such institutions subscribed to the dictum of Professor Tuve N. Hasselquist of Augustana that "it seems to be a prevailing sin among pastors to sleep late in the morning," and were determined to train their future ministers to rise early. No such sin appears to have threatened one of the first Luther students, who wrote: "I now go to bed at ten o'clock and get up at four—yes, sometimes at three; and still I am glad for every spare minute in which to prepare my lessons. . . . I am well, thank God, and never tire of my work. . . . Moreover, our teachers are so outstanding that they make our tasks easier." So wrote Brynjolf Hovde in 1861.[16]

"These early days in the first year of Luther College, were indeed happy ones. Especially do we call to mind how the

lamented Professor Bergh used to wax warm and enthusiastic
on that theme; but his was also an uncommon sense of the
ideal and the beautiful. And beautiful were the bonds that
bound together the members of this colony gathered from
so many parts. The teachers enjoyed the sprightly animation
of youth, not being much older than some of their pupils.
Nature was surpassingly fair. The parsonage lay in a smiling
valley hemmed in by high hills, at the foot of which a prat-
tling brook laughed merrily along. Here, in peace, undis-
turbed by the noise of the world, that plant began to grow
which in later years became so large a tree, with so many
and varied fruits."[17]

When both Larsen and Schmidt were absent, the older
students were expected to work out assignments (usually
review), and one or two of them had the task of instructing
the younger ones. Such proctoring and instruction by advanced students grew out of the Lancastrian system, which
had been practiced in some schools in Norway. At the close
of the first academic year on June 5, 1862, school would
normally have continued throughout the day, but afternoon
classes were dismissed so that students could leave early.
True, arrangements were made that not more than one class
hour should be lost by any section; the point is that the
perennial problem of the exact hour at which vacation starts
was present at Luther College in its very first year.

In the summer of 1862, Reverend B. J. Frich having come
from Norway to occupy the Halfway Creek parsonage, the
college was moved to Decorah. Bag and baggage, the college
and the two professors' belongings were loaded up in ten
lumber wagons and dispatched to La Crosse. There the
travelers stayed overnight and took a Mississippi River boat
to Lansing, Iowa. Apparently there was also an overnight
stay in Lansing, a frontier town which had been founded 13
years earlier, in 1849. On July 31 they reached Decorah.
A building at the northwest corner of Main and Winnebago

streets, later known as the St. Cloud Hotel, and subsequently as the Union Hotel, had been acquired for $1,600 as temporary quarters for the school. At the same time the Judge Griswold residence at the northeast corner of Center Street and Leiv Eiriksson Drive was purchased for the use of Professor Schmidt. Professor Larsen was to live in the larger building. The Griswold residence, across the Upper Iowa River in West Decorah, had its disadvantages, for whenever the river flooded, Schmidt was unable to get to town for his classes.[18]

These structures were smaller then than now, additions to both having been made since. Larsen relates that the St. Cloud building had, in the basement, a large kitchen, a dining room, cellarage, a pantry, and living quarters for the stewards. On the first floor there were rooms for Larsen's family and one classroom. The second floor held an office about seven feet square for the president, two classrooms, and two smaller sleeping rooms that accommodated 11. Above this floor was a large room, where up to 25 might sleep.[19] Registration for the year came to 34, more than double the previous year's attendance.

When the school opened September 8 (one week late because the building was being made ready) Larsen, addressing the students, developed the theme in Psalm 127:1, "Except the Lord build the house, they labor in vain that build it; except the Lord keep the city, the watchman waketh but in vain." At the same convocation Koren took as his subject Proverbs 1:7, "The fear of the Lord is the beginning of wisdom." Thus these two texts, which have been used at so many opening exercises, were introduced at this college convocation in 1862.

First things always have a certain interest. In Decorah, as at Halfway Creek, there was usually, once a month, a cleaning day, when school was suspended and all students scrubbed their rooms and the halls. On February 3, 1863, what might be called the first honors convocation was held; during the pastoral conference at the college the students with highest grades for the first semester were commended before the assembly. On February 21, 1863, Protokol records that "O. Felland, because of repeated complaints about his disturbances during study hours, was punished by *carcer* [confinement to his room] from 3 until 9:30 P.M. and was deprived of his supper." In closing the school year (June 6, 1863), Larsen appealed to the students to conduct themselves worthily during the summer vacation. He also asked them to seek funds for the purchase of a melodeon or piano for the college.[20]

In his printed report Larsen indicated that he had first planned a ten-month school year. It had been impossible to achieve this in either 1861–62 or 1862–63; he now believed it desirable to plan permanently for a shorter term. A briefer term was necessary for the sake of the teachers, he argued; they needed to be relieved of summer duties, so that they would have a greater opportunity to prepare themselves for their tasks. But the shorter year became official only much later.[21]

In 1863–64, because attendance had increased to 51, the lot west of the St. Cloud Hotel property was purchased and a house erected there of bricks made on the West Decorah campus for use in future college buildings. The building apparently was not highly regarded by the students, for it came to be known as "Hututu."[22] Despite this addition, the college in this third year faced the necessity of having students room and board "outside." Four students roomed and boarded at Ole N. Olsen's. Quite a few had to sleep and study in Dale's Hall. "Hututu," the annex, went into use January 7, 1864. During both 1862–63 and 1863–64 there was a great deal of sickness—colds, mumps, typhoid, diphtheria, scarlet fever, pneumonia, measles—and the problems of an administrator whose college lacked a hospital may well be imagined. Dr. John T. Billington, who was a Norwegian, gave his services gratis in 1862–63.[23]

During 1864–65 attendance increased again and more students had to find rooms outside the college buildings. In each of these early years it had been necessary to reject a number of students, some because of lack of room, some because their credentials did not qualify them. In 1864–65 the "social problem" popped up in Protokol, where, on February 1, it was recorded that the students, having given offense, "were given an earnest warning against dancing and loose talk." On April 27, 1865, a memorial service, because of President Lincoln's death, was held and classes were dismissed. On May 17, 1865, for the first time, there was a half holiday in honor of Norway's independence day; a Norwegian flag was presented to the students, and refreshments were served by women and girls of the community.

Meanwhile, progress was being made toward the goal of permanent quarters for the college. The Building Committee, with Clausen as chairman and Koren as secretary, had engaged C. H. Griese of Cleveland, Ohio, as architect; in their plans they had given careful consideration to the aim and scope of the school. The committee report, November 5, 1861, stated that although the duty of the church to prepare preachers and teachers had been the primary occasion for the undertaking and should continue to be its principal aim, nevertheless the church also had an inescapable responsibility to provide opportunities for the youth of the church to receive higher education in the general branches of knowledge. Therefore the committee unanimously resolved so to plan the institution that the department preparing students for the seminary could also accept those who sought other callings in life in which they might serve their country in positions that required more than a common education.[24]

This was by far the best and clearest statement of aim of the college that had been formulated, and since it was printed in *Maanedstidende* for January 1862, it undoubtedly motivated the resolution adopted in June 1862 to make the fees uniform for all students, whether they were preparing for the ministry or not. This statement of purpose was unanimously reaffirmed in 1864. It was broader and more inclusive than those found in some of the earlier discussions; it had a larger scope than is indicated by Larsen's title inscribed in the first Protokol: "The Norwegian Evangelical Lutheran Educational Institution for the Education of Ministers"; it went considerably beyond Koren's statement of 1864, as deposited in the cornerstone, that the first Main Building was erected "to educate teachers of the Church"; and it explicitly stated the objective of providing a broad general higher education for the youth of the church. There can be little question that this formulation was not only a carefully calculated appeal for the support of the laity, but that it also accurately reflected what they wanted in the school they were going to support.[25]

The school, to fulfill its purpose, had to be planned on broad lines. It had to be planned more generously than Concordia College, where additions had been necessary almost as soon as the original building had been occupied. The proposed building, therefore, was to accommodate 80 to 120 students, with provisions for adding a wing later. Although the committee hopefully (and as events proved, much too hopefully) estimated the cost of the building at $28,000, it pointed out that there would also be outlays for houses for the teachers and for necessary sheds and barns, and thus the total would be considerably higher.

At the 1862 Synod meeting in Holden, Goodhue County, Minnesota (a locale later closely identified with St. Olaf College), the report of the Building Committee was well received and its various recommendations were unanimously adopted.

At the same Synod meeting a change in tuition was made

in harmony with the broadened purpose of the college. Following the practice of Concordia, Larsen had recommended, and the Synod had introduced in 1861, this system: Those who had not declared an intention to enter the ministry were charged tuition, whereas those studying for the ministry paid none, and were charged lower fees for board and room. Concerning this practice there was long and thoughtful discussion. The system of 1861–62 had presupposed that the church's duty and obligation extended only to those who intended to serve it directly as preachers or teachers. But it was clearly right and desirable, it was argued, that as many as possible of the young people of the church make use of the opportunities offered. Admission was to be open to anyone who could satisfy the entrance requirements. Those who did not directly enter the service of the church could fit themselves for other respected callings and exercise a beneficial influence as educated laymen in the congregations. The decision was thereupon unanimous to make the fees uniform for all, a policy that has continued since.[26]

The Building Committee was asked to continue operating and, although immediate construction had not been recommended or approved, to carry out such preliminary work as seemed advisable. Under these instructions it contracted for bricks, to be made from clay found on the campus. The site of the kiln was approximately 50 feet east of the north wing of New Main; there, in the spring of 1863, the oak woods and the hazel brush began to fall before the ax, and brickmaking began. The committee also engaged Griese and Weile, architects; made contracts for lumber; and made plans to have the new building under roof in the fall of 1864. At the June meeting of the Synod, Professor Larsen was appointed to the Building Committee. Pastor Koren went to New York for six months in 1865, and thereafter Larsen carried the major burden of the committee's work.

On June 30, 1864, the cornerstone was laid. A procession

formed opposite the courthouse that consisted of the students, the teachers, the president of the Synod, the Church Council, Professors Walther and Craemer from Concordia College, the delegates for the occasion named by the Synod, the Building Committee, and members of neighboring congregations. In the order named the procession marched to the college grounds, where most of those present assembled within the walls of the foundation, the notables finding places upon a platform erected for the occasion.[27]

"The task for which we are assembled here," said H. A. Preus, who used I Peter 2:6 as his text, "is not of importance merely for one congregation, indeed, nor merely for this moment, but for our whole church and for times to come. . . . Let us surround this school with our single-minded and devoted love. Let us always keep it close to our hearts and never fail in our intercessions for it. Let us recognize our privilege of bringing a thank offering by supporting and maintaining it with our temporal gifts. . . . And now, O God, we commend our work to Thee; it is Thine. May the spirit of peace and love dwell within these walls! May the spirit of knowledge and wisdom fill the hearts of students and teachers! May God's blessing rest upon their work to His honor and glory!"

Beneath the stone were placed a brief history of the Synod and of the college in both Norwegian and English, and a prayer for the college from Psalm 90:16–17: "Let thy work appear unto thy servants, and thy glory unto their children. And let the beauty of the Lord our God be upon us; and establish thou the work of our hands upon us; yea, the work of our hands establish thou it." There were deposited also the report of the last Synod meeting, the latest issues of *Emigranten* and of the *Decorah Republic,* a number of coins, a Bible, a copy of the Augsburg Confession, and one of Pontoppidan's *Forklaring* (Explanation). Thereupon the pastors present put the cornerstone in place; President H. A.

Preus struck the stone three times with a hammer, declared that it was laid in the Triune God's name, and concluded with a prayer.

The Synod, at its meeting early in June 1864, had resolved to leave the matter of the school's name to the pastoral conference. At the cornerstone ceremony, in accordance with the pastors' decision, the school was officially referred to as the Norwegian Luther College. It gradually came to be called simply Luther College; in 1918 the latter name was adopted, although legally the change was not incorporated into the Articles of Incorporation of Luther College until 1930.

*Establish thou the work of our
hands upon us; yea, the work of
our hands establish thou it.*
—Psalm 90:17

5

The First Main Building

Under the leadership of President H. A. Preus, the Synod moved vigorously to raise funds for completion of the Main Building by the opening of the school year 1865–66. Great enthusiasm for the college cause had been manifested at the June 1864 meeting of the Synod. There was a greater sense of unity among pastors and delegates as they faced the issues arising from the steady growth of the college, which needed more room, and from the pressures of inflation and the seriousness of the war crisis, despite the prospect of Union victory. They buckled to their task then and later, and the response was extraordinary. The records reveal that more than 9,300 individuals subscribed to the first Luther College building fund. The average subscription was a little over $16.[1]

Two feet of snow on November 8 and subsequent cold weather prevented the roofing of the structure in 1864, but the Church Council and the Building Committee, meeting in January 1865, resolved to push the work with all speed in an effort to complete the building by September 1. But a long winter, a violent snowstorm on April 22, and other difficulties made the attainment of this goal impossible. School opened for the older students in the old quarters downtown; new students were asked to delay their arrival.

On October 10, 1865, however, the college moved into its new quarters; on October 12 most of the new students appeared and were assigned rooms in the new building. On October 14 the dedicatory exercises were held. But there was still much to be done. Because delivery of the windows had been so long delayed that they were barely installed before the dedication, some of the ceiling plaster on the first and second floors had fallen due to water seepage; all of the painting yet remained to be done (and was not completed until November); many minor details needed attention. Yet despite the frustration occasioned by setbacks and incompleted work, the building gave a feeling of triumph to those who had worked so long and hard to see it realized.

It was a structure 126 feet long. The main portion was 52 feet wide and the wing 44 feet. The basement was 10 feet in height, the first floor 14, the second floor 13, the third floor 12 (in the wing it was 16, with no attic above it), and the attic in the main portion 10. The basement contained a storeroom, two kitchens, a dining room seating 100, living quarters for the steward's family and other servants, and two washrooms for students. On the first floor were living quarters for two married teachers and a single teacher and a large study room. On the second floor were eight study and recitation rooms (the three largest were 18½ by 32 feet) and two rooms for guests of the faculty members living in the building.

On the third floor were four sleeping rooms, accommodating 30 students, two rooms to serve as hospital rooms, two study rooms, and in the wing a space which served as a hall for formal gatherings and as a chapel. In the attic were four large sleeping rooms, accommodating 55 students. Lastly, in the second and third story of the tower were quarters, of which one was to serve as a library and the other as a sleeping room. The building could accommodate 100 to 120 students.[2]

Besides the Main Building there were erected a small bakery and a brick stable (later transformed into living quarters

Decorah, Iowa

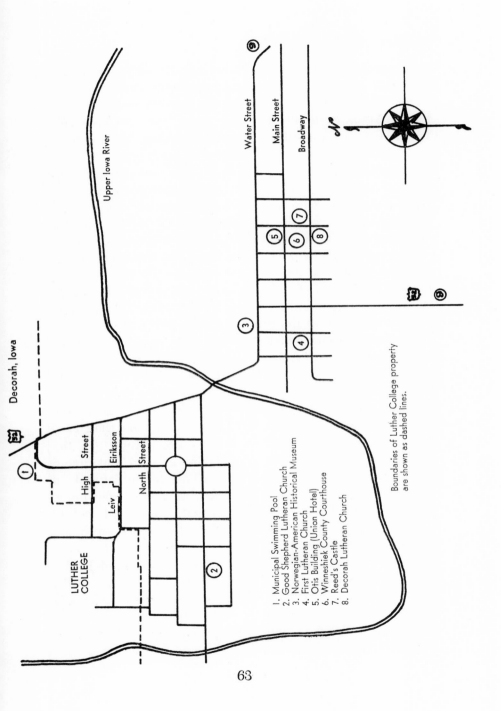

Upper Iowa River

Water Street

Main Street

Broadway

LUTHER COLLEGE

High Street

Leiv

Eiriksson

North Street

1. Municipal Swimming Pool
2. Good Shepherd Lutheran Church
3. Norwegian-American Historical Museum
4. First Lutheran Church
5. Otis Building (Union Hotel)
6. Winneshiek County Courthouse
7. Reed's Castle
8. Decorah Lutheran Church

Boundaries of Luther College property
are shown as dashed lines.

for students and known fondly as the "Chicken Coop"). A hydraulic ram raised water from a spring to a reservoir next to the kitchen; a well was dug just west of the rear entrance to the Main Building; and four large cisterns were constructed. There was still leveling, grading, and seeding to be done. Such was the college plant in October 1865.

In 1880 Lyder Siewers recalled these construction days in an account which illustrates his romantic nature:

"In the course of the summer of 1864 the walls of the new building were gradually rising higher and higher, and the undertaking was embraced with more or less interest by the entire Norwegian population of this neighborhood, though more especially, of course, by the professors and students. If there was no time to take a walk up to the college grounds, one would content himself with a view from the Court House square, to rejoice at the rapid progress of the work.

"One day it so happened that some one was looking in the direction of the college from the office window in what was then the school building, and what a remarkable symbol met his eye! Above the half-finished walls of Luther College rose a beautiful cross, which vividly reminded one of the trials of the cross, but also of 'By this sign thou shalt conquer.' It was no miracle; it was all quite natural. On the bluff on the other side of the river there grew at that time a pine which at a distance bore a striking resemblance to a cross. As the walls of the building rose higher, the cross, though several thousand feet distant, stood out boldly against the sky, thus assuming the appearance of being planted upon the building. This cross gave rise to many thoughts in the minds of those who were occupied in the serious work which was to be carried on within those walls, the work of giving future ministers the necessary classical foundation for advanced study. This was a remarkable symbol when we keep in mind the special object of the new institution of learning.

1. *Claus L. Clausen, taken in 1867, when Clausen was 47 years old.*

2. *Herman A. Preus, president of the Norwegian Synod 1862-94.*

3. *Bernt J. I. Muus. His congregations were among the largest contributors to the college.*

4. *Jakob A. Ottesen. In 1862–63 his congregations sent 14 of the 32 students in attendance.*

5. *Laur. Larsen in 1855. President of Luther College 1861-1902.*

6. *Friedrich A. Schmidt in 1858. Larsen's colleague on the faculty 1861–72.*

7. *Halfway Creek Parsonage (after a sketch from 1890).*

8. *The Otis Building and "Hututu," occupied by the college 1862–65.*

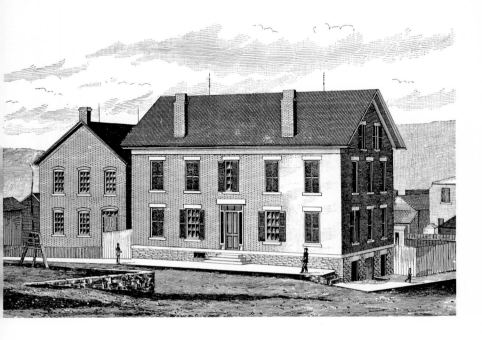

9. Decorah from Pleasant Hill in 1861. From l. to r.—Congregational Church, Methodist Church, Courthouse, Reed's Castle, and Otis Building.
        Courtesy A. J. Ehrhardt, Elkader, Iowa.

9a. The first college bell.

10. *Ulrik Vilhelm Koren in 1853. He selected the site for the college.*
11. *Diderikke Brandt from the portrait by H. Gausta. She was mistress of Campus House 1867–84.*

12. *Dedication of Main Building, October 14, 1865.*

13. *Luther College in 1874 at the dedication of the South Wing. "Chicken Coop" is at the right. Rev. Ingvar G. Monson is at the left on the tower.*

14. *Courthouse Square. The college and the local congregation made use of the large courtroom 1862-65.*

15. *Luther College Faculty, 1869. Standing, l. to r.: Friedrich A. Schmidt and Nils O. Brandt. Seated: Gabriel H. Landmark, Lyder Siewers, Knut E. Bergh, and Laur. Larsen.*

16. *"Chicken Coop"*

17. *Comitia Dumriana, 1873-74. Standing, l. to r.: Thora Larsen, Marie Reque, Margrethe Brandt, Emma Larsen, and Rosine Preus. Seated: Louise Hjort, Caroline Koren, Henriette Koren, and Mathilda Stub.*

18. *The board sidewalk, completed to town in 1880.*

19. *The Egge cabin. This housed the Egges, their two children, and Rev. and Mrs. U. V. Koren during the latter's first winter (1853–54) in America. It is now on the campus.*

"But I have other reminiscences which also deserve being recorded.

"In the early fall of 1865 the new building was approaching its completion, and a couple of rooms had been fitted up for occupancy, while still a great many things were lacking before all would be in proper shape. I moved into these rooms, and alone I sat there evenings in the large and empty building. But soon I discovered that the tower and a window on the west side were already occupied, and that by creatures which serve to symbolize what in this world enjoys and ought to enjoy the highest distinction. In the tower dwelt a pair of owls, and in the moonlight they would sit on their lofty perch, with their large, wise eyes, and send forth their warning cry. The owl, the bird of Minerva, the bird of the Goddess of Wisdom, had taken up its abode where wisdom was to have the foremost place; for 'the fear of the Lord is the beginning of wisdom.' What an omen!

"In the window sill on the west side a dove is lying secure and quiet on its nest; its mate is by its side. They look as if they both are thinking of fulfilling their duties. What a picture! This bird is a symbol of piety and fidelity. Who will ask for a more charming model for the rising generation? If we then in connection with this consider the inscription over the entrance: *Soli Deo Gloria,* i.e., 'To God alone the glory,' we must confess that Luther College entered on its career under the most favorable auspices."[3]

On October 14, 1865, the building was dedicated. No better account of the celebration has been written than that by Knud Throndsen in *Emigranten.* Throndsen, then 35, had come from Valders, Norway, a year earlier, and later taught for a time at the college. His account, quaint in its enthusiasm for the architecture of the structure, follows:

"The recent 14th of October was the greatest festival day which the Norwegian Evangelical Lutheran Church in America has experienced; for on that day occurred the solemn

65

dedication of the university building, in which the school for the training of the Norwegian Evangelical Lutheran Synod's pastors and teachers will carry on its work and which that church body, in an unbelievably short time, by voluntary but extraordinarily energetic efforts, has succeeded in erecting.

"We say these efforts were extraordinarily energetic, and the truth of this assertion everyone will admit. Some few years ago this church body consisted of a few congregations scattered here and there over the land with an entirely inadequate number of pastors and with little strength to survive amid the many enemies surrounding it. But the unusually competent and active spiritual leaders whom it has been the good fortune of the Norwegians to receive to labor among them, by God's help have united the scattered forces, have brought clarity, order, and purpose into their undertakings, and have made their church organization here in this foreign land a spiritual structure, firmly founded, well constructed, and strongly defended, which we hope will stand like a rock against the waves of sectarianism, infidelity, and spiritual confusion.

"And as an expression of the vital spirit which animates the church, its members now have erected this university in the confident hope that through it pure evangelical Lutheran Christian doctrine may be preserved for the present and future generations. Men and women, old and young, rich and poor, having brought their contributions to the builders, now may stand and feast their eyes on the beautiful structure, rejoice in what has been accomplished and in the hope of the blessings which will stream from it.

"The little bustling city of Decorah, which is about 15 years old and is the county seat of Winneshiek County, Iowa, is situated on the banks of the Upper Iowa River in a charming valley, surrounded by picturesque hills, rocky crags, and bluffs covered with beautiful trees. About a good English mile west of the town itself there rises an elevation, which to the south and west descends precipitously to the broad and flat river valley, but to the east slopes unevenly to the valley toward the town, from which it is separated by the river in one of the latter's winding turns. On the highest point of the elevation stands the Norwegian 'Luther College' or university, a grand structure in the noblest style—three imposing stories with their slender, arched windows, above which there is an attic with the usual circular windows beneath the roof line. Above the entry, which faces toward town, rises the square main tower, ending in a pyramidlike peak, on the top of which a tall flagpole points heavenward. In harmony with the chosen architectural style, the somewhat prominent side towers, extending the full height of the building, culminate in conical spires which present a pleasing contrast to the eye and enhance the building's appearance. The plain, ordinary color of the bricks is offset by the many symmetrically designed windows and pilasters, which, like the entrances, have a border of light sandstone, creating an effect that is unusually fortunate and in no small part contributes to the structure's beauty.

"The building, as it stands there on its high foundation, has a remarkably fine appearance; and it is not too much to say that with its mass and its tasteful form, free of all flourishes and architectural affectation, it is an embellishment to the landscape on which the traveler rests his eye with pleasure and which is the pride of all Decorah.

"The fourteenth of October was not a bright, radiant day of sunshine. Yet we can assuredly say, with more truth than many correspondents say of festival days, that the weather favored the festival. At eight in the morning the fog lifted to disclose gray and half-threatening clouds that hid the sky. It really looked as if rain would dampen the festivities. But no one seemed to fear it, and the program was carried out

67

from beginning to end without interruption and in perfect order.

"The American flag on this festal day waved from the top of the tower like a noble symbol of the protecting freedom under which we live and work in this land.[4] The Norwegian flag, with its warm, bright colors, could be seen over the main entrance, which was decked with garlands and leaves and in which was set up a platform which served as a speaker's rostrum. Nearly the whole area in front of the building was filled with improvised benches to seat the assembled throng, and to the rear of the building were set up five exceedingly long parallel tables, at which 400 to 500 persons could be seated at one time to enjoy the good dishes that had been prepared by the members of the local and outlying congregations.

"Very early in the morning the throng began to gather in the valley on the west side of the river, which had been designated as the starting point for the procession. Later in the morning the whole area was filled by a tremendous crowd—some afoot, some in wagons—men, women, and children. Never before on any occasion has so large a crowd of Norwegians been assembled on one spot in this country.

"The procession, which started about 11:00 A.M., followed this order: the steward of the college; the American and Norwegian flags; those who had worked on the building; the architect and the Building Committee; the college students; the college teachers with the German guests, Professor Brauer of St. Louis, Missouri, and Professor Lange of Fort Wayne, Indiana, besides some of the American officials of the county; the president of the Synod; the Church Council and the auditors; the pastors.[5] Then followed the great throng of visitors from town and country; and the line of march was brought up by a long train of teams and wagons, probably numbering 200. As the procession now slowly moved toward the university over the many turns of the road, it extended a distance of somewhat more than an English mile.

"As soon as the procession had disbanded, the whole area in front of the building was filled with people. The president of the Synod and the other pastors, including the above-named representatives of the universities in St. Louis and Fort Wayne, took their places on the decorated platform at the main entrance, and the most important part of the celebration now opened with the singing of the two opening stanzas of the first of the hymns especially written for the occasion. Pastor Brandt then warmly welcomed all those who had come to the festival and offered a fervent prayer of invocation, whereupon the two last stanzas of the same hymn were sung.[6]

"Pastor H. A. Preus then delivered the dedicatory address. Since we have received permission to publish the addresses and these will therefore be available in *Emigranten* as soon as they are received, we shall not here attempt to give a summary of their content, but only observe in general that the quiet, silence, and rapt attention of the great assembly during the addresses was the best proof of how gladly the throng listened to the truths which were expressed so vigorously from the tribune. After the dedicatory address, the second of the festival hymns was sung.

"Thereupon followed addresses by Pastor Koren, Professor Brauer of St. Louis (in German), Professor Larsen, likewise Professors Lange and Schmidt (in English); and finally the dedicatory ceremonies were brought to a close with a prayer by Pastor Ottesen. After the various addresses, stanzas were sung from hymns 284, 157 and 91 in Guldberg's Hymnal.

"The assembly was then invited to the area to the rear of the building, where dinner was ready on the long tables —and great indeed must have been the store of provisions which had been gathered up for this occasion by the surrounding congregations; for the dinner guests, just those who sat down at the tables and had their dinner, were estimated at between 1,500 and 2,000 people.

"By mingling with the crowd we had an opportunity to hear many expressions of opinion about the structure they had come to see. All were unanimous in expressing their satisfaction and joy over what had been accomplished. And when, in the evening on their homeward way, the visitors turned for a last look at the building to which so noble a hope attaches, and the bright light of the illumination streamed toward their gaze from the 50 windows of the building, then they felt that the new university was sending them as its protectors a fresh reminder and greeting; it was as if it would say to the members of the congregations far and wide in the land: 'Yes, here I stand. I will be a beacon of light among you. But without you I can do nothing; therefore, do not forget me. Remember that it is my duty to watch over a different building, one of "living stones," which will become radiant with your love and your prayers.'

"A great step has been taken; but it is only the beginning. Therefore within us there must resound as a dear echo from the festival of dedication: That which has sprung from the heart of the congregations must be nurtured at the bosom of the congregations; only thus will it acquire strength to take its stand and battle for the light and the truth against the darkness of falsehood."[7]

The exalted mood of the occasion was well expressed, and perhaps even heightened, by the welcome with which Pastor Brandt prefaced his invocation.

"Dear festive Christian assemblage: In the name of our Lord be ye welcome to see what the Lord has done for us. Welcome to offer thanks and praise to God, who has made Himself known to us by giving us His pure and holy Word, and for its preservation and extension has built this house for us. Welcome to unite yourselves this day in confiding prayer, to the end that His work here may prosper. Welcome to behold today what an amiable dwelling the Lord has permitted you to erect for your own, your children's, and posterity's spiritual benefit. Welcome, all you who through prayer, labor, and gifts with God's help have built this house. Behold here the proof that the Lord has heard your prayers and given you the fruit of the labors and sacrifices of your hands. Welcome to this festival to be edified by the Word on the foundation of your most holy faith. Welcome to receive from this celebration an exalting, joyous reminder of God's goodness and unspeakable love—a source of strength in conflict and of comfort in distress in future days. Welcome to carry away from here in your hearts and upon your lips glad tidings of the Lord's mercy towards His Church's Zion, joyful tidings for your children and your children's children. Welcome, be ye welcome, one and all, to this joyous festival in Jesus' name."

H. A. Preus spoke upon the text from Psalm 127, "Except the Lord build the house, they labor in vain that build it." He said in part:

"While a terrible Civil War was raging in our land, while our people were afflicted in many places by crop failure, high prices and heavy burdens, means were procured, often in a marvelous manner, and, foot by foot, this building rose; and now after the lapse of a year it stands here before our eyes completely finished. We must say indeed: A wondrous event has come to pass; truly 'the Lord hath done great things for us; therefore are we glad'; for we know that when the Lord has built the house, the work of the builders is not in vain.

"We must first, Christian friends, fix clearly before our eyes what the task is which must be carried out here, what the spiritual structure is, which here must be built.

"With positive contempt and aversion for all superficial knowledge, all sham culture, all coveting of praise and honor before men, the work in our college must be directed towards the training of the heart for God's kingdom with an eye only to the salvation of souls and the glory of God! Behold, my friends, that is the work, that is the 'house which is to be built.'

"But who are the builders? First of all, the teachers and students of the school; but since these both were spiritually nourished in the congregations as in a fostering mother's bosom, have gone forth from the various congregations, are sustained by them, and are expected to return to them, therefore the congregations in their relation to the school have a mother's duty, and each congregational member is a builder in this work. The Lord in His mercy will then bless their work, too, to the glory of His house and to the salvation of many souls among the coming generations. For when the Lord builds the house, then the builders labor not in vain."

F. A. Schmidt addressed the assemblage in English, stating: "The most direct benefit from this institution will, of course, be derived by those for whose good it is directly intended, the congregations who have united in establishing the school. . . . Their children and children's children, throughout generations to come, may derive the most momentous benefit . . . through the service of men who have been trained here . . . in the faith and discipline of that church to which they have the happiness to belong."[8]

Pastor Koren, greeting the representatives of the Missouri Synod, made a skillful defense of the Synod's alliance with Missouri. He said that the hopes embodied in the resolutions of 1857 had been realized, and paid tribute to the Missouri Synod for the assistance it had given the Norwegian Synod. He called attention to the ties of long standing which had linked Luther and Bugenhagen and German Lutheranism to Norwegian Lutheranism. Missouri had passed through the difficult and experimental process of establishing a "free" church in a new land. The Norwegian Synod had profited from its example. Luther College had been patterned after Concordia College. Finally he said:

"The time will come, if God will, when one bond more will unite our children and those of our German brethren, namely, a common language, the language which is spoken in this land and which sooner or later will also be the mother tongue of our children; and we desire therefore to co-operate with each other in such a way that when this happens, our descendants may receive, pure and undefiled, our holy heritage, the pure Lutheran faith and confession, so they may be one in spirit just as they will be one in language; and with joy we will seize every opportunity God may give us to come into ever closer and more intimate ecclesiastical relations with each other, assured that God for Jesus' sake will fulfill for us the promises given to those who hear God's Word and preserve it."[9]

President Larsen, turning to the students, said: "I have long thought that if this happy festival day which we are now celebrating should at last dawn for us, this would be my admonition to my dear students: Guard the right spirit; guard and keep the spirit of humility."[10] Here much was said in little; there was to be no vainglory.

The closing prayer was given by Pastor Ottesen, who said in part:

"Hitherto Thou hast so mercifully helped us when we called upon Thee—helped us even beyond what we could ask or understand. Oh, do Thou so help us still! Should we be sluggish in prayer for this school, then wake Thou us, wake us ever more and more to zeal and loyalty; shouldst Thou send hard times and heavy trials which might cripple our labors, then help Thou, as Thou hast helped hitherto in such times of need; and let them ever be put to shame who would rejoice over our misfortune. And now, O God, we entrust ourselves to Thee; save Thy people and bless Thine inheritance; nourish and exalt it from age to age, and let Thy

73

lovingkindness be over us even in such measure as we trust in Thee. . . . Hear our prayers today; hear us always when we pray that Thy truth may be preserved for us and for our children, and that the work of this school may honor it; hear us when we call upon Thee according to Thy Word; sustain and keep us steadfast in Thy Word and in Thy truth until we die. Hear us now and evermore, to the end that at last we may be gathered unto Thee and everlastingly praise Thee in eternal joy for Thy mercy's sake, in the name of Jesus. Amen!"[11]

Such was the mood and such were the stirring emotions of that distant day. A goal had been reached; a great work had been accomplished. From its humble beginnings in an overcrowded parsonage, the college now began its fifth year in a better than average educational plant with an enrollment of 81, divided among four classes in the college and two in the preparatory department.

6

Rebellion and Slavery

The culmination of ten years of discussion and effort had been reached. The project of eight years earlier, which then had seemed so impossible of fulfillment, was now successfully completed. Although the Civil War disrupted early plans and for the time being placed the undertaking in jeopardy, it also brought a deeper understanding of the scope and purpose of the school. The Norwegian colonists of the Upper Midwest and their children were against slavery to a man and overwhelmingly in favor of the Union cause. In many of the Norwegian settlements not a single able-bodied man remained; all were at war. Husbands, sons, and brothers had fallen; others returned wounded, maimed, or broken by disease. Consequently, in this time of trial there had been a reassessment of values and a deepening of convictions as to the ultimate goal of life.

To the great majority the new college was to be an institution of enduring worth, a center that looked for its strength to spiritual ideals, an expression of things hoped for but not seen, a bulwark of refuge amid the shifting currents of military and political fortunes, a beacon that pointed toward a better day. So, in the midst of war people had continued to give and the work had gone forward. Now the conflict was over; the cause of freedom had triumphed. The cause of the college had likewise triumphed; its physical plant was completed. The October 14, 1865 celebration was

75

the outward manifestation of the great release which all felt after the years of anxiety and tension.

But one seldom stays long upon the heights. There is a return to lower levels, to the humdrum of everyday living, to the problems which plague and destroy pastoral calm at the very moment when it seems most attainable. Thus, it is not surprising that at the moment of victory the college faced certain situations it hardly welcomed.

The first was a minor episode that stirred tempers. The ministers, gathered for the dedicatory exercises, were still in Decorah, holding a pastoral conference in the new college building. Suddenly the news broke that the students were in rebellion. The students, for whom this new plant had been erected and for whom so many sacrifices had been made, were in rebellion! How could this be?

There was hurrying and scurrying, and the leader of the insurrection was summoned. This dangerous person proved to be Rasmus B. Anderson, a youth not quite 19 years old. Because he had written up grievances in what one rebel called a "bill of rights," which the students had signed, he was considered the ringleader of the group. When Anderson refused to retract or apologize, he was expelled and summarily ordered off the campus.[1]

One cannot say that either side to the controversy covered itself with glory in the affair. Rasmus and his associates had picked the worst possible time for their "rebellion." Larsen and his colleagues showed little better judgment in bringing the matter before the assembled pastoral conference. Nor did the Synod pastors exhibit any greater wisdom by passing judgment on a matter of internal school discipline. None seems to have been aware of the comedy in the affair. Nor did Larsen pour oil on troubled waters when, in his official report to the Synod dated June 18, 1866, he stated that "with God's help we got rid of the weed."[2]

But Rasmus and his fellow students were guilty of insurrection against constituted authority; this, to the pastors, was sin. The Synod leaders had received their theological training in Norway, where they had been members of the "official" class, had had the status of "university men," and had been well indoctrinated in conservative ideas. They were, without being aware of it, products of the reaction which dominated Europe after the excesses of the French Revolution and the shattering Napoleonic Wars. The theme occurs again and again in their discussions: Insurrection is among the worst of sins, for all government is of God.[3]

According to Anderson, his "bill of rights" criticized the rigid schedule of classes and study hours imposed on all students and the fragmentation of subject matter which occurred because so many courses were carried simultaneously. It also protested against some of the interior housekeeping arrangements and the lack of windows—and consequently of ventilation—in the attic, particularly in the north wing, which was used for sleeping rooms. One student said the boys thought the rules about going downtown were too strict; moreover, besides sawing and chopping firewood for their own use, they had to cut wood for the teachers; finally, when, during the pastoral conference, some students were assigned to shine the pastors' shoes, they thought that was going too far! "There was not enough freedom."[4]

The rebellion was quelled. Larsen's entry in Protokol is brief and revealing: "A discontented and rebellious sentiment which had arisen among the students disturbed them and kept them from working at the tasks assigned them. This unfortunate situation resulted in the expulsion of R. Anderson, because he was the leader and the one who stubbornly persisted in most shameless judgment and speech about the teachers, his expulsion taking place in the presence of the assembled pastoral conference and with its approval; whereupon the rest of the participants in the conspiracy, one by one, asked for and received pardon."[5]

77

One cannot conclude that by this action the college was saved; nor, unhappily, that the course of history was not to some extent affected.

But if Larsen, as in this case, could display temper and sometimes too long persist in it, he may be forgiven, considering his trials, frustrations, and vexations in trying to get a major building ready, appealing for funds, borrowing large sums of money at the high prevailing rates, opening a school year, moving the college, and preparing for the largest celebration among Norwegians up to this time. Moreover, he was able to rise above the resentment he may have felt. It is interesting that in the subsequent school year there was a slight modification of instruction which met one of Anderson's objections: where, earlier, a teacher had given a class instruction in two subjects, dividing the hours equally between them, he now was to concentrate on one subject until it was completed and only then proceed to the second.[6] The following year the administration agreed that the rising hour in winter should be 6:00 A.M. instead of 5:30. The curious reader may also note that when the south wing was added to the Main Building in 1874, the architect was required to put windows (such as they were) in the attic.

Finally, after Larsen had sent Anderson (no doubt in response to a request) a statement about his work and the quality thereof, Anderson wrote to thank him, adding that the report was "better than I had expected or deserved." And he continued: "Meanwhile I have discovered that the foundation which I laid in Decorah College was broader, deeper, and firmer than what I could have obtained at any American school of which I have knowledge." He closed with friendly greetings to Larsen, Schmidt, and any students who might remember him. Although the exchange appeared to open the way for a full reconciliation, it was 25 years before this came about. Meanwhile, Anderson carried on some bitter controversies, but these were largely with the Synod leaders rather than with the college itself.[7]

About this time a matter of far more fateful consequence, which so far as possible had been pushed into the background during the Civil War, came again to the fore—the question of the Synod's stand on slavery. When Larsen went to St. Louis in 1859, he became closely associated with C. F. W. Walther and other teachers of the Missouri Synod.[8] Among the views held by the highly respected Walther was the Southern theological defense of slavery on Biblical grounds. As early as August 1856 he had expressed his dissent from an article which declared slavery a sin. Later, supporting his position, he quoted approvingly utterances of Luther and Melanchthon, made during the Peasants' War. He also stated that the Missouri Synod subscribed to his views.[9]

Walther's position was that slavery as an institution is an intermediate thing, in itself neither evil nor good; that its use by society, as in Biblical times, did not make it sinful. He admitted the abuses in slavery and urged, "Fight against the abuse, not the use." Of the abuses he said, "They—but not slavery itself—have cried aloud to Heaven." His arguments were those used by the Synod pastors in the controversy that arose.[10]

When Concordia College suspended activities because of the Civil War and the students returned home, Larsen sent a brief notice to *Emigranten,* then the only Norwegian-language newspaper in the country, about this situation. When Solberg printed it, he asked Larsen for a statement of the position taken by the teachers of Concordia College toward the Rebellion. The members of the Synod had shown great confidence in the Missouri institution by sending their future spiritual leaders there for training, the editor said, and this confidence would be strengthened if the teachers at Concordia were shown to be supporters of the Union instead of, like most of the Southern clergy, of the Rebellion. There had been reports from some of the returning students that the teachers sympathized with the South, and his inquiry was designed to clear up the matter.[11]

Larsen did not reply immediately, but after *Emigranten* had printed two articles from subscribers which stirred more comment, he answered in the June 17, 1861, issue "for the weaker consciences' sake." The editorial had inquired about the attitude of the Concordia faculty toward the Rebellion: Were they loyal to the Union? Larsen did not content himself with a simple answer to the question. He injected a defense of the view that slavery is not sin, referred to Roman slavery as far crueler than American slavery, refused to condemn secession because it was not clear that secession constituted rebellion, and indicated that these were the views of the Concordia faculty as well as his own. But he added that, as a states'-rights man, he would take up arms if ordered by the governor of Wisconsin to do so.

Carl F. Solberg, editor of *Emigranten,* knew Larsen and was friendly toward him. He passed over the slavery issue lightly because events had made a discussion of it merely academic; he regretted that the Concordia men were not firmly committed to the Union; and he easily demonstrated the weakness of the states'-rights position taken by Larsen. Were Larsen living in a slave state, said Solberg, he would, at the governor's call, be in duty bound to fight for the South. Solberg clearly did not think Larsen would do this.[12]

Nine days later the Synod convened in Luther Valley, Wisconsin. For more than two days the convention listened to a discussion of the doctrine of absolution. But the question raised by the war — whether the Synod should continue the affiliation with Concordia or should proceed at once with its own college — was the vital one and was tied in closely with the overriding issues of slavery and secession, which loomed large in the minds of all. A minority group, consisting of pastors, urged that the connection with St. Louis be continued until the new institution was established. There were prompt objections because of the disturbing reports about the views of the Concordia faculty. The issue became increasingly clear; the convention therefore proceeded to discuss slavery.

Larsen—whose statement in *Emigranten* had aroused opposition—and several, but not all, of the pastors defended the viewpoint of Walther and the Missourians as to what the Bible teaches concerning slavery. The opposition was led by a layman, Erik Ellefsen (Slen), the "King of Big Canoe."[13]

The Synod leaders were in a difficult position. Feeling bound by the principle of separation of church and state, they hesitated to make a pronouncement on what many regarded as a political issue. They were also bound by their strict adherence to Scriptural authority and were unable to break down the logic of the Southern theological interpretation of slavery. The low-church Eielsen and Augustana groups had early taken the stand that slavery was sinful and were thus sympathetic to the abolitionists; but the Synod leaders and most Norwegian laymen, like the majority of the Northern population, were skeptical of the methods of the abolitionist program. It was no secret that the pastors, like the laymen, were opposed to American slaveholding, and that all but one of them were Republican.[14] The deciding factor, however, was the theological one. What should be the church's pronouncement on slavery?

In an effort to satisfy all parties, the pastors drew up the following declaration:

"Although, according to God's Word, it is not in and of itself sin to keep slaves, nevertheless slavery in itself is an evil and a punishment from God, and we condemn all the abuses and sins connected therewith; furthermore, when our official duties require it and when Christian love and wisdom demand it, we will work for its abolition."[15]

81

All the clergymen present signed the statement. When the laymen were asked whether they were "satisfied with this declaration as a statement of the clergymen's doctrine," 28 voted yes, 10 voted no, 28 did not vote, and 2 were absent. Later Halvor Steensland, C. Smedsrud, and Torkel Gulbrandsen Johnsrud, who had voted yes, indicated they would have voted negatively had the motion been directly on slavery.[16]

Some who were not satisfied with the Pastors' Declaration drafted the following counterstatement, which was spread upon the minutes of the convention:

"Slavery, viewed as an institution, can exist only under definite law, and since the laws upon which it is based stand in manifest conflict with the Word of God and Christian love, it is sin; and since slavery in the United States has been one of this country's greatest evils both for church and state, we look upon it as our absolute duty as Christians and good citizens to do everything in our power, by legal means, to alleviate, lessen, and if possible abolish slavery, when our country's welfare and Christian love demand this of us."[17]

This declaration was signed by Halvor A. Aasen, Isak Aslagsen, Erik Ellefsen, Lars Jaer, Johannes C. Lee, Gudbrand Myhre, Ole A. Ruste, Jørgen Olsen Wraalstad, and Ole Olsen Wraalstad.

As an expression of the strong lay viewpoint which insisted on the founding of Luther College in 1861, says one son of the college, this antislavery, free-labor resolution "should be immortalized in bronze on the Luther College campus."[18]

The vote on the Pastors' Declaration came as a shock to the clergy. For the first time in the history of the young church they had failed to carry the laity with them. To the laity, the declaration seemed to run counter to the fundamental ideals of the Norwegian immigrant: his intense desire for economic freedom, his belief in every man's right to the product of his labor, and his trust in the democratic processes of government. The lay members could not reconcile this pronouncement with what they knew to be the antislavery views of their pastors, and a majority refused to endorse it.

Then, leaving the abstract question for the practical one before them, they wasted no time in deciding to keep their sons up North and to proceed at once with the establishment of Luther College. As to its exact form and its course of study they did not feel competent to judge, and so, as one historian puts it, "left the mysteries of higher education to Professor Larsen and the clergy." Luther College was thus "born of the anti-slavery, freedom-loving, labor-respecting secular tradition, even though its form and its course of study were determined by the ecclesiastical tradition and its strongest representatives, the pastors."[19]

There was some effort to make capital of war sentiment, to say that passions were inflamed and that calm discussion could not be carried on in the war atmosphere. No doubt feeling ran high, but the restraint of the laity in the face of a theological point of view which repelled them and which history has repudiated is remarkable.[20] Despite the searching questions raised by the Pastors' Declaration in a time of war, the laity were so far from fanaticized that they retained Larsen in his position and placed him in charge of the institution which was now to take form up North.

But the matter did not end so easily. The declaration rankled. Before long C. L. Clausen, the warmhearted Dane who many years before had cast his lot with the Norwegians, felt constrained to withdraw his assent to it. His action made the slavery controversy inevitable. It flared up in the press in 1862; was kept in the background from 1863 to 1865; then, after the war was over, was bitterly fought from 1866 to 1869.

At first there was a gentleman's agreement to keep the controversy out of the public eye. With Clausen away, as chaplain for the Fifteenth Wisconsin Regiment, this was possible for a time. Meanwhile, in 1862 the Synod leaders appealed to the theological faculty of the University of Christiania for an opinion. When it came—a carefully worded document prepared by men under whom most of the Synod pastors had sat as students—it offered an escape from the dilemma in which the pastors found themselves. It condemned slavery emphatically as contrary to God's original will to man and as a fruit of sin, but acknowledged that being a slave or holding slaves is not in every instance a sin and that the New Testament nowhere expressly forbids slavery. But the Synod leaders now took issue with their teachers; they carried on long and fruitless negotiations, hoping to persuade the university theologians to change their minds. In the formulation of the Synod rejoinders, Larsen, in particular, took a prominent part.

Synod leaders held conference after conference with Clausen, who, because of ill health, had returned from the war, attempting to convert him to their doctrine, meanwhile withholding from him the knowledge of the Christiania faculty documents until they were finally published in 1866, after the war was over. Clausen was no match for the dialecticians arrayed against him—Larsen, Schmidt, Ottesen, H. A. Preus, and Koren, not to mention the Missourians C. F. W. Walther, William Sihler, and Friedrich A. Craemer, who were brought in to bolster the Synod brethren. Clausen became involved in contradictions that weakened his case. The Synod leaders were therefore able so far to discredit him that at the convention in 1868 they carried the day against him by an overwhelming majority, and felt that they had preserved "the pure doctrine." It was a Pyrrhic victory. In 1869 the Synod again took up the subject (perhaps as a result of A. C. Preus's "Word of Conciliation," in which he defended the Christiania opinion) by declaring that American slavery "in the less precise speech of daily life" was a sin. The Synod also maintained that masters who treated their slaves "in love according to God's word" did not sin by keeping slaves. The Church Council then proceeded to say, "No Christian can be a proslavery man."[21]

"Had there been no connection with the Missouri Synod," says Karen Larsen, "the issue of slavery might never have been raised." She also says, "To uphold the authority of the Scriptures was a *sine qua non* to the clergy. Unless they should change their whole method of Biblical interpretation, they had to maintain that slavery was not necessarily a sin." The Synod men argued from the premise that the words of the Scriptures, inerrant because verbally inspired, were logically identified with the Word of God. Walther confirmed and encouraged them in their position. They persuaded themselves, Walther and Synod leaders alike, that they were upholding the sacredness of Scripture against the mistaken notions of less enlightened men.[22]

Walther did not guide the Synod leaders to a more conciliatory attitude and an abandonment of their early prejudices; on the contrary, he urged them not to yield an inch. "If there should now be the slightest indication that you are contemplating a retreat for pragmatic reasons, the situation would only become worse. . . . America, which is intoxicated with freedom, has to have such people as we are, if it is not to perish without warning. . . . Every period of history and every country has its special temptations and danger; America's is that of the swindle of liberty."[23]

There was something unreal about the controversy; it smoldered while the war lasted and only burst into flame after Southern surrender had settled the practical issue of American slavery. Theodore C. Blegen states: "Each side, for better or for worse, both won and lost. . . . Meanwhile, for Americans north and south, perspective gradually lengthened, and there was a growing tendency to consider slavery, not in theological terms, but as an economic and social institution to be viewed, in its setting of time and circum-

stance, as wise or unwise, just or unjust, humane or in-
human."[24]

Much of this account belongs to the history of the church
rather than to that of Luther College. Yet the slavery controversy, which has been characterized as the "longest,
sharpest, and most bitter" in the annals of Norwegian Lutherans in America up to 1876, had effects upon the college
from which even yet it has not fully emerged.[25]

The issue impaired the finances of the fledgling institution.
Many of the laity were unwilling to contribute to the college
while the Synod pastors adhered to their stand. The grand
total of the cost of the new plant was $87,000, of which
$27,000 remained as a debt. In 1865–66 it was necessary to
borrow money at interest as high as 18 per cent. H. A. Preus,
in a letter to Larsen from Christiania, wrote March 24, 1867:
"The University Fund is a bottomless pit. Last year we
owed $25,000. This year $13,000 was received in addition
to the sale of the old building, yet we owe $30,000."[26] For
years there was a constant struggle to raise necessary funds.

The financial difficulty gave rise to what may be called
the "crisis psychology," which existed even in the college's
first year.[27] There are references to enemies of the institution, as if it were constantly on the defensive and fending
off attacks, instead of joyously carrying on its work, supported and strengthened by warm friends. Walther's advice
usually tended to lend comfort to such an attitude. He constantly urged Larsen and others to stand firm, confident that
God was on their side; they must expect to have earthly foes
but could rely on divine support, no matter how bleak the
outlook. The Waltherian view almost rejoiced in a position
which stirred up opposition and created enemies. It seemed
to encourage a martyr complex.

The controversy also lost the college the support of some
very influential Norwegian Americans. Knud Langeland, who
had wholeheartedly supported the movement for founding

the college, wrote a front-page article in *Emigranten* of October 7, 1861, in which he took issue with the pastors. Later when, with John Anderson, Iver Larsen (Lawson), and others, he founded *Skandinaven* in Chicago, he kept up a running fire at the Synod because of its stand on slavery. And his attack tended to broaden when the Synod leaders made themselves vulnerable by their aspersions on public schools and other elements of American life.[28]

The issue also caused a dozen or more congregations to withdraw from the Synod, notably those associated with C. L. Clausen, such as Luther Valley, Wisconsin, and St. Ansgar, Iowa. Muskego, Wisconsin, home of Colonel Hans C. Heg, Civil War hero, had long stood aloof. Some of A. C. Preus's congregations in Lee County, Illinois, left. Big Canoe, northeast of Decorah, dropped out. Several of these congregations later returned to the Synod, but many individuals withdrew from congregations. Ove J. Hjort wrote, "We hear so many bitter things these days that my wife often weeps because of anxiety for the future of our church." Rumor had it that the position in which A. C. Preus found himself in the slavery controversy was what finally led him to leave America and seek an office in Norway.[29]

The struggle left its mark on the young college president and thereby tended to narrow the outlook and outreach of the college itself. Larsen, having taken his position in the conviction that he was fully sustained by Scripture, labored with youthful fervor and confidence to confute those who opposed his view. The most laborious papers in the controversy are his. With meticulous care he marshaled Bible passages, seeking to buttress his arguments. His opponents showed no disposition to alter their views. Only as the years followed, and time dulled the attraction of mere logical analysis, did a slow and subtle change lead him to the perception of fundamental issues and to a certain distrust of abstractions removed from the practical world. Years later he referred to the "indiscretion of youth" in speaking of the matter.[30]

Larsen was not proslavery or unsympathetic to the Union cause. After Lincoln's assassination there was a memorial service in the Methodist church in Decorah, which all the college attended. Larsen gave the first address, speaking without notes. "I think it was one of the best addresses Professor Larsen has ever given. It was also well received and praised by the citizens. The speech was patriotic from beginning to end."[31]

As late as 1872, however, Larsen wrote that at the Synod meeting of 1861 "a large part, perhaps the majority of the laity" were "confused and fanaticized."[32] That the majority disagreed with Larsen did not justify his describing them thus. It was a time of strong differences of opinion, and the fact that Larsen was the only Democrat among the Synod pastors had little, if anything, to do with the matter. So strong were these differences among the general population that Lincoln in 1860 received less than 40 per cent of the popular vote and was thus a minority candidate.

But Larsen's position was a decidedly uncomfortable one. No partisan of slavery, he was tagged with a proslavery label. He was too honest to deny his own logic; yet there was something false, something hollow in such a situation. So he withdrew more to himself, tending to avoid public issues in the college, made twice shy by his unfortunate sally into a political area. He concentrated more and more on what he felt was of greatest importance to the success of the college and the church—a thorough and liberal training of the young men entrusted to his care, an insistence on high standards of work, an aversion to superficiality, and unflinching honesty and sincerity in all dealings. The program was a narrow one, but it was sound, and it produced able men. In the early days of the college it was perhaps the most thorough schooling offered in the upper part of the Middle West.

*The Lord records as he registers
the peoples, "This one was born
there."*

—Psalm 87:6

7

The Emerging American College

Up to 1861 about 50,000 Norwegians had migrated to this country, but from 1861 to 1880 more than three times as many arrived. There was a strong upsurge of immigration immediately after the Civil War and a falling off during the depression of the seventies. A new and even greater wave of immigration was to follow in the eighties.

The Norwegian Synod, by reaching out to these immigrants, grew rapidly during this period, and the fortunes of Luther College largely paralleled those of the Synod. The slavery controversy, which had caused much bad blood, was thrust into the background when in 1869 the Synod tardily declared American slavery to be sin—a declaration wiser men had been willing to make in 1861. A new conflict, however, arose over the common or public school. President H. A. Preus of the Synod pressed hard for the establishment of religious schools and, by some unguarded intemperate utterances, stirred equally intemperate opposition from *Skandinaven,* Rasmus B. Anderson, and others. But this was largely an internal synodical dispute. In 1872 the Missouri Synod, the Joint Ohio Synod, the Wisconsin Synod, the Minnesota Synod, the Illinois Synod, and the Norwegian Synod met in Chicago and formed the Synodical Conference; this move perhaps came too soon for the strongly nationalistic Norwegians.

Among the Norwegians, the Norwegian Synod still dominated the field—Clausen's Conference, the Augustanans, and the Haugeans comprising a definite minority. A somewhat uneasy truce was broken by what some called H. A. Preus's *banbulle* (bull of excommunication) of 1872 against the Conference, a polemical utterance in which zeal outran good judgment. In 1874 Sven Oftedal and August Weenaas of Augsburg Seminary replied in their "Open Declaration," a violent attack on the Synod that, by its immoderate tone, weakened its effect. It was followed by Weenaas' *Wisconsin-isme* (including, in the second edition, his disavowal of the "Open Declaration"), which stirred replies from Preus and Koren; but the Synod's strong position was not seriously weakened. The seventies were golden years for the Synod. By 1880 it had 145 pastors and 592 congregations. But at the end of the period clouds were gathering.

Like the Synod, Luther College in this pioneer period grew and flourished. Its total attendance rose almost year by year until in 1874–75 it stood at 229, a mark not surpassed until 40 years later. Meanwhile, enrollment in the college division rose from 62 to 146. The panic of 1873, and the drouth and grasshopper plagues of succeeding years, brought hard times which cut the attendance to 165 in 1880–81. Yet the college, although still popularly known as the "preacher school" or the "Decorah school," had emerged from the primitive conditions that marked its birth. It began more and more to take on the character of an American college.

Originally Larsen had used Concordia College as a model, perhaps because Concordia closely resembled the Latin school that he remembered from Norway. But the term *latinskole* was not applied to Luther College in its earliest years. The strenuous efforts required to organize the institution, to care for the many management details, and to plan and supervise the erection of buildings left little time for a formulation of educational theory. H. A. Preus stated, six years after its founding, that the college corresponded most nearly to a Latin school, but was also a boarding school and stressed instruction in Christian doctrine. By 1872 Larsen stated unqualifiedly that Luther College was to be essentially a Latin school, corresponding "approximately" to those in Norway which pastors attended before being admitted to the university.[1]

Larsen, however, always pointed out that Luther College was more than a Latin school, for, unlike its models in Norway, it was a boarding school. Moreover, in Norway they had only one mother tongue; in this country there were two, Norwegian and English, and therefore both had to be studied. In addition, Luther College required all students to take instruction in the history and doctrines of Christianity. Finally, from the very first year of the college, the course included two credit hours of music. These additional requirements therefore made demands upon the student somewhat greater than those of the Latin school in Norway.

Newer men on the faculty who had received their training in Norway were inclined to look back to their own country rather than to Concordia College for a model. Thus A. A. Veblen relates of Thrond Bothne, who joined the faculty in 1875, that his "constant criterion when questions of practice or policy arose, as in faculty meetings, was: Thus we do 'at home' *(hjemme)* and he cared not at all what the practice in a given case might be in American institutions. Neither did he seem to accept as decisive what might be the practice or custom of the Germans, whose standards and opinions in those days counted for so much among the leading lights at the college, as well as among the theologians and laymen generally, of the Synod." But Larsen's "approximately" is worth noting. He was more aware than some that the school had to adjust to American conditions.[2]

In the early years, only a decade or two removed from the frontier, there were grade schools in Decorah and West Decorah, but no high school, although Breckenridge's School and Valder Business College were then operating. In 1874 there were about 30 students at Luther College in Sexta B, one rank below the lowest class, ranging in age from 10 to well over 20 years. Older students, almost without exception, were experiencing their first contact with regular school. Similar conditions prevailed in most of the Midwest area. The University of Wisconsin, which opened its doors in 1849, maintained a preparatory department for about 30 years. The early institutions had to take students at the scholastic level on which they found them. In 1874–75, says James C. M. Hanson, '82, Sexta A was enlarged by "a contingent from Chicago, five in number, readily distinguished from the other students because of their neat and well fitting clothes, the cut of their hair, evidently by a professional barber, not by Nils Flaten at 5c per cut, and that indefinite air of the large city, which the Romans referred to as *frons urbana*."[3]

The same writer states that it was significant that "world history and the history of Norway, Denmark and Sweden were permitted to take precedence over U.S. History. The reason must be sought in the makeup of the faculty and the representatives of the church whose duty it was to outline the courses. Almost without exception they were graduates of the University of Oslo, recent arrivals in America, unfamiliar with its history and even language, who failed to see the changes to come and the drift away from Norwegian to be witnessed in the second and third generations even of their own families."[4]

English had been used among the students from the very beginning. Even in those early years some of them knew very little Norwegian. Larsen, writing a recommendation for Thomas A. Thompson, who had attended 1868–70, stated: "As his knowledge of the Norwegian language, through which most of the instruction here is given, was at the time of his entering rather imperfect, he could not make the progress which else he would undoubtedly have made." Norwegian for some years predominated as the medium of instruction. In part this was a deliberate policy, for the school and Synod leaders were convinced that, for many years to come, pastors in the church would have to be at home in both languages. But the change, though scarcely visible from year to year, was inevitably and swiftly coming. In 1877, according to A. A. Veblen: "English and Norwegian were used to about an equal extent among the boys on campus. Larsen, Brandt and Bothne never spoke English to the boys. The intercourse between the other men and the boys took place in one language or the other indifferently. The language used in the various games or sports would also vary. But baseball could hardly be played except in English. It was the chief sport cultivated at Luther College, and I believe one is justified in crediting the gradual Americanization of the College partly to the influence of this, the national game." Veblen says further: "At the time of my leaving Decorah in 1881, English had practically displaced Norwegian as the language of the campus and largely so in the everyday intercourse between the students, as well as among those of the teachers who had been reared in this country."[5] Not all were happy over the change; nevertheless, it came.

During this period there were several additions to the physical plant. In 1867 Campus House (now the oldest building) was built by the three congregations served by the campus pastor, Nils O. Brandt. Later this building was bought by the college. The Brandts lived there from 1867 to January 1884. Later it housed presidents and professors and, since its renovation in 1937, has been a dormitory for women.

In 1874 the south wing of the Main Building was built. Jens J. Naeset, who served the college well in many capacities, supervised its construction. About the same time changes were made in the older portion of the building to meet the needs of the increasing student body. The new wing was formally dedicated December 2, 1874, with appropriate exercises. One feature of the occasion was the sounding of the college bell for the first time from the tower that evening. The bell, weighing 1,200 pounds, had been procured through the efforts and gifts of the students under the leadership of Bjørn Haatvedt, later Bjørn Edwards. In 1890 the same Bjørn Edwards of Chicago, who achieved distinction as a builder and as founder of *The American Contractor*, gave the college a new bell (the old one having melted in the 1889 fire), which is still in service.[6]

An 80-foot well, equipped with a windmill, was drilled to ensure an adequate supply of water. The "Chicken Coop," originally built in 1865 to be used as a barn, was remodeled in 1871 to provide living quarters for 18 students and again in the latter year to accommodate 30 students. In 1874 it also housed Niffelheim, the famous smokers' society.[7] About the same time approximately two acres of land toward the southwest were added to the campus so that a new frame barn could be erected, farther removed from the Main Building. Although much remained to be done in grading and beautifying the college green (clay for the bricks used in construction had come from a pit northeast of the present Main Building), a good deal was accomplished by students under the leadership of Jacob D. Jacobsen, the first faculty member to occupy himself actively with improving the physical aspect of the campus. In 1877–78 Professors Reque, Narveson, and Veblen supervised considerable work on the grounds. In 1880 the students subscribed $37 and the faculty $19 toward providing a sidewalk about a mile long from town to the college. This was the old wooden walk, familiar to hundreds of students.

First Lutheran Church of Decorah was erected in 1876 at a cost of $22,500. Bricks made on the college campus furnished most of the building material. The church was to be the sanctuary of the local congregation and of the college as well. The two had begun as infant organizations and had

grown up side by side. From 1865 to 1876 they had wor-
shiped together in the chapel in the Main Building. The early
fathers had before them the example of Concordia College
and Seminary, which had been so closely associated with
the congregations surrounding it that there was a mutual
interplay of interest and support. The founders envisaged a
similar relationship for Luther College. The church which
was thus erected to serve both congregation and college was,
and is, a noble structure. But it was located downtown, a
mile from the campus, and so never came to be a college
chapel. Yet the college had a half interest in the structure
and regarded it as its church. When the building was dedicated in 1876, the Synod met for the first time in Decorah;
on that occasion President Larsen stated "that with the
dedication of this church the building program for Luther
College was completed except possibly for some teachers'
residences and minor buildings."[8] Despite certain difficulties that grew out of the dual ownership, the arrangement
came with the years to be regarded as normal; and this
decision to maintain a joint church for college and congregation is responsible, more than any other single factor, for
the fact that to this day there is no chapel on the college
campus.

The joint ownership of the congregation and the college
was not terminated until 1930, when the college turned over
to the congregation its half interest in the property for
$8,134.48.[9] Students continued to be welcomed by the
churches of the city; in addition, since 1959 they have had
their own student congregation on the campus with its own
pastor and worship.

The first piano for the college was bought in 1863 with
funds collected by students under the leadership of Professor
Friedrich A. Schmidt. The first band instruments were purchased in 1878 through the efforts of Hans B. Thorgrimsen,
'79, and other students. Some crude athletic equipment was

set up in the backyard of "Hututu" in 1863. In 1865 such athletic equipment as then existed was set up outside the Main Building. In April 1880, on a motion by A. A. Veblen, it was decided to buy a microscope.

Although the college was burdened by debt in the sixties, its financial condition steadily improved. By 1880 the debt was almost all liquidated and the various improvements of the seventies paid for, leaving only minor financial burdens. During this period the college charged no tuition except first-year fees and the fee of $30 collected, beginning in 1876–77, from the members of Sexta in the preparatory department. It received fairly substantial gifts in kind from supporters near at hand and, through the church, annual student-aid funds. Otherwise, as there was no endowment, income was restricted to the funds received from the Synod. These fluctuated from year to year with the fortunes of the church but did not fail. Except for the few efforts by students, no funds were raised by the college itself within its constituency.

Following the Synod action in 1862 affirming positively its view that the college should open its doors to all young men of the church and that no tuition should be charged whether the student signified his intention to enter the ministry or not, Larsen reported that of 32 in attendance in 1862–63, all 8 of the returning students had entered Luther College to prepare for the ministry. Of the new students, some desired to be teachers, some "have expressly declared that they expect to attend only a short time to acquire certain knowledge, and many are undecided about their future plans." Thus it appears that not a few sought to take advantage of the liberal viewpoint expressed in the church resolution, but there is little doubt that Larsen and his colleagues held firmly to the earlier program he himself had had in mind—that the institution should develop into a college and seminary for leading men directly into the ministry. In the face of the flood of immigration, he was acutely conscious of the overwhelming need of the church for pastors.[10]

It is not surprising, therefore, that in the first decade (1861–71) only four of the school's 26 graduates failed to enter the ministry (if among the four we include Rasmus B. Anderson, whose expulsion in 1865 decided the matter for him). The pressures were strong. Knut Bergh, Anderson's contemporary, wrote to Rasmus on September 2, 1865: "You say you will not study theology. But I can assure you that you will not get permission to do anything else. . . . And do you think they will let you go? No, my good Rasmus." The pressure was there even if it was not openly expressed. Practically all the students had been hand-picked by pastors and were already strongly disposed toward the ministry before they entered the school. Within the college there was an atmosphere of quiet, nonemotional, but pervasive devotion to a cause greater than the individual—the cause of the pioneer Christian ministry on the frontiers of the developing Midwest. Obviously, those who attended Luther College were expected to become preachers. So routine a matter was this that in the early days students were simply "graduated to St. Louis," or "graduated to Concordia Seminary." But in the second decade there was a progressive change, for of the 102 graduates (1872–81) 68 entered the ministry and 34 took up other professions.[11]

The freshman class (Quarta) of 1861 should have been graduated in 1865, but of its six members, three withdrew before the end of the first year because of illness (Knut Folkestad; the highly gifted Knut Bergh; and Niels J. Eide, who later enlisted in the army and served to the end of the Civil War). Knut Aslaksen left in December 1863 because of illness; Iver Larsen withdrew in January 1862 because of dissatisfaction; and Brynjolf Hovde, who was perhaps the most advanced of the six, transferred at Larsen's suggestion to

Concordia College, Fort Wayne, Indiana, in 1862. There was thus no graduating class in 1865.

The first class was graduated in 1866 and consisted of seven members (later eight, when R. B. Anderson belatedly received his degree in 1890). Bergh and Normann entered in September 1861; Anderson and Olsen entered in January 1862; Erdahl and Markhus entered in September 1862; Juve, a transfer from the University of Wisconsin, entered in September 1863; and Stub, a transfer from Norway, entered in September 1865.

There were large increases in attendance after the school moved to Decorah. Because of heavy demands on the staff and the many inequalities in the preparation of entering students, adjustments had to be made, and there was no graduating class in 1867. The second class, consisting of three members, was graduated in 1868.

Whether all members of these two classes received formal diplomas is not revealed by the college records. The records do give us, however, the wording of the diploma granted to Lars S. Reque. He entered in 1862 and was graduated as of the class of 1868, but as he had been absent much of the school year 1863–64 because of illness, he was required to attend school in 1868–69 before he received his diploma in 1869. The diploma was as follows:

"Universitas Norvegica Lutherana
Omnibus has literas lecturis Salutem.

"Vobis notum sit, Dominum *Lars S. Reque* Titulo Graduque Artium liberalium Baccalaurei a nobis esse adornatum, omniaque privilegia, honores, dignitates, quae ubique gentum ad eum gradum pertinent, fruenda ei esse collata. Cujus rei in fidem has literas, Universitatis sigillo et subscriptis nostris nominibus firmatas, accepit.

"Dabamus ex aedibus academicis, in urbe Decorah et re-

98

publica Iowaensi sitis, Kalendis Juliis Anno Domini millesimo octingentesimo sexagesimo nono."[12]

The diploma of Ole G. Felland, '74, was given to the college museum in 1927. It is written in longhand in Latin on official blue-ruled stationery which has a cut of Old Main at the top and bears the official seal of the college in red in the lower left-hand corner. Minor refinements in the wording and form of the diploma were adopted by the faculty May 29, 1879, recommended by a committee consisting of Veblen, Jacobsen, and Sander, and apparently formal printed diplomas have been given since that date. In 1951 the language used in the diploma was changed to English.[13]

The early college seal is found embossed on a recommendation dated June 16, 1866, given to Ole Arnesen Rustad, '64–66, and signed by Laur. Larsen, F. A. Schmidt, N. Brandt, and Lyder Siewers. The seal has in the center a raised imprint of the first Main Building (without the south wing), with the motto, "Verbum dei manet in aeternum," circling the top of the building, and outside this, in a circle, the words, "Norwegian Luther-College Decorah, Iowa."

The following is a list of Luther College students who, before or after entering college, served in the Union armies during the Civil War:

Nehemias Christensen, Port Washington, Wisconsin.

Niels J. Eide, Big Canoe, Iowa; wounded at Stone River and Chickamauga.

Anders Ellestad, Newburg, Minnesota.

Tønnes Møller, Winchester, Wisconsin.

Jacob Ottesen (Lunde), Bratsberg, Minnesota.

Olaf S. Reishus, Rushford, Minnesota.

Peter S. Reque, Deerfield, Wisconsin; he went with Sherman to the sea.

Lars Rydning (Swenson), St. Peter, Minnesota.

Thore P. Schesvold, Mankato, Minnesota.

99

Kristofer Suckow, Washington Prairie, Iowa; died in the war.

Karl Thorsnaes, Norway Grove, Wisconsin.

In 1865 a two-year teachers' training department was organized. Steps toward this end had already been taken by the faculty the preceding year. In 1868 the Synod requested expanded instruction in English. This was provided and the teachers' course lengthened to three years so that students completing it could teach in American common schools. The first graduates of the three-year normal course went out in 1871. Considerable effort was expended on the teachers' training department and it produced some excellent men. But it was never popular. Attendance languished, and finally in 1886 the department was discontinued. In 1889 the church made other provision for this field by opening Lutheran Normal School at Sioux Falls, South Dakota.

The effort to stimulate interest in training teachers was part of a Synod program that eventuated in the academy movement, to which H. A. Preus, president of the Synod from 1862 to 1894, devoted much time and energy. The first such institution was Holden Academy, which opened in 1869 near Northfield, Minnesota, with Tosten Jesme, who had studied at Luther College from 1863–66, as teacher. Holden Academy did not survive but was the forerunner of St. Olaf's School, founded in 1874 in Northfield with Thorbjørn N. Mohn, '70, as president, and staffed during its early years chiefly by Luther College men. Of its 14 faculty members up to 1887, three were women, ten were Luther College graduates, and one was a former Luther College student. Of its 45 faculty members up to 1900, 18 were Luther College graduates, including J. N. Kildahl, '79, its second president. The ties were very close. Reverend B. J. Muus, a moving spirit in the founding of St. Olaf, invited all of Luther College, faculty and students, to the dedication of "the new academy building" on November 6, 1878. There was considerable enthusiasm for the outing, but the Luther faculty finally ruled against it and directed that President Larsen and Professor Reque represent the institution, since both had been invited to speak at the exercises.[14]

In 1876 the Synod decided to establish its own practical theological seminary (the theoretical seminary followed in 1878) in Madison, Wisconsin. This action stirred considerable discussion. (There was some agitation for a joint theological seminary under the auspices of the Synodical Conference, but this project never commanded great support.) Many were unwilling to give up the long-standing connection with Concordia Seminary in St. Louis. But since the Missouri Synod clung as tenaciously to German as the Norwegian Synod did to Norwegian, there was a language problem. Among the rank and file of the Norwegians, national pride also played its part. Moreover, theological opponents in other Norwegian church bodies had taunted the Synod for not having founded a seminary of its own. Some still cherished the plan for locating the seminary in Decorah in connection with Luther College as part of the "university" idea.

But those who wished the seminary separate from the college carried the day and Luther Seminary was established at Madison. Their view, which had far-reaching consequences in modifying the aim and purpose of Luther College, was well expressed by Hans G. Stub, '66, years later, on October 14, 1890. Stub, who received his early education in Norway and spent only one year at Luther College before receiving his degree in 1866, called Luther Seminary an older brother of Luther College, though younger in years. No amalgamation of the seminary and college, he continued, was desirable. "A college must as a matter of course have a broader basis and a more cosmopolitan character." Yet Luther's "ultimate aim is preparation for thorough theological study. . . . But the realization of this aim is not accomplished

101

by making this college a theological preparatory school. Luther College must be a college proper. And I for one think that Luther College in its new form, adapted to the wants and demands of the times by its thorough American training, performed by an efficient and always increasing force of teachers, will have an even larger field of work and exert an even deeper and more widespread influence than the former [theological preparatory school]." This statement, which harks back to the aspirations of the lay-minded founders, and reads in retrospect like a Magna Carta for Luther College, had no spokesman in 1876 and was ahead of its time even in 1890.[15]

Yet in 1890, when this was spoken, it created no great stir; it was regarded more as an expression of what the college was than of what it should become. For the classical course with varying emphasis was found in nearly all American colleges in this early period. Luther, with stress on Norwegian, German, French, and Hebrew in addition to Greek and Latin, was far from being parochial. It demanded of its students a thorough knowledge of the history, institutions, and culture of the peoples whose languages were studied. In short, it gave its students a broad, thorough course in the humanities, and it developed well-rounded men.

Luther College was incorporated under the laws of Iowa February 1, 1865. Its purpose was stated to be "the establishment of a Collegiate Institution in the Town of Decorah of a religious and educational character." The members of the corporation were the duly called pastors of the congregations of the Synod and the chosen representatives of those congregations at the synodical meetings. This membership provision has remained substantially unchanged. On June 29, 1871, at its first meeting the corporation amended the Articles of Incorporation of Luther College to make the Church Council a board of visitors and the president and the professors of the college a board or faculty. An act of the Iowa legislature, approved April 12, 1872, legalized meetings of the corporation held in any state adjoining Iowa.

The bylaws of 1871 provided that the Luther College trustees could not authorize the expenditure of more than $1,000 annually without first submitting their plan to the annual meeting of the Synod for approval. The Board of Visitors, which in effect was the Church Council, was given the power to fix the number of professors and their respective duties and compensation, and also the power to appoint and remove them, subject to the approval of a majority of the pastors of Synod congregations and the professors of Luther College. The Board of Visitors was also made responsible for admission requirements and such other rules and regulations as "they may deem best" for the guidance of the "Board of Professors" in maintaining the good government and discipline of the college.

Under these circumstances the trustees had almost no authority and hence accomplished very little in the early years of the school. The bylaws granting the Church Council and the Board of Visitors their sweeping powers constituted a definite handicap to good administration. Yet this arrangement remained substantially unchanged until the revision of 1930 during Oscar L. Olson's administration, when the Church Council's powers were eliminated to bring the Articles into harmony with what had gradually come to be actual usage, although the Board of Visitors (Board of Education) retained its authority until the revision of 1936. It becomes tedious to observe the ever-recurring reference of minor problems to the Church Council during Larsen's day because of this cumbersome system.

In this period the faculty was composed of young men. Of the 22 who served, 12, including the president, were in their 20's when they started teaching at the college, six were in their early 30's, one was 40, one was 41, and two part-time

103

teachers were 38 and 48. Most of them engaged actively in duties outside as well as inside the classroom and the majority of those who later left the college achieved distinction.

President Larsen, while at Halfway Creek, served four near-by country congregations, and preached on occasion for two others. In Decorah he preached regularly for the congregation there. Beginning July 15, 1868, *Kirkelig maanedstidende* (Monthly Church Times), the Synod's church organ, was edited by the college faculty, but in practice the job was almost wholly Larsen's. In 1874 the journal became a weekly entitled *Evangelisk luthersk kirketidende* (Evangelical Lutheran Church Times), and Larsen continued to edit it until 1889. The establishment of the Lutheran Publishing House at Decorah in 1878 lightened somewhat the burden of his editorial chores. In addition to his editorial and teaching duties, Larsen tended to nearly all the administrative details of the college in its early years, as the carefully kept Protokol, written in his hand, testifies. He was likewise the chief disciplinarian. He and his family occupied quarters in the Main Building. The college provided free housing for the other faculty members in either purchased or rented quarters.

Larsen's first wife, nee Karen Neuberg, who had accompanied him from Norway to the United States, died on February 6, 1871, after an illness of several years. She was an attractive, if somewhat retiring woman, for whom the hardships of early pioneering proved too strong. A year and a half later, on a visit to Norway, Larsen married Ingeborg Astrup, daughter of Judge Nikolai Astrup, August 20, 1872. A devoted and resourceful woman, she took charge of the household in the original drafty quarters in the Main Building, later moving to a much more comfortable apartment in the south wing in 1874, and made a place of serenity and repose for the president and his children. There the family lived until the destruction of the building by fire in May

1889. One of the children has said that no other place could be "quite so much a real home as the old college, where every spot hid a fairy tale and every ray of sunshine lit up a memory."[16]

The faculty included, in addition to Larsen, Friedrich A. Schmidt, who had been educated at Concordia College and Seminary. Schmidt had a long and colorful career. He came to Luther in 1861 and left in 1872 to become the Norwegian Synod's professor at Concordia Seminary. For two years he edited and published, at Decorah, the *Lutheran Watchman*, which was an eight-page, three-column magazine in 1866 and an eight-page, two-column magazine in 1867. He was professor at Luther Seminary 1876–86; at the Anti-Missourian Seminary 1886–90; at Augsburg Seminary 1890–93; and at the United Norwegian Lutheran Church Seminary 1893–1912. He edited *Altes und neues* (Old and New) 1880–85; *Lutherske vidnesbyrd* (Lutheran Witness) 1882–90; and *Luthersk kirkeblad* (Lutheran Church News) 1890–95. He was the author of *Naadevalgstriden* (The Election Controversy) 1881, *Intuitu fidei* (In View of Faith) 1895, and *Sandhed og fred* (Truth and Peace) 1914. Both Larsen and he served the Decorah congregation as pastors from 1862 to 1872. They started work together in 1861. They drifted far apart during the eighties because of theological differences. Both gave up active work in the church in 1912, the year peace in that body was on the way to being restored.

The third teacher at the college was Lyder Siewers, a university man from Norway who taught 1863–77. The fourth, Knut E. Bergh, was the first former student to be employed full time. Before 1865 he had taught part time. He then studied law, was admitted to the bar, and became an excellent public speaker and a member of the state legislature. He was greatly beloved by all; a faculty member 1869–74, he was cut down in his career by tuberculosis. He bequeathed his books and papers to the college. "In his relations with students he was, like Larsen, a gentleman to his fingertips, always friendly and extremely careful not to do anyone an injustice. He found it impossible not to believe the best of everyone."[17] Nils O. Brandt, the fifth teacher, was called to Decorah in 1865 as college pastor and as pastor of the Decorah congregation and the neighboring Madison and Lincoln congregations near Ridgeway. He was active until 1881. The sixth teacher was Gabriel H. Landmark, likewise a university man from Norway. He was at Luther from 1867 to 1876 and served as part-time librarian 1867–74, a position earlier filled by Larsen.

These early men had strong literary interests. In 1870 Siewers, Landmark, and Bergh founded *For hjemmet* (For the Home). This was a "Christian Monthly Magazine for Instruction and Entertainment," published in Decorah. Except for a lack of illustrations, it compares favorably with other magazines of the day. It contained sketches on travel, lands, and peoples; articles on natural history (animal and plant life) and on hunting and fishing; stories and poems; and miscellaneous shorter pieces. In 1874 it published serially the first novel in Norwegian of Norwegian-American life: Nicolai Severin Hassel's *Alf Brage, eller skolelæreren i Minnesota* (Alf Brage, or the Schoolteacher in Minnesota). Later it published Hassel's second novel, *Rædselsdagene: Et norsk billede fra indianerkrigen i Minnesota* (Days of Terror: A Norwegian Picture from the Indian War in Minnesota). The magazine had a respectable if not large circulation. It was taken over and published from 1876 on by K. Throndsen (who had assisted at the college in 1868, 1869, and 1870). It continued until 1887. Lyder Siewers, whose name is perpetuated in Siewers Springs, southeast of Decorah, was later an editor of *Decorah-posten*, 1877–1907. "This stately and friendly man was a popular figure in Decorah to his dying day. His was a poetic nature, rejoicing in children, flowers, and little birds—a true representative of the old romanticism."[18]

Jacob D. Jacobsen, who was one of the faculty, 1872–81, and served as librarian, 1874–81, was one of the original three young Norwegians who went to St. Louis in 1858. In 1863, for three months, he substituted at Luther College, pending the arrival of Lyder Siewers, and was thus the first Norwegian American educated in this country to teach at the college on a full-time basis. (Larsen, however, had often employed advanced students, such as Brynjolf Hovde, for brief periods when he was obliged to be absent from school.) Jacobsen, father of Karl T. Jacobsen, the librarian, and grandfather of Professor Robert S. Jacobsen, was a lover of literature and an inspiring teacher. His revision of an English version of the Augsburg Confession was called the "best translation in the language until the recent one made in 1891 by representatives of all Lutheran bodies in America." It was he who placed the words "The fear of the Lord is the beginning of wisdom" as a motto above the rules of the college. His career was cut short by tuberculosis on April 1, 1881. Students made up a subscription and raised a monument over his grave that same year. In 1883 his portrait in oil, by H. Gausta, was presented to the college by the Alumni Association.[19]

Among other teachers of this period, A. Seippel returned to Norway after one year (1873–74) to become a distinguished professor of Semitic languages, an authority in *landsmaal*, and a translator of the Bible into *landsmaal*.[20] Jon Bjarnason, first Icelander on the staff, taught 1874–75. He later did editorial work on *Skandinaven* (Chicago), *Budstikken* (Minneapolis), and *Sameiningin* (Winnipeg). When the Icelanders formed the Icelandic Lutheran Synod in America in 1885, Bjarnason became its president, serving until 1908. A student in one of Bjarnason's Latin classes relates that one morning Olaf T. A. Stub, '80, being asked to give the principal parts of *fero, tuli, latum, ferre,* blurted out "fero, tuli, lutum, lare." The temperamental Bjarnason rose from his chair, paced the floor, tore at his red beard, and, drifting into verse in his excitement, exclaimed: "Fero, tuli, lutum, lare, Gud bevare, sæt dig ned og skam dig bare!"[21] U. V. Koren, later president of the Synod, Friederich Lindemann, later instructor in the Missouri Synod's Teachers' Seminary at Addison, Illinois, and A. K. Teisberg, later secretary of the Minnesota Railroad and Warehouse Commission, each taught at the college 1874–75.

Cornelius Narveson, '65–67, instructed in mathematics and geography, later in natural history and chemistry, 1873–84; thus he had much to do with the beginnings of science teaching at the college. Like Bergh and Jacobsen, his death came because of tuberculosis, that scourge of the nineteenth century.

Lars S. Reque, '68, was the first Luther College graduate to serve on the faculty, having substituted for Knut Bergh occasionally before being permanently appointed in 1875. He had studied at universities abroad and at home and took a degree in law at the State University of Iowa in 1874. He served the college from 1875 to 1916 except for a term from 1893 to 1897 as United States Consul General at Rotterdam, Holland.

Thrond Bothne had a strong interest in things Norwegian and was a stimulating personality. In Norwegian and history, his favorite subjects, he aroused great interest among the students. After his years at the college, 1875–82, he turned to editorial work—with *Norden* (Chicago) 1882–84, *Amerika* (Chicago) 1884–87, *Skandinaven* 1887–94, and *Decorah-posten* 1894–1907. He is the author of "Kort udsigt over det lutherske kirkearbeid blandt nordmændene i Amerika" (Brief Survey of Lutheran Church Work among Norwegians in America), which appeared in 1898 as a supplement to Heggtveit's *Kirkehistorie.* It is still a useful work.

Adolf Bredesen, '70, taught 1876–78, then had a long and fruitful career in the ministry.

Andrew A. Veblen, who, after a six-year course graduated from Carleton College in 1877, brought some American influences to the school. During his stay at the college (1877–81) he turned Volrath Vogt's *Bibelhistorie* into English in 1879. He later became professor of physics at the State University of Iowa and returned several times to the college to lecture.

Anton B. Sander, '74, has the distinction of being the first graduate of Luther College to earn the Ph.D. degree (at Yale University in 1877). Although very popular with the students, he had the temerity, in a meeting of the Decorah congregation, to challenge certain views of the church leaders. Moreover, he was regarded by some of the faculty as "too American." Accordingly, as not "firmly orthodox," he was dropped from the faculty after one year (1878–79).[22] His promising career was cut short two years later by illness.

Halvard G. Roalkvam, '74, who taught mostly religious subjects, 1878–86, was college librarian 1882–86 and joint editor of *Luthersk skoleblad* 1880–81.

Among the interesting personalities other than faculty members who served the college must be reckoned the stewards and stewardesses: Mrs. Elisabeth Lomen (1862–68) with the assistance of Ole P. Dalemo and, later, of her husband Gulbrand Lomen; J. T. Crøger and his wife (1868–71); Ole A. Larsen (1871–75); B. Fryslie (1878–84). Peer Strømme tells an amusing incident about Captain Crøger. The latter could quickly flare up in anger, regret his action almost as quickly, and become very agreeable again. One summer Strømme was helping him; Crøger also had Thomas Hansen, a Dane from Schleswig-Holstein, as his assistant but did not get on well with him. One day they were putting up a fence around Professor Larsen's garden and Strømme was with them "trying to make it appear that he was help-ing."

Strømme continues: "Crøger dug some holes a couple of inches deep, just deep enough to put the fence posts in and keep them balanced until he could nail boards to them. He insisted that the boards would keep the posts from falling. Hansen knew better; he tried to make Crøger understand that the fence's stability depended on the posts and that therefore they would have to be sunk deeper into the ground. A heated debate ensued and at last Hansen exclaimed, 'Crøger, you don't know any more about this than a woman.' Then what I had feared happened. Crøger could not endure such an insult. He went after Hansen as if to beat him up. Hansen caught a few blows on his chest but they did not seem to bother him. He bore them without striking back, turned, took his jacket from a fence post, and walked off toward the Main Building. 'Yes, go on!' shouted Crøger after him. 'Get out of here! You can go plumb to ————,' a certain warm place. After that Crøger stood there awhile, reflecting on his action, then turned a troubled countenance toward me and said: 'Oh, no—it really wasn't right of me to say that. I am sorry. God forgive me my great sin. Hansen,' he called, 'Hansen—I take back what I said about the place you could go to. You don't need to go there. But you can go to Texas, you miserable Schleswig-Holstein scoundrel!' "[23]

Many another story is told of Crøger and many a story of others who throughout the years served the college so faithfully. These men and women are remembered with re-spect and affection by all who knew them or know of them.

The faculty members of these early years have a special place in the hearts of all friends of the college. They were a dedicated group; they had a strong sense of mission. They were aware of the great migratory movement which was bringing thousands of their countrymen to the Midwest, where amid the crude conditions of pioneer life they were subduing the soil, establishing homes, and founding communities. How were the rites of the church—the solemnization of marriages, the baptism of children, the training for confirmation, and, in the deep hours of sorrow when death struck down dear ones, the consolation of the church at the graveside—how were these to be brought to their countrymen unless the institution they had sacrificed for and founded should fill its students with zeal to serve them?

Fortunately, there *was* this missionary spirit at the college. It was a quiet, pervasive influence that struck deep roots. Hence, the extraordinary achievement of many of the early graduates who went out into the ministry, such as Hans G. Stub, '66, theological professor and president of the Norwegian Lutheran Church of America; Even J. Homme, '62–64, founder of the town of Wittenberg, Wisconsin, in which he established Homme Orphans' Home, Homme Home for the Aged, Wittenberg Academy, Wittenberg Normal School, and a printing establishment, besides editing three magazines; Thorbjørn N. Mohn, '70, first president of St. Olaf College; Bjug A. Harstad, '71, frontier pastor and founder of Pacific Lutheran University (Tacoma, Washington) in 1894; Johannes Th. Ylvisaker, '74, and Olaf E. Brandt, '79, professors at Luther Theological Seminary; John N. Kildahl, '79, second president of St. Olaf College; Thore Eggen, '79, one of the pioneers in Lutheran Brotherhood Life Insurance Society; Nils J. Bakke, '77, the first Norwegian American, so far as known, to devote his life to mission work among American Negroes; and Halvor B. Hustvedt, '73, and Realf O. Brandt, first editors of *Lutheran Herald,* the first general church organ published in English (1906) by a Norwegian-American synodical body.

Among these early graduates were also men who never lost their zeal for serving their countrymen in secular capacities, such as Rasmus B. Anderson, '66, author, United States minister to Denmark, and professor of Scandinavian languages at the University of Wisconsin, 1869–84, the first such post in this country; Peer O. Strømme, '76, author and lecturer; Gisle C. J. Bothne, '78, professor of Scandinavian languages and literature, University of Minnesota; Herbjørn N. Gausta, '72–75, artist (painter); Nils P. Haugen, '68–72, United States congressman from Wisconsin; Gilbert J. Lomen, '67–73, federal district judge, pioneer in the reindeer industry, Nome, Alaska; Andrew O. Nelson, '78–81, Norwegian vice consul, Los Angeles, California; Albert C. Amundson, '78, first graduate to become a physician.

In its earliest years the college did not have the resources to go beyond the narrow field mapped out by those directing its destinies. Within that area it functioned extremely well. Today one can easily see that after the first two decades the time was ripe for some liberalization. External as well as internal difficulties kept the institution from widening its scope and developing a more flexible pattern. And yet within its limited field it had made and it continued to make a notable contribution.

8

Early Student Life

From the very beginning of the college the library received a regular annual appropriation from the Synod, but its collections grew slowly, averaging about 170 books a year for the first 20 years. Student organizations like Mimer, however, had private libraries bought with their own funds; such collections were eventually given to the college. Like other features of the college during this formative period, the library was under the watchful eye of the president. But in the late seventies it was assigned space in the second floor tower room of the Main Building, where it remained until it was moved in 1884 to more commodious quarters on the first floor in the northeast corner.

In *Kirketidende* for February 23, 1877, President Larsen acknowledged the receipt of a collection of 600 birds' eggs and mentioned at the same time that a number of other articles had been received to form the nucleus of a museum. Although the museum grew slowly and had its ups and downs, the idea was never abandoned. In its early years one of its greatest services was the collection and preservation of Norwegian-American newspapers and magazines. Eventually this collection, now impossible to duplicate, was turned over to the library.

The college published its first catalog in 1872—*Katalog for det norske Luther-college i Decorah, Iowa, 1861–1872*. It was prepared by Larsen and ran to 48 pages. It contained

113

a list of officials and faculty members, a history of the college, an outline and a defense of the plan and courses of instruction, a section on discipline and school regulations, and a detailed listing of students at the college from the time of its founding. Larsen's precise scholarship is apparent on every page. Not until 1883 was a second catalog published, this time in English.

In the early years it was usual at commencement exercises for students to read essays or recite declamations. In 1880 the faculty, acting on a petition from the students, agreed that a valedictory might be given by a representative of the graduating class.

In the extracurricular field student societies were soon flourishing. The oldest, Clio, was organized among the Norwegian students at St. Louis March 6, 1860, and was reorganized in Decorah September 16, 1862. It held weekly meetings devoted to speeches, essays, declamations, and debates. English was the official language of the society— that is, such English as it was. "Some of the speakers," reads the report for September 26, 1862, "used such corrupt and akward [sic] language that it made it entirely impossible to correct any of it."[1]

Hetaeria (1863–70) was the name adopted in 1866 by a society founded in 1863, when it was called the Unit. It resembled Clio but used the Norwegian language. Saga (1866–70), Edda (1866–79), and Minde or Ygdrasil (1868–78) all used Norwegian. Edda introduced the practice of levying dues for subscriptions to newspapers, such as *Den nye lutherske kirketidende,* from Norway, and *Skandinaven.* Minde was the first organization to bring up for discussion the rule barring political questions as subjects for debate, a regulation that had been in force until then–and which Minde did not break.

Franklin (1871–79) was very active; it gave public programs, participated in intersociety debates, and kept a con-

siderable file of English, Norwegian, and German newspapers. In 1876, with Edda and Ygdrasil, it organized the
Students' Union (1876–1903). The Students' Union met only
every five weeks, usually for a program open to the public,
and drew its talent from all the other literary societies. It
presented speeches, essays, declamations, debates, and plays.
Its "Journal" soon attracted much attention. Osseo (1879–
81), which used both English and Norwegian, actually introduced debates on political questions; its first debate, won
by the affirmative side, dealt with woman suffrage. Addison
(1879–89) merged with Irving in the next decade. Little
but the names remain of such organizations as Losna, Nordstierna, Det Norske Selskab, Normannalaget, and Breidablik.

The most famous society organized during this period was
originally a smokers' club, which in 1870 received permission
to use a room in the "Chicken Coop." In its palmy days from
1874 to 1889 the group, organized under the name Niffelheim, developed into a "republic" of free souls devoted to
Lady Nicotine, protectress of the more daring who sought
liberation from the rather rigid routine of school rules. It
sponsored frequent debates, orations, essays, poems, and
mock trials. Its "Journal" contains the early work of many
illustrious men. The society had a gay and carefree atmosphere, and stimulated a considerable sharpening of wits.
One of its members wrote:

"Niffelheim was the first society to introduce daily papers
and weekly and monthly magazines at Luther College. She
was the first society to inaugurate trial by jury and regular
court proceedings. . . . Do you call to mind how we replen-
ished our meager treasury by producing the very first small
original farce written at Luther College, entitled 'Studen-
ten'? To say that it was a howling success is putting it mildly.
They crowded in, paying their nickel apiece. And the famous
court cases we had! I remember one especially of how a

115

certain member refusing to pay a fine for having expec-torated wildly was in due course sued by the members of the cabinet. The lawyers were the most illustrious men at col-lege. . . . Do you remember how we at one time felt almost convinced that the jury had been bribed? It seems to me that my ears ring even now with the oratorical denounce-ments uttered on that occasion.

"How did we not willingly contribute part of our small means—and indeed we were not rich in those days—toward securing the first cheap carpet at twenty-five cents per yard and curtains of coarse texture, but neat design? We were the first clubroom to have a carpet and curtains . . . and the feasts we had once or twice a year. They were always oc-casions of enjoyment and good cheer. The members of the faculty that were smokers were always invited and we indeed felt proud when they deigned to be present. There in Niffel-heim we met even the professors under a democratic flag. They often cheered us on and gave us talks full of good hints and advice."[2]

Mimer was organized in 1873 as a reading society, with dues of one dollar a year to provide books of cultural in-terest for the use of its members. Its origin is credited to Jacob D. Jacobsen, '64–65, and it flourished until 1889, by which time most of its functions had been absorbed by the college library. In 1884 it issued a printed catalog of its collection. When it was dissolved, it turned over about 900 volumes to the college library.

Muspelheim, a rival to Niffelheim, was organized in 1877–78.[3] It appealed particularly to those under 18 (who were forbidden to use tobacco) and to nonsmokers (among whom was President Larsen). But it admitted smokers, too. It had the use of a room in the Main Building, supplied with maga-zines and papers bought with the dues. Muspelheim flour-ished until about 1932.

The first student journalistic venture was "Moderlandet"

(The Motherland). This was a biweekly, four-page, hand-written paper, costing twenty-five cents for a half year, which appeared in 1865–66. It was edited by H. G. Stub, '66, and K. E. Nordgaard, '62–66; it had a title lettered by Nils Tønsberg, '65–66, and was copied out by Adolf Bredesen, '70. A satiric rival was "Mamalandet" (The Mamaland), edited in 1866 by K. Bjørgo, '70.

Other early publications, all handwritten, were "Ridderen uden frygt og dadel" (The Knight without Fear or Reproach); "Fluen" (The Fly), official organ of Edda, edited by N. Christensen, '71, in 1869–70; "Svein uræd" (Svein the Fearless), edited by M. Koefod, '70–72, in 1871–72; and "Gjallarhorn," issued one winter in the late seventies by Niffelheim.

Music claimed the interest of many. The first instruction in music, two required class hours a week at all levels, beginning in 1861, was designed primarily to acquaint the students with the rich Lutheran heritage of hymns and chorales.[4] The first concert by students at the college is said to have been performed by a trio consisting of Nils A. Førde, '73, first tenor; Jørgen Nordby, '73, second tenor; and Nils J. Ellestad, '71, bass. The concert was given in a large classroom on second floor.

"The teacher's desk was removed from the platform; and a shawl, stretched from a pole on one corner of the platform to the wall on the right side, hid the singers from the public gaze between numbers. The audience consisted solely of students and others of the college family. The admission was five cents. C. K. Preus, '73, was manager, and his principal duty was to beat eggs and sugar together to keep the throats of the singers in good condition during the concert. . . . A lamp had been placed on a small table close to the shawl which screened the performers, and between numbers the audience was entertained hugely by moving pictures on the wall back of the stage in which gigantic spoons were con-

117

veyed to enormous mouths. It is reported that the troupe was required by the authorities to return the proceeds of the concert to the audience."[5]

The first organized musical ensemble outside the classroom was the Idun Quartette, established about 1869. Members were Nils A. Førde, '73, Jørgen Nordby, '73, Nils J. Ellestad, '71, Magnus M. Koefod, '70–72, Christian K. Preus, '73, Ole P. Vangsness, '75, and Henrik J. Strand, '76. In 1877 the group was reorganized by Nils J. Bakke, '77, to include 12 members. On May 20, 1877, they were given permission to make a tour, provided they used a repertory and adopted rules of conduct approved by the faculty. Pastor Koren, who had been a member of the well-known Behrens Quartet at the university in Christiania, was present, possibly to bolster Idun's cause at the meeting which granted the permission. Professor Reque abstained from voting; Professor Jacobsen voted no.[6]

Idun Society sang some numbers at the concert given by the famous violinist Ole Bull in Decorah in 1879. It is said that Bull, when first visiting the college, which had been involved in controversy for some time, remarked, "Luther College must be like the goat—the more it is abused, the better it thrives."[7]

In 1877 a group of two violins and a cello was organized by John P. Kopang, '77–79. The following year a guitar, flute, and cornet were added, and in succeeding years other instruments rounded out the orchestra. Although no concerts were given by the ensemble until 1883, it has functioned, with some ups and downs, ever since.

In February 1878 a band was organized through the efforts of Hans B. Thorgrimsen, '79, and other students, who raised $250 to purchase a $500 set of instruments from a local city band which was dispersing. The college band made its first appearance in the spring of 1878 and on Decoration Day 1879 performed downtown. The early directors were Thorgrimsen and Ola A. Solheim, '81. Its repertory included selections from Verdi's "Il Trovatore" and Gilbert and Sullivan's "Pinafore," Mendelssohn's wedding march, Beethoven's funeral march from the Fifth Symphony, Suppé's "Poet and Peasant Overture," Rossini's overture to "William Tell," and Norwegian melodies. Gradually, from these beginnings, the Luther College Concert Band evolved.[8]

Organized athletics played only a small role in this early period. More physical exercise would have been beneficial; there would have been fewer illnesses. Most of the boys came from farms still very close to pioneer conditions and were used to hard outdoor work. The confining life of classroom and study was new to them. It was true they had minor chores such as sawing wood, carrying water, and caring for their rooms; but many of them were unaware that their bodies required more exercise than that. There was good reason for Larsen's insistence that during leisure hours students should not read or study but should get out into the open. "Don't become humped over like a question mark," was one of his admonitions. So, various simple outdoor sports were encouraged, such as hiking, running, jumping, wrestling, weight lifting, finger pulling, skating, and skiing.

A popular feature of the early years was the monthly holiday the boys were granted. Once a month the buildings were thoroughly cleaned and scrubbed by hired help. On this day the students were given breakfast and then told to stay away until suppertime. The boys would then set out in larger or smaller parties and explore the surrounding country. Light provisions were taken along. Potatoes and other eatables were procured from the neighboring farms, and dinner was eaten around roaring campfires. These events were so popular that the boys never allowed a month to go by without asking for their holiday.

Baseball, which began very early, was first played by the boys among themselves, later with town teams. A good

119

pitcher in those early days was the one who could throw the ball so that the batter could hit it—not, as now, so that he would miss. In 1874 there were six baseball teams, says James C. M. Hanson, '82, "the members of which had their own special grounds and met once a day, weather permitting. Each team or club had enough players to make up two nines and it was seldom that one club challenged another." Class games and class rivalry were unheard of during 1874–82. The "first nine" (seniors) had the honor of representing the college. Their only opponent was the Decorah team—and once, in 1880, a Dubuque professional team. No intercollegiate contests were even thought of.[9] Ingvard G. Monson, '69–75, Atle J. Lee, '78, Olaf Larson, '78, Isaac B. Torrison, '79, Hans J. Kopperdal, '81, James C. M. Hanson, '82, and the ambidextrous Theodor G. Opsahl, '84, all made names for themselves as baseball players.

Football—apparently a modification of English Rugby and soccer—was introduced in 1877 through the influence of the English colony in Decorah and the efforts of Knut Seehuus, '81. As many as 75 would play on a side; "preps" had to stay on the sidelines for fear they would be injured. The big game was on Founders Day in October. This type of football continued until 1891, when J. C. M. Hanson, '82, on a visit to the college, explained the American game to the boys; later he coached them by correspondence. A team was organized under the captaincy of Erling A. Bothne, '94, who later played guard at Northwestern University.[10]

Organized track and field events were unknown in the early years. Nevertheless, it is recorded that Reinhard T. Bentson, '64–70, jumped 21 feet in the running broad jump and 10 feet jumping backwards, besting all comers in these events.[11] In 1874 foot races were run on a hundred-yard track. Finalists were Thomas E. Torrison, '76, and Hans B. Thorgrimsen, '79, the former winning by a scant foot.[12]

In 1865–66 a military company was formed with P. S.

Reque, '65–67, lately discharged from the Union Army, as captain, to serve in the event of Indian wars. The government furnished old muskets, from which blank cartridges were discharged in an open drill field near Pleasant Hill.[13] In the fall of 1876 there was a military company commanded by Colonel Christian Brandt. In 1877 the "Luther College Phalanx" was formed through the efforts of Jens L. Lee. Fifty muzzle-loading muskets were purchased, besides belts, cartridges, and cap pouches. The officers wore regulation dress swords and belts, the rank and file a blue uniform cap. A. A. Veblen states that, as first lieutenant from 1878 to 1881, he "commanded the company at all drills and target shooting as being the highest in command, and the only 'commissioned' officer attending."[14]

In the early discipline of the college there were certain self-governing features. The president appointed a monitor for each dormitory room and for each study or classroom. Each appointee in turn was a sort of janitor for a day; he was responsible for the care and appearance of the room, and his authority was prescribed by a set of rules posted at the door. Yet many matters were regulated by meetings of the occupants; they were self-governing to that extent.

"Originally all the fuel used was wood and the heating was by stoves. The students were required to cut all the wood into suitable size for the stoves—both for the kitchen and the students' rooms. But, they were required to cut not only the wood used by the school, but also that burned by the members of the faculty, though these of course bought their own individually. For the purpose of this work of wood-cutting, each student had to saw and split wood once or twice a week an hour at a time. The administration of this duty was left in the hands of the student body. They assembled soon after the opening of the school year and elected a superintendent of woodcutters. He appointed a foreman for each day of the week for the college and one

121

for each professor. His appointments, I believe, were subject to approval of the student body. He conducted the assignment of the students in sections of so many for each day of the week and so many for each professor. The foremen, themselves obliged to take their regular turn, saw to it that each man in their contingents did his share in turn. The foremen were accountable to the superintendent. The arrangement gave the student body a sort of co-operative organization of their own."[15]

An alumnus reports: "We college boys were not given a chance to become dainty or fastidious. We had to saw wood for ourselves and our teachers, keep our rooms in order, scour knives and forks, and do other minor chores. It is true that we had heard of a young man who some years earlier had made himself something of a hero by organizing a little revolution against such degrading labor, and who had been expelled from college because of it. But in my time none of us had fortitude enough to follow in his footsteps. We acquiesced in the regulations prescribed for us. We who roomed together took turns week by week in tidying up, bringing firewood, etc. Yes, once a week we had to spend one noon hour sawing wood; well, it was not altogether a very burdensome sort of slavery."[16]

Some of the rules were a bit quaint. For example, in 1879 the faculty solemnly resolved that a monitor be designated for each sleeping room and that his duty would be to rouse those who did not wake up when the first bell rang. "If necessary," continued the resolution, "it shall rest upon whoever first wakes up in the room to rouse the monitor."[17]

On September 12, 1877, the faculty resolved "that the old rule that every student who wished to go to town should write his name in the notebook which hangs on the wall on first floor be abolished."[18] The old order was passing, even though the change took 16 years.

There was not a little effort in these early days to protect the student from contamination by the world. After the unfortunate slavery controversy, it is understandable that Larsen sought to keep political discussions out of the college, although as usually happens, the prohibition perhaps whetted interest in the forbidden. There was a rather strict supervision of the books, newspapers, and periodicals which student societies were permitted to subscribe for, and various attempts were made to censor them. It is perhaps true that Larsen became more liberal in his later years, but the early Luther College was strictly supervised. For example, on January 26, 1881, a committee consisting of Thrond Bothne, Breda, and Roalkvam was elected by the faculty to inspect Mimer's library because certain criticisms had been voiced. On February 23, following the committee's recommendation, Bjørnson's *Magnhild* was banned. Similarly, on May 4, 1881, Turgenev's *Helena* was banned.[19]

But, if such censorship occurred, one may be sure that it was vigorously discussed, especially by students who had been stimulated by Thrond Bothne and respected his honesty, forthrightness, and democratic viewpoint. One of them says:

"We were not mere boys, most of us, whom he *[Bothne]* had to deal with. No, many of us were grown, bearded fellows, who were in class because we wanted to be there, and who often enough found out during summer vacations the price we had to pay for going there. So we had some idea of the value of our time and of the college's worth. And it was the same with conditions in general as with the students: it seems to me they both must have been admirably suited to a plain man of the people like Bothne. For one would indeed have to hunt a long time for a more—in the best sense—democratic society than the little world which in Bothne's time had its home at Luther College. There was no question there of one's ancestry or financial standing or anything like that—only of one's industry and conduct. And I know that Bothne set great store on these. He has talked about them more than once since then. 'True, it was different at college in those days than it is now. Then, at graduation one might walk up to get his diploma in a poor, threadbare suit without a thought of his appearance, and never for a moment fear that everything was not just as it ought to be; and there was never the slightest suspicion that anyone would look down on him.' No, they did not need to fear. There *was* no one who looked down on anyone because of his 'poor, threadbare clothes,' no one among either the teachers or the students. For if there had been, the 'poor and threadbare' would quickly have noticed it. You need have no doubt about that! And it is doubtless because of that simple, plain, comrade-like life that many of us look back on our school days at Luther College in the seventies as among the happiest of our lives."[20]

Of the 128 graduates of the first 20 years, approximately 100 spent a full 6 years or more at the college. Many came as youngsters not much beyond confirmation age. Life was therefore more restricted than today; at times it was perhaps even drab—yet hardly more so than at similar institutions of that day, if as much. But the college was on a hill across the river and almost a mile away from town, with no sidewalk until 1881 to encourage a student to go downtown. One writer says:

"At school we were in a world of our own and we did not get acquainted to any extent with folks in town and its immediate vicinity. In all likelihood it was not very good for us thus to have almost no contact with private family life. Professor Larsen and his family lived in the college building. But that was while his first wife was still living; she was sickly during this time and could not attempt to teach the boys cultivated manners. . . . But only a few steps away was the parsonage, where Mrs. Diderikke Brandt had her home. And she was the dear mother of the whole group of

124

boys. Early and late she was busy helping us and cheering us on. . . . During the Christmas holidays and on other occasions she arranged games and parties for us, took part in them herself, and took care that in everything due attention was paid to the proprieties and the little niceties of decorum. And every Sunday she invited some of the boys to the parsonage for afternoon coffee and cookies. I remember those occasions as great events; I felt compelled to write home about them every time I was one of the lucky ones to be invited."[21]

At Mrs. Brandt's home, says another writer, "Boys could enjoy music, both instrumental and vocal, could take part in happy conversations and, I will admit, could learn and practise good manners. Even if not a word was said, those social gatherings made you consider your own fitness to be there, both as to dress and manners. When the time for the completion of the college course drew near, not a few sought advice from Mrs. Brandt, and she found time to give it, often taking a walk with the student either near the parsonage or north on the campus. She was respected and looked up to as a mother."[22]

Diderikke Ottesen Brandt (March 9, 1827–January 21, 1885), the wife of the college pastor, Nils O. Brandt, was the double cousin of pioneer pastor J. A. Ottesen and Mrs. O. J. Hjort. Brought up in the parsonage of her father, who was dean in Sande parish on the west side of the Christiania fjord, she spent three years at the Moravian Ladies School at Christiansfelt in Schleswig, Denmark, and later traveled in Germany, Holland, England, and Denmark. Upon her marriage in 1856 she came to this country, lived from 1856 to 1865 at Rock River near Ixonia, Wisconsin, and then moved with her husband to Decorah. From 1865 to 1867 they lived in the north wing of the Main Building; thereafter, from 1867 to 1884, in Campus House. She died at the home of her son Olaf in Cleveland, Ohio, and was buried in the Lutheran cemetery in Decorah; students and members of the Decorah congregation raised the funds for a monument over her grave. In 1883 the alumni association had her portrait painted by H. N. Gausta. *College Chips* said she shared the boys' joys and sorrows. "She nursed the sick. She inspired students with love for their work. She extended her hand to them on all occasions when a woman could do it. The doors to her hospitable and entertaining home were wide open to all of them."[23] For many years Mrs. Brandt made clergymen's ruffs and other hand-crafted articles, which she sold to raise money for deserving students.

Mrs. Brandt organized a society of women from the congregation in Decorah which met regularly to patch and mend clothes for students, particularly needy students—a society which other women, notably the second Mrs. Larsen, continued for 40 or more years. She made communion wafers, using the proceeds of their sale to aid students. The sum total of her gifts would not be inconsiderable, says one writer, but of far greater value was "the impression which her self-sacrificing care made upon the hearts of the young and the encouragement which they thereby received to learn to live not for themselves alone, but rather for others. . . . Her efforts were not confined merely to the purely practical. She had one of those sunny dispositions which kept her always young. So she understood that youth needs amusements—relaxation, too, and she tried to do her bit to meet that need in a seemly manner, a proper way. Both in the college and in the parsonage there was life in the party when Mrs. Brandt had a hand in things. At all festive gatherings, both at the college and in the congregation, she took a most active part. In short, for many occasions, she seemed to be quite indispensable."[24]

One of these occasions was Christmas, for in the early days travel was not so easy as now and many students could not afford to go home for the holidays. J. A. Blilie, '77, wrote:

126

"The Christmas vacations at college must not be forgotten. There were always students who could not go home or go visiting with friends in the vicinity of Decorah. Of course, most of the boys were eager to get home, and Peer Strømme wished that vacation could begin before the last day of school. But there were always some who had to remain. At some sacrifice the faculty always saw to it that there was a Christmas tree for the faculty, their families, and the students who were to remain during vacation; and Professor Larsen was careful that each student received a gift. Now followed many evenings that would have become very lonesome if Mrs. Brandt had not come and gathered the boys for games and other entertainment in the college dining room. These meetings became more like family gatherings, taking the place of what might have been expected at home. And her presence was always looked for with joyous expectations."[25]

One organization which cannot be overlooked in this connection is the famous Comitia Dumriana, a female group of transitory existence with a certain fluttering daintiness and elusive fragrance of femininity veiling its hidden strength, which nevertheless hinted of future developments that neither the devotees of the classics, nor the upholders of male traditions, nor the old Synod leaders, nor the shades of Walther and old Missouri were able to stop. The faculty called the group the Comitia (an assembly); the students (or possibly the girls themselves) added Dumriana ("of the silly fair"). The club consisted of nine young women, mostly daughters of pastors and professors. A fire that destroyed the Washington Prairie parsonage and forced Pastor Koren to move to Decorah in 1873 indirectly gave an impetus to the Comitia. The members were: Henriette Koren; Caroline Koren (Mrs. C. A. Naeseth); Thora Larsen (Mrs. J. W. Magelssen); Margrethe Brandt (Mrs. L. S. Reque); Rosine Preus (Mrs. J. Nordby); Louise Hjort (Mrs. C. K. Preus); Emma Larsen (Mrs. Nils N. Helle); Mathilda Stub (Mrs.

127

H. B. Thorgrimsen); and Marie Reque (Mrs. H. B. Hus-tvedt).[26] They studied German, French, English, Norwegian, and history under Siewers, Jacobsen, Landmark, and other college teachers during 1873–74, the year in which the Comitia flourished. For the three or four who were from out of town, the present Campus House served as a dormitory, housing also the Brandt family of seven, the necessary help, college students in the attic, and two or three bachelor professors.[27]

Peer Strømme thus described the effect of this feminine group on his fictional hero: "Almost all these young ladies were so pleasant and attractive that they made poor Halvor's heart ache. When this bevy of girls or Comitia Dumriana, as they were called, strolled down the road, he could not keep his eyes off them. It was not that he was especially concerned over any one member in particular; but collectively—taken all together—they were irresistible. They caused not only his heart but also his feet to ache. For on their account he began to take pains with his appearance. He forced his big feet into shoes so small that they caused him unspeakable agony. He also had to buy clothes oftener than he could afford. What else could he do, even if he sank so far in debt downtown that he did not know where to turn when it came to paying his bills. And what did it all avail him? Not a single one of the silly fair would look at him anyway. When, now and then, he had a chance to talk to one of them, he had no joy of it; he always believed afterwards that he had made a fool of himself. Nevertheless, he continued using hair oil and torturing his feet."[28]

If these were halcyon days for Halvor and other youths at the college, they were also halcyon days for the college itself. The seventies were a kind of golden age for the Norwegian Synod and Luther College. The early tensions had been surmounted. The Civil War had receded into the past. The college had succeeded in supplying more than 125 men to the Christian ministry. These men were not only serving the older settlements but were pioneering on every frontier in the upper Midwest. As the tide of immigration sent new waves of Norwegian settlers into upper Minnesota and Wisconsin, the two Dakotas, and other areas, new and urgent calls came for pastors. Nearly all the early graduates who entered the ministry spent a considerable portion of their time on these new frontiers, organizing congregations and laying foundations for the future church in these areas. Moreover, an increasing number of the college's graduates were entering business, the professions, and public service. They, too, in many cases were pioneers in the communities in which they made their homes. Pastors and laymen played their roles side by side.

It was no small achievement for the fledgling college, even if greater tasks loomed ahead. But the next period was to bring a bitter test to the young institution.

*The glory of this latter house shall
be greater than of the former.*
—Haggai 2:9

9

Crisis and Recovery

As the college entered its third decade, there were prospects of more than normal growth and expansion. The 1880's and early 1890's witnessed a well-nigh explosive population increase in the Middle Western area from which the college drew its students. Despite temporary economic setbacks, these communities were passing, or had already passed, beyond the narrow circumstances of pioneer days and had reached a considerable degree of well-being. Only in the areas to the west and north, in the Dakotas and Minnesota, were frontier conditions still to be found.

The church was trying to keep pace with the spread of Norwegian Lutheran settlements but was not able to keep up with the demand for pastors to serve them. Luther College was still spoken of as a "preacher school." But not all who finished the course were disposed then to take up a three-year course in theology. At Synod meetings there were critical remarks from time to time on this account, for many believed that the college's main function was to furnish promising candidates for theological training. The value of a well-educated laity, friendly to the church and its mission, and the great role the college could play in training such men, had not yet been fully recognized.

But factors in synodical affairs made it increasingly difficult for the college to serve the church as effectively as was desirable.

The storm clouds which had been gathering in the late seventies broke with full force in the eighties. The issue was the theological controversy over election or, as it was also called, predestination. In 1877 Professor O. Asperheim of Luther Seminary in Madison criticized the Missouri Synod on several points, including its doctrine of election. His remarks led his colleague, Professor F. A. Schmidt, also of Luther Seminary, to attack him so severely that Asperheim resigned. In 1879 Schmidt, who by then had come round approximately to Asperheim's point of view, himself launched an attack on the Missouri Synod, singling out particularly Professor Walther's position on the doctrine of election. Walther's view, charged Schmidt, embraced a Calvinistic error in its treatment of the doctrine. When Koren, in January 1880, denied the charge, the issue was publicly joined. From this point on, the doctrinal struggle absorbed nearly all the energies of the church, which in 1878 had celebrated its twenty-fifth anniversary. Not only did the controversy engage the attention of the leaders; it spread also to the rank and file of the congregations and led to schism and heartache.

The Norwegian Synod's connection with Missouri had never been popular with the laity, however warmly it had been embraced by the clergy. The language barrier between Germans and Norwegians and the difference in national origin were one factor. But more deep-seated by far was the hostility to Missouri as the source of a slavery doctrine accepted by the Synod pastors but never by the laity, who had tolerated it only as a kind of theological mystery. On the surface, the slavery issue had been disposed of with Clausen's withdrawal in 1868 and the condemnation of American slavery by the Norwegian Synod in 1869, but below the outward calm the argument still rankled and the animus against Missouri remained alive.

In the election controversy it was charged that the Missouri doctrine involved an interpretation contrary to the Lutheran view of election expressed by Pontoppidan. Soon the opposing factions were known as Missourians and Anti-Missourians. The Norwegian Synod leaders, in an attempt to remove one source of irritation, agreed to withdraw from the Synodical Conference in 1883, but in vain. The Anti-Missouri feeling was too strong. The uneasy solidarity achieved after the settlement of the slavery controversy showed great rifts, patience was easily exhausted, and ultimately there came a violent cleavage that rent the church apart in 1887. Not until 30 years later was the breach healed.

The controversy had a disastrous effect upon the college. The split was felt to some extent even within the faculty, and led to one or two withdrawals.[1] Among the students the effects were even more noticeable. Not a few of those who took up theology after completing college avoided Luther Seminary in Madison because of the sharp division of opinion among the faculty there. It was even charged that the Luther College faculty recommended such action. Some who had contemplated studying for the ministry were so repelled by the violent conflict in the church that they chose other callings. Moreover, the bitter strife in the secular and religious press, in private and public discussion, discouraged many from entering Luther College. As a result there was an almost steady decline in enrollment; in 1887–88 only 118 were in attendance. The break between the opposing forces that finally took place in 1887 came as a relief. Attendance slowly rose again to about 200 and remained constant at about that figure until the close of Larsen's administration.

Although there was relief, once the worst was over, there was no joy in the separation that had taken place. Congregations had been split, neighbors separated, friends estranged. Even families had been divided. When the sister of the president of the college visited Decorah, she went to one church, he to another. Larsen and Schmidt, who, as colleagues, had formed the original faculty of the school were estranged. College classmates, even those who had been bosom friends in student days, were on opposite sides. It was bitter fruit, however much each side clung to its point of view; and there was an uneasy suspicion that truth had been obscured in the heat of conflict. Time was needed to heal the wounds.

Only to a limited degree, however, did this controversy enter into the daily life of the campus. Larsen now, as earlier during the slavery controversy, sought to keep the conflict out of the classroom and to have the students concentrate on their studies. He perhaps came to welcome, more than he had earlier, those extracurricular activities which engaged the interests of students and furnished a constructive outlet for their energies.

For a long time a gymnasium had been needed. In 1886 the first one was erected—a frame structure, 42 by 75 feet. The students had been challenged to raise funds for it. During the summer of 1885 they set to work, and in the fall the building was begun; it was completed the next year. The leading spirit in marshaling students for fund raising was Carlo A. Sperati, later well-known as director of the Luther College Concert Band. In 1895 a 16 by 22-foot stage was built, one that could be folded against the wall when not in use. This was paid for by student subscriptions. In 1886 two large coal stoves were installed in the corridors of the second and third floors, the first heat provided for these drafty areas.

A major disaster, however, struck the college when the Main Building was gutted by fire May 19, 1889. Coming hard on the heels of the election controversy, which had swept away a third of the pastors and congregations of the Synod, the fire was a blow indeed.[2] Moreover, at this time the Synod was in the midst of a campaign for funds for Luther Seminary, which was being moved from Madison to

Robbinsdale, outside Minneapolis, and for Lutheran Normal School, which was being erected at Sioux Falls, South Dakota. The only insurance on the Main Building was $10,000, to cover a mortgage of like amount held by George Phelps of Decorah. Osul Torrison, at a trustees' meeting on June 22, 1883, had urged the necessity of protecting the college against loss by fire. In 1873, however, the Synod had voted not to insure in commercial companies, but to carry the risk itself. The policy proved shortsighted and aroused considerable criticism. But alumni and friends rallied wholeheartedly, and the crisis was overcome.

Immediately after the fire all students were sent home except the seniors, whose classes were conducted in the "Chicken Coop," to which the library collections had been removed during the fire. During the following school year, 1889–90, the college carried on in improvised quarters. The gymnasium served as kitchen, dining hall, and an apartment for the steward and hired help. The three preparatory classes used four rooms fitted up in the basement of First Lutheran Church. College classes were held in "Schmidt's Hall," the Griswold house at the corner of Center Street and Leiv Eiriksson Drive. Rooms were rented in the Arlington Hotel (later the Lutheran Publishing House, the building now housing the Norwegian-American Historical Museum), on the second floor of the Bernatz grocery store, and in one other building. For a reference and reading room, L. E. Davidson lent a large room in his home at what is now 207 North Street.

Meanwhile there had been speculation as to where the college should be rebuilt. Many favored other locations. There were offers from St. Paul, La Crosse, and Decorah. The joint committee, consisting of the Church Council and seven members from each of the three districts of the Synod, to which the matter had been referred, decided to accept the St. Paul site in July 1889. But difficulties arose in reducing the offer to a firm contract; and Pastor Koren was again tireless, and also successful, in rallying support for Decorah. Accordingly, in September 1889 the committee voted to re-build on the original site, provided that water mains were extended to the area from the city without expense to the college.[3] Luther College stayed in Decorah, a small town which, "like some unwooed country beauty, was destined to remain in semi-rustic isolation."[4]

When the structure was rebuilt, the foundation and in large part the walls of the old building were utilized. The work was prosecuted with vigor by A. F. Gauger, the architect. O. K. Simmons of Red Wing undertook to super-vise, without pay, the letting of contracts and the actual construction. Lars Moen of Calmar did the interior carpenter work. The new building had an overall length of 170 feet; the middle section was 52 feet and the two wings each 44 feet in width. There were three full stories and a basement, plus an attic. The basement housed heating and ventilating machinery, a kitchen, a dining room equipped with tables and chairs instead of the earlier large tables and long bench-es, bathrooms and lavatory, storeroom, and living quarters for the steward's family and the hired help. The total cost was $50,000, considerably less than the inflated cost of the first Main Building.[5]

The library was housed in the south wing on the first floor. The rest of this floor contained administrative offices and classrooms. On the second floor were classrooms, and in the south wing a large room, seating about 200, used for a chapel. Third and fourth floors were used for study rooms and the attic for sleeping quarters. A fan ventilating system, it was hoped, would provide fresh air throughout the new Main Building, but the system did not prove satisfactory. The president and his family did not reside in the new build-ing, but moved into the Driggs residence, which the college

135

purchased in 1890—the present home of Sigurd S. Reque, '03, at 208 Leiv Eiriksson Drive.

The city water mains were extended to the campus, giving protection against fire as well as the convenience of a good water supply. The city extended its pipes to the river; the college, with the aid of contributions from congregations in Decorah and the vicinity, and from individuals in Decorah, lengthened them from the river to the college. The mains remained the property of the college until 1905. The first heating plant was also built at this time; steam heat now replaced the old, dangerous, and inadequate stoves.

Opinion in general held that the new Main Building architecturally presented a far more pleasing appearance than the old. It was formally dedicated October 14, 1890. The weather was good, and from 4,000 to 5,000 people were present. The procession, headed by the faculty and students and the college band, marched from First Lutheran Church through the business section of Decorah and up to the college, where seats for 2,000 had been set up on the green before the new building. Johan Th. Ylvisaker, '77, then pastor of First Lutheran Church, opened the services with prayer. J. A. Ottesen, speaking for the congregations, used the text, "I have no greater joy than to hear that my children walk in truth" (III John, 4). Larsen used Joshua 23: 14–16 as his text. L. S. Reque spoke in English. A. K. Bailey, representing Decorah, said in part: "Beautiful as are all these surroundings, they are but a means to an end; they constitute but an habitation in which is to reside the purpose—the soul—which is the real self of Luther College. The shell was burned; the habitation was partly destroyed; but the real college still survived because it was enshrined in hearts that made it the subject of their hopes, their tears and their prayers."[6]

An anthem by Lauritz A. Larsen, '86, was sung. Luren Singing Society of Decorah presented a song of dedication by Thrond Bothne. Torger A. Torgerson, one of the first group of Norwegian students to attend Concordia College in St. Louis, closed the morning exercises with prayer. In the afternoon Hans G. Stub, '66, spoke in English and Henry C. Wyneken of the Missouri Synod in German. On the following day Pastor Koren preached, using as his text II Corinthians 4:13 to 5:1.

In 1891 an attractive music pavilion was built among the oak trees just east of the present gymnasium. Koren, who on many occasions encouraged music at the college, collected the funds for it in his congregations. Here, especially on beautiful spring evenings, musical organizations gave outdoor performances which attracted large crowds of students and townspeople. Few outdoor affairs afforded more genuine pleasure. The pavilion, torn down as a Halloween prank in 1912, was followed by a bandstand in 1913, but this in turn was taken down in 1926 when the C. K. Preus Gymnasium was erected.[7] Many regret that no similar structure has replaced the earlier two.

Koren had selected the site for the college, had persuaded the Synod to establish it in Decorah, and had been the determining factor in having it rebuilt in Decorah after the fire in 1889. He often visited the college, was Larsen's constant adviser, and in many other ways exerted an influence on faculty and students. Of this striking personality, who directly and indirectly played so large a role in the college's development, one of her most distinguished sons wrote as follows:

"In my day he was a rather frequent visitor at the college, especially when there were important public gatherings, at which he often spoke and always with high seriousness and deep effect. I believe that every student soon came to look upon him as having a very special and deep interest in the institution and as exercising, in some to us rather obscure and subtle way, a definite advisory and even super-

137

visory function over the students and the faculty. How clearly one may recall the well-known figure, slender, graceful, impressive; the keen and lively eye; the fine, mobile features; the playful smile! Naturally, the interesting little mannerisms, the invariable and scrupulous neatness of personal appearance, the velvet vest, did not escape observation and comment. 'Gamle Koren' as we youngsters familiarly but by no means and in no sense irreverently called him among ourselves. A striking and noble figure, fixed forever as a distinct and prominent feature in the scenes of Luther College life through nearly half a century. Brief though his visits and briefer still the moment of personal contact, yet he exercised on us a lasting and deep influence, the full value and meaning of which most students probably did not make clear to themselves, perhaps could not understand fully, until long after they had passed out of the college and perchance had had the good fortune to come in contact with him again under widely different circumstances. In large measure his influence was more or less indirect, coming to us through teachers and others who received impulse and inspiration from him, but on this very significant phase of his relation to the students I shall not enlarge. It is the direct influence on us of his gifted and forceful, intellectual yet deeply religious, personality that I wish to emphasize. The peculiar charm of that rare and genuine culture was not without its deep effect on us. His words carried unusual weight because they at once revealed a man of the highest ideals and of determined continuance of lofty purpose. 'His eye was single and therefore his whole body was full of light.' "[8]

In 1893 President Larsen moved into what is now Campus House. In 1899 (the city of Decorah having acquired electric lights in 1897) electric lights were installed in the gymnasium and pavilion. In 1901 a private power plant for the college was installed, the gift of the Luther College Alumni Association and citizens of Decorah. A three-room hospital, later enlarged, was erected south of the Main Building in 1901, made possible by a gift of $1,000 from John A. Johnson of Madison, Wisconsin. The acceptance of this gift, which no doubt was approved by the Church Council under Koren, who succeeded H. A. Preus as president of the Synod in 1894, may mark a liberalizing of an earlier policy, when no gift was accepted except from Lutherans. Johnson in his later years was a Unitarian, but was generous to several Norwegian-American Lutheran institutions, possibly as a token of appreciation for his Norwegian heritage.[9]

With baseball the chief college sport, a diamond was laid out approximately where it was placed in later years, except that the batters faced east. In 1900, when track athletics were introduced, the students constructed a cinder track just north of where the C. K. Preus Gymnasium stands. On February 14, 1896, the faculty resolved to have a telephone installed on trial for the remainder of the year. But on March 9 it was reported that a telephone would not be available for four months, and not until September was it installed. In 1897–98 a vault was built in the basement of the Main building, under the tower, for the storage and preservation of college papers. The Faculty Minutes for April 26, 1898, record this nostalgic note: a solemnly phrased resolution to forbid the tying of horses to trees on the campus; L. S. Reque was designated to arrange for hitching posts at suitable places. Through the efforts of Reque and at the request of the faculty, 1,000 or more replicas of the first college bell were struck from the metal of the old bell. The money received from the sale of these souvenirs (some of which are still preserved) was used to buy scientific instruments and supplies.[10]

There was still no charge for tuition in the college department, although various fees for medical care, library, music, and gymnasium were gradually introduced. In the preparatory department, however, the very limited fees that had been charged, beginning in 1877, were raised in 1889 to $20 per year for each student.

During the late nineties, when considerable criticism of the college and other church institutions appeared to be in the air, a proposal was made to dissolve the corporations known as the Norwegian Luther College and the Lutheran Publishing House and transfer their properties to the corporation of the Norwegian Synod. A committee consisting of John Ollis and Lars S. Reque was elected in 1899 to consider the matter. Their report, made in 1902, so incisively showed the disadvantages of the proposal that no further action was taken.[11]

In 1896 the college divested itself of the responsibility of providing meals for the students. Perhaps following the earlier example of Augsburg College, Minneapolis, the students organized the Luther College Boarding Club and elected a manager, a buyer, and a treasurer. The boarding club functioned for many years. Its elections were hotly contested and gave rise to much campaign oratory. Occasionally eloquence rose to sublime heights in registering complaints about the selection and preparation of food. The college resumed the boarding functions in 1931.

During these two decades first steps were taken toward a permanent policy of pensions and other benefits for college employees. In 1881, by resolution of the Synod, a pension was voted for the widow and children of Professor Jacob D. Jacobsen. In 1884 similar provision was made for the widow of Professor Cornelius Narveson. In 1896 the Synod adopted a plan to provide assistance for all teachers, preachers, and their widows. Although the idea was good, the practical implementation of it was unsound and it never functioned properly.

During the latter half of Larsen's administration the first financially significant legacies were received. Knut Bergh's gift of his library during the first decade has been mentioned.

Professor Ramstad, who, like Bergh, died while in the service of the college, willed a farm whose sale brought $6,400; the income from this sum was to be used for instruction in the natural sciences. Other legacies were: 1882, Halvor Olson Gjerjord, $7,343; 1884, Martin Pederson, $750; 1891, Birgit Ellingson, $300; 1895, Martin Madson, $800; 1901, Gilbert Gulbrandsen, $500, Mrs. Aadnesen, $895, and Knut K. Neste, Jr., $800. These gifts, although not large by present standards, were indications of the good will the college had come to enjoy and of the maturity some of the Midwestern communities had reached; moreover, these legacies held hope of greater things for the future.

The Norwegian language continued to be strongly stressed at the college, although the students used English in daily affairs. *College Chips* was published from 1884 to 1889 as an all-English magazine, but because of pressures from both students and faculty it was enlarged and made bilingual, six pages being printed in Norwegian, ten in English. Not until 1897 did it become all-English again. The Alumni Association decided in 1884 that English should be its official language. The faculty was much more conservative; its minutes continued to be kept in Norwegian. In September 1895, however, a committee report in English was entered—the first such in the minutes.[12] The Board of Trustees kept its record in English from the beginning.

Perhaps the clearest indication of the trend toward Americanization was the founding on June 28, 1880, of that typically American organization—an alumni association. It was first called, in Norwegian, the Luther College Alumni Forening and was founded largely through the efforts of John Koren and Gisle Bothne. The first officers were L. S. Reque, '68, president; Albert Egge, '79, and Johannes Bothne, '78, vice presidents; Halvard Roalkvam, '74, secretary; Gisle Bothne, '78, assistant secretary; and Realf Brandt, '77, treasurer. One of its earliest projects was an endowment fund of

$50,000 for the college. Although $10,000 had been subscribed by 1883, the project languished; it was revived in
1887. In 1888 the Luther College Alumni Association was
incorporated under Iowa law to give the society the proper
legal status for handling funds. But, with the burning of
Main Building in 1889 and the resultant campaign for money
to rebuild it, the plan for an endowment fund apparently
was abandoned. Steps were taken to establish an alumni
paper, but when *College Chips,* published by the students,
appeared in 1884, it was felt that *Chips* might also serve the
alumni, and the project was abandoned.

Although some of these plans of the association did not
materialize, the society nevertheless served the college in
many other ways. It made gifts and loans to the library, the
museum, and the laboratories; it procured and paid for por-
traits of former professors and churchmen; and it was active
in the campaign to build the house presented to Laur. Larsen
in 1897. In 1901, as has been mentioned, the association gave
the college an electric plant. Regional Luther College clubs,
affiliated with the alumni association, began to be formed.
The first, the Minneapolis Luther College Club, was organized in 1886. In 1893 it gave $100 for a scholarship, to be
awarded as the faculty might decide.

It was not an easy period financially, however. In 1886–
87 salaries were three to four months in arrears most of the
time. Larsen sent out letters to 500 ministers and laymen,
urging them to help. The response was gratifying; funds for
education almost doubled over those of the previous year,
other church funds also benefited from the appeal and
showed large increases, and the pensioners, who had not
been paid, also profited.[13]

The second catalog of the college, edited by Lars S. Reque,
'68, Christen A. Naeseth, '74, Gisle Bothne, '78, and Cornelius
Narveson, '65–67, was published in English in 1883. Thereafter the catalog was issued yearly, but beginning in 1886

a Norwegian edition (edited by Larsen) was also published. The two appeared annually until 1905–06. Thereafter the Norwegian edition was dropped. The first illustration in the catalog, in 1900, was a picture of the "Chicken Coop," then housing the museum, which Haldor Hanson was vigorously promoting.

The catalog of 1883 contains the first formulation in English of the purpose of the college. The third paragraph of this careful statement appears to reflect the aim of the institution to be known as something more than a "preacher school."

"The institution owes its origin to the growing demand for educated men who could preach the Word of Life to the rapidly increasing Norwegian population of this country.

"The chief object of the College is to meet this demand; but it also aims to afford the advantages of a liberal education to any youth desiring to avail himself of the same.

"Believing that 'the fear of the Lord is the beginning of knowledge,' it regards mere mental training without Christian faith and love as possessing but a doubtful value. For this reason it desires through its religious instruction and Christian influence to reach as many as it can also of those who do not intend to serve the church directly as pastors or teachers, trusting that those whose education has been based on Christian principles will, also in other vocations, both morally and intellectually, exert a beneficial influence among their countrymen and fellow-Christians."

This statement was later shortened, first in 1888–89 and again in 1894–95.

In the late eighties and early nineties there was considerable interest in the possibilities of coeducation at Luther College. Academy after academy had been founded and all were coeducational. Following St. Olaf's School in 1874 came Monona Academy at Madison, Wisconsin, in 1876; Willmar Seminary, Willmar, Minnesota, in 1883; Bode Academy, Bode, Iowa, in 1887; Stoughton Academy, Stoughton, Wisconsin, in 1888; Luther Academy, Albert Lea, Minnesota, in 1888; Aaberg Academy, Devils Lake, North Dakota, in 1888; and Bruflat Academy, Portland, North Dakota, in 1889. These schools were staffed largely by Luther College men and all were coeducational. Should there not be a place at Luther College, as well as at the academies, for women?

In the eighties Gisle Bothne, '78, was a leading spokesman for this cause. Ole M. Kalheim, '84, then a teacher at St. Olaf's School, in describing conditions there, humorously suggested some advantages of coeducation: "The literary society which flourishes in the upper classes is a composite affair, in which the boys furnish the arguments and the eloquence, and the young ladies the music and the admiration. . . . This combination of talent seems satisfactory to all parties interested." T. O. Tolo, '90, in his lead editorial of the Norwegian section of *College Chips*, stated that "coeducation must be introduced." The same issue contained an article by Thomas Nilsson, '89, in the same vein. In the next issue Tolo returned to his plea and stated that Luther College "needs a Ladies' Hall." The same issue contained a full-page article by George A. Gullixson, '90, urging the admission of women. Finally, the English edition of *Chips* editorially endorsed coeducation.[14]

At the Synod meeting of 1890 it was recommended that a committee be appointed to investigate and report on the desirability of coeducation at Luther College. Larsen and one other member of the committee were opposed to any change. Next year the committee's report was quietly buried; Larsen, in a written communication to the meeting of the Iowa District, asked that consideration of the matter be postponed and this was done. It is said that Park Region Luther College (coeducational) and Lutheran Ladies Seminary, established in 1892 and 1894 respectively, were brought into being to fend off the request for coeducation at Luther College. In any event, this promising effort to bring college policy more in line with the thinking of the rank and file of the church was shunted aside by the conservatives.[15]

An important change in the curriculum, however, was made in 1881, when the course of study was lengthened from six to seven years. It was urged that since Luther College had to teach both Norwegian and English to prepare men adequately for service in the Church, more time was needed than in colleges where only one language was used or required. There is little doubt, moreover, that Larsen was aware of the need for more science courses. Pioneer conditions were a thing of the past; the college had to keep abreast of the times and make its curriculum equal to the best found in similar institutions. Accordingly, the course was lengthened, as Larsen explicitly stated, to increase the requirements for graduation.[16] As a result of this move, there was no graduating class in the spring of 1887, the only break in the record from 1868 to the present.

The change was further implemented by making the lowest three classes into a separate preparatory department in 1889. Professor Herman W. Sheel was made principal of this section, which thereafter had its own organization and head. He was succeeded, 1891–96, by Gisle Bothne, but served again as principal from 1896 to 1911.

In 1889 the school year was divided into three terms—fall, winter, and spring—an arrangement that lasted until 1910. With the building of the gymnasium, a course in physical education was introduced. Since all friends of the school felt strongly that the students should have proper exercise to safeguard their health, this two-hour course was made obligatory in 1886–87 and has remained so since.[17]

Chemistry, the first course in science to be offered in the college department, was initiated in 1891–92 by Professor Sheel. Mathematics had been taught regularly from the start of the school. Other sciences, such as physics, physical geography, zoology, physiology, and chemistry had been given only in the preparatory department.

Although vocal music had been a part of the curriculum from the beginning, the development of music at the college came about largely through the initiative of students. Singing societies, orchestra, and band commanded surprising loyalty among all classes and gradually won more and more support. In 1882 John O. Tingelstad, '85, then a student, established a music library, the humble beginning of what was to become an important collection.

In the 1880's interest in music expanded. Students such as Karl A. Kasberg, '81, Haldor J. Hanson, '83, Carlo A. Sperati, '88, I. D. Ylvisaker, '88, Oluf Glasoe, '83, Ola A. Solheim, '81, Eugene Krohn, '85, Lauritz A. Larsen, '86, and Johan Linnevold, '90, emerged as leaders and directors of the various organizations. The coming of Haldor J. Hanson as a teacher in 1888 gave a new impetus to the development of music. An organ was purchased in 1888 and a piano in 1890. But the program was not moving fast enough. Therefore, the faculty in 1889 decided to establish a Decorah School of Music, hoping later to incorporate it into the college. The second story of P. E. Haugen's shop on Water Street (now 121 E. Water Street) was rented and the school opened October 15. The teachers were Haldor Hanson, principal, Mrs. Sarah Richardson Montgomery, Miss Ella Treat, and Miss Nellie Beaver. The directors were Larsen, Reque, Naeseth, Bothne, and Hanson. The school functioned for one year, but in the fall of 1890 was united with the college, which agreed to provide suitable quarters.[18] Hanson, who had aroused considerable enthusiasm for the project, went to Germany to study in 1891; apparently the School of Music then languished.

In the basic classical curriculum, however, there was no change, although obviously dissatisfaction with it was mounting among the students. In the early eighties there had been

146

numerous requests by students to be excused from the courses in Hebrew. These were regularly denied. Rasmus B. Anderson, who made his peace with the college and was granted his degree in 1890, returned in that year to give two lectures, enthusiastically received by the students, in which, characteristically, he pleaded for the Teutonic heritage, urging that "the rod of the Roman schoolmaster should be broken." The plea was very likely received by the faculty with mixed emotions.[19] The catalog for 1894–95, however, listed economics and French as "electives"—the first mention of electives in the curriculum—and John E. Granrud, '86, taught a course in economics that year. In 1895 William Koren, '82, was engaged to teach elocution, another slight concession to the times. Anglo-Saxon (Old English) and the history of England had been introduced for seniors in 1895.

In accordance with European practice, the college offered the degree of Master of Arts to "graduates of three years' standing who by a thesis or in some other way show to the satisfaction of the faculty that they have made progress in a special study or studies." Later the privilege was extended to graduates of the university in Christiania.[20] From 1882 to 1906, 25 men were granted the Master of Arts degree. Since then it has not been awarded.

*Obedience, humility, faith have
been driven like busy shuttles
through the warp of the fabric
of which the lives of Luther
College men are made.*

—J. Magnus Rohne, '17

10

Close of an Era

During the eighties and nineties some 30 men served on the Luther College faculty. President Larsen, who had been editor of the Norwegian Synod's official church paper for 21 years, resigned this post in 1889. Shortly thereafter he resigned as pastor of First Lutheran Church in Decorah. Lars S. Reque, '68, continued his long period of service with Luther College until 1916. He was also for 7 years treasurer of the Iowa District of the Norwegian Synod, and, for 17 years, secretary of the Board of Trustees of the college.

Gisle Bothne, '78, who, with a one-year interruption, was a member of the faculty from 1881 to 1907, had studied at Johns Hopkins University and abroad; he became professor of Scandinavian languages and literature at the University of Minnesota in 1907. Bothne wrote a 470-page history of Luther College, published in 1897, in the Norwegian language. In 1882 Christen A. Naeseth, '74, began his career at the college, where for varying periods he was teacher, treasurer, and librarian until 1920. His graduate work had been done at Concordia Seminary and at Christiania, Cornell, and Johns Hopkins universities. Haldor J. Hanson, '83, who first taught at the college in 1888–90, returned in 1894, was made its first professor of music in 1895, and continued on the staff until 1904. He had studied at the Chicago Conservatory and in Weimar, Germany. He had a gift for enlisting the cooperation of others and was a vital force on the campus. In addition to his services to the music department and the

148

museum he compiled a 135-page index to *Maanedstidende* and *Kirketidende,* covering March 1855–December 1902.

Herman W. Sheel, '74–75, took over his duties in 1889, succeeding Ola Ramstad, '83, who had done much to improve instruction in scientific subjects. Sheel, whose major interest was chemistry, continued his long and faithful teaching career until 1935. He died March 8, 1937. Another instructor joining the faculty in this period was William Sihler, popularly and affectionately known as "Billy." No student's college experience was complete until he had wandered through the mazes of Sihler's clever and often humorous devices for teaching his subject, which was German. Since "Billy" had some professional baseball experience, he exerted considerable influence upon the development of the game at Luther. He did not give up teaching until 1940; his death occurred July 7, 1941. George Markhus, '85, was at the college from 1892 to 1906 and later became a violin and pipe-organ manufacturer in St. Paul, Minnesota.

Many served for short periods. G. A. Evenson, '80, taught 1881–82; his career was cut short by tuberculosis four years later. Thorleif Homme, '78, taught 1881–82, later returning to Norway. Ola A. Solheim, '81, was a special instructor in music, 1881–82. Emil J. Petersen, author of a book on shorthand, taught from 1882 to 1887. Rudolf Olsen served from 1883–85; R. M. J. Monrad, 1883–88; John G. Halland, '84 (later superintendent of public instruction in North Dakota —one of the first Norwegian Americans to hold such an office), 1887–89; Hans J. G. Krogh, 1890–96; Hans G. Stub, '66, later president of the Norwegian Lutheran Church in America, 1896–1900; Elling O. Hove, '84, later professor of theology at Luther Seminary, 1891–93; and William Koren, '82, later professor of Romance languages at Princeton University, from 1889 to 1892 and again in 1895.

Others who were members of the staff one year or less were George Taylor Rygh, '81, pastor, teacher, and author,

149

who served temporarily in 1883; John Tingelstad, '85, later professor of Scandinavian languages at the University of North Dakota, in 1886–87; Halvor B. Hustvedt, '73, in 1887; Johan Th. Ylvisaker, '77, who produced, in English and Norwegian, the first history of the institution, in 1889–90; Andrew O. Estrem, '86, who had a long and varied teaching career, in 1889–90; Jens A. Ness, '84, whose successive teaching assignments took him eventually to Wittenberg College, in 1893–94; John E. Granrud, '86, later professor of Latin at the University of Minnesota, in 1894; Kristen Kvamme, '94, pastor, editor, and translator, in 1896; Zakarias J. Ordal, '98, pastor and editor, in 1898–99; and Bertinius K. Savre, '96, later a newspaper editor, in 1900–01 and 1912–18. Christian K. Preus, '73, who was to become the second president of Luther College, joined the faculty in 1897; Oscar L. Olson, '93, the third president of the institution, joined it in 1901. Mention should also be made of Charles H. Valder, from 1888 to 1922 head of Valder Business College in Decorah, who taught penmanship, 1881–90; and of Herbjørn N. Gausta, well-known artist, several of whose canvases hang in the college halls; he was an instructor in drawing and painting in 1887. His studies in Europe had been made possible by U. V. Koren.[1] The college physician during this period was Axel C. Smith, who served from 1876 to 1906.

Toward the close of Larsen's administration there was sporadic criticism of the tone and atmosphere of life on the campus. It was said that the students did not attend church regularly, that *College Chips* had too light a tone, and that student conduct was not above reproach. It is difficult at this time to discover what particular items in *Chips* may have given offense; the whole magazine appears to be of solid content, and charmingly innocent. There is some indication that the rigid classical course was a stumbling block to many. The student not interested in or not fitted for it had no choice; no alternative was offered. So there was considerable frustration among some otherwise gifted students, and there is little doubt that the frustration took various forms, some of them objectionable. Attempts to make life more interesting included joint social gatherings for the local congregation and the students. These were well meant, but hardly served the students' needs. A more promising occasion was an invitation from the young ladies of the congregation, asking 38 students to participate in a "literary-musical" entertainment in the basement of First Lutheran Church. But the faculty refused to grant permission. Thirteen found the invitation too tempting and went anyway. The news got out and the president told them that by their action they had separated themselves from the school. But, after individual appearances before the faculty, and apologies, they were reinstated. Some of the later pillars of the church were among these calloused offenders.[2]

During the Christmas holidays one student was sentenced to be expelled because he had been detected taking candy from the college Christmas tree. At the last minute he was saved when it was proved that this was his first offense and that others had been guilty. That same winter a student heated a poker in one of the stoves and burned a hole in one of the bedsteads. For this questionable artistry he was obliged to withdraw from school, but was reinstated two weeks later on promise of good behavior.[3]

Visiting the theater, card playing, dancing, and playing pool or billiards at the Winneshiek Hotel "or otherwheres," were practices frowned upon and occasionally warned against. During the early nineties the use of chewing tobacco became something of a fad. This habit gave rise to unexpected sanitation problems, since the college did not provide spittoons. Finally stern measures banished the practice from all buildings. At times students found it tempting to create a "disturbance" within the college halls. Such stalwarts as Willie Magelssen, Alfred Johnson, and Eli Lewison were

151

required to move to other quarters because, after a stern warning, they had again caused an uproar.[4] At a meeting on April 2, 1898, the faculty was informed that there had been noise and throwing of tin cans in the building. As they discussed various severe measures to cope with the offense, a groan was heard in the hall outside the door. Someone rose to investigate. An eavesdropper, trying to escape, unluckily ran into a teacher coming late to the meeting, and was seen and identified. He was soon on his way home from college.

Although the use of wine at some college functions had been permitted in the early days of the school, the growing Puritanism of the times and the actual problems created by the old-time saloon led eventually to an ironclad rule against visiting saloons or the use of intoxicating liquors by students.[5] To go downtown without permission was a serious offense that brought a warning and a letter to the student's father.[6]

Some reformers felt that churchgoing had been neglected and would be a corrective for such lack of proper conduct as may have existed. The faculty accordingly decided to drop morning and evening devotions on Sundays at the college, with the understanding that students attend morning and afternoon church services. The faculty also made it obligatory for teachers to take turns inspecting the buildings on Sundays to see that students had gone to church. Larsen did not approve of this step and is recorded as not voting for it. At least one faculty member refused to accept the duty assigned him to enforce churchgoing.[7] The testimony of former students indicates that those who found chapel twice a day and church twice on Sunday burdensome, and had to leave the building to avoid inspections, usually went to the woods when the weather was good. Eventually the practice of inspection became a mere formality, and it fell into disuse in the 1920's.

The library, which had grown to about 6,000 volumes in

1889, was saved by students when fire destroyed the Main Building. They toiled a good share of the night, favored by the location of the library in the northeast corner, the last portion of the building to be consumed. Librarians during this period were Olaus J. Breda, 1881–82; Halvard Roalkvam, 1882–86; Emil Petersen, 1886–87; and C. A. Naeseth, 1887–1920. The first classified printed catalog was issued about 1889. In 1893 the librarian was asked to visit other libraries to investigate the best methods for Luther College. During 1899–1900 Torstein Jahr, '96, aided by Joseph Brorby, '99, and Sigurd B. Hustvedt, '02, classified the collection according to the Dewey decimal system and made up a card catalog. Jahr, then a student at the University of Illinois library school, later was a cataloger and reviser, and an expert on Scandinavian, in the Library of Congress.

The museum, which had its inception with a gift of 600 birds' eggs in 1877, grew very slowly until the 1890's. In 1890 Professor Sihler stirred interest by providing some display cases. In October 1895 Haldor Hanson was placed in charge and in the following year was asked to take over the work of gathering books and newspapers about the Norwegians in America. He was energetic and soon enlisted interest in his cause. The museum began to be talked about and visited, gifts came in from unexpected sources, and the files of early Norwegian Americana grew rapidly. By 1897 Hanson was agitating for a fireproof library and museum building and announced one or two subscriptions to the project. On May 15, 1902, the faculty adopted a resolution that a library-museum building of fireproof construction was the first need of the college, but the fulfillment of this project was 20 years distant. Hanson served as curator until September 1902, when he was succeeded by Professor George Markhus.

College Chips, a student publication, encountered opposition before it could begin operation. It was something new.

As early as 1878 students sought permission to set up a press and publish a paper. The report of the faculty meeting of February 12, 1878, states, "All were agreed that this was a dangerous experiment"; the president was asked to confer further with the students concerning the matter.[8] In 1879 the faculty received a similar proposal with interest but offered no definite advice. They thought there should be further investigation. At length, in 1884, the paper appeared as an English semimonthly; later, in 1887, as a monthly.

The editors, Elling O. Hove, '84, and Ole K. Fuglei, '86, stated:

"English is now unquestionably the reigning language of Luther College. It is true, Norwegian is yet used almost equally as much in class as before; but English is the language generally spoken outside of class and English is almost exclusively the language of all our literary societies. English has constantly been gaining ascendancy and is now predominant. We consider this a change for the better."

In the same issue of *Chips* the editors stated, "Luther College is not such an antiquated monastery as some perhaps might be inclined to suppose." Defending the issuance of the journal, they modestly said, "We have thought that a paper of this kind might possibly do something in promoting the interests of the college." Lastly, they called attention to the motto chosen for *Chips* by the editors: *Valeat quantum valere potest;* that is, "Let it pass for what it is worth." It was an auspicious start for a journal that has now passed the three-quarter-century mark.

From December 1889 to December 1892 *Chips* had a Norwegian section; from 1893 to 1896, it appeared in Norwegian one month and in English the next, an experiment that did not prove successful. Although there was doubtless some inclination among the students for a Norwegian section, it seems likely that the faculty had the decisive voice in introducing it. In 1897, for example, when *Chips* proposed to be all-English once more, the faculty objected. But English prevailed.

There were complaints about the editorial policy of *Chips,* and even about publishing *Chips* at all. In 1897 a pastoral conference resolved that there should be "a stricter censorship." And the Committee on Schools of the church recommended that students should not busy themselves with publishing a magazine; such work took too much time, and young folks expressed immature ideas and views which did more harm than good. But, with good judgment, the meeting laid this recommendation on the table.[9] *Chips,* a sturdy child, has survived all attacks to this day.

Among literary and forensic societies, the Students' Union, organized in 1876 and reorganized in 1884, and Niffelheim, both with their popular "Journals," flourished. The Union apparently died out in 1903, Niffelheim in 1888. Muspelheim, a rival of Niffelheim, founded in 1879, was active throughout this period. Irving, founded in 1884, absorbed Addison in 1892. Amphictyonic Literary Society was an outgrowth, in 1891, of a merger of Lowell and Proceedo, both organized in 1890. Other shorter-lived societies were Hamill, 1891–92; Concordia, 1890–93; Minerva, 1891–93; Webster, 1891–93; Athenian, 1892–94; Philomathean, 1895–97; the Sextonian, the Demosthenian, and the Platonian, all in 1898–99. For many years the foremost Norwegian society at the college was Normannalaget, organized 1892. It collected a fair-sized library and was active until 1918; it was reorganized in 1925 and was active for another four or five years.[10] A Shakespearean Club (1885), and a Drawing Club (1887) indicated certain enthusiasms, but had no lasting vitality.

In the early days student and faculty instructors performed yeoman service in developing choirs, band, and orchestra. The following men served as organizers and conductors: Ola Solheim 1881–82; John O. Tingelstad 1883–85; William Sihler 1890–95; Haldor Hanson 1882–83, 1888–90, and 1894–

1904; Carlo A. Sperati 1885–88; Karl A. Kasberg 1878–81 and 1883; Edwin G. Mellem 1889–90; Henry W. Moore 1890–91; Ivar A. Thorson 1892–95; Oluf Glasoe 1879–81 and 1882; Eugene Krohn 1882–85; Lauritz A. Larsen 1885–86; Johan Linnevold 1886–90; Alfred O. Johnson 1890–91; Helge M. Tjernagel 1891–93; and Oscar K. Omlie 1893–94. Ivar D. Ylvisaker organized a flageolet sextet known as the "Nightingale" in 1885. A drum corps and a mandolin club were organized in 1896 and 1898 respectively, but did not long survive.

The first orchestra concert was given in 1883. The first band trip was undertaken in 1886, a fifteen-day excursion; the second, in 1890, was of a month's duration. The first oratorio to be presented, Haydn's "Creation," was given in 1890 under Hanson's leadership. The great expansion of musical activities, however, dates from Hanson's return to the college in 1894. From then on, both vocal and instrumental organizations on campus took on new stature. Ambitious programs became the order of the day under the sponsorship of the Luther College Musical Union, which, under Hanson, came to include band, orchestra, choir, and glee club.[11]

The second two decades of Larsen's administration were marked by an increased interest in sports and by the introduction of intercollegiate athletics. The honorable post of captain of wood sawers passed into oblivion with the introduction of steam heat in the new Main Building in 1890. So also did some of the other chores, such as pumping and carrying water, which had been a part of the early, primitive routine. Each new improvement, such as the installation of water mains and of electric lights, gave both faculty and students more leisure.

Baseball continued to be the king of sports. Early games were played with town teams from Decorah, Waukon, Fort Atkinson, Ridgeway, and Cresco, the major contest usually being the one with Decorah on May 17. In 1891 intercollegiate competition was introduced, the first game being with St. Olaf College May 17, resulting in a Luther victory, 9 to 4. St. Olaf won the next year, 3 to 2. Thanks to *College Chips,* the team rosters of all baseball teams from 1884 on are extant. Opponents included Cornell College at Mount Vernon, Iowa; Drake University, Des Moines; the State University of Iowa; the University of Minnesota; St. Olaf College, Northfield, Minnesota; and Upper Iowa University, Fayette, Iowa. The famous 1893 team took the first extensive tour to be made by a Luther ball club and did not lose a game. The *Iowa Daily Citizen* (Iowa City) for May 9, 1893, gives the following account of Luther's 12–0 win over the State University of Iowa:

"Nine baseball players, one substitute and a manager, all of Norwegian descent, came in on the night train Saturday, and put up at the St. James. On Sunday they sat around the lobby of the hotel, looking curiously at all the diamond-front traveling men; and when the church bells rang, found their way, as was their custom, to a place of worship.

"Two of them, the toughs of the party, smoked cigarettes, and one of them was so far gone, in their eyes, as to smoke a cigar.

"Several times the manager was approached with a view to ascertaining what he thought of the playing qualities of his team. He said: 'We come from a small college of about 180 to 200 attendance, located in the little town of Decorah. We never have been away from home before, all of our games being confined to a few of the neighboring towns. No, we cannot afford to keep a man on a salary, therefore we have no professionals. The oldest man on our team is twenty-two years of age, and most of them are not of age. We are all college boys from the same school.'

"He did not care to talk baseball, nor did any of the team. But when they donned their old-fashioned red uniforms and

157

took their place at the bat or in the field, they played ball, and that with terrific effect. Then they made clear the mystery how they defeated the semi-professional nine at Cornell Saturday. There was no grandstand playing in their work. Their teamwork was like professionals and the individual playing of some of them was very brilliant.

"They went at it in such a matter-of-fact manner that it was really amusing to watch them. When the game was finished, they gathered up their bats—three in number—and quietly found their way to the hotel. They raised not a cry of triumph, not even as much as raised their hats. The story of the game is as short as it is one-sided. For six innings Lindsay put up a beautiful game, when he became disgusted with the support he was receiving and grew very reckless, so much so that the victors pounded out eleven scores. On the other hand the home team could scarcely touch Torrison, the visitors' pitcher. When they did hit one into the field there was always somebody there to take care of it."

Years later, the third president of Luther College, who had been a member of that team, stated: "We were not quite so naive as the article indicates."[12]

On invitation, and after having received permission from President Larsen, the team stayed over to play a second game the next day. The box score of this game shows that at the end of eight innings the university led Luther, 3 to 0. In the first half of the ninth, as speculation began among the fans as to whether the Luther men had been playing possum up to this point, Luther batted in 8 runs. In the last half of the ninth the first two Iowa batters were easy outs; the third lofted a high fly toward second base, a position held down by Karl L. Thorsgaard, '96, later a well-known physician in Chicago. Thorsgaard began backing up, sashayed about a bit as if having difficulty getting under the ball, then at the last moment caught it deftly in his gloved hand behind his back, ending the game. After this last touch of bravado, he trotted off the field, tucking the ball in his pocket.[13]

Football awakened increased interest in the eighties, many interclass games being played, but intercollegiate contests were not introduced until 1892. Games were played with the State University of Iowa, Coe College at Cedar Rapids, Upper Iowa, and Carleton at Northfield, Minnesota. In 1896 the students requested that the gymnasium be enlarged and a football coach hired. But the Church Council, excepting possibly one member, reportedly objected to all intercollegiate athletic contests; they unanimously opposed hiring a coach. The presence of a coach, they thought, smacked of professionalism. The rise of intercollegiate athletics during the eighties and nineties posed new problems and attracted wide attention in educational circles. The value of such contests was seriously debated. The faculty minutes of the college contain numerous references to discussions about intercollegiate athletics and several reports by members who had attended state educational meetings to consider the problems raised by this new development. On June 15, 1897, the faculty, yielding perhaps to outside pressures, banned all intercollegiate football games, but intramural games were permitted.[14] Not until 1919 were intercollegiate games again sanctioned.

After the gymnasium was erected in 1886, turning and other gymnastics became popular. In December of that year the Turning Club was organized through the efforts of Carlo A. Sperati, and in 1888 it gave its first exhibition. For many years thereafter the Turning Club gave annual exhibitions which attracted many enthusiastic spectators. Yet when in 1902 Haldor Hanson requested that the Turning Club be permitted to give an exhibition in the local "opera house" at a concert for the benefit of the museum, the faculty turned thumbs down.[15]

In 1891 William P. Sihler made ready the first tennis court

at Luther, but there is little record of matches at that time; the first intercollegiate contest did not occur until 1904.

Individual athletes had taken part in campus track events from an early date, but the first organized field meet was not held until 1900, and the first intercollegiate meet did not take place until 1902. Upper Iowa then defeated Luther, 59 to 37. Since then track has held a respected place in the college sports program.

A major step in the athletic program was taken when, in 1892, students organized the Luther College Athletic Association. Leading spirit and first president was Oscar L. Olson, '93, later third president of the college. From its inception the association has promoted the cause of athletics at the school.

In the nineties an interest in the adoption of school colors grew out of the athletic program. Navy blue and ivory were the original colors selected by the students, possibly in 1894–95. Later blue and white gradually came to be accepted. A school pin bearing the letters "L" and "C" on blue and white was designed in the nineties; for many years it was a favorite with Luther students.[16]

The college song "To Luther" was written by G. B. Wollan, '97. It was first sung by the Irving Glee Club at Irving's "Entertainment" on February 22, 1897.

The Spanish-American War occasioned interest on the campus, but naval actions played the major role in the conflict and there was no great appeal for man power. Records disclose that the following former students entered the armed forces:

William Bjørnstad, '91–92, St. Paul, Minnesota.
Albert O. Davick, '05, Clinton, Minnesota.
Frank Ellickson, '95–96, Montevideo, Minnesota.
Oscar Fortun, '92–93, Stoughton, Wisconsin.
Eivind Fremming, '96–97, St. Paul, Minnesota.

20. *Student body, 1882. The grass is uncut; the lane of elms is at right.*

21. *First baseball team, 1872. Standing: Peder Helgeland, Gudbrand (Gilbert) J. Lomen, Christian K. Preus, Andreas Torgerson. Seated: Ingvard G. Monson, Halle Røthe, Sjur W. Weeks, Hans Johnson, Olaf Mandt.*

22. *Orchestra, 1878. Standing: Oscar M. Torrison, Ola A. Solheim. Seated: Olaf E. Brandt, John P. Kopang, Karl A. Kasberg, Thorvild K. Thorvildson.*

23. *The Phalanx, 1882.*

24. *Reserve Officers Training Corps, 1919.*

25. *Dining room, first Main Building.*

26. *First gymnasium, 1886.*

27. *Gymnasium, 1903–25. Outlines of a baseball diamond and football field in the foreground.*

The original of this photo and some of the lower parts of the walls in the ruins in the building were re-built.

← south *1st floor* Here was my bedroom.— O.L.O. All my belongings were rescued

Luther College, Decorah, Iowa, burning May 19, 6

28. *Burning of Main Building, May 19, 1889.*

29. *A daily chore.*

30. *Off for college.*

31. *Laur. Larsen.*

32. *G. B. Wollan, '97, author of "To Luther."*

33. *Child and monk by Herbjørn N. Gausta, '72-'75, sketched on a bedroom wall in Washington Prairie parsonage.*

34. *Main Building, 1890–19*

35. *First Luther College B*
1878.
L. to r., front:
J. W. Preus, '82;
Carl O. Lien, '78–82.
Middle: J. M. O. Ness, '80;
Andrew T. Eiken, '75–80;
Engebret P. Haugen, '76–78.
Ole C. Gronvold, '76–81;
Oluf S. Rygg, '82.
Back: Ola A. Solheim, '81;
Hans B. Thorgrimsen, '79;
Erik T. Rogne, '82;
Hans Allen, '83;
Oluf Glasoe, '83.

36. *The hospital.*

37. *Christian K. Preus, president 1902–1921.*

38. *Luther statue.*

39. *Baseball team 1891 and Music Pavilion. Standing: Aaron J. Torrison, Theodor A. Rodsater, Karl L. Thorsgaard, William L. Torrison. Second row: Oscar L. Olson, Sigvard T. Reque. In front: William P. Sihler, Otto G. Juul, Peter A. Reque, Erling A. Bothne.*

40. *Football in 1893.*
Standing:
Ingeman M. Lyngaas,
Sylvester M. Orwoll,
Karl L. Thorsgaard,
Johan E. Winger,
Ingvald A. Kampen,
Martin Teigen,
Bertinius K. Savre.
Seated:
Hildus Ness,
Olav S. Bygland,
Erling A. Bothne,
Lauritz S. J. Reque,
Chr. A. H. Hjermstad.
In front:
H. Gynther Magelssen,
Ivar A. Thorson.

41. *Four student activities,*
1892–93.
Ivar A. Thorson,
Erling A. Bothne,
Helge M. Tjernagel,
Oscar L. Olson.

Eugene Carl Hanson, '95–97, Eau Claire, Wisconsin, died
in Cuba.

Charles T. (Overn) Helgeson, '88–89, Waupun, Wisconsin.

Christopher Jensvold, '97–98, La Crosse, Wisconsin.

Andrew Kleppen, '97–98, Eau Claire, Wisconsin.

Jacob A. Magelssen, '95, Rushford, Minnesota.

Einar E. Opdahl, '95–96, Wausau, Wisconsin.

Samuel Peterson, '97, Chatfield, Minnesota.

Theron Steen, '94–95, Wahoo, Nebraska.

Lars J. Thorsgaard, '93–94, Kindred, North Dakota.

On February 12, 1901, Koren, then president of the Norwegian Synod, delivered at the college his carefully worked-out lecture on Abraham Lincoln, in which he paid a warm tribute to the great leader of the Union cause who had ended the scourge of slavery in this country. One is inclined to believe that the lecture represented an oblique acknowledgment of the great principle of human freedom which had been obscured in the narrow theological interpretation of the sixties.

In June 1902 Larsen had completed 41 years as head of the institution. He was not quite 69 years old. When the college opened in 1861 he had been all things—president, registrar, treasurer, librarian, dean, pastor, and teacher. Gradually many of his functions were set up as separate offices. He had also carried heavy responsibilities as editor. He had served on many important church committees, as vice president of the Iowa District 1876–79, as vice president of the Norwegian Synod 1876–93, and as chairman of the Synodical Conference 1881–83. At the church meeting of 1902, after this long period of faithful service, he tendered his resignation as president. The church accepted it and elected the fifty-year-old Christian K. Preus, '73, as his successor. Larsen was asked, however, to resume the editorship of the church paper (*Kirketidende*). This he did, also retaining his post as professor of Hebrew at the college. He continued teaching until 1911, and kept the editorship until 1912. He died March 1, 1915.

In the long span of years during which Larsen guided the destinies of the college, he could not help putting his mark upon it. There is no doubt that he put the stamp of honesty on it—honesty in work, in play, in conduct. He trusted the boys, he expected honesty, and they responded to his confidence. He also put a stamp of service on the institution. Its graduates were expected to serve first, their church, and next, their country. It was an unwritten law; little was said about it, but it was part of the atmosphere of the place: no one had the right to live to himself alone. He must serve his fellow men. The sense of mission was strong during all the years of Larsen's administration. Up to 1902, at least 322 men from Luther College entered the ministry. Not a few went into other professions, notably law, medicine, and teaching.

Among prominent alumni, not hitherto identified, from Larsen's last 20 years as president are Nils S. Thorlaksson, '81, president of the Icelandic Evangelical Lutheran Synod in America; James C. M. Hanson, '82, internationally known librarian; Ludvig Hektoen, '83, internationally famous pathologist; M. Nelson Voldeng, '83, the superintendent of the State Hospital for Epileptics at Woodward, Iowa; Oscar M. Torrison, '81, judge of the circuit court in Chicago; John H. Lund, '84, judge of county court, Day County, South Dakota; Olaus Dahl, '85, a pioneer in teaching Scandinavian at both Yale and Chicago universities; George A. Torrison, '85, professor of otolaryngology, Rush Medical College; Nils N. Boe, '86, president of the South Dakota District of the Norwegian Lutheran Church of America; Michael A. Mikkelsen, '86, editor of the *Architectural Record* (New York City); Laurits S. Swenson, '86, United States minister to Denmark, Switzerland, Norway, and the Netherlands; Gustav T. Lee, '88, editor of *Lutheran Herald* (Minneapolis);

Carl A. Mellby, '88, professor of economics and history, St. Olaf College; Ivar D. Ylvisaker, '88, president of the North Dakota District of the Norwegian Lutheran Church of America; Isaac Anderson, '90, journalist, New York City; Ole J. Kvale, '90, member of the United States Congress; Johannes Astrup, '93, and Heinrich Otte, '93, missionaries to the Zulus of South Africa; John R. Peterson, '94, medical director, Lutheran Brotherhood Life Insurance Society, Minneapolis; N. Astrup Larsen, '96, missionary to China and president of the Iowa District, Evangelical Lutheran Church; Jacob A. O. Stub, '98, pastor of Central Lutheran Church, Minneapolis; Martin I. Olsen, '99, medical director, Central Life Assurance Society, Des Moines; Hans A. Stub, '00, pastor of Immanuel Lutheran Church, Seattle; Sigurd B. Hustvedt, '02, professor of English, University of California at Los Angeles; Lauritz Larsen, '02, president of the National Lutheran Council; Johan C. K. Preus, '02, educational director of the Evangelical Lutheran Church; Alfred R. Sørenson, '02, surgeon, Minot, North Dakota; and Nils M. Ylvisaker, '02, executive secretary of the Young People's Luther League of the Norwegian Lutheran Church of America.

Despite the fact that the sons of early immigrants were being thoroughly drilled in Latin, Greek, Hebrew, German, and Norwegian—with strong doses of history and Christian doctrine—intellectual areas very remote from those of the farms and small towns from which most of them came, the institution had an attractive atmosphere of modest simplicity which inspired strong loyalties. Moreover, Larsen's religious convictions were deep and abiding and required no outward display. So, chapel during his administration was a brief and simple but satisfying exercise. One student has described it thus:

"We sang two or three stanzas from a hymnbook and President Larsen read a selection from a book of devotions and also one of the prayers in the hymnbook assigned for the morning and evening of each day in the week. These prayers were repeated each week throughout my entire seven years at the college. I knew them practically by heart from having heard them so often, and they were like sweet music to my soul. I never grew tired of them. Every devotion closed with the Lord's Prayer. I cannot recall that President Larsen ever delivered a free devotional talk at chapel exercises. He treated the exercises as family devotions."[17]

Perhaps no better statement has been given of what Larsen sought to accomplish at the college than one he made in 1884, on the occasion of his twenty-fifth anniversary as a teacher:

"In my work here I have striven to accomplish especially three things. In the first place, I have desired that the spirit of Christianity should permeate everything. The instruction, the discipline, all our associations—in short, every part of our school life—should be marked by a true Christian spirit. . . .

"In the second place it has been my aim that the instruction here be thorough; that there be no show or humbug; that everything be pure gold—or, to use a common expression, that it be 'all wool and a yard wide.'

"In the third place, I have wanted such discipline here as would teach the student more and more self-discipline, with each one personally responsible for his own conduct; and still one student restraining the other, so that I might as far as possible be relieved of discipline."[18]

Larsen's record will stand close scrutiny. It leaves an impression of depth and integrity. One student, 35 years after his graduation from Luther, called Larsen "almost the embodiment of Christian faith, hope, and charity"—one who "did not attempt to rob the student of his individuality . . . but to guide, to develop, to really educate." The "latitude in education" at Luther was a heritage from him.

"He was one of her founders; but he was more. He was her first president; but he was more than that. He was the head of this institution; but he was more than its head. Laur. Larsen was the embodiment of the soul of Luther College. He exemplified and inspired a love of truth, of fairness, of justice, of faith in God and faith in humanity. . . . A man who stood for all that was honest and thorough and genuine, and hated hypocrisy and sham and humbug and veneer and make-believe. A man whose whole life with its every talent and all its energy was dedicated to the service of God and his fellowmen. . . . *Soli Deo Gloria,* 'To God Alone the Honor,' the motto of this college, was the motto of his life."[19]

*We should habituate youth to
enjoy the art of music, for it pro-
duces fine and skillful people.*
—Martin Luther

11

Expansion and Growth

When Christian K. Preus became the second president of
Luther College in 1902, the institution was entering a period
in which its task appeared to be to catch up with the material progress all about it. Material progress was evident
not only in the college's constituency but in the nation
generally. Agriculture, still the mainstay of the Middle West,
had emerged from the many years of low prices that followed the post-Civil War collapse; the depression of the
nineties had been overcome; the nation had found new unity
in the Spanish-American War and from that conflict had
dramatically emerged a world power. There was a growth
of prosperity and well-being that was not interrupted until
after World War I. During this time the college, under
Preus, shared in part in this prosperity.

It was still the favored child of the Norwegian Synod.
Other educational institutions, notably many academies,
had sprung up, but only Luther College and Luther Seminary were direct charges on the budget of the church, which
annually footed the bill for their expenditures. This the
Norwegian Synod was amply able to do, for it had now
recovered from the severe blow of the schism of 1887, when
it lost 55 pastors, 211 congregations, and 49,994 members,
more than a third of its numbers.[1] By vigorous home-mission
work in the Northwest and Far West, it had attained approximately the strength it had before the rupture, was a

166

closely knit organization, and was prepared for further growth.

Meanwhile, other Norwegian Lutheran church bodies had begun to repair the breaches of earlier days and had inaugurated a movement toward church union. Although the Norwegian Synod and Hauge's Synod remained aloof, the Anti-Missourian Brotherhood, the Conference, and the Augustanans joined in June 1890 to form the United Norwegian Lutheran Church. But this body became involved in problems which, touching off an inner conflict, resulted in schism and litigation for the new organization. This split resulted in the formation of the Lutheran Free Church; Augsburg College and Seminary, Minneapolis, was its principal institution of learning. The United Norwegian Lutheran Church then supported St. Olaf College, establishing its own seminary (now Luther Theological Seminary) at St. Anthony Park, between Minneapolis and St. Paul.

Despite this setback to church unity, it was evident that the long and bitter doctrinal disputes had brought a reaction. Theological warfare seemed fruitless. Men felt there should be a better way. In 1905, committees were elected by Hauge's Synod, the United Norwegian Lutheran Church, and the Norwegian Synod to confer concerning union. After several years' discussion a successor Joint Union Committee reached an agreement *(opgjør)* at Madison, Wisconsin, in 1912, which formed the basis for ultimate union of the three bodies in 1917. The heart of the agreement was acceptance by the three synods of the doctrine of election set forth in Article XI of the Formula of Concord and in Pontoppidan's *Truth unto Godliness,* question 548. The agreement was made the basis for union, but a sizable minority in the Norwegian Synod still held back. The leaders of this group were C. K. Preus, '73, president of Luther College, and his close friend Isaac B. Torrison, '79. The minority comprised roughly one fourth of the ministers of the Norwegian Synod. Because of the close connection of the two leaders, Preus and Torrison, with Luther College, one as president, the other as college pastor, the school itself was regarded by some as lukewarm toward the idea of union, despite a substantial majority in the Synod who found the Madison Agreement acceptable.

Members of the minority had reservations which to some extent may have been inspired by attacks on the Madison Agreement emanating from within the Missouri Synod; in addition, they were extremely loath to subscribe to an agreement which they feared might result in a complete rupture with their friends of the Missouri Synod. Preus and Torrison, in consultations initiated by John N. Kildahl, '79, and Lars W. Boe, sought a clarification of the Madison Agreement which would be acceptable to their followers. Their joint efforts brought about the "Austin Agreement"; of this proposal the Joint Union Committee stated that "there was nothing in the proposition submitted which is contrary to Scripture and the Confessions, and that we regard the position taken in that document as a sufficient expression of unity in faith." Thereupon the two minority leaders called a meeting of the minority group in Minneapolis for January 17–18, 1917.[2]

Prior to the meeting, Preus and Torrison conferred in St. Louis with Professors F. Pieper, W. H. T. Dau, and Theodore Graebner of Concordia Seminary, who were old friends of the Norwegian Synod. The two came away convinced that the Austin Agreement "leaves the way open for us to go along in the new body with a good conscience and makes it now impossible for us to leave," and with the promise of a letter from the three professors supporting their position. Great was their consternation when the promised letter, dated January 9, 1917, discussed the question of whether the minority should now part company with the majority of the Norwegian Synod, not whether it should

168

enter the union. Despite their explanations to the January meeting, Preus and Torrison found themselves in a very uncomfortable position. Yet they carried the overwhelming number of the minority group with them into the union. Perhaps it is not too much to say that had the letter of the St. Louis professors straightforwardly reported the substance of the conference with Preus and Torrison, the few members of the minority whose doubts were not resolved would not have withdrawn and formed the "Little Synod." Only years later was the truth of Preus and Torrison's position documentarily established.[3]

The story of the minority belongs primarily to the history of the church, but the cloud which for years hung over Preus and Torrison and has only recently been fully cleared away hung also in part over Luther College, creating at times misunderstanding and lack of sympathy. Moreover, the union question, a live and vital one from 1905 to 1917, made considerable drains on the time and energy of many men close to the college and occasionally slowed down their activity in the school's behalf. With the death of Koren in 1910 and the election of Hans Gerhard Stub, '66, to the presidency of the Norwegian Synod, a more conciliatory and liberal atmosphere was apparent, not always welcomed by the more conservative elements in the church. Under Stub's leadership, church union was achieved in 1917 and he then became the first president of the Norwegian Evangelical Lutheran Church in America.

With the union, a great change in the status of Luther College occurred, one not then fully appreciated and one the college recognized only after a succession of shocks that jarred it to its foundations. Hitherto the college had been the darling of the Norwegian Synod. Now it became one of two colleges (the other being St. Olaf) to which the church was fully committed; and it was not many years before it found it was one of four, eventually five colleges, which laid claim to the church's support. St. Olaf, which had had to fight for its life in its early years, had long since learned to order its affairs without too much reliance on the unpredictable vagaries of church politics; Luther, continuing on its course like a carefree child which had always been well supplied by its parent, woke up eventually to discover it would have to assume major responsibilities for its own future.

Christian K. Preus, who was at the helm when this great change occurred, was born October 13, 1852, the eldest child of H. A. Preus, pioneer pastor and president of the Norwegian Synod from 1862 to 1894. His mother was Caroline Dorthea Margrethe Keyser, at 17 the orphaned daughter of Professor Christian N. Keyser of Christiania University. As a youth, C. K. Preus, an attractive, gifted, and well-rounded personality, was greatly looked up to and loved by his brothers and sisters. He early displayed a certain originality, if not whimsey, as when he patiently broke a pair of rams to harness and drove them about the neighborhood to the delight and terror of other children. He had a strong practical bent, became a skillful hunter, and acquired a reputation for having a good eye for blooded livestock and fast horses. He was a born leader among his associates, popular and loved by his companions.

In 1866–67 he and his parents spent a year in Norway. In 1873 he was graduated from Luther College, where he had been a member of the first baseball team in 1872. Forty years later, in 1912, he participated, with traces of his old agility, in a game between the faculty and the seniors. After graduating from Concordia Seminary in St. Louis with highest marks, he was ordained and became his father's assistant in Spring Prairie, Wisconsin. In 1877 he married Louise Augusta Hjort, eldest daughter of the pioneer pastor, Ove Jakob Hjort. In 1883 the Preuses, father and son, had the bitter experience of being deposed from their pastoral office by the De Forest (Wisconsin) congregation during the election (or predestination) controversy.

The elder Preus died in 1894. Christian K. continued to serve the large Spring Prairie parish until 1897, and in addition was pastor of Our Saviour's Church in Chicago, 1893–95. In 1897 his health failed. Because of this, he moved to Decorah in the summer of 1897, occupying the house on the college campus now known as "Sunnyside." In 1898 he was given charge of instruction in religion and Norwegian in the preparatory department, a position he held until he became president of the college. He was called to the office, therefore, without a good background of either teaching or administrative experience, a lack he fully realized when he accepted the post. Although he began his presidential career with a rigor in disciplinary matters that earned him the sobriquet of "Nick Carter" among the students, his friendly nature eventually led him to a mellow confidence in the boys that was cherished by both students and associates.

He is said to have had a sweet tooth; and at one home, when the children spied him approaching, they would cry: "Hide the candy! Here comes Uncle!" One of Preus's great assets was a wonderfully clear and flexible voice. It is said that he used to stand on the steps of Main Building and give directions to Helge Oyloe, the lovably eccentric keeper of the grounds, when the latter was across campus near Koren Library. Preus had not only a remarkably fine voice, but also an unsurpassed facility in impromptu speaking, expressing himself felicitously and incisively. His chapel talks, seldom more than ten minutes in length, were filled with warmth and wisdom and set a standard to which others hoped they might attain.

During Preus's administration attendance remained reasonably constant at about 200 until an upswing after World

171

War I carried the total enrollment, for the first time, beyond the mark established in 1874–75.

Although English was the language of the campus, Norwegian still dominated many classes. It was also used in chapel until World War I brought about its banishment from that forum. The faculty minutes continued to be kept in Norwegian, though English intruded occasionally, until the school year 1915–16, when Norwegian was abandoned and English used exclusively. Beginning in 1907, the catalog was issued only in English, with Oscar L. Olson its chief editor. Up to Preus's last year as president, he wrote his annual reports to the church in Norwegian and often stressed the significance of the word "Norwegian" in the legal title of the college. He had a genuine affection for the cultural roots of the college and of the Synod that lay in Norway. The Norwegian Luther College, nevertheless, resolved in 1918 that the word "Norwegian" be stricken from the official name of the college.[4] Perhaps the fact that Preus's last annual report, in 1921, was made in English was indicative of the trend of times and of the changes which led him then to abandon what he considered his mother tongue.

When Preus took office in 1902, it was clear that improvements and additions to the physical plant were overdue. As the Norwegian Synod was to hold its Golden Jubilee at the college in 1903, steps were quickly taken to triple the size of the gymnasium by adding a center section and a wing to the east. For this meeting, too, an arch was set up at the campus entrance, its two columns having originally adorned the early Winneshiek County courthouse, where in its first Decorah days the college had held Sunday services.[5] The hospital was also somewhat enlarged and improved.

But Preus was disappointed that the Synod failed to provide for substantial improvement in the college plant. In his annual reports he pleaded for a new dormitory, a new library and museum building, and better facilities for music and science. At length he was given permission to go out among the college constituency and raise funds for a dormitory. Singlehanded, Preus started in, and although later, when illness slowed his efforts, he was aided by Professors Naeseth, Bleken, and Thompson, and Pastors Austvold, Ingebrigtson, and others, the lion's share of the effort was his. His final report shows that about $93,000 was raised. With these funds, Laur. Larsen Hall was erected; all necessary water, sewer, and heating connections were made; an addition to the heating plant, with a new boiler, was completed; equipment and furniture for the new building were purchased; and some repairs were made on the Main Building. The new dormitory had a center section 40 by 50 feet and two wings, each 40 by 90 feet, three stories and basement. The basement area, most of which, because of the slope of the site, was at ground level, was utilized for a chemistry laboratory, music room, and lecture rooms.[6]

The dedication of the building took place Sunday, October 13, 1907, with Hans G. Stub, '66, of Luther Seminary, preaching the sermon on I Corinthians 13:1–7. Ulrik Vilhelm Koren, president of the Norwegian Synod, performed the act of dedication. The new dormitory was named Laur. Larsen Hall in honor of the first teacher and first president of the institution. A crowd estimated at 3,000 was present, including 250 pastors of the Synod who had gathered for a general conference. Because Preus had borne the chief burden in raising the funds which had made the new building possible, and because October 13 was his fifty-fifth birthday, the pastors surprised him in the evening with a birthday party when a purse was given him as a token of appreciation.[7]

Meanwhile, West Decorah having been incorporated into the city of Decorah, an agreement was reached about the water mains which the college had extended from the former

173

city limits after the 1889 fire and which the city had been using for several years. In return for deeding over the mains to the city, Decorah contracted to furnish free water to the college for 30 years, beginning November 1, 1905.[8]

In 1906 the grandstand, which was to witness the efforts of many baseball greats until it was torn down in 1959, was erected, largely through the efforts of students.

In 1909 Jens Jensen, the well-known landscape architect, was engaged through the efforts of Chicago alumni, and in 1910 submitted his plan for campus improvement. The elimination of the avenue of elm trees, which extended from High Street to the Main Building, and the grading and leveling of the college green in front of Main Building were done on his recommendation. He also urged that the beautiful view of the Oneota Valley, north of the Main Building, always be left open. On February 12, 1909, the centennial of Lincoln's birth, a replica of Leonard W. Volk's bust of Lincoln was presented to the college by Andrew Gullixson, '97, at a formal public program on the campus. In 1910 T. A. Rossing of Decorah set up a $10,000 scholarship fund.

The semicentennial in 1911 was the occasion for a great celebration and also for notable gifts to the college. The alumni presented a tract of eight acres lying north of High Street and east of the campus. The women of the Synod under the leadership of Mrs. Nora Førde of Starbuck, Minnesota (mother of Mrs. O. J. H. Preus), presented a replica of E. F. A. Rietschel's statue, "Martin Luther at Worms," which was placed a little east of Larsen Hall.

But by far the largest gift on this fiftieth anniversary was the $250,000 endowment fund, which was presented on October 14, 1911. As early as 1898 or 1899 U. V. Koren had negotiated for a site for Luther Seminary with James J. Hill, the builder of the Great Northern Railway, and the two became friends. In 1908 Koren congratulated Hill on the latter's seventieth birthday.[9] In 1909 the Luther College

Alumni Association elected a committee, whose chairman was Laurits S. Swenson, '86, then United States minister to Switzerland, to see about procuring an endowment for the college. Swenson went to see Hill. When Hill told Swenson he would give $50,000 if $200,000 additional was raised by November 1911, the campaign got under way. The committee consisted of Swenson, Hans G. Stub, '66, Christian K. Preus, '73, Ludvig Hektoen, '83, Thore O. Hanson, '75–78, Gustav Livdahl of Velva, North Dakota, and Congressman G. N. Haugen of Northwood, Iowa. The major burden fell on Stub, who headed the appeal, but many others did yeoman work in bringing it to a successful conclusion. One of the pleasant incidents of the campaign took place June 20, 1911. On that date the trustees expressed the thanks of the college to Charles J. Weiser and the Winneshiek County State Bank for the "considerable accommodations" which had been extended during half a century. These cordial relations continued for many years thereafter.

The celebration on October 13 and 14, 1911, included, in addition to the presentation of the endowment, a festival address by Hans G. Stub, '66; an address by Laur. Larsen and another by Ludvig Hektoen, '83; a hymn for the occasion written by Paul Koren, '82; poems, one by John Koren, '79, in English, and a second, by an anonymous author, in Norwegian; the traditional illumination of the buildings; a concert by the band; festival services on Sunday, with a sermon by Olaf E. Brandt, '79; the unveiling of the Luther statue, with an address by Johannes Th. Ylvisaker, '74; and the rendition of Handel's "Messiah" by the Decorah Choral Union and Orchestra, led by Carlo A. Sperati, '88.

Throughout the years, boarding facilities of the college had been located in the basement of the Main Building. In 1916 the students, through Mikkel Lono, '17, submitted a plan for a dining hall. This was found acceptable and the new building, called Loyalty Hall, was erected the

175

same year, with borrowed funds; each student boarding at the college paid $8 a year toward amortizing the loan. The building, 45 by 95 feet, two stories and basement, was dedicated December 20, 1916.

Since the building of Loyalty Hall necessitated moving the hospital, the latter was shifted to its present site and considerably improved and enlarged. A registered nurse, Olivia Peterson, was employed, the first woman to be a member of the college administrative staff except for those who had served in the refectory.[10]

In 1916 the college buildings were connected to the city sewer system which had been installed in Decorah that same year. In 1919 the Driggs residence, which had been college property for many years, was sold to Sigurd S. Reque, '03. In 1920 a tract of land, equal in size to a city square, south of High Street and east of the campus, was acquired from President Preus. The following year, 11 Dayton lots, near but not adjacent to the campus, were purchased and presented to the college by the Alumni Association; in this matter I. B. Torrison, '79, was the moving spirit.

Meanwhile, steps had been taken to erect a new library-museum building. As early as February 1909 the Board of Trustees accepted a proposal by the students (originated by the graduating class) to co-operate in the construction of such a building by making concrete blocks.[11] The student body was divided into squads, each with a leader, which at stated times assembled to mix and mold sand, mortar, and cement into concrete blocks. It was estimated that 27,000 blocks would be needed; more than that were made during three or four years. On June 16, 1910, the Board of Trustees decided that the library building should be placed on the open lot across from the present Campus House, a decision regretted by many.

After this early burst of enthusiasm, the library project languished, perhaps because college leaders were preoccupied with the problems of the church union effected in 1917. The Synod, like the other two parties to the union, raised a fund to liquidate its debts. The campaign ended with a surplus of $25,000. In 1919, with this amount as a nucleus, the Board of Trustees authorized a campaign for funds for the library. Hans G. Stub, '66, now president of the newly formed church, was present and once more lent his influence. Preus again appealed for funds and was so far successful that on February 3, 1921, bids were let for a library building to cost in excess of $125,000.[12] The cornerstone was laid by Stub on April 18, 1921.

In the gathering of funds Michael O. Borge, '70–71, had assisted President Preus; after Preus's death on May 28, 1921, since the total collected up to that time was short of the amount needed, the latter's two sons, Ove J. H. Preus, '01, and Johan C. K. Preus, '02 (joined later by Paul Koren, '82) completed the ingathering. The library building, which was dedicated October 14, 1921, was thus President Preus's last contribution to the physical plant of the college. The building was named the Koren Library in honor of Ulrik Vilhelm Koren, a man who had played a leading role in promoting the college and its welfare from its earliest days.

The structure, which is fireproof, has two large rooms on the ground floor which were originally set aside for museum purposes; these have long since been taken over by the library. The building provides stack space for more than 100,000 volumes and has a main reading room that accommodates 95 persons. In 1921, when the college had less than 300 students, the library was outstanding for a school of its size. One national scholar remarked: "I suppose scarcely any other small college in the country has a better library than this."[13]

By the end of Preus's administration there had been a material expansion of the physical plant, with two major

177

and two minor buildings erected. There had also been many repairs and improvements on the existing buildings and grounds, hardly a year passing without some such work being undertaken. There had also been a stepup in maintenance of the grounds, and with the grading and filling of the area in front of the Main Building (some of it continued in the following administration), the green took on much the appearance it has today. Not a little new equipment was purchased. A biological laboratory, mentioned for the first time in the catalog for 1916–17, was located originally in Larsen Hall and later was moved to the basement of Main Building in 1920–21.

The $250,000 endowment fund of 1911 had placed the college on a more secure financial basis. Gifts and legacies had increased other endowments to $39,111.70 by 1921.[14] The Luther College Alumni Association and the individual Luther College Clubs made several substantial contributions, in addition to supporting fund-raising efforts. Graduating classes made generous and worth-while gifts. Not a few larger undertakings were advocated by alumni and students long before they could become realities. For instance, the plan to raise $500,000 for a library, gymnasium, and music hall was proposed to the trustees by a student committee headed by Rudolph A. Ofstedal, '21, on September 26, 1919, and to the faculty in 1920. No doubt Preus's eyes twinkled as he listened to student expressions of dissatisfaction with what was being done to raise money; nevertheless, he had learned to prize all worthy student enthusiasm.

Another step toward improving the financial situation was taken when, in 1915, the Synod at last authorized the charging of tuition. For years this matter had been discussed; in fact, it was debated when the college was first organized. Its opponents argued that payment of tuition would be a burden on young men preparing themselves for the ministry. So, for more than 50 years, every attempt to introduce tuition charges was beaten down. Even in 1915 President Preus, in his report to the church convention, opposed it. Nevertheless, the church authorized a charge of $20 a year. In 1918 tuition was raised to $40 a year; in 1920, to $60, both increases reflecting the inflation caused by World War I. As an indication of a new concern with financial matters, the first formal budget of the college was prepared in 1918.[15]

The alumni, through their own association and their Luther College Clubs, took an increasingly active interest in college affairs. Apparently the first twenty-five-year reunion of a class was held at commencement, June 6, 1916. The alumni urged an increase in the publicity program. Oscar L. Olson, who joined the faculty in 1901, had shown the way in 1903 when he prepared a 32-page brochure, with 36 illustrations, giving a good descriptive account of the college. Preus encouraged faculty members to be available for public appearances. Under him the old insularity which had kept the college aloof from civic affairs was gradually broken down, and with World War I the institution entered wholeheartedly into every movement that promoted the national interest. An excellent plan for publicity was worked out in 1917 by Halvor M. Normann, '00, and Bertinius K. Savre, '96; provision for newspaper publicity was set up in 1919; a detailed set of recommendations for publicity and for student recruitment was adopted by the faculty in 1920; and in the last-named year Oscar L. Olson, '93, Brynjolf J. Hovde, '16, and Carl W. Strom, '19, were elected editors of the *Luther College Bulletin*, which first appeared in January 1921.[16]

When Preus took over the presidency in 1902, he felt a need to clarify and formulate his ideas concerning the educational policy of the institution. He prepared a paper in Norwegian entitled (in English) "In What Direction and toward What Goal Should Luther College Be Developed to Best Serve the Synod?" This was read before the Decorah pastoral conference in February 1904 and published in *Kir-ketidende* in March and April 1905. It is clear from Preus's paper (and from his later utterances and actions) that he intended no departure from Larsen's central policy of preparing every student of the college for entrance to the theological seminary. He firmly believed that the classical linguistic training would be useful to those intending to enter other professions than the ministry. But he was not prepared to accept in all its implications Stub's statement that Luther College was not to be "a theological preparatory school" but must be "a college proper." To the end of his career he adhered to the narrower view. Because of this, he opposed coeducation (which by then had quite a few adherents), insisted on retaining the preparatory department, deplored the inroads of the high schools which were springing up everywhere and eventually were to drive the academies to the wall, and opposed tuition charges at the college. Despite these ultraconservative views, Preus recognized the need for new developments, stated boldly that the college had not kept pace with the times and needed far more support from its constituency, encouraged the faculty to write more for publication, pleaded for leaves of absence and stipends for faculty members (eight full-year leaves were granted during his administration), and admitted the need of a minor revision of the curriculum. (The new developments which took place in 1906 permitted some elective subjects in the two last college years to form a "modern language" or "literary" course.)

The above major points were in Preus's statement when it was published. There is evidence, however, that it was revised from its original form. On February 9, 1904, it had been read to the faculty. They discussed it at length, for strong opposition arose to the narrow platform proposed. There is no record of the oral debate. But the opposition that was evidenced culminated in the resignations of two faculty members, Knut Gjerset and Haldor J. Hanson, '83. Hanson, who may have had other reasons for his action, let his resignation stand and left the college. Gjerset, after the faculty adopted a statement of aim drawn up by him, withdrew his resignation. Of this statement the two most important points were:

1. Luther College aims to give a sound general education as a preparation for theological study. This is the school's most important objective. But it is not the only one. The college must declare openly that it desires to attract every youth who wishes a sound general education on a Christian basis, whether he intends to study for the ministry or not.

2. A modern-language course shall be introduced in the last two years of college, but co-ordinated in the first two years with the classical course.

The crucial meeting at which this statement was adopted marked the culmination of considerable debate and discussion, and clearly indicates a modification of some of the ideas originally expressed by Preus. Koren, president of the Synod, was present, and it was resolved that none of its proceedings should be released except through him.[17]

The objectives of the college came up again for a thorough discussion in 1918, about six months after the church union of 1917. John E. Granrud, '86, professor of Latin at the University of Minnesota and chairman of the committee on colleges of the Board of Education of the church, which had its headquarters in Minneapolis, and Ole J. Kvale, '90, also a member of the board, met with the faculty. Granrud had taught at Luther College, 1894–97. The main points of his statement as reported by Oscar L. Olson, faculty secretary, were as follows:

1. Luther College is now in a different position from what it was before the church union, being no longer the only college, but one of two or three colleges, all with claims on the church for support.

181

2. The aim of Luther College should be changed; the education of laymen has been largely ignored. The aim of the college should be a liberal and thorough education of as large a number of students as possible, (a) to educate well-qualified students for the ministry and (b) to train laymen for leadership.

3. The curriculum is too one-sided—too one-sided even for future ministers—almost 60 per cent of the credits required for graduation being in language and literature. President Eliot of Harvard introduced the elective system in 1879. In the 38 years since then, Luther College has remained practically stationary. Times have changed. Luther College should introduce more electives. It should teach political economy and kindred subjects, more mathematics and sciences.

4. The existence of Luther College depends on making proper changes.

Although Preus agreed with Granrud in some things, he was opposed to changing the objectives of the college and to offering any course other than a classical one in preparation for the study of theology.[18]

The discussion of Granrud's remarks led to the submission of two proposed curriculums, one drafted at the president's suggestion by Oscar A. Tingelstad, '05, the other submitted by Knut Gjerset, Adolph M. Rovelstad, and Bertinius K. Savre, '96. On February 9 Gjerset, on behalf of himself and his colleagues, withdrew the alternative plan, stating that they did not wish to embarrass the administration. "We do not hold views different from those of the management as to the value of classical studies in higher education or as to their importance to all who wish to enter upon the study of theology. On these points the faculty agree. But we differ as to the policy which ought to be pursued under present conditions. We think that the management take an extreme view when they are unwilling to accede to so slight a deviation from a strict classical course as is represented by the submitted program. It is a rigorism with regard to the classics which we believe endangers the future of the college."

Discussions continued for some time within the faculty and with committees from the Board of Education. Eventually Hebrew was made elective, Latin and Greek requirements were modified slightly, and the faculty proposed the establishment of a chair in economics, political science, and sociology.[19]

The steady succession of problems growing out of the rigid classical course, and the long faculty debates on the curriculum and objectives of the college, had brought about very little change. The Latin-school idea still had too strong a hold. There was no adequate understanding of the new forces at work in society. Although Preus's paper of 1904 and the studies reported in the faculty minutes reveal an awareness of the elective system introduced by Eliot of Harvard and of the curriculums of progressive colleges, they do not indicate a comprehension of the great revolution in education in the nineteenth century. The Latin school was no longer adequate. Planted all over Europe in the fifteenth and sixteenth century, it had made Latin and Greek the core of the curriculum in the Renaissance and Reformation, had served well, but now had lost vitality. New forces to shape the future were coming from scientific investigation, the discovery of the sources of mechanical power, and the industrial revolution. The new instrument of education was to be the laboratory. The struggle between the old and the new was inevitable. The classic statements of the controversy are found in the great debate in England, which ranged humanists and scientists in opposing camps in the late nineteenth century.[20]

Perhaps the Synod leaders had been too isolated. H. A. Preus and Koren, both presidents of the Synod, had resided in rural parsonages, remote from the give and take of daily contact with men of equal intellectual resources and ability. They and Larsen, C. K. Preus, and many other Synod leaders saw the college primarily as a school leading directly to the theological seminary and were not impressed with the need of a modern course in a church college. They defended the classical course as a *sine qua non*. It remained, therefore, for a layman eventually to break "the rod of the Roman schoolmaster."

It should not be assumed, however, that Preus, any more than Larsen, regarded the curriculum as one merely preparatory to theological study. Both regarded the classical course as the best and broadest foundation for the professions, and on this ground recommended it to both those intending to enter the ministry and those intending to enter other vocations. One respected historian states that the founding fathers "refused to inaugurate a policy which might prove unfavorable to thorough scholastic training. They wished to maintain high intellectual standards and genuine scholarship in secular branches. 'Everything should be butter to the bottom and not only on top,' as Professor Larsen expressed it in a speech in 1884. The Augustana Synod, founded by Swedish and Norwegian immigrants in 1860, had founded Augustana College and Seminary. . . . From this school sprang Augsburg Seminary, Minneapolis. . . . Both these institutions had theological departments, but neither of them laid much stress on purely secular branches. Luther College, as a protagonist of classical scholarship and thorough training in secular branches, a school with its own strong individuality, wholly distinct from the theological seminary, occupied a unique position and exerted a profound influence on the development of the whole school system in the Norwegian Lutheran Church in America."[21]

Despite Preus's loyalty to the classical curriculum, he found himself facing constantly changing conditions which, with his practical nature, he tried to meet. The tremendous growth of the American high school and the formalizing of standards for colleges could not be ignored. In 1910–11 the old three-term school year at Luther College gave way to the two-semester school year, an arrangement since followed except for a period during World War I. In 1911 there was a minor revision of the curriculum to provide extra hours for high school students who came with deficient training in classical languages. In 1913 the school year was shortened to 36 weeks to conform to the usual practice in other institutions. In 1915 the college became a member of the North Central Association of Colleges and Secondary Schools, which in 1912 had first begun listing its members as accredited institutions. The course of the preparatory department was lengthened to four years in 1906, and in 1918 to five years, three in senior high school and two in junior high school. In 1919, as stated earlier, Hebrew was dropped as a required course, and a revised curriculum, still classical but with concessions to the times, was adopted. The office of registrar was established in 1914; the offices of dean of men and of physical director in 1919. The college appointed its first full-time librarian in 1920: Karl T. Jacobsen, '02.

A change much more far-reaching, to which the college had to adjust itself, was occasioned by World War I. Voluntary military drill under Oswald B. Overn was introduced in October 1916 and continued for two years, to the end of the school year in 1918. On October 1, 1918, the Students Army Training Corps was officially organized under the command of First Lieutenant Harold H. Fisher, with Second Lieutenant Allen C. Grundy to assist him. The corps consisted of 109 men. Its purpose was to give training suited to commissioned and noncommissioned officers. The removal of doors, desks, chairs, and other furniture except bunks transformed the third and fourth floors of Main Building to military quarters. With the armistice of November 11,

1918, the S.A.T.C. was demobilized and the last man was mustered out December 19, 1918.

Students who were not enrolled in the S.A.T.C. were organized into the Luther College Cadet Corps, in compliance with a church resolution which made military training compulsory at the college. The L.C.C.C. was governed by the same regulations, discipline, and program which applied to the S.A.T.C. and was placed under the command of Sigurd C. Ylvisaker, '03, with Oswald B. Overn and H. Fred Swansen, '14, as his assistants. The L.C.C.C. was abandoned in January 1919.

In that same month a unit of the Reserve Officers Training Corps was established, with Lieutenant Harold H. Fisher as professor of military science and tactics. The company drilled three hours a week, studied a general course in military tactics, both theoretical and practical, and, except during drill periods, was not subject to military discipline. Because seniors and juniors were exempted from this program, the enrollment requirement for the unit could not be met, and the R.O.T.C. was disbanded in January 1920. This marked the end of military training at the college. The course of study had received a shaking up in the process of being accommodated to military requirements, and, although it resumed its old place after the war, it was never again quite so rigid.

The experience of World War I was a wholesome and challenging one. Whereas in the Civil War and the Spanish-American War the college had seemed an island remote from the events of the day, in World War I it suddenly found itself at one with the nation. Perhaps the experience was not unique among colleges. But from the beginning of the struggle, the institution and its resources had been placed at the command of the community and the country. Of students and alumni, 356 saw service in the armed forces; 9 died in service. As its students and alumni were drawn into national service, the college had a new sense of belonging, a new sense of mission, despite the trying ordeal of a small institution watching its student body melt away. The armistice was marked by the ringing of bells and the parading of college units in Decorah. On this occasion the college bell was rung so hard that it cracked.

In 1915, in accordance with Iowa law, the college was reincorporated, but no change was made in its organizational structure. The Board of Trustees continued to exercise only nominal authority and that in a very limited sphere: it supervised buildings and grounds but could not spend more than $1,000 in a given year without authorization from the Synod; it supervised legacies and gifts given to the corporation, but even this right was challenged by some church officials and the board had to resist pressure to turn over to synodical officials funds entrusted to the college corporation.[22] The president and faculty had very limited powers; they were obliged constantly to seek authority from the head of the Synod, from the Church Council, and from the Synod itself, even in matters of trifling importance. The cumbersomeness of the system began to be obvious in the growing number of synodical resolutions which referred problems back to the president, the Board of Trustees, or the faculty with power to act. On April 23, 1913, at a faculty meeting attended by the president of the church, Knut Gjerset proposed that Luther College have a board of regents with power to make decisions; nothing came of it. After the 1917 union, many, both in the Synod and in the United Norwegian Lutheran Church, thought that the Luther College Corporation should be dissolved and that the college, like St. Olaf, should become simply the property of the church. This view did not prevail; about six years later St. Olaf College found it wise to return to substantially its earlier corporate form based on that of Luther College, at the same time making needed changes

187

in its constitution. Thus, the corporate form of Luther College was preserved, but no substantial change in the unwieldy administrative and legislative process took place until much later.

The far-reaching consequences of this failure to alter the organizational structure of the college were not foreseen at that time. Much more vivid to the leaders was the apprehension that change—of any kind—was likely to undermine the character of the school. The transformation that had so rapidly erased the old conditions of pioneer life, coupled with the rise of new institutions to fill the needs of a changing society, were viewed for the most part with alarm by the leaders. They had lost some of the bold pioneering spirit of the founding fathers. They did not place the institution in the van, sweep away old concepts, make it a vital, active force in shaping the changes that were inevitably coming.

School is the golden time to make friends among your teachers and fellow students. —C. K. Preus, '73

12

The Pioneer Passes

During Preus's administration the ties linking the college to its early years were broken, one by one. Laur. Larsen, the first president, who gave up his teaching duties in 1911, died March 1, 1915. Lars S. Reque, '68, died August 8, 1916; he had entered Luther College in 1862 and except for a few years had been a part of its official family ever since. Christen A. Naeseth died February 17, 1921; a student at the college from 1869 to 1874, he became professor of English in 1882 and librarian in 1887. Both Reque and Naeseth served for many years as secretaries of the faculty and the Board of Trustees. In their later years both men were incapacitated by illness from time to time. Since there were no adequate provisions for retirement of superannuated teachers, Preus had problems in keeping them on the staff and in finding replacements when they were ill.

Of the younger men on the staff, Oscar L. Olson, '93, professor of English, who joined the faculty the year before Preus's regime began, often acted as the president's right-hand man, especially when Preus was absent on fund-raising expeditions. Olson was a careful and meticulous worker with a strong sense of order, and Preus quickly came to value these qualities. When Olson took over the secretaryship of the Board of Trustees because of Reque's failing health, and, later, of the faculty when Naeseth became ill, it was apparent that a virile and energetic force was making itself felt.

189

When Preus found his own strength ebbing, he designated Olson as the man to carry on in his stead.[1]

Knut Gjerset, whose graduate work was done at Johns Hopkins and Heidelberg universities, later spent a year at the universities of Christiania and Berlin on leave from Luther College. His two-volume *History of the Norwegian People* appeared in 1915 (New York) and his *History of Iceland* in 1924 (New York). He was an assistant editor of *Symra,* 1912–14, and took a leading part in the formation of the Norwegian-American Historical Association in 1925–26. For this society, besides several short articles, he wrote *Norwegian Sailors on the Great Lakes: A Study in the History of American Inland Transportation,* and *Norwegian Sailors in American Waters: A Study in the History of Maritime Activity on the Eastern Seaboard* (Northfield, Minnesota, 1928, 1933). Under his direction the college museum became the Norwegian-American Historical Museum, and, as curator from 1922 to 1935, he raised it to a level which commanded national recognition. His long career at the college was terminated by his death in 1936.

Another strong force in the affairs of the institution appeared when Carlo A. Sperati, '88, accepted Preus's invitation to become musical director in 1905. He developed the Luther College Concert Band, inaugurated extensive tours by it, including two to Norway and other European countries, reorganized the Decorah Choral Union for the annual presentation of oratorios, and received high honors at home and abroad. Sperati Point in the Bad Lands south of Watford City, North Dakota, was named for him in 1947. His long career at the college was an active one almost to the time of his death in 1945.

Sigurd Styrk Reque, '03, the son of Lars S. Reque, '68, served 1906–08 and 1919–52, teaching French and coaching baseball. Hans S. Hilleboe, '81, was principal of the preparatory department 1912–17, later going to Augustana College,

Sioux Falls, South Dakota. Sigurd C. Ylvisaker, '03, with a doctorate in Semitic languages from the University of Leipzig in 1910, served at Luther College 1911–19, withdrawing when he found the church union of 1917 not wholly acceptable. Adolph M. Rovelstad, professor of Greek and Latin, joined the faculty in 1907 and remained until 1927. Having received his Ph.D. degree from the University of Michigan, he sent a number of his best students to that institution; at least three of them later served on University of Michigan archeological expeditions and one, Enoch E. Peterson, '12, became a leading scholar in the museum of classical antiquities at Ann Arbor. Another young man of exceptional promise drafted by Preus was Oscar A. Tingelstad, '05, who came in 1909 and later was made professor of psychology and education. He received his Ph.D. degree from the University of Chicago. He became the first registrar of the college and gave the registrar's office a standing it has never since lost. He was one of the managers of the 1914 Norway band tour. He was joint editor of *Norgesfærden, 1914* (Decorah, 1914); of *Christian Keyser Preus, 1852–1921* (Minneapolis, 1922); of *Luther College through Sixty Years* (Minneapolis, 1922); and of *Who's Who among Pastors in All the Norwegian Lutheran Synods of America, 1843–1927* (Minneapolis, 1928). He was later president of Pacific Lutheran University from 1928 to 1943, raising it from the stature of an academy to that of a college.

O. M. Norlie, a man of wide experience, joined the faculty as professor of psychology and sociology in 1919. Statistician and collector, Norlie is credited with more than a score of books; he was joint editor of *Christian Keyser Preus 1852–1921*, of *Luther College through Sixty Years,* and of the extremely useful *Who's Who among Pastors 1843–1927* (Minneapolis, 1928) and its Norwegian forerunner *Norsk lutherske prester i Amerika, 1843–1915* (Minneapolis, 1915); he edited and compiled *School Calendar, 1824–1924* (Min-

191

neapolis, 1924). A prodigious worker and collector, Norlie continued at Luther College until 1941. Knute O. Eittreim joined the staff in 1918, teaching commercial subjects and some courses in Christianity. He was college treasurer, 1920–32.

Karl T. Jacobsen, '02, who became the first full-time librarian in 1920, and who had taught one year in 1904–05, has the distinction of belonging to a family which for more than a century has been connected with the college. His father was one of the first group of students who went to Concordia Seminary in 1858; later he taught at the college in 1863. Karl's son Robert, '37, is now actively carrying on the family tradition of service to Luther as professor of mathematics. After a career as cataloger at the Library of Congress and head classifier at the University of Chicago libraries, Karl T. Jacobsen returned to his alma mater, reorganized the library, and trained a number of students who later made very fine records in the library field. His service at Luther College terminated in 1949.

Preus, in the latter half of his administration, turned more and more to what might be called "bright young men" of more than average promise. Almost without exception they went on to distinguished careers. Among those who served longer periods may be mentioned Brynjolf J. Hovde, '16, historian, author of *The Scandinavian Countries, 1720–1865* (two volumes, Ithaca, New York, 1948); Public Housing Authority administrator, Pittsburgh, 1938–44; and president of the New School for Social Research in New York City, 1945–50. Enoch E. Peterson, '12, later became professor and director of the museum of archeology at the University of Michigan. Merriam H. Trytten, '16, physicist and American-Scandinavian Foundation scholar, is now director of the Office of Scientific Personnel, Washington, D.C. H. Fred Swansen, '14, who later became professor of history at Dana College, is the author of *The Founder of St. Ansgar: The*

Life Story of Claus Lauritz Clausen (Blair, Nebraska, 1949) and of many shorter historical articles. Orlando W. Qualley, '18, who is still on the staff as vice president, dean, and professor of classical languages, was a member of the University of Michigan archeological expedition to the Fayoum, Egypt; he has been registrar, and was an indefatigable basketball and football coach in earlier days. Chellis N. Evanson, '18, joined the faculty in 1919 and upon the death of Knut Gjerset became head of the history department. Leonard A. Moe, '12, came to Luther College as principal of the preparatory department in 1920 and administered it very creditably until it was discontinued in 1928. He remained at Luther until 1937. Oliver M. Eittreim, who came in 1920, for some years instructed in physics and mathematics and eventually devoted himself to the operation of KWLC, the college radio station, which he served faithfully until his death on June 18, 1958. Many memories are associated with Marie A. Stephenson, chief cook at the college 1908–18. Born in Norway in 1871, she died in La Crosse in 1949 and is buried in Halfway Creek cemetery.

The library expanded considerably during this administration. Largely through the efforts of Laurits S. Swenson, '86, and Hauman G. Haugan, a banker of Chicago, who donated one fourth of the purchase price, the 5,000-volume library of Bishop A. C. Bang (1840–1913) of the Christiania diocese, Norway, was obtained in 1913. The collection excelled in church history, geography, topography, and the history of Norway. The announcement of the acquisition, received by cable on Founders Day, 1913, prompted the Alumni Association to elect a committee composed of James C. M. Hanson, '82, Christian K. Preus, '73, and Ludvig Hektoen, '83, to take steps toward erecting a new library building at the college. But the hopes of those interested were not fulfilled until eight years later. In 1919 the 3,000-volume library of Markus F. Wiese was purchased. With these and other addi-

193

tions the library, which had about 11,000 volumes in 1902, grew to 27,000 volumes and 5,000 to 7,000 unbound pamphlets and reports in 1920.[2]

In 1905 the Luther College Alumni Association appealed to selected individuals to write the history of early Norwegian settlements and congregations with which they were familiar. The committee in charge was Oscar L. Olson, '93, Zakarias J. Ordal, '98, and Grunde H. Grundesen, '92. Apparently the effort bore little fruit, but it was one attempt to gather and preserve the history of Norwegian pioneers in this Midwestern area.

During this period the museum was housed in the old "Chicken Coop." Haldor J. Hanson, '83, who as curator had given it new stature, resigned in June 1902 and thereafter until his departure in 1905 devoted himself to music. His imagination and vigor were greatly missed. George Markhus, '85, was appointed his successor and served four years. Herman W. Sheel held the office from 1906 to 1911, part of the time greatly aided by Martinus K. Bleken. Thereafter Preus was curator until his death in 1921. Although Preus valued the museum, it was only one of many interests for him; the next and greatest chapter in its development was to come in the succeeding college administration.

Yet a number of things of value were added to the collection: the model of "Maihaugen" (a replica of a medieval Norwegian community) was donated by Martinus K. Bleken; the Erik Egge log cabin, which had housed the U. V. Korens in 1853–54, when they first came to Iowa, was moved from Washington Prairie (about six miles southeast of Decorah) to the campus; and a beautiful altarpiece, hand-carved in wood by Lars Christenson (Kjores), was presented to the museum. Christenson was born in Sogndal, Sogn, Norway, in 1839; emigrated in 1863; and in 1865 settled two miles south of Benson, Minnesota, where he lived until his death in 1910. The altarpiece is an extremely fine example of a folk art that has all but disappeared. In 1953 the National Gallery of Art in Washington, D. C., chose the nativity scene from this altarpiece for one of its Christmas cards, and this scene was photographed and reproduced in color for the *Index of Design.*

The moral welfare of the students weighed heavily upon Preus. In the early years of his regime, his efforts and those of his close friend, the college pastor, Isaac B. Torrison, '79, seemed concentrated too much on the enforcement of rules and regulations. There was some pressure from the outside in this direction too. For instance, "running to town" was the subject of a resolution by the Synod that no student should go downtown after evening devotions without special permission.[3] That thereby hunger for an evening snack if supper had been unusually light or unpalatable was not appeased in healthy and vigorous young men with no access to a family refrigerator seems to have received scant consideration. Preparatory students were placed under even stricter regulations, all Saturday night trips to town being outlawed; these rules were not revoked until 1914.

In 1902 one student went to a light opera which had been forbidden; for this offense he was ordered to attend devotions every evening. But he missed some, had gone downtown, and had also smoked in the Main Building. Anticipating drastic action, he left school. Another student entered a poolroom (to see a cousin, he said) and was suspended for the rest of the term. In 1903 one ingenious student, by unscrewing an electric lamp in the fourth-floor hallway, had put out all the hall lights; faculty action was prompt and decisive: suspension for the rest of the term.[4] Smoking in the Main Building or card playing automatically led to a student's being confined to the campus.

The Church Council delegated a committee of two to make an inspection of the college and discuss its disciplinary problems with the faculty. The spokesman for the two stated, among other things, "There were rumors that girls came up to the college and got boys to go with them to dances." There was perhaps something to the rumors. The modern Eve, enjoying the security and mobility of the automotive toy of the early twentieth century, drove up to the college because she found the young men attractive, while the men, in turn, weary of Bennett's *Latin Grammar* and of chapel platitudes uttered in the Norwegian most of them only half understood, turned to Eve's charms as a welcome relief from social monotony. To the credit of the two inspectors, it should be said that their chief concern was with more serious matters. But the episode has its interest.[5]

Not all of Preus's disciplinary problems were of his own making. For one thing, he had to rely on others when he was away raising the funds so sorely needed. In the second place, the rigid curriculum was a constant source of irritation to those who had no aptitude for languages but whose good parents insisted on keeping them at Luther College. Moreover, there was a restlessness in college circles generally—not merely at Luther. But Preus himself grew in stature and wisdom with his job. He came to understand the boys and their problems, and they to understand him. When they were attacked anonymously in a newspaper article, he sprang to their defense. He was active in the movement which ousted the saloons from Decorah in 1911. Thereafter he was far more liberal in permitting student organizations to take part in civic affairs. He promoted activities which furnished a healthy outlet for student energies. He was always the friend of the sick; during the influenza epidemics of 1918 and 1919, when more than 200 cases developed at the college, his foresight in having procured a trained nurse in 1916–17 and in summoning the additional nurses and doctors needed during the emergency won him the gratitude of many. The Lutheran Brotherhood provided funds to fit up a social room in the basement of Loyalty Hall in 1916.

Even the smokers eventually had a room set aside for them in Main Building. Although the record discloses that a future United States ambassador was reported to have danced with a young lady in the social room, it makes no mention of punishment.[6]

"Professor Preus was unusually fair-minded and possessed a unique ability to catch the other person's point of view," wrote his colleague Oscar A. Tingelstad, "and till the day of his death he stayed remarkably young in spirit. It was therefore no accident that his popularity grew apace during the last half of his administration, so that the original nickname 'Nick' at last came to be a symbol of confidence and genuine affection. Possessed of a keen, warm sense of humor, he would joke about this epithet himself with a twinkle in his eye."[7]

College Chips continued to be the chief student publication. It expanded into a 24-page monthly in 1905 and a 52-page monthly in 1913. With the coming of Knut Gjerset the paper soon introduced a strong "historical department," in which many solid essays by students were included. Illustrations began to appear regularly. Special articles covered outstanding events in college life. The magazine not only maintained the high standard set by its early editors but made several noteworthy improvements.

Since *Chips* had closed its columns to all but an occasional article in Norwegian, those who had a special interest in that language founded *Ervingen*. It was first issued in May 1908 as a 6 by 8½-inch quarterly of 48 pages with Finn Magelssen, '09, as editor in chief. It was discontinued in June 1913 for lack of support.

As early as November 1907 the senior class requested faculty permission to publish a college annual, but nothing came of it. In 1910–11 the junior class made a similar request and met a lukewarm reception. In the late spring of 1911, however, with the semicentennial of the college rap-

197

idly approaching, the faculty apparently saw the matter in a different light and requested the class to undertake the publication. This they agreed to do. The decision was a difficult one because most of the class were members of the concert band, which was preparing for a tour to the west coast, and the others were soon to scatter for the summer. But through the loyalty and hard work of Enoch E. Peterson, '12, its editor in chief, the annual appeared, the first in the college's history, under the title *Luther College Semi-Centennial 1861–1911*, not without its shortcomings, it is true, yet a charming souvenir with some priceless historical material that otherwise might have perished.

In 1920 another annual appeared. At the suggestion of Knut Gjerset it was named *The Pioneer* in honor of the early Norwegian settlers. It was dedicated to the sons of Luther who had responded to their country's call in World War I. Edited by Elmer S. Eid, '21, and his associates, it included a wealth of historical data, as well as the usual material dear to college mates. Succeeding annuals continue to bear the same title.

The Luther College Sunday Association became a factor in student life during Preus's administration. It was organized in the fall of 1901 through the efforts of Pastor Torrison, under the leadership of Oscar L. Olson, '93, its aim being "To advance the members in knowledge of Christian truth, to encourage them in Christian work, and to promote Christian fellowship." It held regular meetings, at which outstanding speakers often were featured. Its influence soon spread into a much wider field. "In the winter of 1903 this association resolved to start a movement for more co-operation and for closer union among its *[the Synod's]* young people's societies. A plan for procedure was presented to the Church Council. The movement received the approval and support of that body and was favorably received throughout the Norwegian Evangelical Lutheran Church." The result was that on May 24, 1906, a convention of 50 representatives of 39 young people's societies of the church met in Decorah and formed the Young People's Association of the Norwegian Synod. Out of this association grew, in part, the Luther League movement in the Evangelical Lutheran Church.[8]

Another organization which displayed great activity in this period was the P. A. Munch Historical Society, organized through the efforts of Knut Gjerset February 11, 1903. Historical study by students was encouraged, the best of their productions appearing in the historical department of *College Chips*. A considerable library was gathered, which eventually was turned over to the college. The society died away in 1919.

Other organizations of this period were Normannalaget, the leading Norwegian literary society until it temporarily dropped out of sight during 1918; Mjølner, another Norwegian literary society, organized February 23, 1907, but inactive after 1918; Idun, an English literary society that originated in the preparatory department in 1907 and survived World War I; and Norrøna, a Norwegian literary society in the preparatory department, organized in 1911, and active only four years. Muspelheim flourished, providing newspapers and magazines for the student body.

The two leading literary societies at the college throughout this period were Irving and Amphictyonic. There was brisk rivalry between them and they sought to outdo each other in their annual public programs. Occasionally, however, they co-operated in putting on these entertainments, which were gala affairs and drew appreciative crowds from the town as well as from the student body. Programs, often elaborately printed, tell of speeches, declamations, music by soloists and groups, farces, minstrel shows, and other dramatic efforts.

Intercollegiate debating made its debut at the college on February 26, 1904, when Martin E. Fretheim, '05, Alfred

T. Felland, '05, and Thoralf A. Hoff, '04, opposed a team from Augustana College at Rock Island, Illinois, and successfully defended the negative side of the question: "Resolved, that the strenuous life of today is detrimental to the American people." Prior to this, debate had flourished for many years on campus, within societies and between societies. There is an almost unbroken record of intersociety debates from 1888 on. In February 1903 the Intercollegiate Debating Association was formed; following the first intercollegiate debate noted above, similar contests were held annually, some with Augustana, some with Gustavus Adolphus College, St. Peter, Minnesota, and Simpson College, Indianola, Iowa.[9]

Oratory was cultivated systematically after the Southern Wisconsin Luther College Club in 1903 offered annual prizes of $25 each for the best English and the best Norwegian oration. When the Luther College Oratorical Association was admitted to the Iowa State Oratorical Association, the local winner in English represented Luther in the state contest. In this period there was also considerable interest in the Iowa State Peace Oratorical Association. Among the debate and oratorical contestants were many who later became prominent: clergymen, a university dean, a university president, several university professors, a judge, and two congressmen.[10]

Music reached a new stage of development during the Preus administration. Under Haldor J. Hanson, whose instrument was the violin, musical forces of the community were linked to those of the college. This policy was continued and expanded, and women, as special instructors in music, played an increasingly important role. Among them were: in voice, Mrs. Walter C. Adams, Pearl Werthwein, and Mrs. Caroline Jacobson Moe; in violin, Vera L. Boice, Mrs. F. Q. Brown, and Mrs. Ruth Downie; in piano, Mrs.

Jessie Ervin Marsh, Katherine S. Hustvedt, and Mrs. Caroline Jacobson Moe.

The band, which had made great progress, met with even greater success under Carlo A. Sperati, '88. His solo instrument was the snare drum. Under his baton the college band performed with a precision of attack and execution which quickly won acclaim.

Son of the organist of the Roman Catholic Church in Oslo, Norway, Sperati had studied violin, piano, and snare drum, and had appeared before royalty in both Denmark and Sweden as a snare-drum soloist. Then, like many a Norwegian youth, he sailed before the mast and ended up in this country. Friendless and without resources, he played for his supper in cheap restaurants and bars, found his way to the Norwegian Seamen's Mission in Brooklyn, where he became organist, and was persuaded by Deaconess Elizabeth Fedde to go to Luther College in 1884; later he entered Luther Seminary and was ordained to the ministry.[11] From his early student days he had sought an outlet for his artistic talents in music. When he was called from his pulpit in Tacoma, Washington, to Luther College, his decision to give up the pastoral ministry was possible only because he felt called in the largest and deepest sense to devote himself to the ministry of music. This sense of mission grew upon him with the years. He was very human, never wordy, never indulged in pietistic bathos; there could be wild flashes of anger; he had a good sense of humor and a fund of stories—was a delightful raconteur. Those who sat under his baton recall his strict discipline, his stern demand for perfection, yet his constant patience with sometimes bewildered youth. He could play a march or waltz with verve and delight and turn to a great symphony with the high seriousness of a master. When, in the Norwegian accent he never quite lost, he paused to interpret what the composer was seeking to express, his musicians were hushed and attentive; and when

201

after long hours of practice the group, in concert, swept on to those climaxes found in great music, the consciousness of the players that they had become a part of a great instrument, the close rapport with an audience that was now oblivious to diverting influences and had surrendered to the spell of the music, and the rapt expression on the director's face—each in its way contributed to an abiding aesthetic experience.

By reorganizing the Decorah Choral Union in 1905, a group founded by Haldor Hanson in 1889 in which town and college musical forces found a common meeting place, Sperati prepared the way for the rendition of great choral works. Haydn's "Creation" was given in 1906, Handel's "Messiah" in 1907, Mendelssohn's "St. Paul" in 1908, Handel's "Elijah" in 1912, Bruch's "Lay of the Bell" in 1913, and Haydn's "Seasons" in 1920. Handel's "Messiah" was often repeated and gradually came to be established as an annual event. Except during World War I, the choral union gave yearly concerts.

But the band received Sperati's chief attention. He very soon organized a second band and a beginners' band as feeders to the concert group. In 1906 the latter took its first extended tour, visiting the Pacific Northwest; again, in 1911, it made a summer-long tour to the Northwest.

In 1905 the Norwegian Student Singers from the Royal Fredrik University, Christiania, visited Decorah, among other Midwestern centers, and invited Norwegian-American groups to visit Norway. In 1911 President Preus represented Luther College at the hundredth anniversary of the Christiania university, gave three lectures which were very well received, and again received a warm invitation for the band to visit Norway. Accordingly, in 1914, the hundredth anniversary of modern Norway's independence, the band made its first tour to Norway. It arrived in time to take part in the great May 17 parade in Christiania (May 17 being Norway's independence day). It also joined in the July 4 celebration, when a statue of Lincoln, presented by the people of North Dakota, was unveiled in Christiania, and when the memorial gift of more than $50,000 from the Norwegian people in America to their kinsmen in Norway was presented by Hans G. Stub, '66, president of the Norwegian Synod. On the same day two teams of band members played an exhibition baseball game. The band gave 73 concerts in Norway, then proceeded through Sweden, Denmark, Germany, Belgium, and France to England, whence it sailed for home July 15; it played a considerable number of concerts in this country, and finished with a gala concert in Decorah August 20. It had been on tour since April 25. Those responsible for the tour arrangements, besides Sperati, were President Preus, Oscar A. Tingelstad, John A. Moldstad, '94, Johan C. K. Preus, '02, and Bertinius K. Savre, '96.[12]

In 1915 the band made another tour, this time to the Panama-Pacific International Exposition at San Francisco, California, and up and down the coast. Many other appearances were made; for example, at Story City, Iowa, in 1907; Chicago in 1908; St. Paul in 1917; Milwaukee in 1917; Red Wing, Minnesota, and Mason City, Iowa, in 1919. Longer tours were taken in 1920 and in 1921; the latter, a sixtieth-anniversary tour, extended to the Pacific Northwest and Canada.

The tremendous success of the band during these appearances undoubtedly was a factor in stimulating the growth of music in communities and schools throughout the Middle West. The number of "Sperati men" who are professional musicians in this area is considerable.

Athletics continued to flourish at the college, the distinguishing feature of this period perhaps being the extension of intercollegiate competition and of interest in additional sports. Baseball was still king and intercollegiate games be-

203

came the rule rather than the exception. Luther's teams regularly met some of the best teams in the area, including the universities of Minnesota, Iowa, Wisconsin, and Nebraska, and colleges such as St. Olaf, Grinnell, Carleton, Cornell, and Upper Iowa.

Old timers love to tell how a faculty ruling sparked one of the most colorful episodes in Luther's baseball history. Six Luther players were reported to have played with a Decorah town team in Calmar on Sunday, April 29. The faculty had some doubt as to whether these players had thereby become ineligible under the rules of the Iowa Intercollegiate Athletic Association; moreover, it frowned on Sunday baseball. Accordingly, the six players were refused permission to play with the team on a big excursion to St. Olaf at Northfield planned for May 17. The team was crippled, the game was cancelled, and the excursion abandoned. On May 17 about 100 students, carrying a box made up as a coffin, staged a procession downtown, returned to the baseball diamond on the campus, and there conducted a mock funeral for beloved baseball. It is said that one innocent and lovable old professor, meeting the students near the bridge on their way to town and absorbed in thoughts of Norway's natal day, greeted them with raised hat and a "Hurrah for the Seventeenth of May!"

The *Decorah Journal* for May 22, 1906, contained the following from the pen of the editor, Fred Biermann:

"Oh, that dim and distant Northfield,
We had hoped to journey there,
In our glad baseball regalia
And Pond's Extract in our hair.
As those rugged hero Vikings
Swore by Woden and by Thor
So we swore to down St. Olaf—
Quoth St. Olson, 'nevermore.'[13]

"So fare ye well, boys, with your tragic grief. Youth is full of emotion, full of life, and irks at restraint. Disappointments hurt keenly and sometimes lead to rashness; but guard against that always and strive to be a credit to yourself, your college, and your country. And remember that the faculty is not your enemy; they conceive nothing in malice. We have been amused by your demonstration and realize that it is only one phase of manifestations peculiar to college life everywhere. Fare you well and march along:

> "Gather up the well worn sweaters
> And the mittens and the bats,
> Walk the *via dolorosa*
> With the crape tied on your hats.
> Put away the sacred relics
> Underneath the yielding sod,
> Where the burdock and the ragweed
> In the summer breezes nod."

Indeed a considerable stir arose about this affair, but cooler counsels prevailed; eventually the students apologized.

Symptomatic of changing mores was a later action of the faculty; although it had frowned on any athletic activity on Memorial Day in the past, in 1916 for the first time it permitted baseball on that day.[14] Another innovation was the engagement of Arthur Laudell, former pitcher for the Detroit Tigers, as baseball coach in 1917. He served until 1921.

Every baseball fan—and the Luther fans are legion—will have his favorites. Yet perhaps one may risk naming such baseball greats of this period as the six Sorlien brothers, all players; Sigurd S. Reque, '03, Alfred Sevareid, '06, Adolph O. Naeseth, '09, Gynther Storaasli, '11, and Henry O. Grangaard, '02. Harking back to an earlier day, one should not overlook the eight Torrison brothers, who were active from the late seventies to the middle nineties, all baseball players and each in his day captain of the team.

Basketball was introduced in 1903, and in 1904 the first

intercollegiate contest was played with Upper Iowa University. Since then basketball has been a major sport. Intercollegiate competition aroused great enthusiasm and the teams acquitted themselves well, winning over 60 per cent of their games up to the season 1921–22. In 1920 Alvin J. Natvig, '18, became the first basketball coach. Ralph Movold coached basketball and track in 1920–21.

The first home track meet took place in 1900. In 1902 intercollegiate meets were introduced. But interest waned, and from 1905 to 1919 the college did not compete with other schools. Intercollegiate meets were resumed in 1921.

The Turning Club, organized in 1886, has given annual exhibitions since that date. In 1909, for the first time, it took part in the state gymnastic meet and captured first place. Thereafter Luther participated regularly in intercollegiate exhibitions, with a surprisingly good record against strong competition, until World War I caused a temporary downswing in the fortunes of turning.

The establishment of the Students Army Training Corps led to the formation of a football team in 1918 which represented it in several contests. In 1919 the college reintroduced the game and engaged Walter Jewell, former tackle on the State University of Iowa eleven, as coach. The following year Oscar M. Solem, University of Minnesota end and tackle in 1911 and 1912, took over the coaching duties and turned out a team that, by winning for the first time in the college's history the championship of a mythical Iowa conference, gave football an impetus at the college which it has not lost.

Tennis, too, took on an intercollegiate hue in this period, the first meet being played with Upper Iowa University in 1904. Since then teams have played in intercollegiate competition, winning the state championship, both singles and doubles, in 1908 and 1909 and the singles in 1910. Players like Henning Larsen, '08, and Lauritz S. Ylvisaker, '10, were outstanding. Other teams made good records, including the

1919 team, of which one member, destined to become a president of Luther College, was said to have played "a consistent game throughout."[15]

The Luther College Athletic Association, controlled and managed by the students, continued to foster and promote the best interests of athletics. In January 1919 it was supplemented by the "L" Club, organized by its first president, Myron W. Larsen, '19, and by Alvin L. Bronstad, '19. Membership was limited to those who had earned the official "L" in forensic or athletic activities.

Among men of some accomplishment graduated during the Preus administration who may deserve mention are: Thaddeus F. Gullixson, '03, president of Luther Theological Seminary, St. Paul; Jacob A. O. Preus, '03, governor of Minnesota and one of the founders of Lutheran Brotherhood Life Insurance Society; Sigurd C. Ylvisaker, '03, president of Bethany Lutheran College, Mankato, Minnesota, 1930–50; Christian E. Bale, '04, professor of English and department head, Concordia College, Moorhead, Minnesota; Louis H. Braafladt, '06, medical missionary to China, noted for his work with kaolin and twice decorated by the Chinese government; Olaf M. Hustvedt, '06, vice admiral, United States Navy; Nils A. Olsen, '09, chief, Bureau of Agricultural Economics, United States Department of Agriculture; Henning Larsen, '08, dean of the College of Liberal Arts and Sciences and provost, University of Illinois; Jacob A. O. Larsen, '08, first Luther man appointed to a Rhodes scholarship, professor of history, University of Chicago; Carl A. Jessen, '09, specialist and chief in secondary education, United States Office of Education; Lauritz S. Ylvisaker, '10, vice president and medical director, Fidelity Mutual Life Insurance Company, Philadelphia; Norman A. Madson, '11, president of the Norwegian Synod of the American Lutheran Church; C. Norman Brunsdale, '13, governor of North Dakota and United States Senator; K. Edward Brunsdale, '14, president of the Pioneer Gravel Equipment Manufacturing Company, Minneapolis; T. Oswald Kraabel, '15, national director of rehabilitation, American Legion, Washington, D. C.; Martin J. Nelson, '16, dean of the faculty, Iowa State Teachers College, Cedar Falls, Iowa; Herman A. Preus, '16, professor, Luther Theological Seminary, St. Paul; Paul J. Kvale, '17, congressman from the seventh Minnesota district; Henry O. Talle, '17, congressman from the second Iowa district; Carl B. Ylvisaker, '17, professor at Concordia College, Moorhead, Minnesota; Knute D. Stalland, '18, dean of the law school, Valparaiso (Indiana) University; Bernhard A. Johnson, '19, brigadier general, United States Army; Christian M. Ravndal, '19, first Luther alumnus given ambassadorial rank, minister to Hungary and ambassador to Ecuador and to Czecho-Slovakia; Carl W. Strom, '19, third Luther man appointed to a Rhodes scholarship and United States ambassador to Cambodia and to Bolivia; Olaf Ravndal, '20, treasurer of American Express Company; and Olaf G. Malmin, '21, editor of *Lutheran Herald*, Minneapolis.

During the last weeks of the 1920–21 school year, it was known that the president's health was failing; yet few, if any, were prepared for his sudden death of angina pectoris on May 28, 1921. On May 27 he carried out a full day's work, presiding at a faculty meeting from 4:30 to 5:30 P.M. His death some seven hours later came as a shock. Funeral services were held June 1.

Almost singlehanded, with his seemingly boundless energy, Preus had moved the college forward and widened its sphere of influence. Perhaps he personally carried too many loads, but his genial nature and great capacity for friendship brought many others, alumni and friends, to the support of the college dear to his heart. To him, with his strong love for things Norwegian, Luther College was still linked to the past, but it was not of the past. Its work was for the future. Yet Norwegian, the language he had learned as a child, which to him was ever a reminder of the rich inheritance from his forebears, was the language of his heart and was used at his funeral. Perhaps its use then was symbolic of the age that was passing and of those who, like him, had played a significant role during that time.

The pioneer period of the college was over. By the end of C. K. Preus's administration all the pioneer leaders had gone to their reward. Even the second generation was beginning to give way to the third. The Norwegian language, despite efforts to preserve it, was becoming a foreign tongue to the young folk attending the school. Moreover, physical and material improvements were altering the whole area served by the college. Other changes had brought the college much closer to its own immediate community; there was no longer a West Decorah separate from the city proper, and even such simple facilities as sidewalks were available the whole distance downtown. Relations between city and college had improved, especially after the disastrous flood in 1902, when the student body en masse, with Preus at its head, marched to town and pitched in to restore a semblance of order in the devastated district. Similarly, in 1918, after a tornado struck Calmar, college students went to its aid and helped clean up the debris. World War I had brought home to all groups the fact that they were first of all Americans. Between the major Norwegian Lutheran church groups there were no longer serious divisions; the Norwegian Lutherans had largely composed their theological differences. Time was still needed to bring about complete harmony and co-operation. But a new spirit was abroad. The time was ripe for a period of constructive effort.

13

Modernizing the College

What was called by one prominent alumnus the "modern era" in the history of Luther College began with the administration of Oscar L. Olson, '93, in 1921.[1] It was a transition period for the college as it was for the nation. But it was not an easy time for a Midwestern college administrator. Thrust into the presidency by the sudden death of his predecessor, Olson faced a turbulent decade that ended in a financial crash which threatened to sweep all before it.

World War I had brought in its wake great upheavals economically, socially, and morally. In the Middle West the farm depression began in 1921; it was a severe shakeup and seriously affected a large part of the Luther College constituency. When the stock market collapse of 1929 was followed by severe credit contractions, the plight of the Middle West was more serious than at any previous time in its history. The "roaring twenties" brought also a dislocation of old values and customs. Military conscription had caused many disturbances. The millions of young men (and not so few young women in auxiliary services) who were exposed to foreign customs and ways of life found it difficult to fit into the old patterns upon their return home. There was a ferment that ran through almost all layers of society. The contrast between lofty ideals and the ugliness of war prepared the way for a wave of cynicism which found expression in the magazines and books of the day. This was the decade, too, of the "noble experiment" and with it the rise of the

210

bootlegger and the growth of rackets. Public morality suffered serious setbacks. Olson's administration coincided roughly with this period.

Oscar L. Olson, like Herbert Hoover, was the son of a blacksmith. His father, Andrew B. Olson, himself the son of a blacksmith, was born at Holmedal, Wermeland, Sweden, in 1843 and emigrated to Sarpsborg, Norway, when he was ten years old. Whether the father was of Swedish ancestry is a question that remains unanswered.[2] His mother was Guroe Larsen Krogstad, born in 1842 near Lom, Gudbrandsdal, Norway. After both had emigrated to this country, Andrew and Guroe met and were married in Chicago; there Oscar Ludvig, their first child, was born February 3, 1872. The family moved to Sycamore, Illinois, in 1874; to Dixon, Illinois, in 1875; and then to Marcus, Iowa, about 45 miles northeast of Sioux City, in 1879. There the elder Olson established his own shop and there Oscar spent his childhood. A sister (Della, later Mrs. J. A. C. Torgerson) was born in 1878. The mother died in 1885 of typhoid fever. Andrew Olson lived in Marcus until his death in 1928. Oscar had the following inscription placed upon the tombstone: "Andrew B. Olson, Jan. 31, 1843, Blacksmith in Marcus from June 24, 1879 until death Dec. 27, 1928."

In the summer of 1886 Oscar was asked by his father if he would like to go to Luther College. "You must remember," said the father with quiet humor, "that students get nothing to eat but salt herring and potatoes." Oscar was willing, even though he had not yet learned that, as Ivar D. Ylvisaker, '88, once put it, he could have New Orleans molasses on his bread three times a day and therein find the paradise that Milton had lost. So, on September 2, 1886, at the age of fourteen, he entered Luther College, where he remained for seven years until his graduation in 1893. He gives the following account of his arrival:

"When I reached the college, which was late in the afternoon, I rapped at Professor Larsen's office door and was told in Norwegian to 'kom ind.' There I stood, a bashful youngster before this dignified, kindly man. He welcomed me in Norwegian and I answered him in Norwegian, which I understood and spoke, but none too well. After making a few inquiries, he assigned me a room on the third floor of the main building and told me to get my trunk from the railroad station and go down to the college barn and fill my mattress with hay. He then told me that for supper I would go to the dining hall, which was in the basement of the building. When supper-time arrived, I went to where I saw others going and thus found my way to the dining hall, where I took a chair at one of the tables. Most of the students were old acquaintances and talked most volubly, as it seemed to me. Also, whenever a plate of bread, or whatever the plate had held, was emptied, it was held up to the waiter's view and rapped with a knife. Such a racket of talking, laughing, and rapping I had never heard or had imagined could be heard in a dining room. It was my introduction to student life at Luther College; nor did it take me many days to get used to a little noise in the dining room. I was soon talking, laughing, and rapping as loud as anyone and heard no noise at all.

"The day after my arrival it rained, and the weather continued dreary for two or three days. I knew no one and was slow to seek acquaintance; furthermore, I had never been away from home before. The result was that I became very homesick. If I had had sufficient money, I would have been strongly tempted to return to Marcus without more ado. On the third day, I think it was, after my arrival, my homesickness seemed to be unbearable. I called on Professor Larsen with tears in my eyes and told him of my plight. He treated me very kindly, and I left his office greatly encouraged. The weather brightened up, some of the boys began to play catch with baseballs, I was invited to join them, and quite suddenly my homesickness left me, never to return. From then on Luther College was my real home for the next seven years."[3]

Olson's chief athletic activity at college was baseball, and for all seven years he was a member of the college nine. For several years he played occasional summer ball, but decided there was no future in that. After graduation as valedictorian of his class, he taught for two years at Bode Academy, Bode, Iowa, then attended the University of Minnesota in 1895–96, where he had the good fortune to study Anglo-Saxon and Chaucer under Professor Friedrich Klaeber, a foremost Beowulf scholar. He received his M.A. from the university in 1903. From 1896 to 1898 he taught at Bruflat Academy, Portland, North Dakota. During part of these two years he studied law, a profession which for some time then and later he thought of entering. On July 8, 1897, he married Clara Gullixson of Bode, Iowa, by whom he had two sons, Walter A., '24, and Paul F., '26. From 1898 to 1901 he taught at Luther Academy, Albert Lea, Minnesota. In 1900 he was called to a professorship at Luther College and entered upon his duties in August 1901.

His decision to cast in his lot with Luther College was a final one and he never thereafter seriously contemplated a change although he was offered a position at Mayville (North Dakota) Teachers College, the chairmanship of the department of English at St. Olaf College, and the presidency of Augustana College, Sioux Falls, South Dakota. He continued his graduate work in English for five summers at the University of Chicago, the first member of the Luther College faculty to spend his summer vacation in studying for a doctor's degree, according to his statement.[4] He was granted the Ph.D. degree in English in 1914 *cum laude*.

During the nineteen years of President Preus's administration, Olson, in addition to teaching regularly, had served in many administrative capacities and was thus thoroughly familiar with the college and its problems. He was the first

213

president educated in American universities and the first layman to become president of a major college in the church. He took office immediately after the death of President Preus. At the faculty meeting of May 19, 1921, when Preus had named Olson as the logical man to take his place in an emergency until an election by the Luther College Corporation could be held, Olson was not present. He has stated that he was surprised when he learned of Preus's statement.[5] No similar situation had arisen in the institution's history. The college had no vice president, nor did the articles of incorporation provide for the contingency which had arisen. Some felt that only a clergyman should be president. Others were equally convinced that the first consideration should be the quality of the man. Not until July 11 did the executive committee of the Board of Education name Olson to serve as acting president until the regular meeting of the board on September 11. Then he was continued as acting president until the regular corporation meeting in 1923. From the time of Preus's death on May 28, however, Olson was expected to take charge of college affairs; this he did, and in the interim period, to 1923, provided such firm and creditable leadership that the corporation unhesitatingly elected him to the presidency.

The time was ripe for a reorientation of the college toward modern American life. English now became exclusively its language, even though the study of Norwegian was required until 1931–32, later watered down to a three-semester hour course in Norwegian culture, which remained in force until 1951–52. Olson sought closer ties with the community in which the college was situated and quickly found a ready response to his overtures. He stepped up the publicity program, being constantly on the alert for such news items as would attract attention to the kind and quality of work done at the institution. Possessed of an excellent voice and a pleasing platform manner, Olson was in demand as a speaker and uniformly acquitted himself well. He excelled in prepared talks, but he was able, as he matured, to make distinguished impromptu addresses. Perhaps the address which received wider publicity than any other was one he delivered at the University of Chicago December 5, 1925, when he commented on George Washington's probable Scandinavian origin, as well as the fact that the patronymic *son* is found in the names of Presidents Jefferson, Madison, Harrison, Jackson, Johnson, and Wilson. A press dispatch on the address went out over the country; Olson's comments on such prominent national figures naturally attracted attention.

From the start of his administration he sought to increase attendance. Enrollment rose almost year by year and by 1927–28 had almost doubled in the college department, standing then at 360, the highest in history. In the preparatory department enrollment declined steadily in the face of competition from the public high school, and in 1928 this department, which had existed since 1861, was discontinued. Because of its dwindling attendance and its consequent deficits, the preparatory department might have been dropped earlier with profit to the college; some defended it stubbornly, deficits and losses notwithstanding. A year earlier the faculty had voted to abolish the granting of the M.A. degree. Thus from 1928 on the college has been concerned chiefly with a four-year course leading to the A.B. degree.

The new president gave a great deal of attention to buildings, grounds, and equipment. In the past the college green during summers had reverted to a hay meadow. Olson arranged for systematic mowing of the green. He extended the open areas of the campus, notably to the northeast, where more than 700 stumps were cleared out, as well as an accumulation of brush. Here Nustad Field, an athletic field made possible by the gift of Nordahl Nustad of La Crosse, Wisconsin, was laid out and made ready; it was dedicated October 21, 1931. The Lina Gjems property, a lot at the southeast corner of Leiv Eiriksson Drive and Ohio Street, was acquired in 1923. More than 100 trees, mostly evergreens, were planted on the campus. High Street, eastward from the library, was graded and curbing installed.[6] Hill Street (years later named Leiv Eiriksson Drive under the resurgence of interest in things Norwegian generated by the Norse-American Centennial), which was the main approach to the college but also was well-nigh impassable in spring or after hard rains, was paved by the city of Decorah in 1922, and the paving was continued into the college grounds. Considerable tree trimming was undertaken, and by the end of Olson's administration the campus had assumed much the appearance it has today. The flagpole, which Preus had suggested to the class of 1921 as their gift, was erected during the summer of 1921 and was dedicated October 13. It is a 95-foot pole.

Koren Library was completed during the summer of 1921 and dedicated October 14. Jacob A. O. Preus, '03, then governor of Minnesota, spoke of the work of Koren and other pioneers; Olaf E. Brandt, '79, using Psalm 86:11 as his text, gave the dedicatory address; and James C. M. Hanson, '82, associate director of the University of Chicago libraries, spoke on the technical aspects of the library and its possible future development.

The celebration was one of the largest of its kind, a very large number of alumni and friends having gathered for it. On Friday, October 14, 7:30 P.M. the time-honored illumination took place. "At the tapping of the college bell the Main Building blazed forth in light while the Concert Band, according to custom, played the battle hymn of the Reformation: 'A Mighty Fortress Is Our God.' The college motto, *Soli Deo Gloria*, shone forth in all its splendor, as did also the numbers 1861 and 1921. Suddenly the Main Building was in darkness and a strong light shone from the east, and there was the newly-dedicated daughter . . . with floodlights

216

playing on the beautiful structure, shifting to the Luther Statue and to the other buildings; and above all Old Glory . . . as it lazily waved with the breeze. The light on Old Glory continued when all was darkness on the campus."[7]

On the same evening the Luther College Concert Band played a musical setting of "In Flanders Fields" by Adolph O. Aaker, '93–96, in which Ove J. H. Preus, '01, sang the solo. When the band next turned to a xylophone solo, "The Mocking Bird," played by C. Vittorio Sperati, '25, the instrument appeared to have a peculiar birdlike ring; the conductor hushed the band and the soloist, and all became aware of a master whistler in the rear of the hall carrying the melody. The whistler was none other than J. A. O. Preus, '03, a former member of the band, who was obliged by the applause to come forward to the stage and repeat the number.

On Saturday evening, at an alumni dinner attended by over 500, the "Luther Field Song" was publicly sung for the first time. The words by Arthur J. Tolo, '18, and music by Norvald G. Maakestad, '21, made it an instant favorite; it is still the best "rouser" the college has.

The major building erected during Olson's administration was the C. K. Preus Gymnasium. Extremely well planned, it has served the college even in ways not originally contemplated. Although Oscar L. Olson, '93, Trond Stabo, Sigurd S. Reque, '03, and Adolph M. Rovelstad constituted the building committee and all offered valuable suggestions, it is generally agreed that the driving force was Olson, who with Charles H. Altfillisch, the architect, meticulously supervised every detail of the planning to get a structure that would serve as gymnasium, auditorium, and social center. The building is constructed of brick with Bedford stone trim. It is 97 by 197 feet, with a stage 35 by 97 feet (proscenium opening 19 by 36 feet), and a main room 80 by 120 feet. Shower and locker facilities are on the floor beneath, as is

217

also a handball court and, as originally constructed, a dirt floor 50 by 100 feet for indoor baseball practice. The building also has team rooms, physical directors' offices, a kitchen, a gymnastics room, various service rooms, space for a swimming pool, and two large rooms in the tower. The latter, dominating the campus, is architecturally harmonious and pleasing.[8]

Kitchen equipment was furnished by an organization of faculty wives, later known as the Luther College Woman's Club. The Luther College Athletic Association provided funds for lockers, nets, benches, and apparatus. Halvor M. Normann, '00, was largely instrumental in procuring two grand pianos. The classes of 1924, 1926, 1927, 1928, 1929, and 1930 made generous gifts toward equipment.

To help finance the building, Olson enlisted the help of the Decorah Chamber of Commerce. Under the leadership of Ray Algyer, the Chamber agreed to raise $25,000, and in fact raised $26,000, a proof of the new era of good will between city and college. The remainder of the total cost of $220,000 was to be subscribed by alumni and friends. But since the amount so obtained fell short of what was needed, provision was made that $100,000 should be borrowed for the gymnasium from a new endowment fund being raised for the college. Even after this had been done, almost $15,000 had to come from money collected for the seventieth anniversary gift in 1931.

Named in honor of C. K. Preus, second president of the college, the gymnasium was dedicated October 14, 1926, by Thaddeus F. Gullixson, '03, who used Hebrews 12:1–2 as his text. Other 1926 anniversary speakers included Jacob A. O. Stub, '98, and Ove J. H. Preus, '01, son of the second president, the latter using John 8:31 as his text.

A property addition of the greatest importance was the acquisition on January 12, 1929, for $60,000, of the Frank Jewell farm of 360 acres. To finance the deal, the Luther

Corporation was then established and title to the farm was vested in it. The farm adjoined the campus to the east, north, and west. It offered the only means for satisfactory large-scale expansion of the college campus. Olson believed also that the farm could be operated to produce needed revenue for the college.

Whatever tribulations arose later from this purchase at a moment when the crash of 1929 was imminent, the wisdom of acquiring this strategically located property has never been seriously questioned by anyone with a long-range view of the college's development. With an enrollment today more than three times that of 1929, expansion would have been seriously hampered, if not absolutely blocked, had not the college possessed this additional area.

Since 1876 the college had had a half interest in the edifice of First Lutheran Church in Decorah, and was therefore responsible for half the cost of repairs and upkeep of the building. The church union of 1917 changed the existing relationship of the college to the two Lutheran congregations then in Decorah. Both churches, which had hitherto belonged to different synods, now belonged to the same synod. It no longer seemed desirable to maintain a special affiliation with one of them; moreover, the relationship required expenditures by the college which could no longer easily be fitted into its budget. Accordingly, in 1930 the college transferred its share in the church to the congregation.[9]

During this administration facilities for study of the sciences were expanded. In 1931 a quantitative chemistry laboratory was equipped in the basement of Loyalty Hall; efforts were successfully made to strengthen pre-professional courses, especially for the study of medicine; and the amount of scientific equipment in the physics, chemistry, and biology laboratories was tripled.

With the aid of Congressman Ole J. Kvale, '90, the college

obtained a broadcasting license December 18, 1926; on January 24, 1927, the call letters KWLC were assigned to the station. At the first broadcast President Olson read Lincoln's Gettysburg Address. In 1931 the station was completely rebuilt with a power of 100 watts. It has carried programs prepared by students and faculty members and some released by the radio services of various educational and religious bodies; for many years it has regularly broadcast college chapel services. Its Friday devotional services for shut-ins have been well received and have brought a large measure of financial support.

Tuition charges, which had been introduced in 1916, increased again. They were $60 a year in 1921–22; $75 in 1923–24; $125 in 1925–26; and $150 in 1929–30, where they remained to the end of Olson's administration. Fees of various kinds increased the basic tuition cost about $30 by 1931–32.

Publicity was stepped up considerably. The *Luther College Bulletin* was established and was published regularly four times a year beginning in 1921, with occasional extra numbers. The first aerial photograph of the campus was taken August 5, 1924, by George C. Henriksen, '24, and was used widely in college literature. In 1927, for the first time, the college embarked on a program of recruiting students by sending representatives into the field, the beginning of work that was later consolidated in the admissions office. In 1928 the Luther College News Service was organized by Chellis N. Evanson, '18, with two students, Frisbie L. Young, '28, and Wilbur A. Nielson, '28, as his assistants. Later, four students were regular members of the staff. The group furnished publicity and news releases to newspapers and other mediums over a wide area. The alumni mailing list, with the aid of Sigurd S. Reque, '03, was brought up to date. Olson, himself, was tireless in calling attention to alumni achievements as a means of stimulating and encouraging others. In 1932 he made a thorough revision of the college catalog, on which, since first entering upon his duties at Luther, he had already expended much time and effort. In 1926 a placement service was organized by Ingebret Dorrum, '04, and Oscar A. Tingelstad, '05, "for the purpose of placing students who desire teaching positions."[10]

The Luther College Alumni Association during Olson's administration did its most effective work in backing the campaign for the new gymnasium and the Luther-St. Olaf Endowment Appeal, presently to be described. It lent its aid to the publication of a study of Norwegian-American Lutheranism by J. Magnus Rohne, '17, and gave its support, limited though it was, to the museum. In 1927 it adopted a revised constitution, in 1930 decided to hold its annual meetings at Homecoming instead of at commencement, and in 1931 abolished the old system of annual dues, substituting therefor an annual roll call for an alumni fund. In January 1932 the *Luther Alumnus* was founded through the efforts of David T. Nelson, who also served as editor.

During Olson's administration the faculty expanded as attendance increased. With the president's approval and encouragement, it undertook in 1921 the project of writing a history of the college. The work was directed by an editorial committee consisting of Olaf M. Norlie, Oscar A. Tingelstad, '05, and Karl T. Jacobsen, '02; the 21 chapters were prepared by individual faculty members; and the volume of 512 pages appeared in 1922 under the title *Luther College through Sixty Years*. O. M. Norlie wrote a 510-page *History of the Norwegian People in America* (Minneapolis, 1925), preparing it against time for the Norse-American Centennial. William P. Sihler published *Fifty Fables,* a translation from the German of W. Hey (Minneapolis, 1927).

Three young men joined the faculty in 1921. Henry O. Talle, '17, organized the department of economics, giving it a stature it has since maintained; he also served as college treasurer from 1932 to 1938. In the latter year he resigned when he was elected to the lower house of Congress, an office he held for the next 20 years. Francis E. Peterson, '09, was on the staff from 1921 to 1924; later he taught in Hawaii, where he became principal of Kawananakoa Intermediate School, Department of Public Instruction, Honolulu. David T. Nelson, '12, Rhodes scholar in 1914, who had served as a member of the Commission for Relief in Belgium under Herbert Hoover, came to Luther in 1921 after army service in World War I and a year and a half in New York City, and has been continuously connected with the institution since that time.

J. Magnus Rohne, '17, was a member of the faculty 1923–32. His *Norwegian-American Lutheranism Up to 1872*, a volume of 271 pages published by Macmillan in 1926, is a pioneer treatment of this subject in English and has proved to be a very useful work. Another addition to the faculty in 1923 was Ingebret Dorrum, '04, who had an easy pen and made a number of translations of poetry from the Norwegian. H. Fred Swansen, '14, rejoined the faculty in 1926 and remained until 1931.

To single out individuals among the many men who served is an invidious task. Among those who were staff members for more than two years may be mentioned Herman E. Ellingson, '24, who later went on to a distinguished research career with the United States Navy; Leo I. Highby, '24, now a specialist in the Office of International Resources of the State Department; Olaf M. Jordahl, '25, later professor of physics and mathematics at Pacific Lutheran University; Thoralf A. Hoff, '04, college pastor and member of the Board of Trustees for many years; William L. Strunk, who joined the faculty in 1927 and developed the department of biology, later going to Pacific Lutheran University. During the difficult period from 1927 to 1931 Skak J. N. Ylvisaker, '95, was financial secretary for the college. Theodore C. F. W. Hoelty-Nickel, who joined the faculty in February 1928, after completing his work at the Conservatory of Music in Leipzig, Germany, had charge of choral work and developed the male chorus, Schola Cantorum; later he became head of the music department at Valparaiso University. Ottar Tinglum, who took his doctorate at the University of Cologne in 1923 and from 1928 to 1932 developed the department of sociology at the college, later became president of Decorah College for Women, thus playing a role in the introduction of co-education at Luther College. Karl Hanson, '08, became business manager of the school in 1928 and served with the greatest diligence and faithfulness until his death in 1948.

In the early years of his administration Olson faced the problem of providing capable coaches for sports, particularly football, who would also fit into the academic program of the college. Ivan Doseff, all-American tackle under Alonzo A. Stagg at the University of Chicago, served from 1921 to 1923, coaching football, basketball, and track. He was succeeded by Franklin C. Cappon, all-American Michigan star, who did an outstanding job from 1923 to 1925 and for many years has been head basketball coach at Princeton University. These men were primarily coaches and had no teaching duties. Olson was convinced that coaches should be regular members of the teaching staff with faculty standing. He had already placed Sigurd S. Reque in charge of baseball and in 1924 made him athletic director also. He put Francis E. Peterson in charge of turning from 1921 to 1924. David T. Nelson coached tennis 1922–33. O. W. Qualley coached basketball in 1923–24.

In 1922 Hamlet E. Peterson, '22, was engaged to teach and coach in the preparatory department. Because of his success there Olson made him coach of football, basketball, and track in the college in 1925. Over the years "Pete" has compiled an impressive and enviable record. He is still active as athletic director and coaches basketball and baseball. In addition to coaching, Peterson has had regular teaching assignments. Thus, with this appointment, Olson achieved his goal of having as coaches men who also carried academic responsibilities and had faculty standing.

Olson sought to expand C. K. Preus's policy of providing stipends and sabbaticals to staff members to encourage scholarship and to improve the quality of the faculty. Because he found it oftentimes difficult to persuade a young man with a doctor's degree to join the staff, he concluded "that the only practicable method of securing a good faculty was to engage promising young men with little graduate study to their credit, give them a trial in order to discover their aptitude for teaching and their interest in preparing themselves for continued service at the college, and then encourage them and help them to continue their studies toward an eventual Ph.D. This was the method that I adopted." He proceeded to put this plan into operation. Had it been worked out more systematically, with conditions for participation made known to all faculty members, it might have been more successful. For the plan had its dangers as well as its merits. For instance, one individual received 30.3 per cent of the amount expended; four received 72.7 per cent. Of the ten individuals so aided, only three, who together received 14.35 per cent of the total expended, have remained on the college staff.[11]

There were also problems in retaining good men. Adolph M. Rovelstad resigned in 1927 to accept a position at St. Olaf College, later going to the University of North Dakota. Oscar A. Tingelstad, '05, and Olaf M. Norlie resigned in 1928, the latter accepting the deanship of Hartwick College, Oneonta, New York; the former becoming president of Pacific Lutheran College, Tacoma, Washington, now Pacific Lutheran University.

In 1930 a group insurance plan was introduced by Hanson to cover teaching and administrative faculty members and other employees, the first attempt by the college to introduce

42. *Laur. Larsen Hall.*

43. *Loyalty Hall.*

44. *College bell.*

45. *First Lutheran Church.*

46. *Hans Gerhard Stub, president of the Norwegian Lutheran Church of America, 1917–25.*

47. *The arch at campus entrance, 1903–22.*

48. *Lars Christenson's altarpiece: wood carving in the Norwegian-American Historical Museum; three panels were left unfinished.*

49. *The Nativity, detail from the altarpiece.*

50. *Koren Library.*

51. *Karl T. Jacobsen, '02, first professional librarian at the college.*

52. *Campus House.*

53. *Oscar L. Olson, president 1921–32.*

54. *Raising the flag, October 13, 1921.*

55. *Luther College from the air, 1926.*

56. *Illumination 1921.*

57. *Fridtjof Nansen's visit, May 11, 1928.*

58. *Silent communion.*

59. *C. K. Preus Gymnasium. College farm in background.*

60. *Football field in the 1920's between Main and Gymnasium.*

61. *Hosei (Japan) University versus Luther, 1931.*

62. *Nustad Field.*

63. *View from a classroom window.*

a welfare program of its own for staff members. The same year the Boarding Club, which had been under student management since 1896, was returned to college control.

The library developed extensively under Olsen. Karl T. Jacobsen, '02, head librarian, carried out a complete reorganization according to the Library of Congress classification system. He greatly augmented and strengthened the reference collections and also filled in gaps in the collections of various departments. In addition, many books, pamphlets, and newspapers from earlier years were accessioned. Substantial purchases were made. The number of bound volumes and pamphlets rose from 36,000 in 1921 to approximately 60,000 in 1932. About 700 volumes of Norwegian-American newspapers and approximately 10,000 manuscripts were sorted and catalogued. Of Jacobsen's work an internationally known librarian said: "Only a librarian who had a chance to see the Luther College Library before and after, and knew what you had to do with, could really appreciate it."[12]

Just as the library made great progress under Jacobsen, so the museum forged ahead under the direction of Knut Gjerset. Placed in charge in 1922, he quickly brought about a complete renovation of the old museum quarters in the "Chicken Coop" and also took over the ground-floor area of Koren Library that had been reserved for the museum. In 1925 he had charge of a Norwegian-American cultural exhibition at the Norse-American Centennial celebration in St. Paul and Minneapolis. The enthusiasm engendered by this occasion confirmed his belief that not only should archival material be gathered as extensively as possible to supplement that already found in repositories such as the libraries of Luther College, St. Olaf College, and the state historical societies of Wisconsin and Minnesota, but that a Norwegian-American historical museum should be created which would help people visualize the living conditions and activities of the Norwegians who came to dwell in America. He asked a small group of interested men to meet in Decorah, and presented them with a preliminary program for an association which should have both the above objects in view. With the active support of Kristian Prestgaard, the editor of *Decorah-posten,* and of Ole E. Rølvaag of St. Olaf College, he spent part of the summer of 1925 traveling about, enlisting interest and support. Largely because of his vigorous leadership, a meeting was held at St. Olaf College at Northfield, Minnesota, in October, at which the Norwegian-American Historical Association was organized with a program essentially the same as that presented to the meeting in Decorah. One of the objects of the association, as specified in its charter, is to help "maintain and develop the Norwegian-American museum in Decorah, Iowa, known as the Norwegian-American Historical Museum," the latter name being officially adopted by the Board of Trustees of Luther College on October 15, 1925.[13]

Upon the initiative of Dr. Anders Sandvig, director of the Maihaugen Museum at Lillehammer, Norway, a large committee was formed in Norway with Professor A. W. Brøgger of the University of Oslo as chairman, for the purpose of gathering a museum collection for Norwegians in America. Gifts were to come from the museums of Bergen, Stavanger, Skien, Drammen, Opland, Hadeland, Christiansund, Sandvig, Valdres, Aalesund, Hallingdal, and Glomdal. Five truckloads of articles, weighing 8,800 pounds, were received. The Norwegian-American Historical Association asked that the collection be placed in the museum at Luther College. In response to this request the Board of Trustees of Luther College on June 5, 1926, agreed to accept the articles as custodian of them for the Norwegian-American people in perpetuity.[14]

During the summer of 1926 Sunnyside on High Street was taken over and remodeled for museum purposes, but the museum was still far short of space. With the purchase of the valuable collection of P. D. Peterson of Eau Claire, Wisconsin, in 1930, the need for room became even more acute. Efforts to raise funds for a new building gave little promise of success. At this point the headquarters of the former Lutheran Publishing House, which on December 15, 1931, was consolidated with Augsburg Publishing House in Minneapolis, became available and in 1932 was leased to the college for museum purposes for ten years at an annual rent of $1.00.[15] Although this three-story brick building is downtown, considerably removed from the campus, and is not fireproof, it nevertheless provides enough space to house the entire collection under one roof. Because of Gjerset's vigorous leadership the institution became widely known and was placed on the recognized list of museums of the Smithsonian Institution as outstanding in its portrayal of the life and history of a national immigrant group.

Few people are aware of the tremendous energy and initiative displayed by Gjerset in encouraging the work of the Norwegian-American Historical Association and developing the Norwegian-American Historical Museum. Although he would have been the first to recognize the efforts of others and of all who preceded him, nevertheless he was a pioneer in promoting both enterprises. He dreamed of having a beautiful building on the college campus to house the priceless collection which he valued so highly, but saw his vision fade with the economic debacle of 1929. Nevertheless, the museum will continue to be a monument to his memory long after the day when his dream eventually comes to fulfillment.

There are other events of this administration which should not be overlooked but can be mentioned only briefly. The Norwegian Student Singers from Oslo, Norway, visited the college May 25, 1925, as part of the Norse-American Centennial celebration.

The first honorary degree granted by the college was a Doctor of Laws conferred on Hans G. Stub, '66, on his seventy-fifth birthday, February 23, 1924. Although students had worn cap and gown at commencement for many years, the first time the faculty appeared in academic dress was in 1931.[16] Neither of these innovations was achieved without considerable debate and some headshaking among certain of the faculty.

The mere statement that the highways into Decorah were paved in 1928 and 1929 may hold little interest for posterity; but anyone who ever had to hurry to put on side curtains at the approach of a storm, or had to leave the shelter of the curtains to fight the battle of putting on chains in mud and water, or struggled, slipped, and perhaps sank all but irretrievably down in the clay roads of Winneshiek County will remember the road improvements as a red-letter event.

Several objects of art were received by the college: a bronze bust of Herman A. Preus by Gilbert Risvold was given by Preus's former congregations in 1926; a bronze bust by Sigvald Asbjørnsen, Norwegian-American sculptor, of an early member of the Board of Trustees, Osul Torrison of Manitowoc, Wisconsin, whose eight sons attended the college, was presented by the Torrison family in 1930; after the death of Herbjørn N. Gausta, '72–75, more than 20 of his paintings were donated to the college, which now has 42 of his works. Other painters represented at the college at this time were Mons Breivik, Yngvar Sønnichsen, N. Hagerup, Alex Grinager, Lars Haukanes, and Arne Berger.[17]

In 1930 the faculty voted to ask Olson to represent the college at the 400th anniversary of the Augsburg Confession in Germany and the 900th anniversary of the introduction of Christianity into Norway. Alumni and friends, as a testimonial to his service to the college, presented a purse to the president so that he and Mrs. Olson might make the trip together.

The seventieth anniversary of the college was observed October 16–18, 1931. A large number of greetings, including one from President Herbert Hoover, were received. Johan A. Aasgaard, president of the Norwegian Lutheran Church of America, who had succeeded Hans G. Stub in 1925, gave the anniversary address and called for a reawakening of the spirit of self-sacrifice displayed by the pioneer founders of the school. Presidents Lars W. Boe of St. Olaf College, John N. Brown of Concordia College, Ove J. H. Preus of Augustana College, Tennis H. Megorden of Gale College, and E. H. Rausch, president of the Iowa District of the American Lutheran Church, took part in a symposium on Christian education. Nustad Field was dedicated, Hans G. Magelssen, '86–94, officiating. The seventieth anniversary gift of $45,507.37 was presented by Skak J. N. Ylvisaker, '95; included in it was the women's seventieth anniversary gift of $4,602, gathered by a committee consisting of Mrs. Stener Turmo, Mrs. Gustave A. Sundby, Mrs. Sibert M. Topness, Mrs. Carelius G. Naeseth, Mrs. Jacob O. Tweten, and Mrs. Realf O. Brandt, chairman.[18] A "Festival Cantata" written for the occasion was given its first performance Sunday evening, October 18. The words were furnished by David T. Nelson, '12, the music by Theodore C. F. W. Nickel, with a closing chorus "Soli Deo Gloria" by Fritz Reuter of the Conservatory of Music, Leipzig, Germany. Participating in the performance were the choirs of First Lutheran Church and Decorah Lutheran Church, the Decorah Choral Union, the Ladies' Glee Club of Our Saviour's Lutheran Church, Minneapolis, the Luther College Chorus, and a choral-speaking choir of Luther College men.

An off-campus event of significance in this seventieth anniversary year was the dedication by Olson on Sunday, October 11, of a memorial at Halfway Creek, Wisconsin: a bronze tablet on a large granite boulder, the inscription reading, "Here Luther College, Decorah, Iowa, was conducted during its first year, 1861–62, in the Halfway Creek parsonage,

229

which was later destroyed by fire." The memorial was erected largely through the efforts of Hartwick C. Smeby, '02.[19]

Only as one becomes conscious of the past does he sense the possibilities of the future. Halfway Creek belonged to a past which seemed remote, indeed. Much had been accomplished since then; many problems had been solved. But the college, even though it had made progress, had by no means exhausted its potential. In Olson's administration many steps had been taken to point the school toward new goals and new academic challenges. But challenges of other kinds, too, were to face it. All these came to focus in the last year of Olson's presidency.

*If we make use of our time, we
have a right to be in college.*
—College Chips

14

The Gathering Storm

In "Retrospect and Prospect," an article written in 1922, one year after he had taken office, Olson stated his views of the aim and future development of the college. In public and private utterances he repeated these views for some years thereafter, phrasing them forcefully and persuasively, as was his manner. He stressed the desirability of a strong and dedicated faculty; pointed out the need for a science hall, music hall, chapel, gymnasium, and new dormitories; asked for an increase in endowment funds; and expressed the hope that the college might soon obtain a financial secretary to solicit gifts. He felt that "the Preparatory Department should be maintained" and believed also that "it should be the policy of the college to plan for an attendance of about 500."[1]

He emphasized the role which the institution must play as a Christian college and took a firm stand for the maintenance of the classical course because the school should provide "the best possible training for the study of theology and subsequent service in the Christian ministry." Although not all students would plan to enter the ministry, everyone could be "accommodated, as at present, by a limited but judicious system of electives." He argued that because the chief aim of the college was to provide a liberal and thorough education for young men who intended later to enter the ministry, Luther College had from the beginning been a college for men. "The aim of the college has not been changed. It never should be changed. . . . Luther stands alone in our church as a college for men." It is clear that his views then coincided closely with those of his predecessor.[2]

Starting from this point of view, Olson made the phrase "A college for men," a slogan that was soon taken up by both students and alumni. Someone added the words "For men who will work." These two phrases were used in connection with much of the college publicity, and not a little enthusiasm was built up around them, especially among the students, who took pride in trying to make them come literally true. The effect was felt in classroom work and in extracurricular activities, in literary fields, journalism, speech, music, and athletics. There was a genuine striving toward a high standard of excellence in every undertaking because such achievement reflected favorably on the school.

The president himself fostered activities that stimulated interest in religious matters. He wished to make the most highly gifted students aware of the challenge to be found in the study of theology and the service of the church. He encouraged chapel speakers to devote some of their talks to the importance of theology among the various disciplines which engage men's minds, brought in speakers from the church at large to address the student body and counsel with individual members, asked students from Luther Theological Seminary to visit the campus and give talks, and himself held many conferences with groups and individuals. In all these efforts he found active allies among the faculty. The Luther College Sunday Association, which he had helped to found, became more active. In 1923, under the leadership of Oscar A. Tingelstad, '05, the Mission Society was organized to study foreign missionary activities. Using the slogan, "An auto for Otte," the Mission Society gave 44 public programs in three states to raise funds to purchase and ship, in April 1927, a Ford automobile to Heinrich Otte, '93, a missionary in Hlabisa, Zululand, South Africa.[3] Local Lutheran pastors were regularly invited to take part in the daily morning chapel exercises. Both morning and evening chapel services were continued until April 1931, when the latter were abandoned.

As a result of the efforts made to present to students the opportunities and challenges of the Christian ministry, the number of men entering the seminary from the college showed a steady upswing, rising from 20 in 1922–23 to a peak of 51 in 1929–30, an increase considerably greater percentagewise than the college growth in attendance.[4]

Some attempts at student self-government were made, but tradition was an effective barrier to action. In 1924 the president reported that the students were taking steps to organize their own council and had drawn up a constitution. He could see nothing objectionable in the movement, "as they had no intention of aiming at student self-government," apparently a defensive statement.[5] The faculty took no action on the document submitted to them. A student council was formed, nevertheless, but it remained a purely advisory body. In 1928, when the document of 1924, with revisions, was again presented, it was "accepted in principle" by the faculty— hardly an enthusiastic endorsement of an effort by the students to assume greater responsibility for their own large stake in the institution.

The church academies held annual conferences alternately at St. Olaf College and Luther College, beginning in 1921. The Academy Conference was formally organized in 1922 and contests were held in debate, oratory, declamation, and basketball. These events stirred a great deal of interest and for a time held out new hope for the preparatory schools. But like the Luther College preparatory department, practically all academies encountered difficulties which led to their discontinuance, one by one.

During this period, too, the Lutheran Students Union made its appearance—an organization whose aim was to bring together representatives of the church colleges to promote understanding and develop interest in all phases of church work. The group held annual conventions, now at one, now at another college, and there is little doubt that it broke down insularity and encouraged co-operative effort.

Because *College Chips,* which for 42 years had maintained a dignified format as a magazine, did not quite meet the needs of the day, *Campus News,* a small four-page news sheet, made its appearance October 15, 1921, with Arthur C. Paulson, '22, and George C. Henriksen, '24, as editors. In October 1923 the rather sprightly *Campus News* was consolidated with *College Chips,* which then was made a fortnightly. But this change did not satisfy the requirements of the growing student body, and in October 1926 *Chips* became a weekly four-page, seven-column newspaper. Under Charles H. Norby, '30, editor, it won its first all-American honor rating from the National Scholastic Press Association in 1930, a distinction it has attained more than a score of times since. Editors of *Chips,* almost without exception, have achieved more than average success in later life.

The Pioneer, first published in 1920 (although preceded by an annual of 1911), appeared again in 1922, 1926, 1929, and 1932. With the improvements growing out of editing, art work, photography, and typography, new standards of excellence were set. The 1932 issue carried some extremely interesting reminiscences by alumni.

Irving and Amphictyonic literary societies continued to flourish. Delphian Literary Society was organized in 1922. In the same year the old Intercollegiate Debating Association and the Oratorical Association were merged to form the Luther College Forensic Association. Debate and oratory, under the leadership of Henry O. Talle, '17, and David T. Nelson, '12, attracted able men, such as Oscar E. Rem, '24, Armin M. Johnson, '27, Norman E. Eliason, '27, and Herbert G. Johnson, '32. Talle was instrumental in the organization of the Economics Club on December 6, 1929.[6] For student society and class dinners Olson introduced the practice of inviting members of the faculty to be patrons and guests.

Music received new attention and witnessed new developments. The Luther College Concert Band under Sperati made tours to the Pacific coast in 1921, 1925, and 1927 as well as four briefer trips. Smaller groups such as the Quintets, the Luther College Entertainers, and the Mission Society groups made many tours, some of them fairly extensive. The various college organizations gave "more than nine hundred concerts and entertainments" on their tours from 1921 to 1932.[7] Youngest among them was the Schola Cantorum, a male chorus which first sang under the name of the Luther College Men's Chorus. Organized by Theodore C. F. W. Nickel, the group took its name from similar organizations, established as early as the fourth century, which exerted a significant influence on the development of church music. The Schola, following the contemporary trend in Europe, sought to revivify the treasures of sixteenth and seventeenth-century church music. In doing so, the chorus sang many of its numbers in Latin, a practice not altogether pleasing to the Norwegian-American press. Nevertheless, the group established itself as an outstanding musical organization and received an ovation from a crowd of 3,000 in the Gold Room of the Stevens Hotel, Chicago, June 1932.

During Olson's administration athletics flourished. The removal of the ban on intercollegiate football in 1919, the erection of C. K. Preus Gymnasium, the completion of Nustad Field, and the greater identification of the college with the main stream of American academic life gave the students new outlets for their energy, and they plunged enthusiastically into team sports as a means of bringing recognition and honor to their school. The former hesitancy about employing coaches disappeared; a coach for each sport was now accepted as routine.

235

Under S. S. Reque, '03, baseball had one of its greatest periods. The baseball diamond was improved, schedules became more attractive, and large crowds came to witness the contests. Such baseball greats as pitchers Ed Hovden, '23, and Ossie Orwoll, '25; Gil Aase, '28–32, who holds the college record of 20 strike-outs in one game; the Olson brothers, Ernie, '29, and Marv, '30; and Tex Rogstad, '33, to mention only a few of the standouts, gave the teams color and enabled them to compile impressive records. Opponents included the universities of Iowa, Minnesota, California, Wisconsin, Hosei (Japan), Missouri, Notre Dame, Nebraska, Iowa State, Michigan State, Northwestern, and Drake, and representative Midwest colleges. Baseball, which had been the first love of the students since the school's founding, perhaps reached its zenith at this time in student support, spectator appeal, and public recognition. One visitor from a foreign land who was fascinated by the hold the sport had on Luther College students exclaimed, "Why, these boys are more in love with baseball than they are with women!"

Football came into its own during this time under coaches Ivan Doseff, Franklin C. Cappon, and Hamlet E. Peterson, '22. Full intercollegiate schedules were played and great spectator interest was developed. Among the "stalwarts" of that decade may be mentioned Bill Olson, '26, Cliff Olson, '27, Lefty Olson, '27, Hoovey Halverson, '31, and Cliff Hansen, '33. In 1926 the team made national headlines because there were seven Olsons in the line-up: Cliff Olson, fullback, Lefty Olson, left half, Ernie Olson, right half, Marv Olson, triple-threat quarterback, Avy Olson, left end, Art Olson, right end, and Tex Olsen, reserve center. The *New York Times* telegraphed a rush order for photographs. The *Parkersburg* (West Virginia) *News* said, "Football is apparently taking the place of other things done best by the Olsons, such as ski jumping, herring scaling, and lutefisk eating." A sports writer in the *Winona* (Minnesota)

Herald wrote: "An unconfirmed rumor has it that Luther's coach almost lost a game once through penalties for stalling when a quarterback lost his head and began to call fake plays with the signal 'Olson back.' There followed an exodus from the line that resembled Napoleon's famous retreat from Moscow." Then he added, "Lonesome and strange as an italicized 'hash' on the menu of a Parisian restaurant is the name of *Patrick* in the Luther lineup."[8]

Basketball entered a new period of development in 1926 when the completion of C. K. Preus Gymnasium made a full-sized floor available. Thereafter the college fielded excellent teams year after year, many of the stars having been outstanding in other sports. Sanford O. Shafland, '29, Erwin L. Haldorson, '31, Olaf J. Kaasa, '31, Le Roy Irgens, '32, Henrik O. Belgum, '28, Garfield O. Sorenson, '26, Joe H. Viker, '26, and Vittorio Sperati, '25, are only a few of the men who helped make basketball history during this time.

Track spurted ahead, especially after the new gymnasium made indoor practice and conditioning possible. New records were established almost every spring, and track began to take its place as a sport to attract crowds. In 1928 the Norse could boast they had not lost a dual meet since 1921; yet they could not muster a well-enough balanced team to capture the Iowa Conference Crown. Melvin N. Tatley, '29, set new marks in the mile run, only to have them surpassed by Harold Leraas, '30; Garfield O. Sorenson, '26, established a new record in the 100-yard dash and Lauren Nesset, '33, in the 220-yard dash.

The turners, first under coach Francis E. Peterson, '09, and then under coach William Janson, continued to make creditable showings, taking the Class C honors twice at the Northwest Gymnastic Meet.

Tennis attracted some exceptional men in the twenties under coach David T. Nelson, '12. The outstanding years were 1925 and 1926, when Luther made a clean sweep of both the singles and doubles championships of the Iowa Conference. Such racket wielders as Einar W. Hove, '24, Paul F. Olson, '26, Walter A. Olson, '24, Walter W. Korsrud, '26, Durwin D. Algyer, '24–25, Fred W. Ronan, '24–26, Lawrence G. Nelson, '27, and Eric Ravndal, '25, were men in the best traditions of the sport at Luther.

Up to 1931 the Luther College Athletic Association, a student organization, controlled athletics. The association did a good job, but incurred some debt. Furthermore, about this time the North Central Association of Colleges and Secondary Schools began to require faculty regulation of athletics in colleges and universities. Olson took the lead in effecting a reorganization on May 27, 1931, by which athletics and all athletic funds were placed under the control of a board in which both students and faculty were represented, although the faculty members had the deciding vote. The body thus set up, with minor modifications, still regulates athletics at the college.

The curriculum continued to receive attention, but no substantial progress was made in altering it despite long and wearisome debates in 1926, marked by several faculty proposals, including one suggesting coeducation, and by a protracted meeting with the Board of Education of the church. A revision of the curriculum worked out by an evenly divided faculty committee was adopted, but it was a compromise between opposing views and failed to reach the heart of the problem.[9]

Other minor changes fared better. On October 8, 1924, the faculty adopted the honor-point system and, in 1925, the practice of granting degrees *cum laude, magna cum laude,* and *summa cum laude* in recognition of superior scholarship. An "orientation" course for freshmen was introduced in 1927–28. In 1929 the college made arrangements for students to do practice teaching in Decorah. In 1929 also the faculty adopted a classification of teachers as professors, assistant professors, and instructors; a designation of men charged with supervision of student conduct as deans; and a grouping of the academic departments into divisions. On May 5, 1931, the old requirement of 16 units of high school work for entrance was changed to 15.[10] The final breakthrough in the whole curriculum had to wait until 1931.

A number of problems that arose during the twenties made a revision of the Articles of Incorporation of the college appear desirable. The revision, largely the work of Olson, legalized dropping the word "Norwegian" from the name of the college; arranged for the establishment and maintenance of the Norwegian-American Historical Museum; set up the office of business manager; and made provision for a senate of the faculty. The revision inserted in Article II words from the catalog which stated that the purpose of the institution was to "give young men a good Christian college education and, in particular, prepare young men for the study of theology with a view to subsequent service in the Christian ministry," and also specified that only teachers of the Lutheran faith should be employed, two stipulations not found earlier.

In Olson's eleven-year administration there were 601 graduates, as against 804 graduates in the 60 years that preceded it. A few of the men whose careers are of general interest are: Oscar E. Heskin, '22, head of the department of economics, University of Florida; Paul B. Jacobson, '22, dean of the school of education, University of Oregon; V. Trygve Jordahl, '22, president of the South Central District, Evangelical Lutheran Church; Arthur C. Paulson, '22, professor of English, St. Olaf College; F. Hjalmar Carlson, '23, and Roy E. Carlson, '22–25, road contractors, Decorah; Gunnar J. Malmin, '23, director of choral music, Pacific Lutheran University; Sigvart J. Steen, '23, professor of music, Wagner College, Staten Island, New York; Harald T. Reishus, '21–24, vice president, International Harvester Company, Chicago; Carl N. H. Otte, '25, missionary, Untunjambili, Natal, Africa;

Harry R. Gregerson, '26, founder of Lutheran Vespers, "an international religious broadcast" in its thirteenth year, now carried by 111 stations, which plans a $300,000 "Chapel in the Hills" on a 20-acre site on a mountain top in the Black Hills, South Dakota; Oswald K. Sagen, '26, chief of special studies, national health survey, United States Department of Health, Education and Welfare; O. Hjalmar Hove, '27, general secretary, Evangelical Lutheran Church, 1952–60; Norman E. Eliason, '27, professor of English, University of North Carolina; Clifford O. Olson, '27, and Leonard A. Olson, '27, two of the "seven Olsons," the former, football coach at Pacific Lutheran University, the latter at Augustana College, Sioux Falls, South Dakota; Reuben I. Jacobson, '28, vice president of Lutheran Brotherhood Life Insurance Society, Minneapolis; Oscar E. Nybakken, '28, chairman of classical languages, State University of Iowa; Walter L. Rugland, '29, president of Aid Association for Lutherans, largest fraternal insurance society in this country, Appleton, Wisconsin; John W. Torrison, '29, president of Aluminum Specialty Company, Manitowoc, Wisconsin; Allen V. Lee, '30, who, although crippled by poliomyelitis, became an evangelist for the church; Sigurd J. Ode, '30, principal of Morgan Park High School, Duluth, Minnesota; Eldo F. Bunge, '31, professor of English, Washburn Municipal University, Topeka, Kansas; Ernest M. Espelie, '31, librarian, Augustana College, Rock Island, Illinois; Gerhard E. Frost, '31, professor, Luther Theological Seminary, St. Paul; Wallace A. Moen, '31, president, Wally Moen Organization, Chicago, Illinois; and Herbert G. Johnson, '32, vice president, Jones and Laughlin Steel Corporation, Pittsburgh.

A major step forward in Olson's administration was an increase in endowment funds. The North Central Association of Colleges and Secondary Schools, of which Luther and St. Olaf were members, had passed a resolution requiring member colleges to have minimum endowment funds by Jan-

240

uary 1, 1927, or lose their accreditation. The additional amount needed by Luther College was $250,000; by St. Olaf College, $300,000. Since both appealed to the same constituency within the church, it was decided to put on a joint compaign for $550,000, Luther to receive five elevenths and St. Olaf six elevenths of the sum obtained. O. H. Pannkoke, who had had considerable experience in fund raising, was engaged to manage the campaign.

A surprising thing that came to light was the opposition expressed by many of the clergy and some others of the alumni to the campaign because it had been made necessary by a body not related to the church. The requirement was resented, partly as an infringement upon the sovereignty of the colleges, partly because some felt, and also voiced the opinion, that colleges with such funds at their disposal might become too worldly. The Norwegian-American Lutherans of the Midwest had not yet fully emerged from the limited circumstances of the pioneer period. Echoes of this view persisted even into the 1940's.

Even more of a surprise was the response of the rank and file to the campaign. A total of $1,392,000 was pledged. Up to October 31, 1931, the amount of $1,081,000 had been received in cash, lands, and securities. More than $310,000 then remained unpaid; some of these pledges were eventually paid fully or in part, but many lapsed because of illness, death, and indifference once the success of the campaign was assured, or because of the swift economic deterioration after the collapse of 1929. Nevertheless, the campaign succeeded beyond expectation and gave friends of both schools reason to believe they continued to enjoy the good will and confidence of their constituency.

Early in his administration, Olson had stressed the need for a financial secretary to solicit funds. His views were seconded by the alumni. Nevertheless, despite repeated efforts to fill this post, he did not succeed until 1928, when he per-

241

suaded Skak J. N. Ylvisaker, '95, who had raised the Luther Memorial Fund for liquidating synodical indebtedness prior to the church union in 1917, to devote full time to Luther College. In the same year, as a further measure to improve the financial status of the institution, Olson named Karl Hanson, '08, then in charge of the office for the Luther-St. Olaf Endowment, business manager. In the fall of 1929 he engaged H. Gynther Magelssen, '87–94, to join Ylvisaker in soliciting funds; he did this largely at the insistence of Knut Gjerset, whose interest in the museum was a powerful, driving force and who at this time entertained high hopes of a new museum building.

During Olson's presidency about $65,000 was received in special gifts, testamentary bequests, and annuities, in addition to three farms totaling 400 acres. These were apart from the sums raised for the endowment, the C. K. Preus Gymnasium, the Koren Library, and the seventieth anniversary gift. Moreover, some results of Ylvisaker and Magelssen's work were not apparent until much later.[11]

Meanwhile, despite efforts to augment the resources of the college, its financial position had deteriorated alarmingly. The accumulated deficit, which had been $7,700 on December 31, 1922, showed only a nominal increase to $12,200 on December 31, 1927. But by July 31, 1930, the deficit had soared to $74,100, an increase of almost $62,000 in two and one half years. The period was not an easy one for administrators. The church's annual appropriation for the college had been reduced from $48,600 in 1923 to $35,000 in 1925 and $30,000 in 1929. During the same time the old endowment fund, then controlled by the Church Investment Committee in Minneapolis, had suffered severely. By June 25, 1929, this fund showed $143,300 in real estate foreclosed, an impairment of $12,100 in capital, and only eight mortgages current in payment of interest. The new endowment was to exhibit a record only slightly better. Consequently, income from endowment funds was drastically short of college needs. Expenditures for paving the approach to the campus, increased insurance on buildings, expenses for the repair of First Lutheran Church, and the still unpaid balance on the C. K. Preus Gymnasium, all of which had been carried forward from year to year, had helped to swell the deficit. Bank loans of over $100,000 became pressing.[12] Accordingly, the Board of Trustees and the Board of Education recommended forcefully that the college, for its seventieth anniversary, launch an ingathering to reduce its indebtedness, and this was done.

At the meeting of the corporation in 1930 Olson was elected for a second term. There was some opposition to his candidacy, for there were those who feared all was not well; he had been requested privately by a committee of pastors from the Decorah circuit to decline to be a candidate; he had also been approached by an influential member of the Board of Education; and later, when that appeal failed, by the president of the church. To all, Olson's reply was substantially the same: he did not wish to interfere with the selection of a president. Some voices were heard to oppose him on the floor of the convention, but he was elected by a large majority.[13]

The fiscal year ending July 31, 1931, brought a $23,900 deficit, raising the accumulated deficit to $98,000.[14] Moreover, enrollment figures of September 1931 showed a sharp decline in attendance. For the full year 1930–31 the enrollment was 345; for the full year 1931–32 the number dropped to 283. Because of the critical financial situation in the church and in the country at large, the Board of Education decreed a 10-per-cent cut in salaries. This was announced to the faculty by the president October 3.

Thoroughly alarmed by the drop in enrollment, by the reports of student solicitors, and by the financial situation, the president proposed that the curriculum be completely

243

modernized and the old classical requirements dropped entirely. The proposal was adopted by the faculty September 23, 1931, and a few days later was approved by the Board of Education.

Thus the modernization of the curriculum was completed. It had taken 70 years to break away from the classical course. Olson himself had traveled a considerable distance from the position he had defended so forcefully in 1922. It is perhaps not surprising that others connected with the college moved but slowly toward the same goal. On nearly every occasion when change was proposed, the cry was raised that the aim of the college must never be altered, that the college must keep faith with the founding fathers, and that it must not lose its Christian character. Defenders of the classical course tended to picture the proponents of change as destroyers of the religious character of the school. Even the clarity of Hans G. Stub's plea of 1890, not to make Luther College "a theological preparatory school" failed to move the men who controlled the college's destiny. Granrud's strong appeal, ably seconded by Gjerset, had not succeeded in making C. K. Preus see the potentials of a broad program by which men interested in the ministry and those interested in lay professions might pursue, side by side, the different preparations best suited to their future life work. But conditions change, and in Olson's decade they changed fast. Olson had the good sense and courage eventually to change with them. For this the college must remain in his debt.[15]

On September 24, 1931, the president stated to the faculty that he had decided to advocate coeducation for Luther College. After a discussion which took up most of the evening, the faculty endorsed this plan. On October 16, 1931, the Board of Trustees likewise supported the president by proposing an amendment to the articles to permit the admission of women.

The suggested changes were on everyone's lips as the seventieth anniversary celebration got under way the next day. There was an unusually large gathering of alumni, for not only was it a time for a Founders Day celebration, it was also a time for a discussion of the proposed changes and of the problems to be faced. The alumni, whose mail from the college had carried for a decade the slogan "A college for men" and whose memories in many cases included fond recollections of Luther as they had known it in the past, were a little bewildered at the abrupt switch of front by an administration which so often had pleaded the virtues of a classical school for men. They came prepared to hear the issues discussed. So the alumni association meeting, which normally would not have attracted large numbers, on this occasion drew not only practically every alumnus on campus, but many interested spectators as well. A morning meeting which commenced at 9:30 was adjourned barely in time for a light snack before the football game. The session reconvened immediately after the game at five o'clock.

At the morning meeting Olson introduced the discussions in a statement dealing with finances, recruitment of students, and the curriculum. He then laid before the alumni the proposal to introduce coeducation. That the question to be faced was not merely a simple issue of whether to admit women to the college was apparent in the first speech from the floor. J. A. O. Preus, '03, a member of the Board of Trustees, pointed to the dangerous financial situation of the institution despite the large sums raised for it in the last few years. Was it lack of coeducation that had created this situation? Would coeducation abolish the causes that had brought it about? Might not coeducation call for new and unforeseen expenditures?

As the discussion wore on, it was clear that the financial question was inextricably interwoven with the question of coeducation. The one could not be separated from the other.

Some were strongly in favor of coeducation; some, likewise, were staunchly opposed to it. Many who were not hostile to the plan were uneasy over the mounting college debt. This middle group held the key. As afternoon drew toward evening, speeches were limited to five minutes. At last, after easily reaching a decision to approve the sweeping change in the curriculum, the alumni passed a resolution to table the motion endorsing coeducation.

News of this action soon reached the Board of Education, which, under the Articles of Incorporation of Luther College, had to pass on the resolution of the trustees. The Board of Education did not hurry its decision; it had pressing problems of its own. The finances of the church and most of its institutions were in an unhappy situation; and those in administrative positions at church headquarters faced the task of cutting away at the proliferation of offices and functions which had helped to swell the church's deficit and, in the face of the deepening depression, of bringing the debt under control. Hence, all new enterprises were regarded doubtfully. What expenditures would the church commit itself to if it sanctioned coeducation at Luther College? Olson had consulted an architect concerning the remodeling of Laur. Larsen Hall as a dormitory for women and had received an estimate of $45,000 as the probable cost. Would this be only the beginning of required expenditures? Moreover, among those who had opposed changing the character of the school there had been some very influential alumni voices. The Board of Education, said Aasgaard, president of the Norwegian Lutheran Church of America, would have had to hold convictions as individuals in favor of coeducation to sanction it; lacking these it was unwilling to hasten the normal two-year period required for a constitutional change. On December 16, 1931, the Board of Education refused to concur in Olson's proposal that the Articles of Incorporation be amend-

246

ed at the corporation meeting in June 1932 to permit coeducation at Luther College.[16]

On January 7, 1932, J. C. K. Preus, '02, who had become executive secretary of the Board of Education in 1931, met with the president and faculty for a discussion of the problems facing the institution. A committee was elected to make a "thoroughgoing investigation of the whole financial situation of the college at the present time and report to the faculty." To the faculty, as to the alumni, the news of the large indebtedness of the college had come as a shock; like the alumni, the faculty was groping for the causes, not wholly convinced that the administration's explanations were adequate. In the course of its deliberations the committee encountered sentiments within the faculty which caused it to ask each member to write out and sign a statement embodying his judgment of the situation at the college. Nearly all faculty members did this. Through the statements, moderate in tone, there was repeated one theme, although phrased in various ways: the confidence of the college constituency in the incumbent administration was so far impaired that it was doubtful the administration could rescue the college from its precarious situation.[17] On January 11 Olson met with Aasgaard, who stated that the Board of Education desired his resignation, mainly because of the financial situation at the college. Olson resigned. At Aasgaard's request he agreed to continue as president until the end of the fiscal year, July 31, 1932.

The resignation changed the situation but it did not solve the financial problem nor that of coeducation.

The college Board of Trustees, at its meeting October 16, 1931, had expressed disappointment that the college accounts for the year ending July 31, 1931, had not yet been audited. Reports later showed a deficit of $23,900. In 1931 the college farm (the Luther Corporation) showed a loss before depreciation of $2,800. At a joint meeting of the

Board of Trustees and Board of Education of the church and the Board of Trustees of Luther College, the college treasurer reported that the indebtedness of the college and of the farm totaled $218,000, exclusive of a $100,000 loan from the endowment fund that had financed the C. K. Preus Gymnasium. Most of the debt was in short-term loans, and the banks, especially, were beginning to ask questions. The situation was an uneasy one. In an attempt to take care of it, the three boards, with only one dissenting vote, authorized a loan of $100,000 to the college under specified conditions. But unforeseen obstacles arose, and it remained for Olson's successor to struggle with the unwieldy debt of the institution, most of it current.[18]

Those who favored coeducation were not content to let the matter drift for the next two years. They sought action at the meeting of the college corporation in 1932. The Board of Education, expressing the view that "coeducation will not solve the financial situation at Luther College as an emergency financial measure," had recommended that the problem be referred to it and the Board of Trustees of Luther College. Those desiring a stronger statement found a spokesman in Attorney J. A. Nelson of Decorah and secured the passage of a resolution submitted by him providing "that the matter of admitting a limited number of girl students at Luther College for credit be left to the best judgment of the newly elected president, subject to the consideration, approval and power to act on the part of the Board of Trustees of Luther College and the Board of Education." This resolution had enough loopholes to allow for considerable differences of opinion when the new president took office.[19]

Responsibility for arrangements for the ensuing year was assumed by the Board of Education. The budget for 1932–33 was cut more than 30 per cent. "Much as such action is to be regretted," said the board, "and realizing that the school will be deprived of the services of a number of very able teachers, the Board, nevertheless, has found it necessary to ask for the resignation of several teachers. Salaries have also been reduced, some of them very sharply." Certainly the adjustments made were drastic; yet so swiftly did the deterioration of the economy proceed that even this budget produced a deficit.[20]

Olson's administration drew to its close. After his resignation from the presidency he continued his long and unwaveringly loyal service to the college as professor of English, retiring finally from all teaching at the end of the school year 1951–52. At Homecoming, October 13, 1951, the college conferred on him the honorary degree of Doctor of Letters. In 1955 a new dormitory for men was named Oscar L. Olson Hall in his honor. His 51-year span of teaching is the longest in the college's history.

Olson spent his life in the service of the schools of the church, beginning with Bode Academy at Bode, Iowa, and ending with Luther College. During his administration Luther College took on the definite characteristics which are associated with a modern liberal arts college. He succeeded in practically doubling the attendance. It was his misfortune to encounter the sharpest deflation and depression in American history. In his efforts to increase the financial and other resources of the college, he was led to increase its overhead almost at the moment when the financial storm was descending. Nevertheless, the college farm, an invaluable property for future expansion, was secured; the curriculum was modernized to serve the needs of all Christian youth—not merely those intending to enter the ministry; and coeducation, if not actually introduced, was made an issue which had to be debated, not shunted aside, and which soon thereafter triumphed.

Olson stressed scholarship to both students and faculty. Not that sound scholarship had been ignored by his two predecessors. But in the period following World War I, when many of the values associated with the Norwegian pioneer fathers seemed remote to a generation shaken loose from its moorings, it was necessary to reinterpret and reinstill the ideal of scholarship. This Olson did well. He gave the sciences new impetus. He likewise encouraged a broad athletic program, with all its intercollegiate aspects. Debate and oratory flourished. Journalism took on new life. Although Olson was not musical himself, he encouraged musical organizations and brought a highly trained church musician to the college. According to his own statement, he found his greatest satisfaction in seeing many of the most gifted students go on to study theology and enter the ministry. Of 601 who graduated during his term of office, 122 entered Luther Theological Seminary.[21] Olson's chapel talks, straightforward and well prepared, were listened to attentively. Many cherish even more his reading of choice Bible passages in chapel. Certain of the Psalms, selections from Isaiah, and, especially the Beatitudes were favorites. His voice was clear and strong, his enunciation and articulation well-nigh perfect, his inflections faultless; and the sincerity of his interpretation, without artifice or flourish, made the hearer aware of new beauty and power in the old familiar passages. To the end of his life on November 19, 1956, he was a familiar figure on the campus, delighting in the youthful vigor of a growing student body, keenly alert to extracurricular contests and triumphs, and rejoicing in every step forward by the institution which he so staunchly cherished.

*Will we meet the challenge of the
pioneering few who said, "We
will build, if you will maintain"?*
—M. O. Grangaard

15

Struggle for Survival

The man who was selected to lead the college at this critical
moment in its history and who remained its president for
the next sixteen years was Ove J. H. Preus, '01, oldest son
of C. K. Preus, '73, second president of the institution. Born
at Spring Prairie, Wisconsin, January 21, 1880, Ove Preus
attended Luther College 1895–1901, completed the course
at Luther Seminary in 1904, and spent a year in postgraduate
study at Johns Hopkins University in 1904–05. His first pas-
torates were at Tacoma, Washington, 1905–10, and Los
Angeles, 1910–16. In 1908 he was married to Amanda Magdalene Forde, the attractive, vivacious, and musically gifted
daughter of Nils Førde, '73, and his wife, the former Nora
Otilia Erickson. To this union were born one daughter and
five sons.[1]

Ove Preus studied law at Southwestern University, Los
Angeles, receiving the J.D. degree in 1916. Thereafter he
shepherded parishes at Beloit 1916–18 and at De Forest
(Norway Grove) 1918–28, both in Wisconsin. In 1926 he
became president of the Eastern District of the Norwegian
Lutheran Church of America; he held this position until he
resigned to accept the presidency of Augustana College,
Sioux Falls, South Dakota, in 1929.

Preus was a man of versatile talents. In college he was a
star baseball pitcher and a member of the college band. He
had a pleasing bass voice and was often heard in solo work,
particularly in Handel's "Messiah." As a determined young

251

preacher in Tacoma, he had the task of convincing an equally determined young couple that it would be a grave injustice for them to saddle their baby daughter with the name Beelzebub, even though their intentions were good. He was equal to the occasion.

Ove Preus, as he was known to his close associates, was strongly devoted to his church and single-mindedly dedicated to its service. His strength lay in his sympathetic nature and his great capacity for extending a friendly and helping hand. Moreover, he had a strong conviction of the need for right principles and right conduct in public affairs; hence he showed an active interest in movements which affected the life of the state or nation. When the elder La Follette headed a third-party movement in 1924, Preus, who had admired him both as governor and senator, actively promoted his candidacy for the presidency. This action caused not a little lifting of eyebrows among his conservative fellow Norwegian-Lutheran brethren, lay and clerical, with their traditionally strict views on separation of church and state. It would be interesting to speculate whether Herman A. Preus, his grandfather, would have frowned on such activity; at any rate Ove went his own way, convinced that as a citizen it was his duty to support a candidate of La Follette's probity and stature.

Preus had been president of Augustana College only three years when he was offered the presidency of Luther College. He had gone to Augustana, he said, "with the thought of giving my remaining years of service to this institution of the Church." Was it right for him to leave after only three years? As a pastor, it was not his function to dictate or suggest where he should serve. Although the problems at Luther College appeared "far more complicated and formidable than at Augustana," he yielded to the decision of the church.[2]

Not all alumni of Luther College favored his candidacy, although his name received support at an informal meeting of alumni, friends, and faculty in Decorah on February 22, 1932. Preus had had three years' experience as the head of a coeducational institution, but rumor had it that he had expressed opposition to coeducation at Luther College.[3] The alumni, however, at a meeting on June 2, 1932, in Minneapolis, united in support of him and selected N. B. Hanson, '99, then the president of the Luther College Alumni Association, to express their views at the meeting of the college corporation. Preus was elected without a dissenting vote.

Pressing financial problems demanded some solution by the new administration. One attempt to relieve economic distress had been made by the Board of Trustees and the Board of Education of the church on February 26, 1932, in co-operation with the Board of Trustees of the college. The three groups authorized a loan of $100,000 to the college on certain conditions; but legal and other difficulties arose and nothing came of the plan. On May 30, 1932, the Board of Trustees of the college suggested that a temporary loan of $30,000 be made, secured by bonds and stocks of the endowment fund, to provide funds for current expenses; but this suggestion was not acted on at the time. At the meeting of the college corporation on June 7, 1932, a resolution was adopted, providing for the flotation of a bond issue of $250,000, secured by a mortgage upon the college's real property, the proceeds of which were expected to meet the urgent demands of creditors. The college treasurer had reported earlier that Luther College and the Luther Corporation (the college farm) were $218,000 in debt, exclusive of the loan of $100,000 from the endowment funds that had been used for the gymnasium.[4]

Up to the time of Preus's election and taking office, none of the plans had made any funds available. Meanwhile, creditors were becoming more insistent, the general economic situation was deteriorating, and news of the serious difficulties of the college was spreading. Such was the financial picture when Preus took over.

The issue of coeducation, moreover, had split the ranks of the alumni. Many favored the admission of women, and this sentiment was particularly strong in the communities geographically closest to the college; but a very considerable group was firmly opposed to a change in school policy. Even among those who did not take a pronounced stand, some feared that the introduction of coeducation would entail increasing expenditures instead of decreasing the acute financial problems of the school. As late as August 13, 1934, when a representative group of alumni met to propose ways and means of strengthening the college, it was not possible, despite the earnest efforts of a committee elected to deal with the issue of coeducation, to reach a solution which commanded united support. Even the committee presented a divided report.[5]

There was a third complicating factor. Although the faculty and Board of Trustees of the college had endorsed coeducation, the matter could not legally come before the Luther College Corporation without the endorsement of the synodical Board of Education, for under the peculiar stipulations still in force in the articles and bylaws, the latter board had wide and sweeping powers over the school. Not a few of those opposed to coeducation made their views known to the members of the Board of Education, which thus found itself caught in the crosscurrents of controversy. In addition, because of the increasing financial problems of the church, the board had taken a firm stand against any measures which might involve new or increased demands upon the educational budget. Thus the Board of Education was likewise an uncertain factor in the problems confronting the new president.

Possibly a determined and aggressive leader might have moved more swiftly and surely on the course which ultimately was followed. But no single step could be taken that did not affect more than one of the pressing problems. Only gradually did a pattern emerge that won general support and enabled the college to rally its supporters.

The economic condition of the country in 1932 and the years immediately following was such as to discourage the strongest of heart. The depression was felt in the remotest hamlet. On January 19, 1932, the Winneshiek County State Bank closed its doors, as did also its affiliates in the county. For decades this institution, known as the Weiser bank, had been the principal financial agent of the college. Most of the college paper was held by it and its affiliates and, with its failure to reopen, the college not only lost a principal banking support, but was forced to try to raise funds to liquidate its indebtedness. On July 5, 1932, the Decorah State Bank also suspended operations, but shortly thereafter arrangements were made by which it reopened on a restricted basis. But it was hardly strong enough to offer the college financial assistance.

By pledging bonds and stocks from its endowment funds, the college obtained a loan of $30,000 from the First National Bank of Minneapolis in July, 1932. With this money the new president had a little elbowroom in which to operate, and he set to work strenuously to secure students for the coming year. By the time school opened in September he could report that the decline in attendance had stopped and that the gain in students, although slight, held out hope of a reversal of the downward trend.

Considerable time was expended on the proposed $250,000 bond issue, but the project was never popular, the times militated against its success, and the effort yielded little save expense. More productive of results was a plan to have deposit claims against the closed Winneshiek County State Bank assigned to Luther College to offset debts of the college to the bank. A committee headed by Charles G. Stoen, '22,

255

president, and Charles Altfillisch, secretary, soon procured the assignment of more than $14,000 in deposit claims and thus reduced the college indebtedness by that amount.[6]

Unfortunately, although the Board of Education assumed full responsibility for the college budget for 1932–33 and drastically curtailed all expenditures, general economic deterioration was so rapid that the year showed a deficit of $5,763.[7] The net result was therefore discouraging. In the following year, as creditors' demands grew more urgent, a plan was devised, formulated in a resolution by attorneys Carl F. Granrud and Knute D. Stalland, '18. It stated that whereas the 1926 endowment fund of Luther College amounted to $349,000 [sic], of which $250,000 had been raised specifically to preserve Luther's accreditation in the North Central Association of Colleges and Secondary Schools; and whereas the balance of $93,000 was a surplus which had been raised in addition to the required $250,000, therefore the balance of $93,000 might be loaned by the endowment funds to the college to liquidate its indebtedness. This resolution passed. M. O. Grangaard of the First National Bank of Minneapolis was selected as agent of the college to effect a settlement with bank creditors; this he did within the next few weeks. Apparently the success of this settlement suggested a further use of the endowment funds, for on June 7, 1934, the Luther College Corporation passed a resolution authorizing the use of up to $200,000 of these funds to liquidate college indebtedness. Later, this authority was extended to include the indebtedness of the farm, a separate corporation. These actions, although they did not solve the financial problem, nevertheless relieved the college of pressure from some of its largest creditors.[8]

Meanwhile, coeducation was receiving considerable attention. On June 17, 1932, A. C. Bishop, Ben Bear, and B. B. Anundsen, representing the Decorah Chamber of Commerce, appeared before the college trustees to urge the advisability, in view of the times, of permitting women to matriculate at Luther College that fall. In pursuance of the resolution passed at the church convention in 1932, the trustees then resolved, subject to the approval of the Board of Education, that the college should admit "a limited number of women for credit at the beginning of the next school year."⁹ This action came up for consideration by the Board of Education on July 6, 1932. Hans B. Thorgrimson, '79, and Knute D. Stalland, '18, appeared before the board and strenuously opposed the proposal; Preus and Sigurd T. Sorenson, for the trustees, supported it. The Board of Education, asserting that Luther College had its best future as a school for men and that coeducation would afford only a slight temporary advantage, refused to concur in the action of the college trustees; at the same time, however, it pledged itself "to stand by Luther College in every way possible in an earnest effort to insure the permanency of the college."¹⁰

For the moment this action appeared to have settled the matter. But the grass roots were yet to be heard from. Small informal private meetings were held in Decorah in June and early July to see what provision could be made in the city for the education of women.¹¹ Following the July 6 action of the Board of Education, a public meeting was held in the parlors of First Lutheran Church on July 21, followed by another on July 25 at which 30 or 40 people were present. The meetings were undenominational and such men as Reverend Thoralf A. Hoff, '04 (Lutheran), Reverend O. Sandbach (Methodist), Reverend J. P. Burling (Congregational), members of the Luther College faculty, and other citizens were present. On August 1, 1932, a permanent organization was effected and articles of incorporation, prepared by Jacob A. Nelson, were adopted. The name of the new institution was "The Decorah Junior College for Girls"; it was to offer a two-year course.

257

The first officers of the corporation were Jacob A. Nelson, president; R. G. Isenberger, vice president; Herman F. Dale, '14, secretary; L. K. Knight, treasurer. Other trustees were J. C. Hammond, publisher of the *Decorah Journal;* A. C. Bishop, publisher of the *Decorah Public Opinion;* Georg Strandvold, associate editor of *Decorah-posten;* Ben Stortz, businessman; Mrs. E. Kathinka Hanson, fourth district president, American Legion Auxiliary; Reverend Thoralf A. Hoff, '04; Reverend O. Sandbach; Mrs. Karl T. Jacobsen, wife of the librarian at Luther College; and Ottar Tinglum, from 1928 to 1932 professor of sociology and Norwegian at Luther College. Preus and T. R. Roberts, superintendent of the Decorah public schools, were named advisory members.

A large frame dwelling at the corner of Fifth Avenue and Ohio Street (the former J. J. Marsh residence) was considered first, but later the large brick seventeen-room C. J. Weiser residence on Broadway was secured for the girls' college. Tinglum, who had been active from the beginning in organizing the college, was chosen president. He had completed the course of the Christiania Cathedral School in 1917, studied from 1919 to 1924 at the University of Cologne in Germany with sociology as his major subject, and there received the Ph.D. degree in 1923. He had joined the staff of Luther College in 1928.

Preus reported to the Luther College trustees that bank closings in the county had left many parents without funds to send their daughters away to college; therefore they were promoting the new school. They had given him assurances of only the friendliest feeling toward Luther College; he had assured them that Luther College "would try to be a good neighbor and show the same courtesy toward this school as it would naturally show to any school which happened to be its neighbor."[12] Preus therefore agreed that students of the new college might use the libraries and laboratories of Luther College, that there should be certain advantageous exchanges of professors' services, and that student privileges for lectures, concerts, and athletic contests should be extended to the new school. The calendar of the Decorah Junior College for Girls for dates of opening, closing, and vacations, was the same as Luther's, as were the class schedules, tuition charges, and other fees.

After operating for one year under these arrangements, the two schools entered into a formal contract for 1933–35. Under it Luther gave instruction to the women; Decorah Junior College agreed, upon the termination of the contract, to turn over its assets to Luther upon request, provided its debts were paid.[13] Under this new arrangement women registered at Luther College, paid their dues at its business office, attended classes and regular chapel exercises, were admitted to various student societies, and were given positions on *College Chips*. The girls' college building downtown became simply a dormitory. Women were not yet admitted to the Luther College dining room, and at the completion of their course, although they participated in the Luther College commencement exercises, they received their certificates from the college for girls through its president. (The school had been accredited by the Iowa State Board of Examiners in April, 1934.) Luther College had thus virtually become coeducational, although technically there were still two student bodies.

Another step toward coeducation was taken when Luther College organized its first summer school in 1933, with Olaf M. Norlie as director. Both men and women were admitted to the course, which ran June 12–August 19. The summer session was repeated in 1934, but was dropped thereafter until 1941.

The measures providing for the education of women at Luther College met with mixed reactions. Most friends of the college welcomed them, but some thought the administration a little out of bounds, considering that the Board of Education had not officially altered its stand. On July 26, 1933, the college trustees, in an effort to appease such critics, again proposed that women be admitted, but at the same time stated officially that it was the policy of the board to continue Luther College as an institution for men unless the corporation by resolution expressly changed it.

Somewhat later the faculty, which in 1931 had gone on record as favoring coeducation, again endorsed it, their views being formulated by a committee consisting of Henry O. Talle, '17, and David T. Nelson, '12. These two men and Carl W. Strom, '19, then registrar, presented the resolutions to the Board of Education on February 1, 1934; whereupon the college trustees and the Board of Education each passed a resolution to amend the articles of Luther College to provide for the introduction of coeducation.[14]

Thus it appeared that the matter had finally been disposed of. But such was not the case. Barely two months later, on April 11, 1934, the Board of Education conferred with Preus concerning future prospects for the school. The board had before it three proposals: 1. Luther College should be continued as a college for men; 2. The college should become coeducational; 3. Luther Seminary should be moved to Decorah, and Luther College and St. Olaf College should be reorganized into one institution at Northfield, Minnesota. After some discussion, "further consideration of this matter was by common consent referred to the Executive Committee, which was authorized to confer with other groups interested in a special way in the last proposal and finally to determine upon and formulate a pertinent report to go before the convention in case it is deemed advisable to lay this proposal before the convention."[15] This was a strange reversal, indeed. Moreover, to the amazement of the faculty members who had been present at the February 1 meeting when the synod's attorney had been called in to draft a proper resolution for coeducation at Luther College, the report of the Board of Education to the convention in June 1934 stated that "when this Board decided to reverse its original action on this question at its meeting on February 1, 1934, it was not that its fundamental conviction in the matter had changed."[16]

This was news to the faculty members who had presented the faculty's views to the two boards. The point made to them by members of the Board of Education was that co-education at Luther College would have to be coeducation as a settled policy, not something to be turned on or off at will. When assured that a permanent policy of coeducation was what the faculty desired, Chairman Aasgaard asked, "Well, gentlemen, have you a resolution ready?" One of the Luther College trustees stated that there already was a resolution in the hands of the Board of Education. At this point the chairman opened a dossier before him, drew out the only document in it, and said, "This will never do, gentlemen," and proceeded to show why the resolution of July 26, 1933, which he held in his hand, would not be satisfactory. Thereupon, it was agreed that a new resolution should be drawn, and Carl F. Granrud was called in to draft it. There was no talk of this action as "a mere enabling act" to bring the matter before the convention for final decision.[17]

Nothing in the minutes sheds light on this change of front by the Board of Education. It is true that in 1933 a statement in the public press had suggested a merger of Luther and St. Olaf, but this was accompanied by other suggestions so farfetched it was hard to take any of them seriously.[18] Evidently there were strong forces at work behind the scenes. This was a period, too, of "planning" on a national scale. The term had become popular. So it is not surprising that the planning of new setups in the church and new setups in its educational system should have become popular. Moreover, this was a time when academies were going under. There was a good deal of defeatist sentiment in the air.

261

Whatever the cause, the 1934 convention of the Norwegian Lutheran Church of America, instead of voting on a change in the articles which would provide for coeducation at Luther College, elected a special committee to report on the church's educational system. This report, delivered by Seth C. Eastvold, centered on a merger of Luther College and St. Olaf College (described as a marriage) to meet the financial crises confronting the schools of the church. The debate dragged on throughout the afternoon until Henry O. Talle, '17, caused the delegates to stir uneasily by frankly stating that the proposed marriage would result, not in a blissful honeymoon, but in civil war. From the talk in the corridors, it was evident that closing the oldest church college merely because of its temporary financial difficulties was likely to create more problems than it would solve. The planners had overreached themselves. Accordingly, it was with a feeling of relief that the meeting, acting on a suggestion in Talle's speech, referred the educational problem to the president of the church, the Board of Trustees of the synod, and the Board of Education for a solution. This resolution was interpreted to include also the question of coeducation for Luther.[19]

The debate in this 1934 convention about the future of Luther College was a great shock to her alumni and friends. The sentiment of the rank and file was expressed by one writer as follows: "It was apparent to everyone present that Luther was being pushed out on a limb, that the oratorical saw had begun to cut, and that the sawdust of over seventy years was beginning to trickle down. But the 'woodsmen' spared the limb when a group of our loyal men stepped into the breach and halted the attack. A truce was established and a commission set up to make a detailed study of the educational program of the Church."[20] This statement undoubtedly expressed the feelings of a majority of Luther graduates. Some, however, felt that a milder assertion would have been more politic. But the frank expression of the sentiment raised some questions as to the statesmanship of those who had been busy formulating plans as if colleges were pawns on a chessboard. There were, moreover, many friends of the college outside the ranks of its alumni and immediate supporters who found the convention proposals little to their taste. One of them, W. B. Ingvoldstad of Decorah, on June 12, 1934, was moved by the turn of the debate to offer the college a gift of $1,000. In any event, the convention discussion and the comment in the *Luther Alumnus* stirred the alumni to action, and shortly thereafter they turned their attention to a positive, constructive program.

On August 13, 1934, about 50 representative alumni gathered at the college to discuss its welfare. C. Norman Brunsdale, '13, was elected chairman. The group, after hearing reports from college officials on finances and other problems, made provision for a committee whose duties should be to arrange for a celebration of the college's Diamond Jubilee in 1936 and for the ingathering of a fund to be known as the Diamond Jubilee Chest, title to which should be vested in the Luther College Alumni Association. The committee consisted of Nils S. Magelssen, '03, chairman; M. O. Grangaard of Minneapolis; George J. Ulvilden, '16; George W. Johnson of Decorah; and David T. Nelson, '12, executive secretary. The alumni group, as indicated earlier, failed to agree, however, on the subject of coeducation.[21]

This August meeting may be regarded as a turning point in the financial fortunes of Luther College in this decade. Through the counsel and advice of M. O. Grangaard the bank debts had been liquidated, as related earlier, and provision had been made for the use of endowment funds to pay off other pressing obligations. Now an organization was set on foot to gather funds to bolster the weakened financial structure of the college, to plan for its seventy-fifth anniversary, and to unify the alumni, whatever the decision about coeducation might be. Moreover, 1934 turned out to be a remarkable year for the church; it not only raised its budget of $663,000, but $100,000 over and above that figure.[22]

Events on other fronts augured well. On March 13, 1933, the Luther College Woman's Club was established in Decorah, membership being open to any woman interested in the aims of the college. The club, a direct outgrowth of an older organization of faculty wives, was headed by Mrs. Karl T. Jacobsen; later, when she retired because of ill health, by Mrs. David T. Nelson.[23] On April 13, 1935, a Twin City chapter was organized, with Mrs. J. R. Peterson as president. The Decorah club had as one of its projects the raising of what was called the Laur. Larsen Student Loan Fund, which has grown to respectable size and has helped many students. Both clubs also made contributions to the Diamond Jubilee Chest.

In October 1933 the centennial of Laur. Larsen's birth was celebrated at Homecoming. To honor the first president, alumni erected a Laur. Larsen Memorial (completed in 1934) on the slope southeast of Koren Library; it consists of a likeness of Larsen in bronze on a giant boulder set in honeycomb limestone, with an explanatory bronze plaque beneath. Tarkjel Landsverk of Peterson, Minnesota, designed and built the monument.[24]

During these difficult early years of the O. J. H. Preus administration, various gifts reached the college. Arthur Andersen of Chicago gave "Trade Wind," a 25-foot Norwegian sailboat, 9 feet wide and 3½ feet deep, which had left Norway March 26, 1933, crossed the Atlantic Ocean, and arrived August 29 at the Century of Progress Exposition in Chicago. With it came its log, kept by Hans and Harald Hamran. From Andersen also came a painting by E. L. Blaamater of "Sørlandet," the training schooner which brought a group of Norwegian naval cadets to the exposition; in 1935 Andersen gave a semiantique Kermanshah rug (portraying a shah of

Persia) valued in excess of $1,750, which was hung in the Koren Library; still later a second Persian art rug; and in 1938 and 1939 valuable gifts to the library. A gift of $2,500 was received from the Dr. Otto Svebakken estate in 1935, and one of $1,000 from the Norwegian-America Line.[25] Another gift was a small pipe organ for the chapel in the Main Building, provided through the initiative of William Sihler by the students of Luther College and of the Decorah College for Women and dedicated May 22, 1935.

The Schola Cantorum, under Theo. C. F. Nickel, made a tour to the west coast in 1933 which was highly successful, and the Luther College Concert Band under Carlo A. Sperati, '88, filled an engagement that same year at the Century of Progress Exposition in Chicago.

The Decorah Junior College for Girls, by an amendment to its articles of incorporation, became the Decorah College for Women on April 3, 1935, and then sought and received accreditation from the North Central Association of Colleges and Secondary Schools as a four-year college. George A. Works, then professor of education at the University of Chicago and executive secretary of the North Central Association, was a good friend of Henry O. Talle, '17, who carried on the preliminary negotiations for accreditation and went to Chicago for the meeting of the executive committee of the association. Works's blessing brought approval. When he came out of the meeting to report to Talle, who was waiting for the decision, he said: "We have done a unique thing. We have accredited a college that has no plant, no campus and no faculty."[26]

The Decorah College for Women was now operating in closest harmony with Luther College. Its first two B.A. degrees were conferred on Doris A. Erickson and Esther M. Hanson at Luther College commencement exercises on Tuesday, June 4, 1935, by President Ottar Tinglum, "with an evident appreciation on the part of the audience of the his-

265

toric nature of the occasion." Two-year normal certificates were given to Viola E. Bagley, Eleanor G. Isenberger, Mary F. Kendrick, Janice W. Relf, Dorothy A. Swaren, Clarysse A. Trytten, and Selmer A. Hellen.[27] In 1936 five were granted the B.A. degree: Ruth A. Graeber, Helen M. Hoff, Dorcas V. Jacobson, Laura M. Monson, and Lily B. Nelson. Since the women students were for all practical purposes members of Luther College, the combined enrollment, which for Luther College alone had stood at 283 in 1931–32, increased as follows:

	LUTHER COLLEGE	COLLEGE FOR WOMEN	SUMMER SESSION	UNDU-PLICATED TOTAL
1932–33	285	24	—	309
1933–34	300	60	39	393
1934–35	313	50	26	383
1935–36	341	67	—	408

Obviously, the presence of women on the campus did not discourage men from entering Luther. It is also clear that the substantial increase in attendance because of the inclusion of women made possible a much better utilization of the plant and did not require a proportionate increase in the staff; consequently, finances improved more than had been anticipated.

On the whole, the women who pioneered coeducation during this transition period took in stride the problems associated with elbowing their way into an old established college for men. By some of the die-hards the women were accepted only grudgingly; at times they were the victims of pranks, most of them designed to draw laughs and harmless enough. By 1935 coeds were admitted to Irving Literary Society, the Linné Society, and the Delphian Sister Society. *College Chips* welcomed them as early as October 25, 1933, and the women fittingly labeled their column "The Ride of the Valkyries."

> For ages Norsemen stood supreme,
> Never of Valkyries did they dream.
> Time and tide for no man wait.
> With triumph Valkyries crashed the gate.[28]

The problem of coeducation, however, had not even yet been officially settled. The Board of Education, which in February 1934 had passed a resolution providing for coeducation and had apparently reversed its position at the 1934 convention, reported on June 26, 1934, at a meeting in Decorah that it had "an open mind on the question of coeducation at Luther." Next day it urged that the discussion of debt problems and coeducation be discontinued in Luther College circles.[29] This was like commanding the tide to stand still. But it was doubtless well meant, for these matters had been referred to a joint committee consisting of the Board of Education and the Board of Trustees of the Norwegian Lutheran Church of America.

M. O. Grangaard, who had carried through the measures which relieved the college of its pressing bank obligations, now organized a special four-man college committee without official standing to propose solutions to the problems left unsolved by the 1934 convention. Several meetings were held in Minneapolis and Rochester, presided over by Grangaard. In May 1935 the group agreed on a program for the four colleges which included coeducation for Luther College, an improved plan for allocating appropriations to the four major colleges of the church, and means for promoting co-operation and harmony among the colleges. Substantially this program was adopted by the joint committee (of which Grangaard was a member) elected by the 1934 synodical convention.[30]

Two sentences in the report of the joint committee to the 1936 convention spelled coeducation for Luther College:

"The Church supports four Senior Colleges. The four Senior Colleges shall be coeducational institutions."[31] The report, with only a minor change, was adopted by the 1936 convention. Later the Luther College Board of Trustees made the alumnae of Decorah College for Women alumnae of Luther College.

Meanwhile, the need to revise the Articles of Luther College, something voiced by the alumni early in 1932, was translated into action. The Luther College Alumni Association took the lead in 1935 by electing a committee to prepare a revised set of articles.[32] The proposed new Articles, after being approved by the trustees, were submitted to the Luther College Corporation and adopted June 5, 1936.

They provided for:
1. Coeducation.
2. An enlarged board of trustees of 7 to 11 members.
3. Election of the corporation officers by the Board of Trustees.
4. Decorah as the place for all regular meetings of the board.
5. A vice president for the college.
6. Designation of the chairman of the board rather than the president of the college to preside at meetings.
7. Trustees to have a voice in the nomination of the president of the college.
8. The Board of Trustees to have the power to appoint faculty members and to fill temporary vacancies, even in the presidency.

The Board of Education retained its power of nominating, in conjunction with the trustees, the president of the college. But the revised Articles did away with the system of divided authority and vested in the trustees the responsibility for administering the college. The change was long overdue. It should have been made when the Norwegian Lutheran Church of America was formed in 1917. But apparently no one thought the matter through then. St. Olaf College revised its articles in 1930 to get away from an even more cumbersome setup than that of Luther College. The earlier revision of the Luther College Articles in 1930 did not provide the autonomy needed by a collegiate institution. Because of this lack, important and unimportant decisions were constantly being referred to the Board of Education in Minneapolis. The board, trying to deal with the depression difficulties of a dozen or more schools of the church, had more than enough troubles of its own without trying to run the affairs of Luther College. From January 1931 through December 1935 there were 52 entries in the minutes of the Board of Education dealing with Luther College, whereas in the same period there were only four entries dealing with St. Olaf College, with its more autonomous structure. The affairs of Luther College were to a considerable degree being run from Minneapolis by those not familiar enough with its problems to make wise decisions. No wonder there were misunderstandings and considerable friction. So, in 1936, those who had been prescribing various panaceas for Luther College from Minneapolis, with only as much cooperation on the part of the patient as she was willing to give, decided to turn her loose and give Nature a chance. Once the change was made, there is little doubt that the Board of Education was as relieved as was the college.

The revised Articles quickly received an affirmative vote at the corporation meeting. The coeducation amendment was submitted, and adopted by a vote of 472 to 31. *De facto* coeducation became *de jure*. The sometimes acrimonious issue was resolved with surprising unanimity and with no loss of support for the college. In fact, by opening its doors to women, the college gained a host of new supporters. The results have more than justified the change. It was coeducation "which cut the cord of slow strangulation."[33]

269

Alma Mater, thou shalt yet, by the grace of God, live to see ever greater things. Vivas, crescas, floreas!

—J. A. O. Stub, '98

16

The Triumph of Coeducation

With the formal introduction of coeducation, Luther College ended a seventy-five year period as a men's college and entered upon a new era. No longer would it be known as just a "preacher school" or as a home for monks, as some, on occasion, were inclined to twit it with being. It had become a place where the youth of the church, regardless of sex, might receive an education. It had realized an ideal which had been voiced in the earliest discussions concerning the college, but one which the most influential early leaders, because they were children of their time and background, and because they faced the alarmingly urgent need for pastors and the tremendous problem of financing an institution of learning, failed to bring to fruition.

Now the die was cast. The old order had passed. Just as the college had relegated the early university idea to the limbo of forgotten things, just as it slowly and sometimes painfully had shed the pattern of the European *gymnasium* with its rigid classical course and had emerged as a full-fledged, accredited, four-year, American liberal arts college, so now it recognized the conditions of the times and returned upon itself to realize the aspirations of some of its earliest promoters and later supporters by opening its doors to students of both sexes.

The shift to coeducation was hailed with satisfaction by the overwhelming majority of the constituency; even the minority who had their doubts or who looked back with nostalgic regret to the good old days were not reluctant, as the years passed, to admit the desirability of the change. But in 1936, when the college had survived the severe financial crisis of the depression, when the coeducation issue had been settled, and when it seemed a new period of peaceful development lay ahead, no one anticipated that only a few years more would bring another world war, a fire to destroy the loved Old Main of the college, the loss of nearly all male students to the armed forces, and, with the end of the war, the manifold problems of postwar adjustment. It is perhaps well that man cannot see too far into the future.

The Diamond Jubilee year was a memorable one. The college introduced coeducation; it also revised its articles and bylaws to give it the degree of autonomy without which no institution can function properly. The Luther College Concert Band under Carlo A. Sperati, '88, its vigorous seventy-five-year old conductor, made a triumphant tour to Europe. Alumni and friends raised and presented a Diamond Jubilee Chest to strengthen the school financially. Some of the same group, most of them direct descendants of the pioneer founders, erected the Pioneer Memorial on the campus; others with a special interest in music presented the Olaf Angelo Sperati Memorial Organ. Karen Larsen's biography of her father, first president of the college, appeared. Inga Bredesen Norstog translated into English Peer Strømme's novel of early life at Luther College. The faculty, with the newly admitted women in mind, introduced a two-year teacher-training course. Pi Kappa Delta, the first national honor society to be represented on the campus, granted Iowa Xi chapter to the college. Two other student organizations took form, the Classical Club and the Campus Players, the latter replacing an earlier Dramatics Club organized in 1932. In this year, too, the city of Decorah built its municipal swimming pool on land originally part of the campus.

Against the background of these events, the Founders

Day festivities October 14–18 drew one of the largest crowds in the history of the institution. "The crowd on Sunday was estimated at from 3000 to 5000. People came and went during the whole course of the festivities and it is safe to say that from 5000 to 10,000 visited the campus during the week of the celebration. Though threatening for a time on Friday, the weather was favorable, and on Saturday and Sunday delightful." More than 60 of the 69 classes of graduates were represented. Each of the seven and a half decades that had elapsed since the founding of the college was represented. More than a handful present could recall when the institution was moved to its chosen location at Decorah, then 50 miles west of the nearest rail terminal. Some had walked that distance to enroll. They, and others, had been present at the laying of the cornerstone for the first building on the campus in 1864. No later anniversary observance would see the presence of most of these.[1]

On Thursday evening, October 15, "Voluspaa," by the modern Norwegian composer David Monrad Johansen, was given its first rendition in this country by a chorus and orchestra under the direction of Theodore C. F. Hoelty-Nickel. The English translation was by Ingebret Dorrum, '04.

A historical pageant on Friday preceded the dedication of the Pioneer Memorial, designed and constructed by Tarkjel Landsverk. Sigurd S. Reque, '03, had dug out the names for the nine bronze plaques from old records. Laurits S. Swenson, '86, speaking at the dedication, quoted Laur. Larsen as follows: "Our people want to hold fast to that which is good in the old heritage and let it be of benefit to this new nation. Therefore we will all guard our old memories. . . . The pioneers have represented our nationality at its best, and they have brought to this new land . . . forces that should influence its history, as the Normans of the Middle Ages influenced the countries to which they came. They have already done so, and the mark they have made will never be erased."[2]

The alumnae of Lutheran Ladies Seminary and the alumni of Luther Academy had been invited to hold reunions at Decorah during the celebration; subsequently both groups were extended membership in the Luther College Alumni Association. Later the Gale College alumni were similarly welcomed. The festival address was given by Jacob A. O. Stub, '98, of Central Lutheran Church, Minneapolis, who reviewed the progress of the college from its "Heroic Period" (1861–1902) through its "Period of Adjustment and Growth" (1902–21) to the "Modern Era" (1921–36), with a final look into the future. The festival sermon was preached by Thaddeus F. Gullixson, '03, president of Luther Theological Seminary, who used as his text the words found on the seal of the college: *Verbum Dei manet in æternum* (The Word of God Abideth Forever), I Peter 1:25. He praised the founding fathers for their faithfulness to this text, concluding in a tribute that many would second: "God let the breezes today touch lightly the leaves and grasses on their graves wherever they may be, and rest the souls in His presence who so boldly sent forward the banner of their confidence in God's revelation."

The Diamond Jubilee tour of the Luther College Concert Band was recorded on film by Martin Elstad, '35, and his associates; the Diamond Jubilee Founders Day festivities were filmed by Mabel Thorstenson of Chicago. Both of these records are deposited in the college library.

The Diamond Jubilee Chest reached a total of $51,137.81 in cash, plus $926 in pledges. Frisbie L. Young, '28, helped greatly in organizing alumni committees; H. Gynther Magelssen, '86–94, and Sigurd S. Reque, '03, served in the field; the executive secretary was responsible for the central office and the city of Decorah. The committee's policy was to concentrate on cash gifts rather than pledges. Despite the fact that the ingathering took place during the upset economic conditions of the time and the severe drouth of 1936, the sum raised was the largest received in the interval between the second endowment campaign of 1926 and the emergency appeal of 1942. More than 2,173 contributions were made, averaging $23.53 each. The sum raised for the Pioneer Memorial was $2,586.27. In addition several sizable annuity gifts were an indirect result of the campaign, but were not included in the chest totals.

With these funds the college was enabled to make settlements with its remaining creditors and clear up its external debt. Not a few gifts and legacies, some large, some small, were received in the next few years. At the same time the administration and the Board of Trustees pursued so sound and conservative a financial policy that Preus in his 1939 Christmas letter was able to point to audited figures showing a reduction in the deficit during the previous six years of $67,500.

In 1934 the Gardner Cowles Foundation of Des Moines gave the college $500 for student scholarships, and since then has made a similar grant annually. The Harold Fardal Student Loan Fund was established during this period. The Norwegian Evangelical Lutheran Congregation of Zumbrota, Minnesota, upon its dissolution, gave its remaining property to the college. The assets remaining after the closing of Willmar Seminary likewise were given to the college. Gifts and bequests came also from Mrs. Rachel Johnson, Decorah; C. N. Smedsrud, Lansing, Iowa; Ben Bear, Decorah; O. C. Johnson, Decorah; W. H. Klemme, Ridgeway, Iowa; Nordahl Nustad, La Crosse; Oluf Gjerset, Montevideo, Minnesota; and Olaf Halvorson, Los Angeles. The Smedsrud bequest was the second largest gift received by the college up to this time.

Up to 1938 the general endowment funds of the college had been administered by the Investment Committee of the

Norwegian Lutheran Church of America. This procedure, which governed the funds of St. Olaf College as well as Luther, appears to have originated partly from a desire to keep a close control over the finances of the schools lest they become too independent of the church and partly from the belief that a central investment committee could do a better job of investing than the individual colleges could. The policy was not popular; it was cumbersome and gave rise to differences of opinion between the college authorities and the Investment Committee as to the most satisfactory employment of endowment funds. In 1938 the policy was changed and the endowment assets were returned to the college.

A large part of the endowment assets had originally been invested in farm mortgages; many of these were now in default; in many instances the land covered by the mortgages had been forfeited to the college. The administration and the Board of Trustees set to work vigorously to rehabilitate these funds. Karl Hanson, business manager, was tireless in his efforts. The Board of Trustees, with such men as M. O. Grangaard, George W. Johnson, T. A. Hoff, and Nordahl Nustad, likewise devoted a tremendous amount of time and energy to the problem. The minutes of the board record instance after instance of offers, recommended for acceptance by financial agents, which the board declined, making counter-offers at a higher figure. In almost every instance the latter sum was obtained. Thus, by a cautious and prudent policy and through the general improvement in economic conditions, the board had practically completed the rehabilitation of the endowment funds by the end of Preus's administration. With the reduction of the deficit and the restoration of the endowment funds to a productive status, finances, by the end of Preus's term, had reached a stability in marked contrast to what they had been at the beginning.

A. C. Bishop, publisher of *Decorah Public Opinion* and a

warm friend of the college, was eager to see the school provide better housing for its women. Going back to the "pig club" idea promoted by Ben Bear of Decorah in World War I to raise money for the American Red Cross, Bishop proposed in his newspaper that funds for a women's dormitory be raised in the same way. Farmers were to be asked to set aside a baby pig in the spring; when it had been raised to market size and sold, the proceeds were to be given to the dormitory fund. Others might give sums equivalent to what was realized from the sale of a pig. As the idea grew, "piggy banks" were suggested and procured, to be filled and turned in by donors.

The "pig club" idea never won wholehearted support, partly because linking it to a dormitory for women afforded too many opportunities for good-natured chaffing. But it did have the merit of stirring the alumni into action. In 1939 they elected a committee of ten, held an organization meeting January 2, 1940, and launched a campaign that by June 1942 had netted $46,000 in cash and $39,000 in pledges. Once more Ray Algyer headed the solicitation in Decorah. The campaign was halted when Old Main burned on May 31, 1942. Perhaps it was as well that the interruption came. Original plans for the dormitory were hardly adequate, for they envisaged a first unit to cost $125,000. Although this figure reflected the prewar price level, a structure of the size first planned would hardly bear comparison with the $1,000,000 Brandt Hall erected later.[3]

The first sound and permanent retirement policy was adopted in 1936 and went into effect in 1937, when the college became a member of the Teachers Insurance and Annuity Association. The plan, worked out by a committee, provided for a funding and amortization of accrued liabilities and a minimum contribution toward a retirement fund. As the soundness of the project and its advantages to both teachers and college became increasingly clear, contributions were increased to the standard 10 per cent in 1945, and a collective insurance policy was added for each member. In 1946 Blue Cross and Blue Shield protection was also provided.[4]

Other "internal" improvements were a great step-up in personnel, counseling, and health services; inauguration of "Freshman Days" in 1937; preparation of a printed student handbook; and the establishment of freshman and senior honor societies in 1939. In 1940 city and college collaborated in inaugurating the Decorah Concert Series. The art department had its beginnings in 1936 with Eldrid Thorpe as the first instructor. Its quarters have been successively the first floor of Koren Library, the north classroom beneath the stage of C. K. Preus Gymnasium, the north portion of what later became a part of the bookshop and canteen, and lastly the second floor of the Korsrud Heating Plant. In 1941 the departments of instruction were grouped in six divisions, an arrangement that is still in effect: 1. Religion and philosophy; 2. Languages and literature; 3. Education and psychology; 4. Mathematics and sciences; 5. Social sciences; 6. Fine arts.[5]

A faculty exchange program was attempted in 1939–40, when Professors Edvin Tingelstad and Paul Highby of Pacific Lutheran University spent a year at Luther and Professors O. M. Norlie and David T. Nelson in turn spent the year at Pacific Lutheran. Similar exchanges have been advocated by various Lutheran faculty groups. There can be little doubt of their value in creating friendly understanding and in stimulating ideas.

An innovation in publicity was the president's Christmas letter, inaugurated in 1937—a chatty, informal review of the year, addressed to the alumni. In 1935 the "Alumni Register," which had been printed annually up to that time as part of the college catalog, was omitted. To replace it, the *Alumni Directory*, edited by David T. Nelson, appeared in

1939. In 1938 Karl H. Nordgaard, '25, became "fieldman" for the college, performing duties later centered in the office of admissions under his direction.

For many years a canteen run by students had been conducted in the basement of Old Main, dispensing candy bars, soft drinks, and miscellaneous articles. In September 1938 Adolph Arveson took over the canteen, enlarged it, and made it the Luther College Bookshop. Arveson was a quiet, unassuming man, but it was soon apparent that as manager of the bookshop he exerted a pervasive spiritual influence that attracted students and faculty alike. His untimely death September 11, 1940, was a great loss. The bookshop was carried on by his widow for a time, was moved to what is known as the "Visiting Team Room" in the C. K. Preus Gymnasium, later to a CCC (Civilian Conservation Corps) building from the Decorah Fair Grounds set up on a site between Main and the gymnasium, and after World War II to a war-surplus frame building northwest of the gymnasium. In 1960 it was removed to temporary quarters in the ground floor area of Valders Memorial Hall of Science.[6]

In 1937 Mr. and Mrs. Simon Hoegh of Rushford, Minnesota, gave $1,200 to Station KWLC, making it possible, in 1938–39, to move the transmitter to rooms in the tower of C. K. Preus Gymnasium with a vertical radiator nearby. A radio exchange with KGLO of Mason City resulted in the complete rebuilding of KWLC in 1941 with a 205-foot vertical radiator; since then it has broadcast on a frequency of 1240 kilocycles with a power of 250 watts. In 1946 the college retained the hours from 9:30 A.M. to 1:30 P.M., but leased the remaining time to KDTH of the *Dubuque Telegraph Herald*. This agreement was terminated; a new one, August 1951, gave this time to the Scenic Broadcasting Company of Decorah, which operates KDEC. The last arrangement is still in effect. In 1959 the vertical radiator was moved to the river bottom west of the Korsrud Heating Plant.

Each day except Sunday, college chapel services are broadcast. Other hours in the station's time are filled with informative, dramatic, literary, and musical offerings. Many individuals have given time and effort to furnish programs for KWLC, among them members of the Decorah community, the college faculty, and the student body. Programs which were fixtures for many years were those of Reverend Thoralf A. Hoff, '04, and Georg Strandvold, foreign-news editor of *Decorah-posten.*[7]

As the thirties, decade of depression, tribulation, and angry revolt, drew to a close, few looked forward to another World War. Possibly the visits of European royalty to the United States in 1939 were more deeply motivated than historians have yet recorded. In any event the visit of Crown Prince Olav and Crown Princess Märtha of Norway stirred tremendous interest. Their only stop in Iowa was at Decorah, May 6 and 7, 1939. They were met at the Leiv Eiriksson Bridge on their arrival from La Crosse and escorted by the Luther College Concert Band to the Winneshiek Hotel, where they were welcomed by Governor George A. Wilson. In the evening, at a public meeting in C. K. Preus Gymnasium, Crown Prince Olav was given the honorary degree of Doctor of Literature. Sunday, May 8, the royal couple, after a visit to the Norwegian-American Historical Museum, attended divine services in First Lutheran Church. Then they were guests at a luncheon, and the crown prince addressed the crowd from the steps of the gymnasium before departing. This visit drew the largest crowds in the history of Decorah. The sentiment of those present was perhaps best expressed by one old Viking as he shook hands with the prince, "Det var godt du kom, Olav." ("It was nice of you to come, Olav.")

Hardly had the glowing memories of this event begun to recede when news came of the outbreak of hostilities in Europe. Following the "phony" war of the winter of 1939–40,

279

Americans (and especially those of Norwegian ancestry) listened incredulously as they heard the news of Hitler's occupation of Norway. As time passed, America began preparations for defense, the war became a central theme, and few felt safe from its repercussions.

A pilot-training program under the Civil Aeronautics Authority was inaugurated in 1940, with Emil C. Miller in charge. When the attack on Pearl Harbor came on December 7, 1941, a pledge of loyalty and support from the faculty, student body, and alumni was immediately forwarded to President Franklin D. Roosevelt. Units of the V-5 and V-7 Naval Reserve groups were formed on the campus; Lieutenant Commander T. H. Jones visited the college frequently, both during and after the war; and Chellis N. Evanson '18, crew member of the flagship "Pennsylvania" in World War I, became almost a symbol of the United States Navy at the college. The Luther College women, who, as the men were swept into service, gradually dominated the campus, organized a Red Cross unit, took charge of the sale of war stamps and war bonds among students, and in other ways aided the general effort; later, as careers in the armed forces opened to women, almost a score joined the new units. Accelerated scholastic programs became the rule. More than 12 of the younger faculty members entered various branches of the service.

Some effort was expended on a projected military or naval unit on the campus, but this came to naught when on Sunday, May 31, 1942, Old Main caught fire and in a matter of hours was reduced to a smoldering ruin. For the second time fire had destroyed the stately structure which, more than any other, symbolized Luther College. Apparently a bolt of lightning struck with great intensity minutes before the blaze was discovered in the attic. Fire departments from Decorah and four neighboring communities were powerless to halt the flames, once they gained headway. Volunteers assisted faculty and students in removing valuable biological equipment from the basement, and college records, furniture, and other supplies.

At 7:30 that evening the faculty met in the Tower Room of the gymnasium to take the measures necessary to enable the summer session, scheduled to begin the following morning, to open without delay or inconvenience. The secretary recorded that "as the flames were still rising from the ruins of Main Building, Laurence N. Field opened the meeting with Scripture reading and prayer."[8] Vice president O. W. Qualley, '18, was chairman. Preus, who had hurried home from Rio, Wisconsin, arrived during the meeting. Administrative offices were set up in Larsen Hall, and temporary classrooms were arranged in the library, gymnasium, music hall, and Larsen Hall.

Expressions of sympathy and offers of help streamed in from all quarters. President L. W. Boe of St. Olaf College, then under doctor's orders to rest, sent a warm message of sympathy and a personal contribution toward the rebuilding of the structure. Hall Roberts of Postville, Iowa, sent a $500 war bond to the college. J. A. Aasgaard, president of the synod, made a special trip to Decorah to confer with the college trustees. Boe later sent a special report (supplementary to his regular annual report) to the church convention, scheduled to meet June 9, mentioning the help given St. Olaf College when its chapel burned in 1923 and urging all in the St. Olaf family to come to the assistance of Luther College. Under Aasgaard's leadership the church authorized an immediate emergency appeal for $300,000 for Luther College; A. J. Bergsaker, stewardship secretary, agreed to head it. For its slogan, the words of Boe were adopted, "When calamity strikes, we are one." Other colleges and organizations within the church gave it their approval. The unanimity of support led Preus to write: "Luther College will be given new vitality and be enabled in

281

turn to give of her strength as never before to the church and the country that have nourished her so well. If we have needed one more cord with which to bind the amalgamated parts of our church together through the performance of a common task, God has given it to us in this disaster."[9]

The campaign for funds was successful, more than the specified amount being raised. Bergsaker, ably assisted by Torstein H. Rossing, '20, was tireless in urging that as large an amount as possible should be raised. The wisdom of his words was fully vindicated later when war inflation shrank the value of the dollar. Meanwhile plans were being discussed, preliminary drawings made, and steps taken to secure priorities (wartime authorizations) for building the new structure. But none of these came to fruition during Preus's administration, and new efforts were necessary before a new main building could rise in 1950–52.

As the war continued, it swept away all but 80 male students in 1943–44, the low point in attendance during the war, although an increase in the number of women to 166 in that year was a saving factor. Thoughts of those on campus turned to the men and women on the far-flung fronts of the conflict. *College Chips,* mailed to every serviceman, went to unexpected corners of the globe. *Scuttlebutt,* begun as a private letter from old navy man Chellis N. Evanson, '18, to some of the naval recruits, gradually expanded until it was reaching everyone from Luther in the armed forces. It was a cheerful sheet with the typical Evanson touch, made possible by his singlehanded, devoted efforts.

Perhaps the mood of the home front was well expressed in the Christmas 1943 *Bulletin:* "The war has dominated activities at the College during the year which now draws to a close. Outwardly the campus has been peaceful. Nor has it ever seemed lovelier, whether gowned in the white of last winter's snow, clothed in the richness of spring and summer's verdure, or decked in the flaming beauty of autumn's changing colors. Perhaps the starkness of the ruins of Old Main, now leveled and only a memory of the past, has been a symbol of a grim reality which lies just below the surface of everyone's thinking as he goes about his daily tasks. For the day's work goes on—goes on amid these beautiful and peaceful surroundings. But every week brings news of more men and women, former students of the College, who have been drawn into the service of their country. And scarcely a week passes that some of them do not return, if only for a few hours, for a fleeting visit to the scenes that hold so much that is dear to them. Perhaps these visits are also a symbol—a symbol of the longing for a better and more beautiful world of peaceful, constructive pursuits when the present struggle is ended."

Memorial services for Luther men killed in action were held at the college from time to time; the final one after the war included full participation by patriotic organizations such as the American Legion, Veterans of Foreign Wars, and their auxiliaries. Chellis N. Evanson, '18, assisted by David T. Nelson, '12, was largely responsible for the honor roll memorial in New Main facing the entry. The memorial contains the names in bronze of those who served in the armed forces of the United States in both wars: 354 in World War I, of whom 9 gave their lives; 1,358 in World War II, of whom 35 gave their lives. The roster reveals that 17 Luther women served in World War II.[10]

As early as 1936, two acres of the campus were sold and two acres leased to the city of Decorah on which to erect a municipal swimming pool. Two lots east of the campus and north of 409 High Street were purchased in 1935. In 1937 Sunnyside and Campus House were completely renovated as women's dormitories. The "Chicken Coop," which in its day had housed many and various activities, was remodeled in 1938 to provide facilities for the music department. There were two large studios on the second floor; a classroom and music library, one studio, and four practice rooms on the first floor. The venerable structure continued to serve the musicians until it was torn down in 1951 during the construction of New Main.[11]

Melody Manor, a residence at 500 High Street, was purchased for $7,500 in 1943; and Vanaheim, a residence at 509 North Street, was purchased for $8,500 in 1944, both as residences for women. The Chandler residence at 508 Center Street and the Weiser residence at 612 Broadway were purchased for $7,800 and $14,000, respectively, in 1946, both for apartments for faculty members. From the government, 17 barracks with facilities for 31 families and 64 single men were obtained in 1946; these were set up as a veterans' village on the east side of Highway 52, opposite the Municipal Swimming Pool, to accommodate the men, many with families, who returned to college under the G. I. Bill of Rights. Two large buildings from the prisoner-of-war camp at Algona, Iowa, were also obtained from the government and erected north and west of the gymnasium to provide classroom and office space. They were named Norby Court for Charles H. Norby, '30, and Lane Court for Gerhard A. Lane, '31, whose deaths occurred during their war service. The college purchased two Civilian Conservation Corps barracks, placing one north of the gymnasium for classrooms and one south of it for a canteen and bookshop. A lot bought in 1943 enabled the college to make a 220-yard straightaway for the cinder track which had been completed in 1938 on Nustad Field. The same year 25 acres of bottom land below the bluff were purchased for $2,010; and two years later a lot needed for a new heating plant.[12]

With the coming of peace in 1945 the attendance, which had reached 301 in 1944–45, rose to 418 in 1945–46, 735 in 1946–47, and 887 in 1947–48. The growth of the student body brought increases in staff, buildings, and campus area, and new instructional procedures.

Coeducation had triumphed and women had taken their place on the campus. The fears expressed by some had proved to be imaginary. Not only was there a refinement of manners and tone on campus; there was also a quickening of interest among parents attached by strong ties to the school who had daughters to educate. It was as if there were an infusion of new blood, giving fresh vitality to an old and honored institution.

Almost at the moment when it seemed that the college was ready for a long step forward, World War II had come. The draining away of men had been inexorable. Then had followed the burning of Old Main, a blow that stunned and disheartened. But misfortune also stirs sympathy and loyalty. So it was now. *Resurgam,* "I shall arise," was a word that comforted many a heart. Moreover, as the men on campus dwindled to a mere handful, the women took over. They manned the chief posts in student organizations; they carried on the old traditions—and made a few new ones of their own. The home front was theirs. They manned it gallantly. They needed to make no apologies when the veterans streamed back from the war and a new crop of freshman men entered. Women had carried on. Their place was assured.

*Why not examine into some of the
old, stable, going objectives that
we have seen weather many storms?*
—N. B. Hanson, '99

17

Postwar Adjustments

The Board of Trustees had authorized the remodeling of
C. K. Preus Gymnasium before Old Main had burned. After
the fire the work was swiftly carried out. The former ground
floor batting cage and adjacent areas were transformed into
a gymnasium for women, with dressing rooms, showers, and
lavatories, and a playing floor 50 by 96 feet. The space under
the stage, originally set aside for a swimming pool, was
utilized for four good-sized classrooms. The turning room
and the second-floor Tower Room of the gymnasium also
became classrooms.[1]

A modernization of Laur. Larsen Hall, extending over the
period 1944–46, included new fireproof stair wells and stair-
ways; modern washrooms; replastering of all rooms and
halls; new doors; new desks, wardrobes, and dressers in all
rooms on second and third floors and, in the west wing, on
first floor. The project cost about $60,000.[2] The ground-floor
level of Larsen Hall continued to house the biology and
physics departments and most of the chemistry department. The biology department, which had previously occupied quarters on the ground-floor level of Old Main, had
moved to Larsen Hall after the fire.

After Morrell and Nichols, architectural firm of Minneapolis, had prepared a revised campus plan in 1946, the
Board of Trustees authorized the construction of a new
heating plant and tunnels as the first step in the postwar
building program. The old plant had served long and well,

but it was inadequate for the new buildings contemplated, and its boilers had a very limited remaining life. The new plant was erected in the southwest corner of the campus at a cost of $138,600.[3] The campus had never been so torn up and disrupted as it was during the work on the tunnels, essential as they were. The new building was named the Korsrud Heating Plant in honor of Ole Korsrud, who had served as electrician, night watchman, and engineer at the college since 1901. He was given the honor of breaking ground for the structure on May 6, 1946, and lived to see it substantially completed before his death January 13, 1947.[4] The building, 42 by 72 feet, nestled into the hillside, has a second story, used for classrooms. This area first housed the Bible department and student offices; later, after the completion of New Main in 1952, the art department.[5]

To provide more space for the music department, six practice rooms were constructed in the north portion of the old heating plant in 1946. These served until the whole structure was razed in 1952. To make room for 25,000 more volumes in the library, a fourth tier of stacks was added in 1946 at a cost of $7,000. In 1947 the library began microfilming to preserve and make more readily available the invaluable Norwegian-American newspaper material in its possession. Lights were provided for Nustad Field in 1946; roll-away bleachers were installed in C. K. Preus Gymnasium in 1947, thus greatly increasing seating capacity; and an I. B. M. clock system was put into operation on campus the same year. A public-address system had been installed in the gymnasium in 1946.[6]

Finances continued to improve, particularly because gifts and bequests came from friends of the college. Donors of special gifts from 1942 to the end of the Preus administration were: Mr. and Mrs. W. B. Ingvoldstad, Decorah; Thomas O. Nelson, Whitewater, Wisconsin; A. N. Fardal, Stanhope, Iowa; Dr. Hildus A. Ness, '89–94, Mabel, Minnesota; Mr. and Mrs. William Nelson, Belgrade, Minnesota; Mae Johnson, Rio, Wisconsin; Aneken Halvorson, Davis, Illinois; Martha Brye, La Crosse, Wisconsin; brothers and sisters of Charles H. Norby, '30, Fergus Falls, Minnesota; Mrs. Carrie O. Henryson, Story City, Iowa; J. C. M. Hanson, '82, Chicago; Olaf Halvorson, Los Angeles; Reverend and Mrs. C. A. Fritz, Albert Lea, Minnesota; Mrs. Inga Remmen, Chicago; the Brunsdale family, Mayville, North Dakota; Lou Ellefson, Decorah; the family of Dr. George Kessel, Cresco, Iowa; the family of Junior Bickle, '41–43; and the family of Knute Preus Stalland, '40–42. There was an anonymous gift of $9,000, later considerably increased, for a carillon, and a bequest of $10,000, for a chapel, from Dr. T. Stabo, who served on the Board of Trustees with great faithfulness for 30 years and as college physician for 33 years. In addition to the above, thousands of generous gifts were made by individual donors to the dormitory building fund and the emergency appeal.

The collection of 20 paintings and etchings of Dr. Nils E. Remmen, '79–84, was presented to the college by his family in 1941. This well-chosen group included an etching by James A. McNeill Whistler and one by Anders L. Zorn. In 1944 the family of Nils O. Giere, '79, gave Koren Library a copy of the rare first edition of Henrik Ibsen's *Catiline*, the second one now owned by the library. Only four copies are known to be in this country.[7]

The first dean of women of Luther College was Emily Frank, who held the position 1936–37. Orlando W. Qualley, '18, was elected vice president in 1936, the first to hold that office. In 1946 he was made the first dean of the college.[8] In 1941 the summer school, which had been discontinued in 1934, was revived with Rolfe A. Haatvedt, '29, as director. It has been conducted every summer since then.

In 1941, under the sponsorship of the North Central Association of Colleges and Secondary Schools, summer work-

64. O. J. H. Preus, '01,
president 1932–48.

65. Inaugural procession,
1932. J. A. Aasgaard, president of the Norwegian
Lutheran Church of Amer-
ica and Preus in the lead.

66. Sunnyside.

67. *Pioneer Memorial.*

68. *Baseball, faculty versus seniors, 1934. Standing, l. to r.: Eittreim, Dorrum, Hanson, Reque, Strunk, Jacobsen, Olson, Strom, Nickel, Sihler, Norlie. Kneeling: Preus, Nelson, Qualley, Peterson, Evanson, Talle, Ellingson.*

69. Decorah College for Women.

70. Class of 1935. Doris A. Erickson (Mrs. Adolph I. Buckneberg); Esther M. Hanson (Mrs. Harold Hoff).

71. Original L. C. "Floradoras." L. to r.: Eleanor Dorrum, Ruth Luzum, Solveig Dorrum, Agnes Engell, Dorcas Jacobson, Helen Hoff.

72. Class of 1936. L. to r.: Helen M. Hoff (Mrs. R. A. Haatvedt); Dorcas V. Jacobson (Mrs. B. B. Wrolstad); Ruth A. Graeber (Mrs. F. D. Boots); Laura M. Monson (Mrs. M. K. Elstad); Lily Nelson (Mrs. H. T. Knutson).

LUTHER COLLEGE CONCERT BAND
CARLO A. SPERATI, MUSICAL DIRECTOR
EUROPEAN DIAMOND JUBILEE TOUR 1936
W. A. MOEN, MANAGER
ORCHESTRA HALL   JUNE 19,   CHICAGO, ILLINOIS

73. *Luther College Concert Band, 1936, Carlo A. Sperati, director.*

74. *Morning chapel.*

75. *Olav V, king of Norway (then crown prince) receiving honorary LL.D., 1939. Lictors: Evanson and Norlie. Governor George A. Wilson is visible in the immediate background.*

76. *Crown Princess Märtha receiving a gift at the hands of Karlyn Nordgaard and Erick Ellingson.*

77. *Winter on campus (Ruth Mikelson).*

78. *Norwegian-American Historical Museum.*

79. *Knut Gjerset.*

80. *Melody Manor.*

81. *Vanaheim.*

82. *Reading room, Koren Library.*

83. *Korsrud Heating Plant.*

OSCAR A. TINGELSTAD
first registrar

KARL HANSON
first business manager

OLAF M. NORLIE
*first summer school
director*

EMILY FRANK
first dean of women

ORLANDO W. QUALLEY
*first dean and
vice president*

CLARA M. HOYT
*first director of
women's chorus*

OTTAR TINGLUM
*president of Decorah
College for Women*

GORDON A. SELBO
*first student
congregation pastor*

91. *Postwar canteen, 1947–52.*

92. *Canteen in the gymnasium,
1942–47.*

shops were inaugurated to promote a program of educational experimentation and self-analysis among colleges in the area of the association. Luther was one of 30 colleges participating in the group at the University of Minnesota, Conrad R. Waldeland being its representative that year. The workshops have been held annually since and the college has regularly been represented.

Largely as a result of the stimulus afforded by the workshops, the faculty established a postwar planning committee in 1943 which later was enlarged and renamed the Committee on Educational Research. In the spring of 1945 the former committee sent the alumni a twelve-page questionnaire. Upon the basis of the replies the committee drew up a series of recommendations which the faculty adopted. Many of the proposals would doubtless eventually have found their way into the college academic structure; but the decisive weight of alumni opinion encouraged the faculty to adopt these ideas immediately.[9]

Among the recommendations adopted were the following: preparation and distribution to the alumni annually of a condensed financial statement and a report on the work and progress of the college; direct representation by the alumni association on the college Board of Trustees; an annual roll call or appeal to alumni for gifts; establishment of a system of stipends for faculty members for summer study; a new formulation of the aims and objectives of the college; inauguration and expansion of a program of visual aids in teaching; a review of the Norwegian-language requirement with a view to its elimination; great emphasis for prospective theological students on courses in philosophy and social problems; expansion of work in testing, vocational guidance, and counseling; limitation of the number of students by a selective admission policy; expanded social and recreational programs and more adequate facilities for them; a regular monthly convocation, planned by the Committee

289

on Lectures and Entertainments; the appointment of a chapel committee and the use of the Lutheran Common Service at least once a week in chapel. Practically all the above recommendations have been carried out; as many more, of greater or less importance, have been studied and, in many instances, adopted.[10]

The curriculum during the decade preceding 1944 was expanded by the introduction of major sequences in music, physical education (for men), speech, and business administration; and by minors in art, Spanish, sociology, secretarial training, library science, and elementary teacher training. In 1946, after setting up new and higher standards, the faculty established a number of scholarships from student aid funds to assist outstanding students. The first regular faculty institute at the opening of the school year was held September 14 and 15, 1945, with Dean W. E. Peik of the college of education, University of Minnesota, as consultant.[11]

The Committee on Curriculum and Scholarship, with Dean Qualley as chairman, struggled through 22 meetings over more than two years to formulate a new statement of the objectives of the college. This was adopted by the faculty in 1948. The following general statement summarizes what was enlarged upon under 12 subheads:

"The objective of Luther College is a liberal and thorough Christian education of men and women. In the attainment of this objective the college is mindful of responsibility to the individual student, its supporting church, and society.

"Luther College aims to serve the individual student by providing an integrated program of spiritual, mental, and physical development; to serve the Evangelical Lutheran Church by helping to supply consecrated and enlightened leadership, both ordained and lay, in every field of Christian service; to serve society by fostering Christian ideals of patriotism and world citizenship."[12]

After the liberalization of the curriculum in 1931–32 and

the introduction of coeducation in 1936 it was clear that
the aims and objectives of the college were in need of re-
statement. The college had come a long way since Larsen
designated it as the "Norwegian Lutheran School for the
Education of Ministers." It had always been something
more than a Latin school, strongly as it was influenced by
the Latin-school pattern. Despite the reactionary defense
of the classical program and insistence that the college's
primary role was to prepare men for the ministry, the college had refused to become "a theological preparatory
school." It had actually developed "a broader basis and a
more cosmopolitan character," as Stub had suggested. It had
finally returned to the idea of educating "the youth of our
church," a phrase so many times uttered by Claus L. Clausen.
Clausen, influenced by his great compatriot N. F. S. Grundtvig and also by his admiration of American institutions, had
been the best spokesman for the laymen's democratic aspirations. The laymen wanted a school open to all the youth
of the church. They objected to exempting from tuition
those who declared an intention to study for the ministry
and insisted that all students be accepted on an equal foot-
ing. Moreover, the laymen were never enamored of the
rigid classical course; nor were all the clergy, for that matter.
Finally changes came. The new formulation of the college's
aims and objectives expressed the broader viewpoint, one
which had already won acceptance in every other college
of the church and which quickly received the support of the
overwhelming majority of the college's constituency. The
old order had passed.

With the growth of the college and the enlargement of
the student body through the admission of women, a change
took place in the composition of the faculty, which, up to
the end of Olson's administration, had consisted of men
only. Gradually women were engaged, at first only in posts
made necessary by coeducation, later in any teaching posi-

tion for which they were qualified. The transition was not complete when O. J. H. Preus's administration ended; nevertheless, women had taken over many posts of responsibility and numbered about a third of the faculty in 1947–48.

A number of veteran faculty figures passed from the scene during Preus's presidency. Knut Gjerset died in 1936; Herman W. Sheel in 1937; William Sihler in 1941, after 50 years as an active faculty member; Knute O. Eittreim in 1942; Carlo A. Sperati, '88, in 1945; Karl Hanson, '08, in 1948. Alumni will remember the latter's classic remark as business manager: "Someone's got to pay." His devotion to duty was exemplary, both at the college and at First Lutheran Church, where he was superintendent of the Sunday school for 15 years.

Among other familiar faculty names may be mentioned Oscar A. Tingelstad, '05, who returned in 1944 to serve for six more years; Olaf M. Norlie, who returned in 1932 and left in 1941 to accept a position at St. Olaf College; Carl W. Strom, '19, who entered the United States Foreign Service in 1935; William L. Strunk, who left in 1938 to join the staff of St. Olaf College; Henry O. Talle, '17, whose career as head of the department of economics and college treasurer closed in 1938 when he was elected to the lower house of Congress, where he served for the next 20 years; Theodore C. F. Hoelty-Nickel, who accepted a position in 1941 with Radio Station KFUO and Concordia Theological Seminary in St. Louis, and eventually became head of the department of music at Valparaiso University.

Among new names to appear on the faculty roster are those of Sherman A. Hoslett, '30, who began full-time teaching of biology in 1933; Emily Frank, who capably supervised elementary-education programs, 1935–51; Morton O. Nilssen, who, after heading the Bible department 1935–41, became president of Waldorf College, Forest City, Iowa; Oivind M. Hovde, '32, assistant librarian 1935–38, associate librarian

1944–49, and head librarian since Karl T. Jacobsen retired in 1949; Donald O. Rod, '38, who was assistant librarian 1940–43, and left to become head librarian at Augustana College, Rock Island, Illinois, and later, head librarian at Iowa State Teachers College; Rolfe A. Haatvedt, '29, who taught 1936–42, returned in 1946 after a war career, but left in 1950 to enter the United States foreign service; Clara Maude Hoyt, an extraordinarily fine influence on campus from 1936 until her retirement in 1958; Adrian M. Docken, '37, on the staff since 1938 and from 1942 head of the department of chemistry, which Conrad R. Waldeland had directed 1932–42 (Docken was a faculty fellow, Yale University 1954–55, and is a science faculty fellow, University of London 1961–62); Donald J. Larson, whose untimely death on May 23, 1948, was a great loss to the department of music; Karl H. Nordgaard, '25, head of admissions since 1938; Rudolf Kyler in the economics department 1939–46; and Arthur O. Davidson, '31, staff member since 1941, who in 1961 became president of Wagner College, Staten Island, New York.

Other well-known faculty figures of this period are Ralph M. Dahlquist, '28, college physician since 1939; N. Lewis Fadness, '22, in political science and psychology; Emil C. Miller in physics; Robert S. Jacobsen, '37, in mathematics; and Clara J. Paulson in English, all since 1939; Kenneth L. Berger, under whose leadership the department of speech was developed and enlarged 1941–57; Laurence N. Field, head of the department of Bible 1941–44 and, a few years later, professor at Luther Theological Seminary; Frank R. Barth, '40, in business administration and economics 1942–53; Sigvart A. Hofland, who was active as a composer and music director from 1942; Sigvart J. Steen, '23, who had charge of the choir and band from 1946 to 1948, when he left to accept a position at Wagner College, Staten Island, New York City; Vera Bucknell Thompson, assistant librarian 1942–48; Gerhard E. Frost, '31, campus pastor 1944–56, until he became professor at Luther Theological Seminary; Charlotte B. Schilling Grue, a member of the health service since 1944; Helen Adams Bodensteiner, in speech and dramatics since 1946; George E. Knudson, in chemistry, and Orville M. Running as head of the art department, both since 1946; Kathryn M. Ulvilden, '41, in music from 1946 to 1956; Barbara Bahe in German; Frederic A. Giere, '47, in biology; Clair G. Kloster, '38, in psychology and education; and Inga B. Norstog, director of the Norwegian-American Historical Museum; the last four joined the staff in 1947.

The museum did not make great progress during the depression and the war. After Gjerset's death Knute O. Eittreim was curator from 1936 to 1939. He was succeeded by Sigurd S. Reque, '03, who held the post until Mrs. Norstog succeeded him in 1947.

Despite difficulties, student organizations flourished until the war. The Luther College Concert Band, under Sperati, made a tour to the Century of Progress Exposition in Chicago in June 1933 and was heard on a coast-to-coast radio network on Norway Day. In 1936 it made a European Diamond Jubilee Tour, a three months' journey that included appearances in Norway, Denmark, and England, and a stand at the Great Lakes Exposition in Cleveland.

Other appearances included concerts at the Tri-State Fair in La Crosse, Wisconsin, the National Dairy Cattle Congress at Waterloo, Iowa, and, in April 1942, a Midwest tour, the last to be made with Sperati as conductor. From 1943 to 1946 Sigvart Hofland, more gifted as a composer than as a director, headed the band. In February 1946 Sigvart J. Steen, '23, director of the navy choir at the Great Lakes Naval Base during the war, returned to take over directing duties. During the two years of his leadership, extensive tours were again undertaken.[13]

The Schola Cantorum, an *a cappella* male choir directed by Theodore C. F. Hoelty-Nickel, had its greatest successes in this period. In 1933 it made a memorable trip to the west coast and in other years made briefer tours in the Midwest, with many radio appearances. After the departure of Nickel in 1941, the drain of men in the war, and the changes in the composition of the student body, the organization languished.

With the admission of women, the Women's Chorus, under Clara M. Hoyt, was organized and soon won a place for itself, enrolling more than 60 members. Soon a mixed chorus was established. Under Sigvart J. Steen, '23, this developed into the Nordic Cathedral Choir, later known as the Luther College Choir, and quickly took its place among similar outstanding groups of the Midwest.

The student council gradually developed into an important factor in campus government, particularly with the return of veterans from the war. As the servicemen had a maturity beyond their years, it seemed natural to entrust more and more problems to the students themselves. Nevertheless, in 1947, the students, possibly because there were complicating factors little evident on the surface, rejected a proposal to introduce an honor system at the college. The Men's Senate dealt with all men's problems on campus; the Women's Self-Governing Association performed a similar role for women.

Many veterans were married and had children. They had to be housed and cared for. The old policy (not unique at Luther College) by which a student marriage was treated almost as a moral delinquency, was relegated to oblivion overnight. The ex-servicemen, after life in foxholes and subsistence on the delights of army rations—especially canned ones—were determined to have homes of their own and enjoy normal peacetime life. Although barracks and other makeshift quarters could hardly be called normal, the young married folk, happy to be together, took them in stride. Everyone caught the spirit. A delightful and charming postwar event was a faculty party for married students and their

295

families. The guests were youthful husbands and wives (many of the latter pregnant), babies and toddling children —a wholesome, thankful, and responsive group, future builders of church and state. The old era, with many of its taboos, was gone.

Religious activity among the students broadened. In 1939 the old Mission Society was renamed the Braafladt-Brevig Mission Society in honor of two men: Louis H. Braafladt, '06, medical missionary to China, who had been twice decorated by the Chinese for his work during the cholera epidemic of 1919 and the pneumonia epidemic of 1921; and Tollef L. Brevig, '72–76, missionary to Alaska, who pioneered Lutheran mission work among the Eskimos beginning in 1894. The Lutheran Students Union functioned until 1947, when the Lutheran Students Association, an intersynodical society of broader scope, took its place. The Lutheran Daughters of the Reformation was organized in 1937. A board of religious activities co-ordinated the efforts of the various religious groups, which included the Fellowship Forum for the discussion of current controversial spiritual problems.

Debate, oratory, dramatics, and radio work flourished again in the postwar period under Kenneth Berger's leadership. "Dark Encounter," an original student play born of the burning of Old Main, had a successful run with such stars as Justin Hammond, Jerry Rosholt, Marv Lore, Georgiann Johnson, Helen Trilhus, Victor Tinderholt, Jack Lien, and Bob Inman, with Bob Seegmiller directing. The proceeds went to the fund for New Main. Radio audiences had a chance to hear Great Dane, detective, "the crackerjack of criminology," assisted by such eminent personalities as Dave Preus, Rosemary Leitch, Nels Strandjord, Ted Jacobsen, Chellis Evanson, Jr., Marjette Fritchen, Harold Wheaton, Jean Baker, Mildred Comisrud, Betty Colby, Ruth Barth, Barbara Baker, Lloyd Townsend, Curt Eittreim, and the "incomparable KWLC summer crew," consisting of Helen Trilhus, Jerry Karlton, Styrk Orwoll, and Jack Aaker. The show's star, Roland Dain, was eloquently labeled "the peach of Redondo Beach."[14]

A more serious effort was that of Karlton J. (Jerry) Rosholt, '48, who won first place in the seventy-fourth annual interstate oratorical contest at Northwestern University on April 16, 1948. It was a double first: the first time a representative from Luther College had won; the first time a representative from an Iowa college or university had won. A similar honor came to Georgiann Johnson at the Glenn Burke centennial tournament at Tulane University in February 1948; she walked off with the Carnot Cup for original oratory, the first woman to win a Glenn Burke trophy since the awards were endowed in 1848. She had previously won first in women's oratory in the national Pi Kappa Delta tournament in 1947.[15]

College Chips, now as earlier, was the foremost student publication. The first woman to take over the editor-in-chief's duties was Louise Helen Nelson (Mrs. Cliff Knapp) on January 24, 1940. In 1943 a smaller format, 12 by 17 inches, was adopted under Ruth Kalnes, '44, as editor. March 19, 1946, with Helen E. Stoen, '48, as editor and Nancy Ney, '48, as her associate, the paper went modern in make-up, abandoning the old vertical style for a horizontal one, with a floating name plate and sans-serif display type. In October 1946 the paper reverted from a biweekly to a weekly.

The first woman to be editor in chief of *The Pioneer* was Louise Helen Nelson in 1940. The news bureau, manned by students under Chellis N. Evanson's direction, continued to furnish college news to daily and weekly papers over a large area. Several of the men who tried their hands at editing or news writing went on to responsible newspaper positions.

The first Homecoming queen in the college's history was crowned October 10, 1941—Lillian R. Stadsvold of Starbuck,

Minnesota. In 1945 two students from Norway were welcomed to the campus, the first of a steady stream of foreign undergraduates brought here by the college or by college groups. Overseas students have come from Latvia, Lithuania, Estonia, Germany, Puerto Rico, Colombia, Nigeria, Union of South Africa, Ethiopia, Iran, Hongkong, Formosa, China, Indonesia, and Norway.

Although the thirties were years of drought and depression, college athletics managed to flourish. Coaches Hamlet E. Peterson, '22, and Orlando W. Qualley, '18, both of whom taught the classical languages, continued to turn out winning combinations in football and basketball; the college won the conference football championship every third year from 1929 to 1941. Peterson was also successful in track. In March 1958 he was elected to the Hall of Fame, basketball section, of the National Association of Intercollegiate Athletics. Sigurd S. Reque, '03, whose academic interest was teaching French, was successful with his baseball teams until he resigned in 1942 to do field work for the department of public services. His overall record of 244 games won, 139 lost, and 9 tied in 21 seasons made him known throughout the baseball world. In 1960 he was one of the first four named to the Hall of Fame, baseball section, of the National Association of Intercollegiate Athletics.[16] In tennis and turning there were very creditable squads. In track, the half-mile relay team of Adolph L. Belding, '35, Clifford H. (Cliff) Hansen, '33, August A. (Augie) Luther, '36, and Lauren B. Nesset, '33, was outstanding; their college record time of 1:30.6 was set in 1932. Nesset set a conference mark of 9.09 in the hundred-yard dash. Four-letter winners in sports were Cliff Hansen, who later played with the Chicago Bears, and Augie Luther. The latter ran 102 yards for a touchdown against St. Mary's of Winona in 1933. Other stars of the prewar period were Anton J. (Butch) Stolfa, '39, football great, who later played with the Chicago Bears, and during whose four college years only two conference games were lost; Arthur M. (Beech) Grangaard, '37, versatile three-sport man; and David W. Preus, '43, a brilliant defensive basketball player.

When Reque retired as athletic director, he was succeeded by his colleague Hamlet E. Peterson, '22, who also coached basketball and baseball. After the war, athletics swiftly regained prominence. The return of veterans raised interest to fever pitch and overflow crowds turned out for every contest. Among the early standouts were Norman Everson, '48, who set a new school scoring record in basketball, only to have it surpassed by Arnold (Judge) Veglahn, '49, hook-shot artist; and Donald R. (Rufe) McDowell, '48, effortless expert in basketball and baseball.

Women had organized the Women's Recreation Association in 1939. Women's athletic activities grew to include badminton, volleyball, basketball, softball, archery, tennis, field hockey, and such winter sports as skiing and tobogganing. Women also took a prominent part as cheerleaders.

A number of social groups sprang up, such as, in 1945–46, the freshman social societies for women—Prima, Secunda, Tertia, Quarta; Phi Theta Theta, for students in elementary education, in 1940; Pi Kappa Tau in 1938 and Sigma Alpha Phi in 1947–48, both social organizations for women; and Sigma Alpha Delta in 1939 to develop professional interests among prospective teachers.

Mary Margaret Roberts, '44, received a Ph.D. degree in 1959, the first Luther alumna to earn this honor. She is director of debate at the William Pitt Debating Union, University of Pittsburgh. Georgiann Johnson, '48, is the first Luther alumna to win a place on television and the Broadway stage.[17]

Among the many men and women who served the college in administrative capacities during this period, former students will recall Ole L. Korsrud, August O. Korsrud, Adolph Running, C. Nickoley, Martin Bergan, George Dirksen, Peter

Eggen, Florence A. Thompson, Ferneva F. Weinkauf, Lois L. Flickinger, Alma Malli, Grayce O. Larson, Charles A. Osborne, C. W. (Colonel) Leikvold, Mrs. Julia Bloomfield, Bernice G. Forde, Mrs. Marie Fjelstad, Ralph Olson, Joseph Thomas, Erling K. Knutson, and Mrs. Anna Lionberger.

Following the surrender of Germany May 7, 1945, and of Japan September 2, 1945, new problems descended upon colleges throughout the country. They were urgent and demanded early solutions. They were faced first by administrators. Luther College was no exception to the general rule. Preus, who had a strong physique, had never spared himself, nor did he now. It is not surprising, therefore, that after the arduous years of depression, drouth, fire, and war, his health gave way. On December 18, 1945, he suffered a heart attack, was confined to his home for some weeks, and thereafter was obliged to curtail his activities.

In February 1947 Preus addressed a message to the alumni indicating his desire to retire at the end of his term in 1948: "I can no longer conduct three to five services on Sundays, as I did regularly for about twenty-five years. In other words, while my general health is good, my heart is not 100% as it used to be. Luther College needs a man in good health and vigorous at the helm, particularly at this time of expansion and building operations. Much as I love to continue to work, I should therefore be permitted to retire from my present position in 1948—if the Lord lets me function up to that moment. And if there then is strength left, one may perhaps be permitted to draw on that in a less arduous corner of the church."[18]

The way was thus open for the alumni to take counsel concerning his successor, and this they proceeded to do. With Preus's health still precarious, the sudden death from a heart attack of Karl Hanson, '08, indefatigable treasurer and business manager, on January 27, 1948, caused the Board of Trustees considerable uneasiness. Accordingly, at their suggestion and urging, David T. Nelson, '12, on February 25, 1948, was made acting business manager, an office he held until August 1, 1948. To meet the insistent demand of the alumni for action on the building program, Nelson enlisted Frank R. Miller, '37, Ralph M. Dahlquist, '28, and Reinert N. Svendsen, '34, all of Decorah, in reactivating the campaign for funds for a women's dormitory. With the assistance of Orlando W. Qualley, '18, Hamlet E. Peterson, '22, Sigurd S. Reque, '03, and others, about $70,000 additional was raised, and before the end of the school year the trustees awarded the contracts.[19] Work on the new building was thus finally under way before Preus stepped down as president.

On June 30, 1948, at the expiration of his third term, Preus retired. He was made president emeritus, joining Oscar L. Olson, who had been given the same title in 1942. To meet a minor emergency Preus taught part time at the college in 1949–50; in a similar way, with characteristic self-sacrifice, he served the Burr Oak, Iowa, Lutheran congregation for a time. He died February 13, 1951.

Preus's administration had been one of the most eventful in the history of the college; yet the factors that made it so were not of his own choosing. The severe financial depression of the thirties, the problems raised by the issue of coeducation, the impact of World War II, the destruction of Old Main by fire, and the urgent postwar adjustments resulted in a succession of crises. By the end of his presidency they had in large measure been successfully overcome, and secure foundations had been laid to build upon. In retrospect it can be seen that the tremendously patient and painstaking husbanding of the college's resources by the president, the treasurer, the business manager, and the Board of Trustees had rescued the school from the brink of disaster and assured its financial soundness. If there was some dissatisfaction at war's end, it was because the college did not move forward fast enough.

301

Preus's great strength lay in his appeal to the hearts of friends and supporters. In a Christmas message in 1932 he reminded alumni and friends that God had opened a way leading directly to his throne of mercy. But: "Many a day, perhaps many a year, you have not trod that way very faithfully for your Alma Mater. She has not been carried on the arms of prayer to the throne of mercy every day by every alumnus." Not money, not endowments, not students caused him most concern. "It is the soul of Luther College that I am thinking of. And the soul of Luther is a reflection of your soul and mine."[20]

To appeals such as the above there were responses of many kinds. Preus welcomed them all. Sometimes the suggestions growing out of them were poorly conceived, but they nevertheless received a hearing. Moreover, the difficulties and crises of the college challenged friends and supporters to come to its aid. All were warmly welcomed. They proved to be far more numerous than most men had dared hope. What was accomplished surpassed what had been deemed possible. It was therefore with confidence and assurance, despite the looming problems of a large building program, that Preus turned over the reins of administration to his successor.

To be worthy of the name Christian,
the education we offer must be
thorough and sound.
—J. W. Ylvisaker, '21

18

Planning for Growth

On June 10, 1948, J. Wilhelm Ylvisaker, '21, was elected to
head the fifth administration of the college. His choice had
been clearly foreshadowed at two meetings of the Luther
College Alumni Association and by two polls of the alumni
taken in 1947 to ascertain their sentiment.[1]

Ylvisaker was born April 18, 1900, at Robbinsdale, Minnesota, the youngest child of Johannes Th. Ylvisaker, professor
at Luther Seminary. He attended Central High School in St.
Paul, Minnesota, and completed his undergraduate work at
Luther College. After teaching a year at Luther Academy,
Albert Lea, Minnesota, he attended Luther Theological
Seminary, St. Paul, three years followed by a year at Princeton Theological Seminary, receiving his master of theology
degree in 1926. He then accepted a call to Northwood, Iowa,
thus becoming one of 14 members of the two branches of the
Ylvisaker family to serve as pastors and missionaries in the
Lutheran Church in this country. After 11 years at Northwood, he accepted a call to Our Saviour's Lutheran Church
of Minneapolis, where he remained until 1948. He was active
in youth work, was a delegate to the Lutheran World Federation at Lund, Sweden, in 1947, and traveled in Norway and
Denmark. In 1930 he was married to Lucille Torgerson of
McFarland, Wisconsin. Their two children are Martha Elizabeth (Mrs. James Limburg), '56, and James William, '60.

Although his experience had been largely that of a parish
pastor, Ylvisaker was always deeply interested in the college

of which he was a graduate, and kept in close touch with its progress. Modest concerning his own abilities, he was perhaps taken aback to discover that strong alumni sentiment favored him for president. But once aware, long before the event, that his election was all but assured, he gave himself to an analysis of the college's needs, a reassessment of its objectives, and a formulation of policies needed to reach them. Therefore when he took office he was prepared to launch a new period of development. Basically, he wanted growth—growth in attendance, in material resources, in academic excellence, and in spiritual life, firmly believing that alumni and friends would support such a program.

In the twelve years of his administration there has been a little backing and filling, a reappraisal from time to time of projects contemplated or undertaken, but always there has been a rebound toward larger goals, to a greater vision of what the college may be and what it may accomplish.

His relations with faculty and students, with alumni and friends, have been cordial and warm. He has encouraged discussion, welcomed ideas, sought advice, been friendly in counsel, and shown patience in difficulties. His flashes of wit, never caustic and always friendly, have brightened many a situation. He was president of the Association of Iowa College Presidents, of the Iowa College Foundation 1953–55, and of the National Lutheran Educational Conference in 1959. In 1960 he was elected to his third six-year term as president of Luther.

Ylvisaker was present, by invitation, at the trustees' meeting when contracts were let for construction of the west wing and center section of Brandt Hall. Because it was necessary to borrow money if both were to be built, there was some sentiment for omitting the center section. Ylvisaker urged that both be carried through; his view prevailed.

The college plant had undergone practically no expansion during the years of depression and war; it was therefore essential that a major building program be undertaken. Ylvisaker has carried this out; with the completion of Valders Science Hall and the College Union in 1961, about $5,500,000 will have been spent in new construction since the Korsrud Heating Plant was begun in 1946.[2]

The west wing and center section of Brandt Hall, for which ground had been broken as early as October 14, 1945, were finally under construction in the summer of 1948. The structure cost $620,000; furnishings required an additional $55,000. A bond issue of $280,000, the first successful one in the history of the college, was needed to complete its financing.[3] The Luther College Woman's Club of Decorah furnished the main lounge, and the Luther College Woman's Club of Chicago, the recreation room. The building, which accommodates 225 women, was completed and occupied the second semester 1949–50. It was dedicated on Mothers' Day, May 14, 1950, V. Trygve Jordahl, '22, officiating.

Seven years later the east wing of Brandt Hall was built, thus completing the original design of the structure. The east wing with furnishings cost $550,000 and was financed in part by a loan of $400,000 from the federal government. It was ready for occupancy in September 1958. Brandt Hall now has accommodations for 392 women.[4]

The second major building erected during Ylvisaker's administration is New Main. President emeritus Preus broke ground for it October 12, 1950, and work on the foundations proceeded during the fall and early winter. Construction was resumed in 1951 (the old heating plant and the "Chicken Coop" were then razed); the cornerstone was laid June 3. The structure, ready for occupancy when school opened in September, 1952, represents an expenditure of $613,000, with $58,000 additional for furnishings.[5] It contains 18 classrooms, 21 administrative offices, and 27 faculty offices, most of the latter in a six-story tower which has a faculty lounge on its top floor. A foundation stone from Old Main with an outline of Old Main carved upon it was mortared into the wall beside the entrance. The keystone from the original Main Building bearing the inscription "1864" is in place beside the corner-stone. New Main, like Brandt Hall, has attracted much favorable attention for the simplicity of its modern design.

Ever since the war there has been a need for more dor-mitory space, especially for men. In 1954, with funds from a federal loan of $535,000, work was begun on a dormitory with built-in beds, dressers, and desks, to house 233 men.[6] Total cost was $594,000. With some temporary inconvenience because of unfinished details, students occupied the building in September 1955. The cornerstone was laid May 17, 1955; the building was named and dedicated as Oscar L. Olson Hall in honor of the third president of the college on October 16, 1955. Located slightly east and south of Larsen Hall, it has ramps which run from its second story to the sloping knoll directly north of it.

Originally it had been thought that the mathematics and physical science departments might be accommodated in New Main. But it was soon clear that this was not practical, and the sciences graciously agreed to await their own build-ing. Their patience was rewarded beyond their fondest dreams as plans gradually took shape for a new science building. At the request of Mr. and Mrs. Louis W. Olson, principal donors toward the project, the hall is named the Valders Memorial Hall of Science in honor of the area in Norway (Valdres), from which the forebears of Louis W. Ol-son came, and of Valders, Wisconsin, where they settled in this country.

The building, with two wings, one of three stories, the other of two, will house the departments of biology, chem-istry, physics, and mathematics. (One of its features will be an air-conditioned lecture hall seating 300. A planetarium and elevator are planned for completion later.) It will con-tain 85,000 square feet of floor space and will cost, equipped and complete, $1,500,000.[7] Construction began November 16, 1959. The cornerstone was laid May 12, 1960; Sidney A. Rand, executive director of the Board of Education of the Evangelical Lutheran Church, delivered the address. It is expected the building will be ready for occupancy for the opening of the school year 1961–62. Valders Memorial Science Hall is the first million-dollar building on the campus.

The sixth major building of the Ylvisaker administration is the College Union. After preliminary planning by faculty and student committees, the college in 1958 engaged Porter Butts of the University of Wisconsin as a consultant. In September 1959 a student fee of $12.50 per semester for use of the Union was initiated. The federal government authorized a loan of $750,000. The structure with equipment will cost $1,250,000. On May 17, 1960, ground was broken by Ronald S. Lee, '61, student body president for 1960–61, in a ceremony presided over by Ylvisaker; others who participated were Gordon A. Selbo, Paul H. Lionberger, '49, Fayetta Paulsen, J. C. Magelssen, '42, and Curtis A. Rotto, '60. Construction began October 4, 1960. The cornerstone was laid May 5, 1961, by A. Alvon Nelson, '29, who used Joshua 24:27 as his text.[8]

On lots purchased in 1948, four hard-surfaced tennis courts were constructed to the south and west of Larsen Hall. The same year a receiving warehouse was erected immediately north of Korsrud Heating Plant. In 1949 a concrete bleacher was erected on the south side of Nustad Field to provide permanent seating for 700. Eight lots south of Larsen Hall were purchased in 1954, and a strip of land to provide an approach to Oscar L. Olson Hall from the south. On Leiv Eiriksson Drive the Engebretson-Gjerset lots were acquired in 1955 to extend the campus eastward in that area. In 1956 the Mattie Moore farm of 160 acres was acquired for $24,000. This property, lying north of Bluffton Road directly opposite part of the college farm, has significant possibilities. The campus and the adjacent farms now comprise almost 600 acres.

The building program and the expansion of the campus foreshadowed the need of a revision of older plans and a reorientation of the college to the larger potentials revealed by its steady growth. In 1954 Arthur O. Davidson, '31, who had left the staff in 1948 to accept a position at Dartmouth College, returned to his alma mater as vice president in charge of development. The Campus Planning Committee, composed chiefly of faculty members under Davidson's chairmanship, carried out exploratory studies that indicated the need for a new and larger view of college problems. Their conclusions were reinforced by the report of Algo D. Henderson to the Cowles Foundation, which stated with regard to the physical plant that the college "needs fresh perspective, such as could be given by an imaginative land planner."[9]

In the summer of 1956 Orville Dahl, now president of California Lutheran College, was engaged to make a survey of the college, report on its probable future growth, suggest a development program, and draw up a new campus plan. His comprehensive report, accompanied by a model layout for display purposes, was ready in the spring of 1957. The report, which has been the subject of much study and discussion since, undoubtedly encouraged a larger and freer outlook upon the college's future development.

By 1948 attendance had almost doubled the prewar total. Except for the relatively mild disruptions caused by the Korean War (1950–53), the enrollment figures continued to climb. The number of men enrolled during the regular school year ending 1948 was 614; the number of women, 273. In the regular school year ending 1960 the number of men was 737; the number of women, 548. Total unduplicated enrollment, including the regular school year, summer sessions, and extension courses, expanded from 1,081 in 1947–48 to 1,517 in 1959–60. Enrollment in the regular school year for the same periods was 887 and 1,285. Both sets of figures show approximately a 50 per cent increase over the twelve-year period from 1948 to 1960. No single factor can be assigned to account for this. Although the national trend toward greater college enrollments after World War II played a significant part, the increase at Luther College appears to have exceeded the average. The academic program at Luther College has been attractive, building operations have had a strong appeal, admissions officials have been active, and sound standards of scholarship, coupled with a friendly atmosphere, have been potent influences. A new factor has been a program of loans to students from funds distributed through the United States Office of Education under the National Defense Act of 1958. These federal funds now exceed the amounts offered by the college's private loan funds and are important in bolstering attendance. The total available from both now exceeds $284,000.

The increase in attendance, expansion of campus and farm areas, and the extensive building program have gone hand in hand with a large growth in financial resources. Here again no single factor can be pointed to as all important; several have played their part. The significance of the general economic improvement of these years may be illustrated by the history of the Norswing Foundation. The foundation grew out of pledges made by the late Knut Norswing to the church and to the Luther-St. Olaf Endowment Appeal, and out of other assets for which the church, St. Olaf College, and Luther College advanced $100,000 in 1933, and an additional $33,000 by 1941. As conditions improved, the assets, which were under the supervision of M. O. Grangaard, were set up in 1946 as the Norswing Foundation. By 1958 all debts had been paid and the fund had grown to $200,000, the amount contemplated when the foundation was established. These funds and the Norswing properties are held in trust by the American Lutheran

309

Church and the income is distributed, 30 per cent to Luther College, 30 per cent to St. Olaf College, 25 per cent to the American Lutheran Church, and 15 per cent to Pacific Lutheran University. Considerable sacrifice was necessary in the 1930's to conserve the assets but, with careful supervision and the general economic improvement, they have grown to be a substantial addition to the endowment fund of the sharing institutions.

The supporting church, through its improved finances, has been able to increase its annual appropriations to the college. In 1948 the appropriation was $43,200; in 1960, $116,200, more than two and a half times as much. In 1949 the church launched a United Christian Education Appeal for its educational institutions. Luther's share of these funds was $185,000 as of January 31, 1951. To meet the spiraling living costs that were working hardship on faculty members at all its institutions, the church distributed grants for salary bonuses in 1945 and again in 1951. Its Church School Cost of Living Appeal, up to January 31, 1952, netted $347,900 for distribution to its schools and colleges.[10]

The expansion of college activities placed additional burdens on the business office, which since 1949 has been headed by Wilbert O. Kalsow. He has introduced standardized national college and university accounting procedures and in 1959 began a complete switchover to mechanized office records.

Many special gifts and bequests were received in this twelve-year period. The Luther College Woman's Clubs of Decorah and Chicago, which had raised more than $10,000 earlier, made additional contributions for furnishing the lounges in Oscar L. Olson Hall and for equipping the college hospital. Bequests and special gifts were received from Ida Goelberg of Mabel, Minnesota; Mr. and Mrs. John Dieseth, Fergus Falls, Minnesota; Mrs. C. H. (Lena) Ostrem, Viroqua, Wisconsin; Blanche Christy, Bismarck, North Dakota; Dr. and Mrs. J. C. K. Preus, Minneapolis; Mathilda Gilbertson, La Crosse, Wisconsin; Helga Gunderson, La Crosse, Wisconsin (a bequest which, through the generosity of the Wiley Piano Company, Minneapolis, was stretched to purchase pianos worth twice the amount given); Mr. and Mrs. Olai Steen, Clinton, Minnesota; Solva J. Strom, Albert Lea, Minnesota; Christine E. Johnson, Capron, Illinois; Ida Marie Henderson, Oshkosh, Wisconsin; Christine Miner, Albert Lea, Minnesota; Ingrid Landsrud, Englewood, Colorado; and Bertha S. White, Sturgis, South Dakota. George Benson of Osage, Iowa, bequeathed 100 shares of General Motors Corporation stock and 15 shares of Montgomery Ward and Company stock, both for the benefit of the Norwegian-American Historical Museum; the stock was received in 1950.

The period was marked by several bequests larger than any which had come to the college earlier. From the estate of Andrew A. Linde of De Forest, Wisconsin, came a bequest to the church to be shared by Luther College and St. Olaf College. Luther's portion was $48,200. In 1955–56 the college received $72,400 from the estate of Miss Lou Ellefson, a lifelong resident of Decorah and for years a member of the Decorah Luther College Woman's Club. In 1959 Beatrice Brevik of Albert Lea, Minnesota, bequeathed an estate valued at $50,000. Her husband, Reverend Olaf Christian O. Brevik, had been pastor of Glenwood Lutheran Church, Decorah.

The largest amount assigned to the college by one family came in the form of gifts and bequests from Mr. and Mrs. Louis W. Olson of Mansfield, Ohio. Louis W. Olson, born in Manitowoc, Wisconsin, January 12, 1878, was the adopted son of Knud and Gjertrud Olson of that city. Olson took a degree in electrical engineering at the University of Wisconsin and, after three years with J. G. White and Company of New York City, became associated with the Ohio Brass Company of Mansfield, Ohio. There he was engineer, salesman, factory manager, plant and design engineer, and, from 1936 until his death, vice president. "He pioneered in the field of employee relations and introduced innovations in this area which have been widely accepted."[11] He married Nell W. White September 16, 1908. Both were civic-minded; they gave a building in Mansfield to the Boy Scouts, a park to that city, and a carillon to Wittenberg College, Springfield, Ohio. Testamentary gifts included those to the ministerial pension fund of the Evangelical Lutheran Church; St. Luke's Lutheran Church, Mansfield, Ohio; Skaalen Sunset Home, Stoughton, Wisconsin; Mansfield General Hospital; the Y. M. C. A. and Y. W. C. A. of Mansfield; the Salvation Army; and the Camp Avery Scout Reservation.

Olson's boyhood chum was Gustave A. Sundby, '00, with whom he maintained a lifelong friendship. Through him Olson had made some small contributions to Luther College; then in June 1952 he wrote Sundby that he was planning a testamentary gift of $20,000. Two months later he stated that he was establishing a fund for a Valders Memorial Hall of Science and that his bequest would probably total $200,000 or more. In the same letter he recalled a visit paid him by President O. J. H. Preus, some years earlier. Both he and Mrs. Olson became more and more interested in the development plans of the college and made careful provisions for these plans to be realized. When Mrs. Olson died May 14, 1955, she left a substantial bequest to Luther, in addition to what she had given outright earlier.[12]

Olson had several discussions with Ylvisaker and Davidson, and later with Davidson alone, concerning the future of the college and the needs of the projected science hall. On August 5, 1957, he drew up a new will in which he substantially increased his bequest to the college. He died December 16, 1958. The cash, securities, real estate, and other items given and bequeathed to the college by Louis W. and Nell Olson total over $900,000.

An alumnus and his wife who desire anonymity have agreed to deed fruit-ranch properties valued at $100,000 with certain stipulations. A second gift of great potential is tied in with a Florida land development. Louis W. Ehrich, '40–42, and his wife have made an agreement with the college by which net profit, not to exceed $300,000, from their 270-acre tract, known as Hill 'n Dale, near Brooksville, Florida, will inure to the college when the property is sold. Each of these gifts, when they materialize, will set new marks in alumni giving.[13]

A development of great assistance to private colleges in recent years is the Iowa College Foundation. Organized in 1953 by a group of associated private colleges, it solicits support and funds for the non-tax-supported educational institutions of the state. In its first year (1953) the foundation raised $47,500. In its second year, with Ylvisaker as its president, it received $105,700. Operating thereafter with a full-time executive secretary, it has annually obtained substantial sums for distribution among associated colleges. In 1953 Luther College received $2,800; in 1959, $11,300.

The largest amount received by the college from a foundation was a Ford Foundation grant of $229,500. Two equal payments were made, one in 1956 and one in 1957. The objective of the Ford Foundation in making these grants was to improve the quality of college teaching. It stipulated that the funds were to be invested, and the income was to be used for supplementing faculty salaries. The church, to show its appreciation, gave the college an additional appropriation equal to the income from the Ford grant. To invest the Ford funds, Ylvisaker set up an investment committee, to which the faculty elected one member as its representative. At the suggestion of the committee, the administration secured Durwin D. Algyer, '24–25, a partner in one of the larger New York City banking firms, as consultant for investment policy. Later, the Board of Trustees asked Algyer to serve as adviser for the college's whole investment program.

Generous and valuable as all the above gifts are, they would very likely not have materialized had it not been for the great response of alumni and friends to the current needs of the college during the present administration. When the time came to erect New Main, funds available were no longer sufficient, so rapid had been the increase in building costs. At this point the Luther College Alumni Association agreed to raise $150,000, the amount then believed necessary for the completion of the new structure. Eventually alumni and friends pledged $171,000 and businessmen of Decorah $40,000 toward the building.[14]

On November 30, 1949, officers and directors of the Alumni Association initiated the practice of holding meetings to discuss college problems, to suggest solutions for them, and to prepare an agenda to be brought before the association at its annual meeting. This practice has been continued and expanded, with very beneficial results. In 1952 the association decided to reactivate the Alumni Fund by inaugurating a system of monthly giving. A report on the first eleven months of the new program revealed that $20,700 had been received. For several years the association had urged the college to employ a full-time field man to promote its interests. It was in response to this sentiment that A. O. Davidson, '31, returned to the college.[15]

Under Davidson's direction a campaign for funds for a new science hall was begun in 1954. By August 1955 faculty, staff, and students at the college had pledged $84,000; the city of Decorah, $83,000. Somewhat later the pledges reached a total of more than $200,000. In the city of Decorah George A. Baker was the general chairman; F. Hjalmar Carlson, '23, and William N. Johnson were co-chairmen.

Alumni meetings in 12 different cities in January and February 1956 revealed a strong sentiment for enlarging the goals of the campaign. On February 17, 1956, the Board of Trustees of the college, encouraged by the enthusiasm of alumni, approved a broader campaign, to be known as the Centennial Development Fund, with an over-all goal of $700,000 from the alumni. In two months $215,000 in pledges had been received. For this achievement the college was awarded third place in national competition in the capital gifts fund-raising division by the American Alumni Council in 1956. On December 8, 1956, total pledges were $377,000. By February 1958, total cash and pledges in the fund had reached $727,000.[16]

The loyalty of the alumni in reaching and surpassing the campaign goals is noteworthy. Another accomplishment was the stepup in the size of gifts by graduating classes. The development program caught their attention and stirred them to action. Class pledges were as follows: 1956, $29,000; 1957, $26,300; 1958, $30,800; 1959, $20,900.[17]

The Kresge Foundation of Detroit, Michigan, gave $25,000 toward the new science hall in June 1957, the achievement of the alumni in surpassing their goals enabling the college to qualify for it. The United States Public Health Service, a division of the Department of Health, Education, and Welfare, granted $25,000 for constructing and equipping health-research facilities. The Woods Charitable Fund, Incorporated, of Chicago awarded $500 for the science hall.[18]

In March 1957 the college launched the Lutheran Alumni Mobilization Plan, for convenience called LAMP. The goal of the project is to encourage alumni participation in all phases of college development—disseminating information about the institution and its aims, finding and attracting able students, and promoting a method of systematic financial support. The plan has been well received by the alumni, who have already laid the groundwork for making it effective. In

1960 LAMP was cited as one of the top ten alumni programs in the country for "outstanding service rendered to an institution and to the cause of education by organized alumni effort."[19]

Among the factors that brought about the large increase in gifts to the college there are reciprocal stimuli, as all will admit. Increased alumni and student support undoubtedly stimulated giving by friends; and giving by friends was a spur to the alumni. The total of all gifts and grants to the college was $224,000 in the fiscal year ending June 30, 1955; $140,000 in the following year; $460,000 in 1957; $379,000 in 1958; $538,000 in 1959; and $882,000 in 1960.[20]

The response from students, faculty, townspeople of Decorah, alumni, friends of the college, and foundations made it possible to announce in March 1959 that the combined goal of $800,000 for the Science Hall and Centennial Fund had been exceeded, and that cash, pledges, property, grants, and bequests had reached a total of $1,927,000.[21] With these and the additional funds which flowed in later, the college reduced its indebtedness by $250,000, thus clearing up external debts except for loans from the federal government on Brandt Hall, Olson Hall, and the College Union. The preliminary long-range development program of 1954 contemplated a building program of $2,054,000 by 1960. Buildings completed and contracts now let indicate that by 1961 $3,900,000 will have been expended.

Comparative figures for this administration show that current income in 1947–48 was $530,000; in 1959–60, $1,535,000. Net assets on June 30, 1948, were $2,335,000; on June 30, 1960, they were $6,444,000. Although inflation accounts for a portion of the increase above, substantial growth is evident as well.

The enlargement of the student body, the expansion of the college plant to more than twice its former size, and the substantial increase in college funds and in annual gifts have brought swift changes in the outward aspects of the institution.

Returning alumni and friends invariably are struck by the changes that have taken place in the appearance of the campus. Even those on the staff who have watched developments day by day are impressed by the evidences of physical growth on every hand. The expansion of the plant was long overdue. The depression and the restrictions imposed by World War II halted all normal expansion for almost two decades. After these restrictions were removed, the institution was hard put to it to catch up with the demands on its resources. Nor has the college yet won the race despite the addition of six major buildings in twelve years.

But there has been growth in other areas. Here, too, the development has been rapid and has touched every aspect of the college—an expansion that has involved the organizational structure of the school, the faculty, the curriculum, the admission policies, the standards of scholarship, and the welfare of students.

May the spirit of truth, of fairness,
of justice, of faith in God and
humanity be the spirit of Luther.
                              —O. J. Kvale, '90

19

Raising Standards

The Norwegian Lutheran Church of America, which is older than the college, in 1946 decided to drop the adjective that indicated the national origin of its founders, and named itself the Evangelical Lutheran Church. This action was one more evidence of the obliteration of old national ties. In the following postwar years, the synod expanded at an astonishing rate. Its latest move was an amalgamation, January 1, 1961, with two other synodical bodies—one of German origin, one of Danish — to form the American Lutheran Church. Luther College today is one of the nine colleges of this synod.

The Articles of Incorporation and Bylaws of the college were amended June 22, 1950, to bring them into harmony with the change made in 1946 in the church name (Evangelical Lutheran Church); the amendments also specified that officers of the corporation and of the trustees be elected for one-year rather than two-year terms and that the trustees should meet four times annually in Decorah.

The corporation made a much more sweeping revision June 19–20, 1958, this time with the new American Lutheran Church in mind. The revised articles, in setting forth the objects and purposes of the college, incorporated the essence of the faculty statement of objectives of March 1948. They also provided that the governing body be called the Board of Regents and consist of not less than 12, nor more than 24 members. A significant change was the enlargement of the duties and powers of the board. The regents, together with the president of the church and the chairman of the Board of Education, henceforth were to elect the president of the college from nominees selected by the regents. The regents were empowered to appoint teachers, fix their rank, and grant tenure. Many refinements were incorporated in the revision. In general, the latest articles attempted, within the framework of ownership which has existed since the college was first incorporated, to give the college that measure of autonomy without which no institution can grow and prosper.

As early as 1950 Ylvisaker had recommended that the president of the Luther College Alumni Association be invited to attend meetings of the Board of Trustees. The trustees welcomed the suggestion. The alumni president is now an advisory member of the enlarged Board of Regents. In 1955 and in 1956 the trustees recommended that women be admitted to membership. Hitherto they had not served on the board. Mrs. Elizabeth Branstad, Forest City, Iowa, president of the national Woman's Missionary Federation, served a short time as an advisory member and in June 1956 was elected the first woman trustee of Luther College.[1]

Throughout the Ylvisaker administration the board has worked harmoniously with the president and other officials of the college. Frank R. Miller, '37, who became a trustee in 1948 and chairman of the board in 1951, has been closely associated with the growth of the college in this period. He has been forward-looking, has unhesitatingly and consistently encouraged expansion, has been a very competent legal adviser, has given generously of his means as well as of his time, and must be accounted an important influence in the progress made in recent years.

Within the college there was a clearer division of duties among the administrative offices and an increase in the number of administrative officers and employees. The faculty, which had managed its affairs in an informal way for most

319

of a century, took steps to give formal standing to the structural organization which had grown up as need arose. Qualifications for faculty status were formulated, the functions of the faculty and of the faculty senate were clarified, and a policy on tenure was formulated. Practically all these details, as well as many others pertinent to the life of the college, were set forth in 1957 in a *Faculty Handbook.*[2]

Ylvisaker has been a persistent and vigorous advocate of adequate salaries and of other measures to improve the status of faculty members. Salaries in 1960 were considerably more than double those of 12 years ago. As early as 1949, $25,000 was made available for 15-year loans to faculty members to assist them in building or buying their own homes. More has since been made available, notably from the Ford Foundation grant.[3]

When the college was approved in 1951 under the federal Old Age and Survivors Insurance program, Social Security was made a supplement to the earlier retirement provisions established with TIAA (Teachers Insurance and Annuity Association), thus substantially increasing ultimate benefits to retired teachers. This action appeared to be the most practical way of combating the eroding effects of inflation. After TIAA inaugurated CREF (College Retirement Equities Fund), by which up to one half of a teacher's accumulations toward his retirement annuity may be invested in equities (i.e., common stocks), the trustees approved this policy also. In 1955 the college adopted a more comprehensive Blue Cross and Blue Shield contract to cover its employees. In 1959 it further increased the hospital and surgical benefits payable under the plan and extended the insurance against poliomyelitis to cover ten other dread or "catastrophic" diseases. In 1958 the college lumped all health and annuity charges except the social security tax under the general term "fringe benefits" and assumed their cost. This policy resulted in tax savings for all affected and thus indirectly

93. J. W. Ylvisaker, president
1948– .

94. Ylvisaker with F. A. Schiotz,
president of the American Lutheran
Church.

95. Seventeenth of May, Norway's
natal day, at outdoor museum on
campus.

96. *Diderikke Brandt Hall.*

97. *Christmas transparencies.*

98. *Night view, Brandt Hall.*

99. New Main Building.

100. War Memorial in New Main.

101. Entrance arch keystone of Old Main and cornerstone of New Main.

102. *Oscar L. Olson Hall.*

103. *Campus bulletin board.*

104. *A student social hour.*

105. *"The Messiah," 1960.*

106. *View from faculty lounge in New Main. L. to r.: Nelson, Rebassoo, Miller, Hoslett, Knudson.*

107. *Valders Memorial Hall of Science.*

108. *Louis W. Olson.*

109. *Nell W. Olson.*

110. *College Union, overlooking the bluff.*

111. *Faculty, 1959–60.*

112. Strolling toward town.

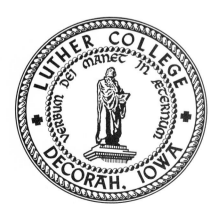

113. College motto in entrance to New Ma

114. Early college seal.

increased take-home pay. In 1959, to round out its annuity and retirement program, the college increased the collective insurance it carries to $12,500 per teacher. Collective insurance is decreasing insurance, worth most when the annuity accumulation is smallest. At the present time the health and insurance provisions in force are the most liberal in the college's history and rank very well with those of other educational institutions.

Measures have been taken to stimulate professional competence within the faculty. The program of leaves of absence followed in other administrations was enlarged. A report from the faculty affairs committee requesting $2,500 annually for in-service research and independent study was approved in 1956. In 1959 a faculty forum research program was developed "to encourage research, promote a Christian community of scholarship and stimulate writing for publication." The teaching staff of approximately 80, of whom more than 20 have doctor's degrees, averaged 25 months of graduate study per member; in 1959 on this basis the college ranked above the 75th percentile among colleges included in a North Central Association survey.[4]

Among the scholarly achievements of faculty members is that of Karl T. Jacobsen, '02, who retired as librarian in 1949. "While still at Luther College he directed the reorganization of the library of Luther Theological Seminary, St. Paul, Minnesota. After his retirement from Luther College he served as librarian of Luther Theological Seminary. During this period he also served as consultant in the re-organization of the library at Chicago Lutheran Theological Seminary at Maywood, Illinois, and of the library of Central Lutheran Theological Seminary, Fremont, Nebraska. He directed the organization of the library of Pacific Lutheran Seminary, Berkeley, California, and initiated the organization of the library at Luther Seminary, Saskatoon, Saskatchewan."[5] He devotes most of his time now (gratis) to the organization of materials deposited in the library archives.

Publications by members of the faculty include *Plain Talk in an Arctic Chapel* by Knute W. D. Lee, '37; *Chapel Time*, a collection of chapel talks given at the college by Gerhard E. Frost, '31, and Gerhard L. Belgum, '36; *The Diary of Elisabeth Koren*, translated and edited by David T. Nelson, '12; and *Halvor* by Peer Strømme, translated and adapted by Inga B. Norstog and David T. Nelson.[6]

Emil C. Miller, head of the department of physics and a member of the Committee for Atomic Energy Education in Iowa, was selected in 1948 by the Iowa Department of Public Instruction to assist in the preparation of study manuals on atomic energy for all educational levels, from elementary grades through college and adult classes. Five volumes were published. Miller contributed chapters, reviewed and edited material, and supplied the bibliography for college and adult manuals.[7]

Erling O. Naeseth, '47, collaborated in the chapter, "Functions of the Federal Reserve System," in *Money and Banking*, likewise in a chapter, "Death and Gift Taxes, and Miscellaneous Revenues," in *Public Finance;* Warren G. Berg, '48, collaborated in a chapter, "Voucher System," in *Principles of Accounting*.[8] Frederic A. Giere, '47, has published articles on problems in biology; George E. Knudson, the results of chemical researches; and Robert W. Getchell, four books of studies for brass musical instruments as well as other material helpful to teachers and students in the field.[9]

Weston H. Noble, '43, head of the department of music, has been in demand as a director, conductor, and clinician. He was director of the All-State Chorus in Iowa in 1953, in Minnesota in 1954, and in South Dakota in 1956; of the All-State Band in Oklahoma in 1955 and in Nebraska in 1958; of the Summer Music Camp, Eastern Illinois State College, Charleston, Illinois, in 1954; of the Iowa Junior College Festival in 1958. From 1952 to date he has conducted the thousand-voice all-Lutheran benefit performance of "The Messiah" in the Minneapolis Auditorium annually. He was codirector, with Roger Wagner of Roger Wagner Chorale, of an all-Texas vocal music clinic (high school-university) at the University of Texas in the summer of 1947; he was also clinician at the Colorado State Music Association contest and festival in 1957. In 1958 he was conductor of the High School Choral Directors' Workshop in South Dakota and of the Big Horn Basin Music Festival at Greybull, Wyoming. In 1960 he was director of the high school symphonic band and the Michigan all-state band at the National Music Camp, Interlochen, Michigan.

Orville M. Running of the art department has designed liturgical furniture and equipment for at least half a dozen churches and has likewise planned and supervised church decoration. He and his associates, Ernest C. Schwidder, Karl Christiansen, and Abner Jonas, have exhibited paintings in galleries in this country and abroad.

A venture that brought national and international scholars to the campus was the five-year series of Martin Luther Lectures, inaugurated in 1956. The project was developed by members of the division of religion and philosophy under the leadership of Gerhard E. Frost, '31, and Gerhard L. Belgum, '36. Ylvisaker had challenged them "to think of some way of observing the centennial which would be something other than a nostalgic, backward look." What could be done, he asked, "to enter into our second century in a creative way, a way consonant with the heritage and the upward thrust of Lutheran higher education?"[10] The lectures were made possible by a supporting grant from the Lutheran Brotherhood Life Insurance Society of Minneapolis. They dealt with the relevance of Luther for today's world, and treated him as theologian, churchman, professor, pastoral counselor, musician, educator, man, father, and friend. Among the lecturers

323

who took part were Professors Roland H. Bainton, Yale University; E. Gordon Rupp, Manchester University, England; Regin Prenter, University of Aarhus, Denmark; Willem J. Kooiman, University of Amsterdam, the Netherlands; Jaroslav J. Pelikan, University of Chicago; Theodore G. Tappert, Lutheran Theological Seminary, Philadelphia; Harold J. Grimm, Ohio State University; Warren A. Quanbeck and Herman A. Preus, Luther Theological Seminary, St. Paul, Minnesota; Theodore C. F. W. Hoelty-Nickel, Valparaiso University, Valparaiso, Indiana; George W. Forell, Chicago Lutheran Theological Seminary; Lowell C. Green of Canby, Minnesota; D. Peter Brunner, University of Heidelberg; and Bernard J. Holm, Wartburg Theological Seminary, Dubuque, Iowa.

The lectures appeared in printed form in five volumes. To promote their publication, the Luther College Press was established. Its official founding date was August 31, 1956, when the press entered into a formal contract for the printing of the first volume of the series; all five were edited by Gerhard L. Belgum, '36.[11]

The Knute Preus Stalland Memorial Fund was originally set up to provide prizes for student essays on some aspect of the ideological conflict between Christianity and materialism. In 1958 the donors, Mr. and Mrs. K. D. Stalland, proposed that the income be used to bring outstanding lecturers to the campus. The three who so far have spoken in this series are Russell Kirk, editor of *Modern Age*, Chicago; Congressman Walter H. Judd of Minnesota; and L. Arthur Larson, director of the World Rule of Law Center.

In 1959 the Adolf Gundersen Medical Foundation, La Crosse, Wisconsin, established the Adolf Gundersen Lecture Fund at the college. Under its provisions distinguished men are brought to the campus annually. The first lecturers were Dr. Willy Ley, authority on rockets and space travel, and

John Ciardi, poetry editor of the *Saturday Review*, who appeared March 8 and 30, 1960, respectively.

Several staff members have been lost by death since 1948. They are (with date of death): Ingebret Dorrum, '04, translator and master of an easy pen in Norwegian, January 6, 1952; Sigvart Hofland, composer of symphonies, string quartets, choral preludes, piano concertos, vocal solos, and incidental music, March 13, 1956; Oscar A. Tingelstad, '05, professor at Luther and former president of Pacific Lutheran University, April 4, 1953; Mrs. Inga B. Norstog, who became director of the Norwegian-American Historical Museum in 1947 and infected all who came to know her with her enthusiasm for its significance, July 13, 1960; Oliver M. Eittreim, who had been chief engineer of KWLC since it began operations in 1926, June 18, 1958.

Kenneth L. Berger, head of the speech department since 1941, resigned in 1957 to accept a position in Sacramento State College, California. Clara M. Hoyt, who joined the faculty in 1936 and directed the Women's Chorus for ten years (1936–46), retired in 1958. Vivian A. Peterson, catalog librarian since 1952, left in 1960 to become head librarian at Midland College, Fremont, Nebraska. Esther J. Olson of the speech department accepted a post at Luther Theological Seminary, St. Paul, in 1960. In 1959 John Gimbel took a position in history at Humboldt State College, Arcata, California.

On October 29, 1954, Orlando W. Qualley, '18, was given the J. A. O. Preus Award of $500 by the Lutheran Brotherhood Life Insurance Society for outstanding and faithful service to the college and the church. In 1960 Chellis N. Evanson, '18, who had served as director of the news bureau for 25 years, became the third Iowan to receive a citation from the College Sports Information Directors of America, the first representative of a small college to be so honored.

Two visiting Norwegian teachers, both from Bergen,

served on the faculty: Lektor Sverre Rasdal, 1948–51, and Lektor Finn Glambek, 1951–53 and 1954–55.

New staff members who are veterans of five years or more, and the years in which they began their full-time duties, are: in 1948, Gerhard L. Belgum, '36, in Bible and philosophy, and Warren G. Berg, '48, and Erling O. Naeseth, '47, in economics and business administration; in 1949, Herbert J. Rebassoo in mathematics and Wilbert O. Kalsow, business manager and treasurer; in 1950, Ruth Mostrom, registrar and Latin instructor, Edsel K. Schweizer, psychology instructor and football coach, and Constance E. Dahl, '45, secretary to the president; in 1951, Sigrid R. Harrisville, coordinator and head resident, Brandt Hall, Angeline Jacobson, reference librarian, and Irene J. Langlie, '38–40, assistant director of public services; in 1953, John C. Bale in English and Knute W. D. Lee, '37, in Bible and religious education; in 1954, Bartlett R. Butler in music, Ruth N. Fjelstad in Spanish, David Torrison Nelson, '49, in physics, Curtis Reiso, '54, assistant director, office of development, and Helen A. Strand in education and psychology; in 1955, Robert W. Jenson, '51, in Bible and philosophy, Paul H. Lionberger, '49, Bible instructor and dean of men, Martin A. Mohr, in English, and Fayetta Paulsen, psychology instructor and dean of women; in 1956, Leona Alsaker, assistant reference librarian, John W. Bruemmer, '53, assistant business manager and assistant football coach, Donald Pilgrim, in mathematics, and Elliot R. Wold in music.

Not all faculty effort is directed toward higher scholarship and professional advancement. There are also numerous attempts through small group meetings, round tables, and social events to encourage and maintain close faculty-student relationships. Once every four years the faculty "lets its hair down" and puts on a "Faculty Follies." This is a full evening's entertainment in light vein which always draws a packed house of students and others in the college family.

The admissions policy has been revised periodically to insure the selection of a student body of high quality. In general, during pioneer days colleges took students at the levels where they found them and tried to give them work suitable for their stage of development. With the spread of common-school and high-school education, colleges have found it more and more important to require of candidates for admission certain levels of attainment. In most instances a high-school diploma is no longer a sufficient qualification. At the present time Luther College requires that a student, to be admitted, rank in the upper half of his high-school class.

A similar upgrading of standards has taken place in athletics. The college requirement goes beyond the passing grade in 12 semester hours of work specified by the Iowa College Conference regulations. A student, to qualify for travel with a touring organization such as an athletic group or the bands and choirs, must attain a C average (the four passing grades are A, B, C, and D in descending order).

Scholarship honors have continued to come to Luther students. George C. Mohr, '51, and Anthony A. Preus, '58, were awarded Rhodes scholarships. Seven students have been given Woodrow Wilson national fellowships. Four have received Danforth graduate fellowships, as have two faculty members. At least five National Defense graduate fellowships have been awarded Luther graduates. Sixteen have been given Fulbright awards.

A steady effort has been made to upgrade and stimulate the faculty to greater professional competence. The college has granted full and half-pay sabbaticals and leaves; has offered encouragement in the form of leaves and grants for summer study; has stimulated research by authorizing full or partial remission of instructional duties and by making funds available for the proposed projects; has subsidized faculty members to the North Central Association Workshop at the

University of Minnesota for 18 consecutive years; and has provided funds annually to subsidize faculty attendance at meetings of professional organizations on the college and university level.

The library has continued to make progress, although it is greatly hampered by lack of space. Its needs have been placed on the priority list. The Scandinavian library of Brynjolf J. Hovde, '16, consisting of 200 volumes, was given by his widow, the former college nurse Theresa Arneson, in 1954.[12] The library now contains 115,000 volumes; 1,000 volumes of Norwegian-American newspapers which are in process of being microfilmed; a collection of more than 20,000 manuscripts; and a sizable collection of Gausta paintings. More than 290 periodicals are received regularly. Library expenditures per student were $40.70 for 1959–60.

In 1954 the curriculum was expanded and strengthened. A general education course in science and mathematics was introduced for students who were not concentrating on those subjects. At the same time the science requirement for all students was raised from 8 semester hours to 12. The former graduation requirement of one major subject and two minor ones has been changed to one major and one minor subject; but students preparing for teaching in secondary schools must take a second minor in education. Major sequences in music education, business education, and physical education were strengthened. Foreign-language requirements were reviewed and made more uniform. The teacher-training program was reviewed and strengthened and more uniform policies were formulated with regard to intercollegiate athletics. In 1958 the two-year elementary-teacher program was discontinued to conform with the changing standards which became effective in Iowa and Minnesota in 1960. In 1958 revisions were also made in requirements in social sciences and in Bible and religious education; a requirement in the humanities was added for all students; an art major and a sociology major were established; 15 courses were dropped and about 30 new ones added.[13]

In general the changes in admissions standards and in course requirements and offerings, and the emphasis on faculty competence point toward higher levels of scholarship throughout the college.

Reports by examiners for various organizations were gratifying. In April 1950 the college was accredited by the Iowa Board of Educational Examiners for offering curriculums leading to the Advanced Elementary Certificate (four-year course for teachers in elementary grades).[14]

In 1952 Algo D. Henderson of the University of Michigan made a survey of non-tax-supported colleges and universities in Iowa for the Gardner Cowles Foundation of Des Moines. In 1956 he made a second survey. His reports on Luther College were both favorable. He commented in 1956 that Luther "has the largest campus acreage, with vistas of unusual beauty and excellent topography for building sites and playing fields. . . . Next to Drake, it is now the largest of the colleges visited (full-time students). . . . The library is one of the largest and is distinctive in having a collection relating to Norwegian-American culture. . . . The student body continues to rank at the 60th percentile on the ACE national scholastic aptitude test, which makes it one of the best in Iowa. . . . The curriculum is a conservative one. . . . Some desirable experimenting is being done. . . . Salaries have been increased by 80% since 1948."[15]

In 1958 the American Association of University Women, after a survey and inspection which extended over several years, added Luther College to its approved list, thus making the 686 women then holding the bachelor of arts degree from Luther eligible for membership in the association. This recognition was very welcome to an institution which is relatively young as a coeducational body.[16] Clara J. Paulson played an important part in early steps leading to this approval and was ably seconded later by Ruth Mostrom, Fay-etta Paulsen, and Dean O. W. Qualley.

On April 13–14, 1959, inspectors from the North Central Association visited the college in accordance with its policy of reviewing accredited institutions at least once in ten years. The report "lauded the college for its adherence to the ob-jectives of the accrediting agency, the quality of instruction, and the competency of conception and execution of plans for constant evaluation and improvement."[17]

The National Council for Accreditation of Teacher Educa-tion, after its five-member committee had visited the campus in November 1959, granted full accreditation to Luther Col-lege for the preparation of elementary and secondary teach-ers with the bachelor's degree. The committee reported "evidence that there have been significant changes in the teacher education program at Luther College in the past ten years." It is estimated that half of each year's graduating class will benefit from the accreditation.[18]

The favorable comments in the reports of official investiga-tors and the recognition accorded by national associations bear their own testimony to the upgrading of students and faculty, of curriculum and instruction, which has been in progress for many years.

Women have a particular interest in the celebration of the twenty-fifth anniversary of coeducation at Luther in 1961. They have long since ceased to be regarded as curiosities on campus, have a leading role in all student activities, and are making their mark as graduates. The two first alumnae to enter the medical profession are Mrs. Joyce Everson Lee, '56, and Mrs. Arlene Kalsow Ellis, '57, both of whom were awarded M.D. degrees in June 1960, the former by the Uni-versity of Wisconsin, the latter by the State University of Iowa. Another and different achievement of alumnae was recorded in the 1952 survey of the Population Bureau of Washington, which reported that "women graduates of Luther College place first in the state of Iowa for 1942 alumnae with an average of 1.77 babies each. This ranks them sixth in the nation."[19]

The Norwegian-American Historical Museum began a new period of activity after World War II. In 1948 Mrs. Inga B. Norstog took over the position of curator and later was named director of the museum, a position she held until she resigned shortly before her death in 1960. She made many improvements in the displays of the museum and had a flair for getting publicity for it. Acquisitions of this period include a notable collection of more than 20 tapestries given by Georg Unger Vetlesen, shipbuilder, yachtsman, and founder of the Scandinavian Airlines System; articles of clothing, china, and silver, chiefly from Norway, given by the late Mr. and Mrs. Louis W. Olson; three pieces of sculpture by Sigvald Asbjørnsen and a portrait of the artist, given by his daughter, Mrs. Borghild Heitmann, of Chicago; a painting of Mrs. Samuel Mather (Ellen Knudson) by George Plasse and articles of china and clothing, given by Mrs. Frederic P. Lord of Hanover, New Hampshire.[20]

On May 21, 1961, a set of carillonic bells was dedicated. These were purchased with funds (mentioned in chapter 17) given by Alfred R. Sorenson, '02, of Minot, North Dakota. The electronic controls are in C. K. Preus Gymnasium, the amplifier on the tower of New Main. The instrument, which can be played mechanically or manually, is set to sound the Westminster chimes and strike the hours. In addition, daily programs may be played.

Student activities took on new dimensions in this period, as was natural with the large increase in enrollment. There was development not merely in size but in depth as well. The practice inaugurated in 1946 of having monthly college convocations, at which a prominent speaker appears, was continued and has brought some stimulating figures to the campus. There is a Religious Emphasis Week, usually each

331

autumn, at which outstanding church personalities give lectures and conduct informal meetings. In 1956, members of the senior class were made responsible for their attendance in classes and at chapel. Beginning the same year, faculty members, once a week, have had their own chapel services, separate from the students.

In February 1959 the Board of Regents authorized the students to form their own congregation and call a pastor. Gordon A. Selbo of the Bible department became the first minister of the newly formed group. It has a congregational organization with deacons and trustees, conducts regular Sunday services on the campus, and has its own budget for local and benevolent expenditures.

Changes were made in 1949 in the machinery of self-government with a view to placing more responsibility upon the students. Since that date various refinements have been introduced into the student-faculty relationship to promote greater understanding and co-operation. Most decisions in issues affecting student welfare are vested by faculty resolution in a committee consisting of the president, the dean of men, the dean of women, the president of the student body, and the president of the Women's Self-Governing Association.

There has been a proliferation of clubs and special groups —professional, social, political, athletic, literary, musical, and religious. More than a score are active. Each appears to have a place, and each flourishes insofar as it meets the needs of its particular group. In 1952 the canteen and bookshop were moved to Lane Court; these quarters were abandoned after the start of construction on the College Union (temporary quarters were found on the ground floor of the east wing of Valders Science Hall), but they nevertheless provided a popular spot for relaxation and fellowship for a decade.[21]

A fine arts festival, sponsored by faculty and students, has been an annual event on campus since 1957. Lecturers in the fields of literature, art, and music have appeared, musical programs and plays of unusual interest have been presented, and artists from half a dozen states have exhibited during the festival.

Since 1958 the college has sponsored a "Men for the Ministry" conference which each year attracts more than a hundred high-school juniors and seniors to the campus. Men of outstanding ability and personal appeal are the speakers, and college students play a prominent part in hosting the visitors on campus.

Since 1950, when Beth Lien, '51, was in charge, students have sponsored an annual style show. The affair, which is held in the C. K. Preus Gymnasium, has proved very popular. Closely allied to this event is the competition at the local level for the "Miss America" title. In 1956 Martha Barsness was named Miss Iowa and participated in the Miss America pageant at Atlantic City. Judging is on the basis of personality, talent, and beauty. The rewards in scholarships and other ways are considerable.

Journalistic ventures attract some of the ablest students. *College Chips,* published as a weekly newspaper, frequently enlarges its normal four-page size to six pages to give adequate space to campus events. It continues to provide the most complete coverage available of all aspects of the college community. Since its first recognition in 1930 with an all-American honor rating from the National Scholastic Press Association (later superseded by the Associated College Press), *Chips* has won more than 23 all-American awards.

New Impressions, an annual of student writing, appeared in April 1949. The first editor was William L. Lester, '49; his assistants were Thalia Wittman, '49, Ruth G. Wold, '50, and Alfred Waters, '49. The magazine, at first devoted exclusively to literary material, now frequently includes interesting sections devoted to the graphic arts.

The Pioneer appears annually. On the whole it presents

the best pictorial history of the wide range of college activities from year to year—scholastic, artistic, religious, political, athletic, dramatic, forensic, musical, and social. Many an ephemeral moment is snatched from oblivion, and for the participants the record remains a source of satisfaction and enjoyment over the years.

Speech activities have exhibited unusual vigor in this period. Campus Players have presented three and four major plays a year under the direction of Esther J. Olson and Helen A. Bodensteiner, who worked sometimes singly and sometimes in collaboration. Among plays presented were "Oedipus Rex" in 1951 in a new translation by Robert Jenson, '51, and with special music by Sigvart Hofland; Norman Williams, '51, played the lead and Beth Lien, '51, Jocasta. "A Penny for a Sparrow," a three-act religious drama by Mrs. Erling Wold (Margaret Barth) '41, was given in 1953. Among other plays may be mentioned Eliot's "Murder in the Cathedral"; Coward's "Blithe Spirit"; Ibsen's "Ghosts" and "Brand"; Anouilh's "Antigone"; Shaw's "Arms and the Man" and "Pygmalion"; Molière's "Imaginary Invalid"; Dostoevski's "The Brothers Karamazov"; and Truman Capote's "The Grass Harp." The dramatic groups have also given many shorter skits which have enlivened public programs at Homecoming and on other occasions. At the ninetieth college anniversary in 1951 a pageant, "Soli Deo Gloria," written by Norman Williams, '51, was given an effective presentation.

Forensics and oratory attract many excellent contenders. In 1959 the squad, under Harold C. Svanoe, won the debate and sweepstake trophies in the Iowa Forensic Association tournament at Dubuque. In 1960, for the second consecutive year, the group won the sweepstakes championship in the tournament at Grinnell.

The Winter Carnival is a student undertaking that has been zealously promoted for several years. But the failure of the weatherman to co-operate has been a source of difficulty on more than one occasion. Skating, skiing, and toboggaming are featured.

Musical organizations have grown in number. Well-established groups, such as the Luther College Concert Band and the Luther College Choir, have made numerous and extensive tours. The band, in addition to its short annual trips, went to New York City in 1953; to Cleveland, Ohio, to appear before the convention of the National Music Educators Association in 1955; to the east coast in 1957; and to Norway and other European countries in 1961. The choir made trips to the west coast in 1955 and 1959, and other shorter tours annually.

During this period the Women's Chorus and the Schola Cantorum were discontinued. The Chapel Choir, under Bartlett Butler's direction, came to the fore and is now one of the major musical organizations on campus. The Varsity Band, organized in 1952, has achieved an enviable place for itself and furnishes an outlet for the energies of many musicians. The college orchestra, which has attracted new talent to its ranks, has offered public concerts during the last few seasons and has assisted in larger choral works. Each year "The Messiah" is given the week before students disperse for the Christmas holidays. Three performances are sold out well in advance. For almost a score of years all soloists have been students. The Pep Band, object of affection and rhubarbs, carries on at more public functions than any other musical group on campus. Recordings of the Luther College Concert Band, the Luther College Choir, and the Luther College Chapel Choir have been made.[22]

On October 18, 1958, under the direction of Wade Raridon, Puccini's "Gianni Schicchi" was given to an enthusiastic Homecoming audience, the first rendition of a light opera on campus. Four other minor operas which have been produced are "Sunday Excursion" by Alec Wilder, "The Devil and Daniel Webster," with music by Douglas Moore, "Down in

335

the Valley," by Kurt Weill, and "The Telephone" by Gian Carlo Menotti.

The department of music, which has more teachers than any other department, is still unable to concentrate its work in a single building or complex of buildings. Some instructors give private piano and voice lessons in Sunnyside; others, however, moved to Norby Court in 1952; and the band and choir use the rehearsal room under the stage of C. K. Preus Gymnasium.[23]

A major factor in carrying on the undertakings of this department is the Dorian Society, which includes in its membership practically all students with musical interests. The first Band Music Festival was held April 25, 1950, under Dorian's auspices. The first Choral Music Festival was held in 1951. The first Piano and Organ Festival was held in 1956. Annually these events attract hundreds of high-school students, whose performance is reviewed and evaluated by members of the college music staff and by guest critics from leading musical schools and centers.

Recitals by individual student musicians and by small musical groups have become popular of late years. Recitals by music faculty members have also been welcomed by the college and the community.

Sports, which since the earliest days of the college have enlisted the ardent loyalties of students and given joy to older spectators as well, continue to flourish. *Mens sana in corpore sano*, the motto engraved in stone on C. K. Preus Gymnasium before the introduction of coeducation, appears to have won as much loyalty from women as from men. Hence there has developed a broad and constructive program of physical education, of intramural sports, and of intercollegiate competition. Of competitive sports the faculty stated in 1954: "We believe that athletic competition under proper administration is a constructive and satisfying part of student life for both participants and non-participants. We strongly resist both the tendency to abandon so desirable an element in the development of a well-rounded student and also the tendency to engage in any practice which we recognize as educationally unsound." It is not always easy to maintain this middle ground in what is oftentimes a controversial area; but in the long run there is satisfaction in doing so. One inspector wrote: "There are no athletic scholarships; yet the football record of 20 wins in 2½ years is the second highest among the smaller colleges of the Middle West." The record in other sports is also impressive, as in 1954, when the college won an Iowa Conference football championship, a basketball championship, a tie for the championship in wrestling, a championship in tennis, a championship in the Northern Division in track and field, and a tie for the championship in the Northern Division in baseball. A perusal of the college paper reveals that hardly an issue fails to record such events as hikes, picnics, nature jaunts, square dances, and intramural competitions. There is a strong emphasis on participation in all forms of wholesome physical activity.[24]

In 1949 the erection of concrete bleachers for about 700 in Nustad Field gave football and track improved facilities. Robert M. Bungum, '32, who was head football coach, 1946–50, was followed by Wallace Johnson, and the latter in turn by Edsel K. Schweizer in 1952. Under Schweizer, who first joined the staff in 1950, football has enjoyed some of its best years. The 1954 team was the only undefeated one among Iowa colleges and universities and was the first undefeated and untied team in Luther's history. The undefeated club of 1955 on Thanksgiving Day won the Corn Bowl game, 24 to 20, at Macomb, Illinois, against Western Illinois University, the only bowl game participated in by a Luther team. Luther won the Iowa Conference championship in 1957.

Schweizer's men have won "Little All-American" honors 18 times. Richard R. Rundle, '56, quarterbacked his teams to 20 consecutive victories. Brad K. Hustad, for a three-year period

337

prior to his graduation in 1959, was the leading ground gainer in the nation in the history of football. His 98-yard run for a touchdown against Central in 1958 ranks with Augie Luther's performance.

Basketball, baseball, and track continued to attract many able athletes. Luther won the Iowa Conference basketball championship in 1949 and again in 1954; the cinder-track men won three conference titles, the last by the unusual margin of one fourteenth of one point because of a freakish situation in the final relay race; and the baseball team carried off the Iowa Conference championship in 1960. In basketball Arnold Veglahn, '49, Harlan D. Wilson, '56, and William M. (Clay) Lyon, '60, set successive college scoring records. In the two-mile run Hans R. Schink set an Iowa Conference record of 9:35 in 1953. In 1960 Gregory M. Dotseth set a new school mark of 4:33 in the mile run. In 1954 Arthur R. Piper became the first Luther athlete to win a national championship when he took first place in the discus throw at the National Intercollegiate Athletic Association field and track meet at Abilene, Texas, June 4–5, 1951, with a toss of 151 feet, 11⅜ inches. Piper also holds the school shot-put record

Tennis, which has seen a revival of interest since new permanent courts were constructed in 1949, has produced, under Coach Gerhard L. Belgum, head of the Bible department, Iowa Conference championships in 1954, 1956, and 1958, and conference singles champions in 1957 and 1960. Outstanding in this period were Donald C. Paulson, '57, Keith W. Paulson, '58, Ira J. Melaas, '54, Ronald G. James, '58, Alan T. Heggen, '58, and Robert C. Speed, '60.

The turners, under William K. Janson, who has coached the sport since 1924, turned in a number of creditable performances, most of the time competing against very strong competition from the relatively few larger schools which keep up this activity. Golfers have trained annually and in 1960 tied with Wartburg for the conference title. Fencing was introduced in 1949 by Madeleine Fried, then director of women's physical education. She organized the first fencing clinic in the Midwest with more than 100 guests participating. The sport has not, however, won many adherents.

Wrestling as a formal intercollegiate sport was introduced by Wallace Johnson in 1950–51. It became popular immediately and attracted enthusiastic crowds. Under Howard Schutz the squad won the Iowa Conference championship in 1952–53; the team won a tie for the championship the following year; and under Merle Foss took the championship for a second time in 1961.[25]

Cross-country running was introduced in 1955 and has been continued since. The harriers are a determined lot, each one running his race as an individualist, yet with a strong sense of team effort in striving for victory.

Intramural sports receive a great deal of attention, the number of teams taxing the facilities available. Physical education has made several other sports popular for both men and women, such as volleyball, bowling, badminton, and archery. Hiking, skating, tobogganing, and skiing attract many participants.

These athletic programs give nearly every student an outlet for healthful physical activity. In addition, however, there are so many other opportunities for the expression of talents that few, if any students, fail to participate in extracurricular effort of some kind. Beginning with frosh testing programs and orientation, there is a plethora of student activity: frosh initiation, beanies, stunts, student programs; greased pig and greased pole contests; serenades, campus society invitations and initiations; cheerleading; Homecoming, with queen, floats, music, parade, and other ceremonies; picnics, steak fries, pizza parties, teas, and coffees; student government problems—elections, the dancing issue; political rallies in state and national election years, with active party clubs; jazz concerts, student follies, society programs, carnivals; formal parties, Valentine parties, Sadie Hawkins weekend; winter carnival, snow frolics, beard contests; fashion shows and bridal shows; Syttende Mai (Seventeenth of May) programs, with folk dancing; honor society dinners, lectures, and musical events; honor awards for excellence in scholarship, dramatics, oratory, forensics, journalism, music, and athletics; the beautiful Christmas transparencies on the picture windows in Brandt Hall; Christmas parties and Christmas carols; daily chapel, evening dorm devotions, campaigns for far-off missions and for assistance to foreign students. It is a full and often exhausting life, especially when teachers "pile it on," and examinations bring the inevitable stern accounting. Now and then these active young folks take time off to sleep.

But these are happy years. Each new activity opens up vistas and encourages development. And if the pace grows too fast, student common sense asserts itself; deceleration takes place and books get more attention; the sound, serious business of getting a college education is not lost sight of.

The upsurge in college attendance has not yet leveled off, if indeed it will in the foreseeable future. More, not less, education is forecast to meet the demands of the present swiftly developing era. Greater enrollments and increasing problems loom ahead. The requirements of a "space age" will be more, not less rigorous than those of the past. Standards will not be lowered; they are likely to be made higher. The mounting costs of education haunt administrators and parents. They are also the concern of legislators and public officials. There is no end in sight to the problems confronting education.

To meet the past needs of the college and to face up to the challenge of the future, the Ylvisaker administration has moved vigorously on all fronts. It has appealed to the constituency for increased support; has pushed a building program to provide six major buildings in thirteen years; has welcomed a greatly enlarged student body and set much higher entrance standards; has increased the number of faculty members and has upgraded the quality of their training; has made a substantial increase in the curricular offerings; and has strengthened the financial resources of the institution. The administration has given careful attention to the welfare of both students and faculty by promoting conditions conducive to good work and sound development. It has sought better accreditation and an expansion of the areas in which it can serve its supporters. Not all the problems have been taken care of. In fact, with growth, new ones arise as soon as those in hand have been disposed of. But the achievements of the Ylvisaker administration must be gratifying to all friends of the college, and they provide a sound basis for a step forward into the future.

Enlarge the place of your tent, and let the curtains of your habitation be stretched out; lengthen your cords and strengthen your stakes.
—Isaiah 54:2

20

A Last Word

This history began with a glance at the first Norwegians who made voyages to the North American continent, with a brief reference to those scattered groups who, prior to 1825, settled in the colonies which later became the United States of America, and with a bare summary of the great migratory movement which, beginning in 1825, eventually made the Upper Midwest the promised land of Norwegians seeking a home in the New World. In the Upper Midwest, and later in the far Northwest, Norwegians have left their indelible mark.

Now, after more than a hundred years, national lines among immigrants to the Midwestern area have largely disappeared; the third and fourth generations are American. New loyalties assert their claims. New streams of influence surge irresistibly forward. Luther College is carried along on this strong new tide. But the college does not, and will not, turn its back on its past.

Since the homeland of the Norwegians was a Lutheran country, the immigrants brought a Lutheran heritage with them. It was a deep-rooted heritage, one they did not slough off in the course of their migration. Their earliest records contain accounts of household devotions and of lay leaders—a testimony to the loyalty of the Norwegian immigrant to the Christian teachings he had absorbed at home. Small wonder that congregations were formed at a very early date and pastors called. But in this new land there were no pastors who could speak to the immigrants in their native tongue; the settlers had to turn to the mother country for help. They sought in Norway the trained leaders needed in their new homeland.

A number of pastors, urged on by a missionary spirit, were soon among them. Approximately half of them represented the strong lay revival which had swept Western Norway; these were on the whole nonconformist. The other half represented the established church, which insisted on a thorough university training as a prerequisite for the ministry; these were for the most part highly orthodox.

When the rapid increase in immigration completely outran the limited supply of pastors from the homeland, steps were taken to found schools in this country to train men for the pastoral office. The earliest surviving institution founded by Norwegian Lutherans is Luther College. It was the result of their first great united effort.

"In a certain sense Luther College is the lengthened shadow of the intellectual and spiritual hopes, aspirations, and ideals of the hardy Norse pioneer men and women of the Northwest. As pioneer times recede, it becomes increasingly hard for us of our time to appreciate fully with what painful toil and sacrifice, yet with what gladness, intensity of purpose, and faith in the future, Luther College was launched upon its mission. . . . No tricks of expediency, no false gods, no obscurity of purpose, no ambitions of men, no spurious standards have cut her adrift from her original moorings. . . .

"With the progress of time many ideas and many material things, and the men who wrought with them, become worn out, obsolete, and pass away. The fundamental principles underlying Luther College are as fresh, applicable, necessary, and indestructible today as ever and will so continue to the end of time."[1]

Such sentiments represent the mature appraisal of many

343

who have been the beneficiaries of the planning, toil, and sacrifice of those who founded the institution. The pioneer founders deserve no lesser praise.

This narrative is an attempt to record the story of the struggling formative years of the institution; of the subtle ways in which it gradually adjusted its European traditions to an American background; of the place it filled in the swift expansion of the church among Norwegian Lutherans; of the difficulties which beset it because of church controversies; of the internal adjustments made to bring it into harmony with the needs of the times; of the gradual changes, scarcely noticed from day to day or from year to year, which transformed its student body and its constituency from Norwegian to American; of the expansion of its curriculum and the growth of its intellectual interests and aesthetic endeavors; of the enlargement of aim and extension of opportunity which have won for it the continuing loyalty of an ever-widening constituency. In short, this history is an attempt to tell the story of Luther College in such a way that understanding of its place and mission may grow. It is not an account of an unbroken succession of triumphs. No institution is so fortunate as to warrant such a narrative. It is rather an attempt to tell the story simply and directly, as it has been unfolded by the principal actors in the drama. They, not the historian, make the record.

Through the years Luther College, a child of Norwegian Lutherans strongly attached to their church, has been loyal to its founders. For evidence of this one may point to the more than 1,100 pastors who have gone out to serve in every field of Christian endeavor. One may point to their self-sacrificing efforts on advancing frontiers, their steadfast perseverance despite poverty and discouragement, their faithful ministrations, their acts of charity and love wherever they were called to serve. One may point to the congregations they established, the churches they built, the schools they founded. These, although there is danger that they may be obscured by being taken for granted, are known to everyone. Not so easy to single out is the tremendous role played by Luther College laymen. This has not yet been fully appraised, perhaps not even fully appreciated. Teaching, medicine, law, public office, business—in all these fields Luther laymen are active in large numbers.

Luther graduates are found predominantly in the professions of public service. According to one survey, the fields in which Luther College has contributed most to national leadership are education, the clergy, and business, in that order. In education Luther's percentage is 150 per cent of the average; in the ministry it is 350 per cent; in business it is approximately equal. Another area in which Luther College graduates exceed the average is the Foreign Service. Three of the four fields named are what may be termed the "dedicated professions."[2]

The testimony of outsiders is significant. It is definitely weighted in tribute to the solid worth, the friendly spirit, the willingness to help, the ready response from the rank and file of Luther men and women when important values are at stake. Those who have entered the ministry and those who have gone into other professions have stood together for the spiritual values that make a society strong. It is not a loyalty that is worn on one's sleeve. But men have come to recognize its genuineness and to know that they can rely on it.

One well-known, lovable layman of low-church leanings made this statement: "There is something solid and substantial about Luther College which commands respect. From the very beginning it has stood for orthodoxy, scholarship, and culture. Orthodoxy has become more tolerant, scholarship broader, culture more democratic."[3]

It is not that there have been no shortcomings during the century; far from that. But mistakes fade as vision is centered on positive accomplishment. On the latter, in the last analysis, the institution will be judged; on this it can continue to appeal to an ever-widening community of friends.

One of the recurring themes of commencement and Homecoming speakers is that Luther College has not changed, that she stands where she has always stood, and that she must never change. Any reader of this history will see that this point of view cannot be substantiated. It is a law of life that there must be change. No institution will survive that does not constantly adjust to the shifting world about it. Such adjustments are feared by some. They often involve fairly fundamental concepts. But life cannot be ignored. Wise men are not dismayed because the world has been transformed, because old concepts must be abandoned, because life is not static but dynamic. They chart their course in full acceptance of the facts; and they move forward, relying on the soundness of their guiding principles.

Nevertheless, the theme of "no change" has its place; one is still able to subscribe to the idea if it may be interpreted in the fresh atmosphere of faith. The motto of the college, *Soli Deo Gloria,* engraved on the entrance stone of New Main, still fills the hearts of men and women who go in and out of the college portals. Christian idealism is still the touchstone to transmute all baser metals into those which will stand the test of time. In this sense the college is anchored on the rock; no changes in the superstructure will shake its foundations.

Luther College has passed through infancy, boyhood, and youth. It now stands in its young manhood, ready for the tasks ahead. Those who know the college best will understand it best and love it most. This study, whatever its imperfections, seeks to contribute to knowledge, understanding, and love.

APPENDIX

Appendix

STATEMENT OF OBJECTIVE

The objective of Luther College is a liberal and thorough Christian education of men and women. In the attainment of this objective the college is mindful of responsibility to the individual student, its supporting church, and society.

Luther College aims to serve the individual student by providing an integrated program of spiritual, mental, and physical development; to serve the American Lutheran Church by helping to supply consecrated and enlightened leadership, both ordained and lay, in every field of Christian service; to serve society by fostering Christian ideals of patriotism and world citizenship.

In carrying out its objective the college aims to help the student to:

Grow in grace and the knowledge of Jesus Christ; appreciate the place of the Bible in education and in life; establish habits of conduct based on Christian ethical principles; cultivate the virtues requisite to Christian stewardship; be loyal to the highest ideals of achievement.

Take an active part in the building of the church; respond to the call for men and women to devote full time to its service; worship regularly; increase in knowledge of all that honors the Christian message.

349

Appendix

Arrive at a mature comprehension and application of evangelical Lutheran doctrine and a tolerant understanding of the various denominations within the Christian church.

Develop his intellectual curiosity, habits of reflection, methods of reasoning, and criteria for judgment.

Increase his knowledge of words and of other symbols which men use in communicating with each other, interpret them correctly and use them effectively; broaden his acquaintance with the records of man, particularly with the world of books.

Appreciate literature, music and other arts; employ his talents in creative activity.

Understand the phenomena of the physical world and the influence of science on the development of thought and institutions; apply the methods of scientific study to the solution of concrete problems.

Gain the historical perspective and ethical insight needed to assist in the solution of social problems; share in the responsibilities and privileges of citizenship; recognize the dignity of man and the interdependence of peoples; foster international understanding, justice, and peace.

Acquire the knowledge and habits necessary during work and play to physical and mental health.

Understand the significance of the family and prepare for successful family life.

Enter into friendly personal relations with teachers and fellow students; achieve a well-balanced social and emotional adjustment to the world in which he lives.

Understand the place of work in the life of man; discover his own vocational interests and aptitudes; develop scholarly aims and ambitions; exalt every honorable vocation as a ministry under God.

TO LUTHER

Air: There's Music in the Air.

To Luther let us sing
　A joyous song of love and cheer.
Let our voices loudly ring
　In praise of Alma Mater dear!

CHORUS

May our thoughts to thee oft turn
　When we're absent far away.
May we then sincerely yearn
　To return to thee some day.

Thy mem'ry dear we'll cherish
　And ever recollect thy care;
That thy fame may never perish
　Is the burden of our prayer.

Our hearts are light and free
　Whene'er we to old Luther sing,
May she now and ever be
　Faithful to our Heavenly King!

GUSTAV B. (GEE BEE) WOLLAN, '97

THE FIELD SONG

Our boys go in to fight and win,
The spirit of old drives them on.
　With a "Pri Sec" shout,
　We all come out
To yell for Luther who wins today.
　And Luther's team is strong;
　They fight as long
As victory hangs in doubt.
　　Rah! Rah!
　Opponents fall
　'Fore Luther's wall.
All hail to our college dear!

Words by ARTHUR J. TOLO, '18
Music by NORVALD G. MAAKESTAD, '21

351

Appendix

EARLY RULES AND REGULATIONS

(The following rules, in Norwegian, were in effect from 1861 to February, 1878)

I. The first bell rings at 5:30 A.M., at which time all students rise, dress, make their beds, and proceed to their study rooms, where they immediately begin studying their lessons.

II. The bell rings again at 6:30; then all students go to the dining hall where, after morning devotions, breakfast is served. After breakfast all return to their study rooms and study till 8:30.

III. 8:30–9:00: Recess, during which those charged with that duty tidy up the rooms.

IV. 8:30–12:00. Classes and study periods; 15-minute recess about 11:00.

V. 12:00 noon. The dinner bell rings. Recess till 2:00.

VI. 2:00–5:00. Classes and study hours; 15-minute recess about 4:00. There are no study hours, however, from 4:00 to 5:00 on Wednesday and all of Saturday afternoon. Nevertheless, those who desire to do so may study, but otherwise no studying is permitted during recess periods. In bad weather, however, the hours from 1:00 to 2:00 and from 6:00 to 7:00 may be used for leisure reading.

VII. 5:00–7:00 P.M. Recess; supper at 6:00.

VIII. 7:00–8:30. Study hour followed by evening devotions. After devotions the older boys are allowed to stay up till 10:00 P.M., during which time they may either study their lessons, read such books as are permitted at the school, or write letters. But everyone must be in bed by 10:00 P.M.

IX. Sunday morning the bell is rung at 6:30. Everyone gathers for devotions at 7:00 A.M.

X. No one is permitted to study during recess (except Wednesday afternoon from 4:00 to 5:00 and all of Saturday afternoon—See VI). On the contrary, students, as far as possible, shall get some exercise outdoors.

XI. There must be silence in the rooms during study periods. No one may ask for help with his lessons until he has first diligently tried to help himself; if he does ask a question, he must

352

do so very quietly so that the other students are not disturbed. During study periods everyone is to study and no one is to occupy himself with anything else. Should anyone have learned his lessons for the next day before the study period is over, he must either continue studying for the following days or review.

XII. No one is to take his place at table before the table prayer has been read by the student whom the president has appointed. When the meal is over, all stand, and the same student returns thanks.

XIII. During leisure hours students may not only amuse themselves on the campus but are also allowed to hike a mile or two toward the country. Unless they have had permission from the president, however, they are not allowed to go farther than the river in the direction of town.

XIV. In each classroom the teacher, if he finds it necessary, may appoint one or more monitors to make certain that the students are orderly at all times. Moreover, it is the duty of all students to supervise themselves, to admonish and reprimand one another and, if this does not help, to notify the teacher of all breaches of good order.

XV. In each classroom the students take turns weekly as janitor. As such, they must clean and air out the room and carry up water and firewood.

XVI. In the bedrooms the students also take turns in cleaning. But no one must be janitor in his classroom and bedroom at the same time. If by following the prearranged schedule this should happen, an exchange must be made with some one who is to be janitor the following week.

XVII. The students also take turns in keeping the washrooms clean, with the same understanding as in the preceding paragraph if perchance the same student should be assigned as janitor in two places at the same time.

XVIII. In general the duty rests on each student to keep his room clean and everything in order. His bed must be made, his books must be in good order on the bookshelves, when they are not in use; he must not splash and make a mess when washing and must always pour out the dirty water when he is through.

XIX. All books and printed matter must be kept on the bookshelves where they can be inspected at all times by the teachers. No book or periodical may be brought into the school building without the permission of the class instructor. In general political newspapers are not allowed.

XX. Every student should be willing to help his teachers with various jobs in the house, yard, garden, etc., and also to help the college servants when they ask him to lend a hand.

XXI. Each student who is strong enough must spend at least one hour a week sawing wood for the school or the teachers. More specific rules for regulating this work will be given by the president of the school as he sees fit.

XXII. No one under 18 is permitted to use tobacco. Neither is one permitted to smoke in the building or on the city streets.

XXIII. When weather does not permit the students to spend their recess out of doors, they are to avail themselves of the hallways for walking back and forth; but noise, running about, or carrying on other strenuous exercise is never allowed either in the halls or rooms.

XXIV. Students must always go up or down stairs quietly, especially when many are going up or down at one time. There must be no sliding on the bannisters. The small south stairway is not for the use of students.

XXV. Ashes from the stoves must be emptied in the cans placed in the halls for that purpose and must never be emptied in the trash box or any other wooden box. If the ashcans and trash boxes are full, they must be carried outside and emptied.

XXVI. Rubbish must not be left in the hallways or in vacant rooms, nor in general must anything be left that does not belong there.

XXVII. If students desire to organize a society or anything similar, they must first request the president's permission and apprise him of the purpose and plans of their undertaking.

XXVIII. No one is to go to the top story or the tower unless he has work to do there. At no time is anyone to go out onto the roof.

XXIX. All doors are to be closed quietly, never slammed or closed violently, and are not to be left open. The outside cellar doors, especially, must be closed very carefully so that the glass panes will not be broken. On first floor the students should generally use only the west door.

ATTENDANCE
1921–1932

(Complete figures on attendance, 1861 to 1921, are found in *Luther College through Sixty Years.*)

	COLLEGE	PREPARATORY DEPARTMENT	UNDUPLICATED TOTAL
1921–22	185	87	272
1922–23	223	84	307
1923–24	282	65	347
1924–25	313	46	359
1925–26	307	38	345
1926–27	346	28	374
1927–28	360	24	384
1928–29	353		353
1929–30	344		344
1930–31	345		345
1931–32	283		283

1932–61

	MEN	WOMEN	TOTAL REGULAR YEAR	SUMMER SESSION AND EXTENSION	UNDUPLICATED TOTAL
1932–33	285	24	309		309*
1933–34	300	60	360	39	393*
1934–35	313	50	363	26	383*
1935–36	341	67	408		408*
1936–37	330	103	433		433
1937–38	327	116	443		443
1938–39	348	142	490		490
1939–40	320	123	443		443
1940–41	333	161	494		494

*Includes Decorah College for Women.

1941–42	319	146	465	56	511
1942–43	297	138	435	127	516
1943–44	80	166	246	133	347
1944–45	83	218	301	167	419
1945–46	217	201	418	169	539
1946–47	494	241	735	263	869
1947–48	614	273	887	381	1081
1948–49	669	241	910	385	1099
1949–50	641	249	890	496	1197
1950–51	556	275	831	438	1132
1951–52	448	280	728	419	1035
1952–53	445	286	731	425	1080
1953–54	508	360	868	371	1156
1954-55	576	422	998	370	1242
1955–56	632	460	1092	317	1293
1956–57	654	462	1116	353	1346
1957–58	706	468	1174	325	1395
1958–59	735	522	1257	387	1523
1959–60	737	548	1285	334	1517
1960–61	727	559	1286	321	1482

BOARD OF TRUSTEES 1921–58
BOARD OF REGENTS 1958–61

(The list for 1861–1921 is found in *Luther College through Sixty Years.*)

1. T. Stabo, 1914–44. Emeritus, 1946.
2. A. H. Dahl, 1914–23.
3. Oscar L. Olson, 1917–32.
4. L. S. Swenson, 1920–22.
5. O. E. Schmidt, 1920–24.
6. J. C. M. Hanson, 1920–23.
7. J. A. O. Preus, 1921–32.
8. I. A. Thorson, 1922–23.
9. O. A. Tingelstad, 1923–28.
10. S. J. N. Ylvisaker, 1923–32.
11. Gilbert Knudson, 1923–32.

12. Joseph M. Green, 1923–30.
13. J. A. Berg, 1925–26.
14. Sigurd Gunderson, 1926–30.
15. Z. J. Ordal, 1930–38.
16. B. K. Savre, 1930–38.
17. Emil Estenson, 1932–42.
18. N. Nustad, 1932–48.
19. S. T. Sorenson, 1932–40.
20. O. J. H. Preus, 1932–48.
21. George W. Johnson, 1936–48.
22. T. A. Hoff, 1936–48.
23. Carl Estrem, 1936–42.
24. M. O. Grangaard, 1936–40.
25. J. O. Tweten, 1938–44.
26. A. E. Hanson, 1938–44.
27. Laurence R. Lunden, 1940–52.
28. S. T. Severtson, 1940–46.
29. N. M. Ylvisaker, 1942–47.
30. O. G. Fjeldstad, 1942–45.
31. Einar R. Larson, 1944–56.
32. H. P. Skoglund, 1944–56.
33. Roy O. Storvick, 1944–56.
34. C. H. Megorden, 1945–60.
35. A. O. Storvick, 1946–52.
36. Frank R. Miller, 1948–
37. T. P. Solem, 1948–54.
38. Erling Johnson, 1948–60.
39. Olin Lokken, 1948–54.
40. J. W. Ylvisaker, 1948–
41. Alf M. Kraabel, 1952–
42. Henry A. Olson, 1952–
43. Roy A. Harrisville, 1954–
44. Arthur J. Smaby, 1954–59.
45. Elizabeth Branstad, 1956–58.
46. A. Reuben Gornitzka, 1956–60.
47. Martin Jenson, 1956–
48. Anita P. Nelson, 1958–
49. C. Norman Brunsdale, 1958–

Appendix

50. Hazel I. Halvorson, 1959–
51. Lavern R. Hanson, 1958–
52. Wallace A. Moen, 1958–
53. Roy E. Carlson, 1958–
54. John Dieseth, 1958–
55. Reuben I. Jacobsen, 1958–
56. George Ulvilden, 1958–
57. V. T. Jordahl, 1958–
58. Karl M. Torgerson, 1958–61.
59. John W. Torrison, 1958–
60. P. O. Brunsvold, 1960–
61. M. H. Trytten, 1960–

FACULTY 1921–61

(Special instructors as well as regular faculty members are included. The letter A after a name indicates that the individual was a student assistant. For a list of faculty members from 1861 to 1921 see *Luther College through Sixty Years.*)

Ahl, Hildegard D., 1939–40.
Allison, Mary Clara, 1952–56.
Almlie, Magdalene M. (Mrs. Christian Bruland), 1948–52.
Alsaker, Leona, 1956–
Ambuel, J. Philip, 1941–42. A
Ambuel, Louise, 1957–
Amland, Harold J., 1925–28.
Ammondson, Clayton J., 1943–44. A
Amundson, Gerald A., 1947–48. A
Andersen, Esther (Mrs. Peter Peterson), 1947–48. A
Andersen, Gordon W., 1951–52. A
Anderson, Carrie M., 1937–41.
Anderson, Gerald S., 1949–52. A
Anderson, Henry O., 1940–41.
Anderson, Roger W., 1958–
Asmus, Dorley M. (Mrs. L. Reuben Lerud), 1947–50.
Bahe, Barbara, 1947–
Bahr, Vernon H., 1951–52; 1955–57.

Bale, John C., 1953–
Barns, Shirley, 1958–59.
Barth, Frank R., 1942–43; 1946–53.
Beaver, Lyle B., 1946–49.
Belgum, Gerhard L., 1948–61.
Benson, Gordon M., 1948.
Berg, Warren G., 1948–
Bergan, Kenneth N., 1938–39.
Berger, Kenneth L., 1941–57.
Berger, Marion, 1942–44.
Bergland, Allan, 1959–60.
Bergstrom, Richard, 1944–46.
Bernsten, Maxine, 1959–61.
Berven, Luther H., 1934–35. A
Bestul, Valborg E., 1937–39.
Birkestrand, Harold O. S., 1928–31.
Bjerkness, Odell, 1959–
Bjorkquist, James, 1960–
Bodensteiner, Helen Adams, 1946–
Borge, Paul D., 1947–49.
Braaten, Lila M., 1957–58.
Bratlie, Otto M., 1938–39.
Brattland, Shirley, 1960–
Bredeson, Lewis B., 1934–35.
Breiland, John, 1935–38.
Brekke, Arne, 1954–58.
Bremness, Gladys Glesne, 1946–48.
Brendsel, Thomas A., 1957–59.
Brudos, Alan R., 1958–59.
Bruemmer, John, 1956–
Bunge, Wilfred F., summer 1953.
Bungum, Robert M., 1946–50.
Burstrom, Warren F., 1949–50.
Butler, Bartlett R., 1954–
Cappon, Franklin C., 1923–25.
Carey, DeVere, 1950–51. A
Carlson, Ruth M. (Mrs. Frank Summerside), 1952–56.
Christiansen, Karl, 1958–

Appendix

Crown, Keith A., 1940–41.
Dahlberg, Lida, 1949–50.
Daniels, Perry C., 1958–
Daniels, Phyllis McFarland, 1959–60.
Davidson, Arthur O., 1941–48 (war service 1942–46); 1954–61.
Dennis, John R., 1940–43; 1947–48.
Docken, Adrian M., 1937–38; 1942–
Docken, Orene Madson, 1936–38; 1950–60.
Dorrum, Ingebret, 1923–52.
Doseff, Ivan, 1921–23.
Eitel, Eleonore, 1960–61.
Eittreim, Knute O., 1918–39.
Eittreim, Oliver M., 1920–24; 1928–58.
Eitzen, Leroy V., 1950–53.
Eitzen, Leslie Mong, 1950–53.
Ekern, Sallie R., 1958–61.
Eliason, Norman E., 1928–29.
Ellefson, C. Ashley, 1955–57.
Ellefson, Elmer O., 1954.
Ellingsen, Daniel J., 1924–28.
Ellingson, Clifford T., summer 1953.
Ellingson, Herman E., 1924–47 (war service 1942–46).
Elvestrom, Victor A., 1923–28.
Engelstad, Paul, 1954.
Erdman, Lowell P., 1955–59.
Evanson, Chellis N., 1919–
Fadness, N. Lewis, 1939–
Fadness, Signe Adolphson, 1942–55; 1957–59.
Fagerhaugh, Kenneth H., 1936–38.
Field, Laurence N., 1941–44.
Finanger, Kenton E., 1957–
Fiskerbeck, Victor A., 1927–28.
Fjelstad, Ruth N., 1954–
Fletty, Valborg, 1948–53.
Forde, Betty Mae (Mrs. John Baccarini), 1944–47.
Forde, Janet Jerdee, 1949–50.
Foss, Merle, 1960–
Frank, Emily, 1935–51.

Fried, Madeline M. (Mrs. William Hurster), 1949–53.

Frings, Hubert W., 1939–40.

Fritz, Luther E., 1942.

Frost, Gerhard E., 1944–57.

Gaalswyk, Arie, 1947.

Gamelin, Francis E., 1938–40.

Gattiker, Godfrey, 1958–60.

Gattiker, Irene, 1958–60.

Gedstad, Vilera, 1948–49.

Getchell, Robert, 1958–

Giere, Frederic A., 1947–49; 1953–

Gimbel, John, 1950–51; 1953–59.

Gjerdrum, Donald W., 1952–56.

Gjerset, Knut, 1902–16; 1917–36.

Glambek, Finn, 1951–53.

Goddard, Lorene J., 1940–41.

Goellner, Karl E., 1946–48.

Goulson, Hilton, 1951–52. A

Graber, Paul A., 1946–47.

Grant, Lane, 1959–60.

Grimes, Marjorie Ann (Mrs. Robert Broward), 1946–47; 1948–50.

Grue, Charlotte B. Schilling, 1944–

Gullickson, Gerald L., 1956–59.

Gulsvig, Elmo L., 1938–42.

Gundersen, Knut T., 1959–

Gunsolus, Victoria L., summer 1952.

Haatvedt, Rolfe A., 1936–42; 1946–50.

Haeussler, Helmut H., 1953–55.

Haines, Eleanor Dorrum, 1960–

Halbakken, David S., 1946–47.

Hallen, Lois J. (Mrs. C. V. Thomas), 1949–50.

Halverson, Paul M., 1932–33. A

Halvorson, Jeanne (Mrs. Jack V. Peters), 1946–48.

Halvorson, Ruth E. (Mrs. Wayne Gunness), 1949–50.

Hamre, James S., 1959–60.

Hansen, Clifford H., 1942–43.

Hansen, Erling M., 1959–61.

Hanson, Karl, 1928–48.

Appendix

Hanson, Sarah V. (Mrs. Lawrence Bremmer), 1940–43.
Harvey, Margaret (Mrs. Oscar Aspenson), 1957–59.
Hass, Mrs. Arthur, 1948–49.
Hasvold, Paul M., 1957–59.
Helms, John, 1957–60.
Hendrickson, Edwin H., 1924–27.
Hendrickson, Kermit T., 1947–48; 1950–
Hennings, Ralph Waldo, 1942–43.
Henriksen, George C., Jr., 1924–25.
Hervig, Richard B., 1942.
Herwig, Lloyd O., 1942–43.
Highby, Leo I., 1927–30.
Highby, Paul R., 1939–40.
Hill, Ordelle, 1960–61.
Hiller, Philip C., 1951.
Hjelle, Albert E., 1958–
Hjelle, Lester C., 1938–39.
Hobart, Richard M., 1949–52.
Hodges, Lucianne (Mrs. George P. Elmore), 1945–46.
Hoelty-Nickel, Theodore C. F. W., 1928–41.
Hof, Lawrence, 1938–39.
Hoff, Harold E., 1935–36.
Hoff, Thoralf A., 1927–30.
Hofland, Sigvart A., 1942–56.
Holey, James M., 1949–51.
Hommen, Donovan L., 1958–59.
Hoslett, Martha Sundby, 1939–44; summer 1953, 1955.
Hoslett, Sherman A., 1930 (one semester); 1932–
Hovde, Brynjolf J., 1916–17; 1919–23.
Hovde, Oivind M., 1935–38; 1944–
Hoyt, Clara M., 1936–60.
Hustad, Alice M., 1947–48.
Hustvedt, Lloyd M., 1951–55.
Iversen, Iver, 1960–
Iverson, Hazel L. (Mrs. John V. Halvorson), 1942–46.
Iverson, Lloyd A., 1946–47.
Iverson, Ralph G., 1949–51.
Jacobsen, Anna, 1943–44.

Jacobsen, Glenn D., 1959–61.
Jacobsen, Karl T., 1904–05; 1920–49.
Jacobsen, Robert S., 1939–
Jacobson, Angeline, 1951–
Janson, William K., 1924–
Jensen, Dinniemaud V., 1944–46.
Jensen, Olive M. (Mrs. E. J. Nordby), 1938–39.
Jenson, Robert W., 1955–
Jerdee, Joseph C., 1958–59.
Johnson, Clare I., 1945–47.
Johnson, David C., 1957–
Johnson, Einar O., 1954–58.
Johnson, Georgiann, 1947–48. A
Johnson, Guy C., 1959–
Johnson, Miles B., 1955–57.
Johnson, Theodore, 1949–50. A
Johnson, W. C., 1925–28.
Johnson, Wallace T., 1950–52.
Johnston, Gladys C., 1954–57.
Johnston, Stanley L., 1948–55.
Jonas, Abner, 1960–
Jordahl, Leigh D., 1960–61.
Jordahl, Olaf M., 1927–31.
Josephson, Robert M., 1947–48.
Julsrud, Ingrid, 1957–
Kaasa, Harris E., 1953–55.
Kjorlaug, Eunice, 1946; 1947–48; 1951–52; 1959–
Kloster, Clair G., 1947–
Knepple, Beth Evanson, 1956–57 (first semester).
Knispel, John, 1954–57.
Knudson, George E., 1946–
Knudtson, Glenn W., 1935–36.
Kohn, James D., 1957–61.
Kolstad, Gertrude M. (Mrs. O. Rolf Olson), 1957–60.
Kruse, Elouise, 1960–61.
Kuhl, Paul, 1940–41.
Kvammen, Alfred G., 1949–50.
Kyler, Rudolph H., 1939–46.

Langhammer, Franz, 1955–56.
Larsen, Marie Weltzin, 1941–42.
Larson, Donald J., 1937–48.
Lee, Knute W. D., 1953–61.
Lee, Milo E., 1933–34.
Lee, Norlan J., 1953–54.
Legvold, Sam, 1937–39.
Leidal, Floyd L., 1936–37.
Leland, Earl J., 1959–
Leraas, Harold J., 1942–43.
Lerud, L. Reuben, 1940–42; 1946; 1947–50.
Lewison, Nora V. (Mrs. Thomas H. Major), 1936–38.
Lien, Jacob A. O., 1942–43.
Lionberger, Justine Holum, 1950–51 (one semester).
Lionberger, Paul H., 1955–
Locks, Joyce O., 1955–57.
Lomen, Oscar M., 1926–31.
Malmin, Olaf G., 1925–26.
Mathees, Arnold J., 1948–51.
Matthews, James T., 1953–55.
Mattson, Martha M., 1933–34.
Melaas, Ira J., 1960.
Mickelson, Harlan, 1955–56.
Mikkelsen, Anna S., 1935–36.
Miller, Emil C., 1939–(war service 1942–46).
Miller, Frank R., 1941–43.
Minge, Margaret, 1940–42.
Moe, Leonard A., 1920–37.
Moe, Lois (Mrs. Robert S. Jacobsen), 1943–46; 1951–53.
Mohr, George, 1950–51. A
Mohr, Martin A., 1955–
Monhardt, Maurice, 1959–
Monson, Laura M. (Mrs. Martin K. Elstad), 1935–36. A
Monson, Paul H., 1952–56.
Morris, Eloise M., 1938–39.
Mostrom, Ruth, 1950–
Naeseth, Erling O., 1948–
Nasby, Helge, 1938–39.

Nelson, Allen E., 1927–28.

Nelson, Anita Pleuss, 1945–46.

Nelson, David T., 1921–

Nelson, David Torrison, 1953–

Nelson, Marjorie Moore, 1953–56.

Nelson, Wendell A., 1952–56.

Nesheim, Obed J., 1957–61.

Nilssen, Morton O., 1935–41.

Noble, Weston, 1946; 1948–

Norby, Charles H., 1931–32.

Nordsieck, Henriette (Mrs. Stuart Pierson), 1947–50.

Norlie, Olaf Morgan, 1919–28; 1932–41.

Norstog, Inga Bredesen, 1947–60.

Norstog, Knut J., 1949–51.

Nybakken, Oscar E., 1930–31.

Ofstedal, E. Dorothea (Mrs. John Helms), 1949–50; 1957–59.

Oien, Arthur, 1960–

Olsen, A. Loran, 1955–57.

Olsen, Jervis D., 1950–51. A

Olsen, Theodore L., 1960–61.

Olson, Doris M. (Mrs. A. Lee Warbington), 1948–51.

Olson, Esther J., 1956–60.

Olson, Louise N. (Mrs. Virgil Butts), 1949–51.

Olson, O. Rolf, 1958–60.

Olson, Oscar L., 1901–52.

Olson, Roger M., 1952–56.

Opsahl, Alert M., 1924–25.

Opstad, Iver A., 1953–58.

Orton, Lambert S., 1941–42.

Orwoll, Harold S., 1940–42.

Osterkamp, Daryl, 1954–56.

Otte, Carl N. H., 1951.

Owen, Christine N., 1936–38.

Owen, Ernest M., 1951; summers 1951–55.

Owen, Marguerite H., 1950–52.

Paulsen, Fayetta, 1955–

Paulson, Clara J., 1939–

Pederson, Pernie C., 1947–48.

Peterson, Agnes, 1950–52.

Peterson, Enoch E., 1912–21.

Peterson, Francis E., 1921–24; 1952–53; summer 1955.

Peterson, Hamlet E., 1922–

Peterson, Helen L. (Mrs. Jack Hustad), summer 1953.

Peterson, Henry C., 1926.

Peterson, Vivian A., 1952–60.

Pfabel, Wolfgang, Jr., 1957–58.

Phelps, Betty Lou (Mrs. Paul H. Monson), 1949–50 A; 1952–53.

Pilgrim, Donald, 1956–

Posson, Shirley A. M., 1947–48; 1960–61.

Preus, Nelson F., first semester 1950; 1951.

Preus, Ove J. H., 1932–48.

Preus, Ove J. H., Jr., 1951–52.

Qualley, Orlando W., 1918–

Radzin, Hilda, 1957–58.

Ramsland, Dorothy E. A., 1944–45.

Raridon, Wade, 1957–59.

Rasdal, Sverre, 1948–51.

Ravndal, Eric, 1925–26.

Rebassoo, Herbert J., 1949–

Reque, David, 1956–57.

Reque, Peter R., 1957–59.

Reque, Sigurd S., 1906–08; 1919–52.

Ritland, Lloyd O., 1931–32.

Rober, Norlin E., 1959–

Roberts, Mary Margaret, 1949–50.

Rod, Donald O., 1940–43.

Rod, Herbert L., 1958–

Roe, K. S. N., 1929–31.

Rohne, J. Magnus, 1923–32.

Rollefson, Arthur M., 1936–39.

Rollins, Dean B., 1933–34.

Rølvaag, Ella V. (Mrs. Thorliff Tweit), 1941–43.

Romig, Mary R., 1939–40.

Ronning, Sharon F. (Mrs. Leonard S. Smith), 1957–60.

Rood, Phyllis (Mrs. Theodore Cleys), 1947–48. A

Rosholt, Karlton J., 1947–48. A

Rosholt, Robert L., 1957–59.
Rossing, Thomas D., 1949–50. A
Rousseau, Eugene E., 1956–60.
Rovelstad, Adolph M., 1907–27.
Rowe, Helene (Mrs. Edward J. Furst), 1950–51.
Rude, Leslie G., 1953–58; 1960–
Rugland, Sigvart L., 1927–28.
Ruid, Lloyd W., 1940–42.
Running, Orville M., 1946–
Sagen, Oswald K., 1928–31.
Sagvold, Enid Erickson, 1954.
Salaverria, Helena C., 1959-61.
Sauer, Theodore C., 1948–49
Scarvie, Walter B., 1925–27.
Schilling, Elsa E., 1945–46.
Schroder, Fridtjof C. M., 1941–43.
Schroeder, Paul C., 1949–50.
Schutz, Howard A., 1952–54.
Schweizer, Edsel K., 1950–
Schweizer, Helen Pearson, 1950–54.
Schwidder, Ernest C., 1956–57.
Selbo, Gordon A., 1957–
Selbo, Warren K., 1951–52. A
Selness, Martha E. (Mrs. Paul F. Henzler), 1939–42.
Sheel, Herman W., 1889–1935.
Sihler, William, 1890–1940.
Simonson, Laura, 1946–50.
Skarshaug, Emry C., 1934–36.
Skirbeck, Thora, 1956–58.
Skogsmark, Helen A., 1946–51.
Skramstad, Marie O., 1958–
Smale, Charlotte, 1944–47.
Smith, Leonard S., 1958–60.
Snow, Ruth Gordon (Mrs. Clarence E. Williams), 1939–41
Sovik, Gertrude S., 1941–43.
Sparhawk, Ruth M., 1953–55.
Sperati, Carlo A., 1905–45.
Stansberry, Lucile (Mrs. Robert L. Rosholt), 1955–59.

Appendix

Stavig, David, 1960–

Stearns, Gretchen Woldt, 1949–51.

Steele, Evelyn, 1940–41.

Steen, Margery Mayer, 1947–48.

Steen, Sigvart J., 1942–48 (war service 1942–46).

Steinau, Stanley, summers 1952, 1953.

Stephenson, Audrey (Mrs. Lowell P. Erdman), 1955–57.

Stokke, Myrtle G. (Mrs. Walter W. Korsrud), 1946–49.

Strand, Helen A., 1954–

Strandjord, Nels M., 1942–43.

Strom, Carl W., 1919–23; 1927–35.

Strunk, William L., 1927–39.

Struxness, David F., 1945–46.

Struxness, Erling B., 1940–42.

Sundby, Gustave A., 1945–46.

Svanoe, Harold C., 1957–

Swansen, H. Fred, 1926–31.

Talle, Henry O., 1921–38.

Tatley, Helen (Mrs. Robert Barber), 1955–57.

Tawzer, Hannah Stevenson, 1958–

Thayer, Jean M., 1935–36. A

Thomas, Shirley Mortenson, 1950–53.

Thompson, Ted R., 1951–52

Thompson, Vera Bucknell (Mrs. O. W. Harris), 1942–48.

Thomte, Reidar, 1946–48.

Thorpe, Eldrid M. (Mrs. Cyrus Running), 1936–38.

Tingelstad, Edvin, 1939–40.

Tingelstad, Gertrude B., 1942–43.

Tingelstad, Oscar A., 1909–28; 1944–50.

Tinglum, Ottar, 1928–32.

Tolo, Arthur J., 1958–61.

Tolo, Harold M., 1929–30.

Tonning, Ole, 1926.

Torgrim, Marie Hjelle, 1951–58.

Torrison, Isaac B., 1902–29.

Trytten, Merriam H., 1917–18; 1919–20; 1921–24.

Ulvilden, Kathryn M. (Mrs. Norman W. Moen), 1946–57.

Vischer, Christine D. (Mrs. Gerald L. Gullickson), 1956–59.

Wagner, Beulah O., 1934–35.
Waldeland, Conrad R., 1933–42.
Waller, Martinus C., 1923–25.
Walstad, Orlow M., 1945–46.
Wanberg, Larrie D., 1959–
Westly, Malcolm K., 1959–
Wiener, Elaine, 1957–59.
Wik, Esther I., 1953–58.
Winterlin, DeWayne E., 1959–
Wold, Elliot R., 1956–
Wold, Erling H., 1950–53.
Wold, Margaret Barth, 1951.
Wollan, Pernille L., 1955–
Woolery, Arlo D., 1942–43.
Wulfsberg, Einar, 1932–33.
Ylvisaker, J. Wilhelm, 1948–
Youngberg, Karin, 1960–61.
Zaiser, Carol Freshwater, 1961–
Zastrow, Joyce R., 1953–56.

ADMINISTRATIVE OFFICIALS 1921–61

President
    Oscar L. Olson, 1921–32.
    Ove J. H. Preus, 1932–48.
    J. Wilhelm Ylvisaker, 1948–
Vice president
    Orlando W. Qualley, 1936–
    Arthur O. Davidson (in charge of development), 1954–61.
Dean of the College
    Orlando W. Qualley, 1946–
Librarian
    Karl T. Jacobsen, 1920–49.
    Oivind M. Hovde, 1949–
Registrar
    Oscar A. Tingelstad, 1920–27.
    Carl W. Strom, 1927–30; 1931–35.

Oscar M. Lomen, 1929–31.

Bernice G. Forde, 1935–36.

Rolfe A. Haatvedt, 1936–42; 1946–50.

Orlando W. Qualley, 1942–46; 1950–56.

Ruth Mostrom, 1956–

College Pastor

Isaac B. Torrison, 1901–29.

Ole Glesne, 1917–32.

Thoralf A. Hoff, 1929–32.

Laurence N. Field, 1941–44.

Gerhard E. Frost, 1943–57.

Gordon A. Selbo, 1957–

College Physician

Trond Stabo, 1906–39.

Ralph M. Dahlquist, 1939–

College Nurse

Nora Walhus, 1921–24; 1925–27; 1929–36.

Christine R. Strom, 1924–25.

Mrs. Dagny Johnson, 1927–29.

Loyes M. Henningsgaard, 1936–39.

Martha Sundby (Mrs. Sherman A. Hoslett), 1939–41; 1943–44.

Margaret Naeseth Hegland, 1941–42.

Eunice Strandjord, 1942–43.

Charlotte B. Schilling Grue, 1944–47. (Since 1947 Mrs. Grue has been supervisor of the health service.)

Director of the Norwegian-American Historical Museum

(Prior to 1958 the title "Curator" was used)

Knut Gjerset, 1921–36.

Knute O. Eittreim, 1936–39.

Sigurd S. Reque, 1940–47.

Inga Bredesen Norstog, 1947–60.

Mrs. Ralph M. Olson, 1960–

Dean of Men

Leonard A. Moe, 1925–37.

Walter B. Scarvie, 1925–27.

J. Magnus Rohne, 1925–27.

Chellis N. Evanson, 1925–29.

Herman E. Ellingson, 1927–30.

Harold O. S. Birkestrand, 1929–30.

Morton O. Nilssen, 1937–39.

N. Lewis Fadness, 1939–47.

Clair G. Kloster, 1947–50; 1951–54.

Edsel K. Schweizer, 1950–51.

Einar O. Johnson, 1954–55.

Paul H. Lionberger, 1955–

Dean of Women

Emily Frank, 1936–37.

Carrie M. Anderson, 1937–39.

Arla Gredvig Nesset, 1939–40.

Clara J. Paulson, 1940–43; 1944–47.

Lois Moe (Mrs. Robert S. Jacobsen), 1943–44.

Valborg O. Fletty, 1948–53.

Ruth Mostrom, 1953–55.

Fayette Paulsen, 1955–

Director, News Bureau

Chellis N. Evanson, 1928–50.

Director, Sports Publicity

Warren G. Berg, 1952–

Director Radio station KWLC

(From 1928 to 1944, the station was under the direction of committees. From 1928 to 1958 Oliver M. Eittreim was engineer and operator.)

Richard Bergstrom, 1944–46.

Kenneth L. Berger, 1946–47.

Paul D. Borge, 1947–50.

Leroy V. Eitzen, 1950–54.

Leslie G. Rude, 1954–56.

Esther J. Olson, 1956–60.

Harold C. Svanoe, 1960–

Director of Summer Session

Olaf M. Norlie, 1932–34.

Rolfe A. Haatvedt, 1941–42; 1949–50.

Orlando W. Qualley, 1943–49; 1950–

Director of Placement Bureau

(The bureau was organized in 1926 by I. Dorrum and O. A. Tingelstad)

Appendix

Carl W. Strom, 1934–35.

Bernice J. Forde, 1935–36.

Helen M. Hoff (Mrs. Rolfe A. Haatvedt), 1936–39.

Rolfe A. Haatvedt, 1939–41.

Arthur O. Davidson, 1941–42; 1946–48.

Jacob A. O. Lien, 1942–43.

Hazel L. Iverson, 1943–45.

Stanley L. Johnston, 1948–55.

Clair G. Kloster, 1955–58.

Albert E. Hjelle, 1958–

Director of Admissions

Karl H. Nordgaard, 1937–

Director of Public Services

Erling H. Wold, 1950–53.

Arthur O. Davidson, 1954–61.

Ass't Director, Irene J. Langlie, 1951–

Ass't Director, Office of Development, Curtis Reiso, 1959–

Ass't Director, Centennial Development Fund, Eldred J. Nesset, 1958–

Director of Office of Development, Karl M. Torgerson, 1961–

Treasurer

Knute O. Eittreim, 1920–32.

Henry O. Talle, 1932–38.

Karl Hanson, 1938–48.

L. Reuben Lerud, 1948–50.

Wilbert O. Kalsow, 1950–

Business Manager

Karl Hanson, 1928–48.

David T. Nelson, 1948.

Wilbert O. Kalsow, 1948–

Engineer and electrician

Ole Korsrud, 1910–46.

Ralph M. Olson, 1946–

Cecil H. Peterson, 1952–

Superintendent, buildings and grounds

Clarence W. Leikvold, 1942–51.

Erling K. Knutson, 1947–

Bibliographical Notes

a. The capital was Christiania until January 1, 1925, when it was renamed Oslo. In the present volume, place names given in citations will follow the practice that was in effect at the time of publication.

b. Translations of quoted passages, not otherwise credited, have been made by the author.

c. Maanedstidende (Racine and Inmansville, Wisconsin), the official church organ, was a monthly paper known by that title 1851–53. There was no publication from 1853 through 1855. The successor was *Kirkelig maanedstidende* (Inmansville and Madison, Wisconsin, and Decorah, Iowa) from 1855 to 1874; it became *Evangelisk luthersk kirketidende,* a weekly, which continued as such until 1917, when it merged with *Lutheraneren* (Minneapolis). Both *Maanedstidende* and *Kirkelig maanedstidende* are here cited as *Maanedstidende,* and *Evangelisk luthersk kirketidende* as *Kirketidende.* Inmansville is a little north of the church of the congregation named "Luther Valley" by Claus L. Clausen; the congregation is still known by this title.

d. For the Norwegian Synod's first convention, 1853, there was no printed report. The second meeting, 1855, was recorded in *Forhandlinger* (Proceedings). Reports for the conventions of 1857, 1859, 1861, and 1862 were printed in *Maanedstidende* and are here cited simply as page references in the latter. The year 1863 marked the publication of *Beretning om det sjette ordentlig synodemøde for den norsk-evangelisk-lutherske kirke i Amerika afholdt i Rock River kirke fra 10de til 17de juni, 1863.* From 1863 to 1917, such a *Beretning* (Report), popularly known as *Synodalberetning* (Synodical Report), for each convention was issued variously from Madison, La Crosse, and Decorah. The Norwegian Lutheran Church of America, after its establishment in 1917, published *Beretning* from Minneapolis, 1917–23. Reports 1863–1923 are here cited as *Beretning,* mentioning the specific year. From 1924 to date, the reports, in English, have been issued from Minneapolis—by the NLCA until 1946, and since then by its successor, the Evangelical Lutheran Church (ELC). The first was Norwegian Lutheran Church of America, *Report of the Third Regular District Conventions Held in 1924* (Minneapolis, 1924). Any of these is here cited as *Report,* mentioning the specific year.

e. The first of this series, *Katalog, 1861–1872,* was printed in Norwegian. Succeeding numbers, 1882–85, were printed in English; from 1885–86 to

373

1905–06 they were issued in English and Norwegian. From 1906 on, only English was used, with the title, *Luther College Catalog*. It is cited as *Katalog* or *Catalog*, according to which form was in use at the time. The catalog now appears as one number of the quarterly *Luther College Bulletin*. See bibliographical note *j*.

f. College Chips, published by Luther College students, was established in 1884 and continues to the present; it is hereafter referred to as *Chips*. It was a magazine until 1926, when it became a newspaper.

g. Luther College Faculty, *Luther College through Sixty Years*, was edited by O. M. Norlie, O. A. Tingelstad, and Karl T. Jacobsen.

h. Symra, an annual, had ten issues, 1905–14. It was edited and published in Decorah by Johannes B. Wist and Kristian Prestgard; Knut Gjerset and Peter J. Eikeland joined them in editing the 1914 number. The volumes contain more than 200 articles, poems, and sketches by pioneer Norwegian-American clergymen, professors, authors, poets, and lecturers. The Symra Literary Society, limited to 25 members, was organized in 1907 to assist the publishers. The magazine ceased with the 1914 volume, but the society continues. Normally it meets every two weeks throughout the school year, with a speaker and a discussion following.

i. Protokol (Protocol with Daily Register for the Norwegian-Evangelical Lutheran Educational Institution for the Education of Ministers) is a handwritten record beginning August 17, 1861, now on file in the registrar's office, Luther College. It was first kept by Larsen himself. Protokol No. 1 has a list of the first 434 students, in order of their enrollment, and also *attester* (recommendations) numbered from 1 to 80. The latter were statements about students who had requested recommendations or letters of dismissal, besides a few references for men who had taught at the college. Protokol No. 2 has only the faculty minutes. There are seven such "protokols," continuing until June 10, 1916; all were kept in Norwegian but included occasional reports in English. Beginning September 14, 1916, Protokol was replaced by the minutes of the Luther College Faculty, which were typed, signed, and bound. They also are on file in the registrar's office. They are here referred to as Faculty Minutes.

j. Luther College Bulletin has been published quarterly in Decorah since January 1921; henceforth it will be cited as *Bulletin*. The catalog is now issued as one number.

k. A single date after the name of an individual indicates the year of his graduation from Luther College; for anyone who did not take a degree, the inclusive years of attendance are given.

l. Pioneer is published by the junior class; it appeared in 1920 and in 1922; triennially 1926–38; biennially 1940–46; and annually 1948 to date.

m. "Record of Proceedings of Board of Trustees and Corporation of the Norwegian Luther College," beginning June 9, 1871, is the official manuscript record of the board, deposited in the Koren Library. It will be cited as Trustees Minutes. The Board of Trustees became the Board of Regents in 1958. The record of the latter is cited as Regents Minutes.

Footnotes

I. THE BACKGROUND

1. See Theodore C. Blegen, *Norwegian Migration to America, 1825– 1860,* and *Norwegian Migration to America: The American Transition* (Northfield, Minnesota, 1931, 1940) for a well-documented account of the whole migratory movement; and Ingrid Gaustad Semmingsen, *Veien mot vest: Utvandring fra Norge til Amerika* (Oslo, 1942, 1950). See bibliographical note *a.*

2. Carlton C. Qualey, *Norwegian Settlement in the United States,* 47 (Northfield, 1938).

3. Qualey, *Norwegian Settlement,* 213.

4. The cornerstone statement was formulated by Ulrik Vilhelm Koren. See Oscar A. Tingelstad and Olaf M. Norlie, *Christian Keyser Preus 1852– 1921,* 309 (Minneapolis, 1922).

5. Qualey, *Norwegian Settlement,* 82.

6. For an account of religious development among Norwegians in this country, see E. Clifford Nelson and Eugene L. Fevold, *The Lutheran Church among Norwegian-Americans* (Minneapolis, 1960).

7. Nelson and Fevold, *The Lutheran Church,* 1:12.

8. Knut Gjerset, *History of the Norwegian People,* 2:403 (New York, 1915).

9. Blegen, *Norwegian Migration, 1825–1860,* chapter 2.

10. The words quoted are from J. Magnus Rohne, *Norwegian American Lutheranism Up to 1872,* 41 (New York, 1926).

11. In 1852 the Synod of Northern Illinois founded Illinois State University at Springfield. It was not, as its name seems to imply, a state-supported institution. It comprised an academy, a college, and a seminary. The total attendance in 1852 was 82; in 1858, 146. In 1853, seven young men of Norwegian descent were students there. The college offered four-year courses in Greek and Latin, and mathematics through calculus; there were no electives. Olaf M. Norlie, *History of the Norwegian People in America,* 204, 216 (Minneapolis, 1925).

12. That is, the German Evangelical Lutheran Synod of Missouri, Ohio, and Other States; and the Lutheran Synod of Buffalo.

13. As a result of this withdrawal, membership in the Northern Illinois Synod dropped from 5,319 in 1859 to 1,551 in 1860. Illinois State University languished and in 1867 it closed. In 1874 the building became the

property of the Missouri Synod, which since then has conducted its "practical" seminary (i.e., one that does not emphasize languages) there under the name Concordia Seminary. Norlie, *Norwegian People*, 204, 216.

14. Blegen, *Norwegian Migration: American Transition*, 528. Andreas A. Helland in *Augsburg Seminar gjennem femti aar, 1869–1919*, 378 (Minneapolis, 1920), gives the number of students as 24, divided 11 and 13.

15. J. W. C. Dietrichson, *Reise blandt de norske emigranter i de forenede nordamerikanske fristater*, 3, 42 (Stavanger, Norway, reprinted by Rasmus B. Anderson at Madison, Wisconsin, 1896). See bibliographical note *b*.

16. See supplement by Thrond Bothne, "Kort udsigt over det lutherske kirkearbeide i Amerika," in Hallvard G. Heggtveit, *Illustreret kirkehistorie*, 839 (Chicago, 1898). N. F. S. Grundtvig, 1783–1872, was a Danish theologian and poet who awakened new impulses in church and nation.

17. Einar Haugen, "Pastor Dietrichson of Old Koshkonong," in *Wisconsin Magazine of History*, 24:312 (1945–46).

18. E. Clifford Nelson, "The Making of a Constitution," in J. C. K. Preus, ed., *Norsemen Found a Church*, 202 (Minneapolis, 1953).

19. The other eight are: Augustana, Sioux Falls, South Dakota; Capital University, Columbus, Ohio; Concordia, Moorhead, Minnesota; Dana, Blair, Nebraska; Pacific Lutheran University, Tacoma, Washington; St. Olaf, Northfield, Minnesota; Texas Lutheran, Seguin, Texas; and Wartburg, Waverly, Iowa.

II. TEN YEARS OF DISCUSSION

1. Blegen, in *Norwegian Migration: American Transition*, 159, 160, mentions a letter of Dietrichson, August 23, 1847, that was printed in *Nordlyset* (Trondhjem), November 19, 1847.

2. David B. Owens and others, *These Hundred Years*, chapters 1 and 2 (Columbus, Ohio, 1950). Capital University underwent a crisis between 1840 and 1850. The liberals wanted English authorized as a medium of instruction; the conservatives clung to German. After the victory of the former, some of the conservatives resigned from the Ohio Synod and joined the Missouri group. Professor William F. Lehmann, later president of Capital, was able to build up the student body and restore morale. "So successful was he with his students that in June 1848, when the Ohio Synod met again in Columbus, he could risk having them give a literary entertainment in the new Court House for the benefit of the visitors; it was received with great enthusiasm by an audience that crowded the courtroom"; Owens, *These Hundred Years*, 27.

3. *Maanedstidende*, 5 (May, 1852). Gisle Bothne, *Det norske Luther College 1861–1897* (Decorah, Iowa, 1897) errs in saying, page 27, that the recommendation carried. Members of the committee were A. C. Preus, H. A. Stub, Johannes Johannesen, G. Gulbrandsen, and Torgeir Vinger. About the church papers, see bibliographical note *c*.

4. "The Emigrant" (Inmansville and Madison), was the leading Norwegian-language newspaper of the period.

5. *Emigranten,* June 11, August 13, 1852.

6. *Maanedstidende,* 5-9 (October, 1852). The "literary entertainment" criticized by Grabau is mentioned in note 2 above.

7. *Maanedstidende,* 6–9 (December, 1852).

8. *Emigranten,* January 14, 1853.

9. *Maanedstidende,* 7–9 (August, 1853). The committee consisted of A. C. Preus, H. A. Preus, J. Landsverk, L. Lie, G. Myhre, O. Knudson, and P. Jacobson.

10. Halvor Halvorsen, *Festskrift til den norske synodes jubilæum 1853–1903,* 75 (Decorah, 1903).

11. *Maanedstidende,* 76 (1855). Present were A. C. Preus, H. A. Preus, Lars Lie (precentor), and John Fosmark.

12. For the quotations from the committee report and from H. A. Preus's motion, see *Forhandlinger i den norsk-evangelisk-lutherske kirkes synodalmøde,* 7, 19–21 (Inmansville, Wisconsin, n.d.). See bibliographical note *d.*

13. *Maanedstidende,* 154 (1856). See also *Emigranten,* February 8, 1856.

14. *Maanedstidende,* 211–216 (1856).

15. *Maanedstidende,* 370 (1857).

16. *Maanedstidende,* 472 (1857).

17. *Maanedstidende,* 476–489 (1857).

18. Jenny Lind's association with P. T. Barnum, who had brought her to this country, was perhaps enough to discredit her with the "university men" in general.

19. Presumably the delegates also visited Illinois State University at Springfield, but this was not mentioned in their report; *Katalog for det norske Luther-College i Decorah, Iowa, 1861–1872,* 5 (Decorah, 1872). See bibliographical note *e.*

20. *Maanedstidende,* 489 (1857). Present at the meeting were A. C. Preus, H. A. Preus, G. F. Dietrichson, Iver Ingebretsen, Christian Henriksen, and Jens Johnson Skipsnaes.

21. In 1850, in the aftermath of the struggle over English and German, Reverend William M. Reynolds, at that time associated with Pennsylvania College (later Gettysburg College), then the chief college of the General Synod of the Evangelical Lutheran Church, became president of Capital. He was of Scotch-Irish descent, did not speak German easily, favored English as the medium of instruction, and was broadly tolerant in religious views. He soon became suspect to the culturally isolated and intensely orthodox in the Joint Ohio Synod; the cleavage grew, and he resigned in 1854. It is by no means certain that all would have been well with Capital had he remained as president; but in the five years following his resignation, the college had a hard fight for survival. See Owens, *These Hundred Years,* 46, 64, 65, 77.

22. The Norwegian word *læreanstalt* was used to designate this new venture. It is a difficult term to translate, indicating more than an academy in the American sense. It was not a college, for the American term "college" had not yet attained standing among the "university men." The

Footnotes

term "seminary" was associated in the minds of those from Norway with the seminaries or normal schools which had been established in Norway, most of them in the 1830's. So the institution was designated as one for the training of "teachers" or ministers of the church, and the fund for its establishment was regularly called the "University Fund." Popularly the school came to be known as the "preacher school," the Decorah school, and Decorah college.

23. Members of the committee were H. A. Stub, J. St. Munch, Gudbrand Myhre, L. J. Lie, and Thor Helgeson.

24. For the above and following details, see *Maanedstidende*, 4–16 (January, 1858).

25. *Maanedstidende*, 10 (1858).

26. *Maanedstidende*, 41 (1858).

27. Not until a pastoral conference at Black Earth, Wisconsin, in July, 1860, was a decision made to send students to the Missouri Synod's practical seminary at Fort Wayne, Indiana; *Maanedstidende*, 305 (1860).

III. GETTING STARTED

1. A. W. Meyer, "The Organization of the Synodical Conference," in W. H. T. Dau, ed., *Ebenezer*, 326 (St. Louis, 1922).

2. Owens, *These Hundred Years*, 64–77.

3. Concordia Seminary was founded in 1839 in a log cabin in Perry County, Missouri, about 85 miles down river from St. Louis, by Saxons who had followed Pastor Martin Stephan to this country that year. In 1850 the college and seminary was moved to a new building in St. Louis. By the school year 1859–60, two buildings had been added. In 1854 Professor C. F. W. Walther became president of the seminary division. In 1860 the institution had a library of 5,000 volumes. See *Maanedstidende*, 237–244, 258 (1860).

Larsen said later, "I remember well when I was in St. Louis in 1859–61, how imposing I then found the college and seminary of the Missouri Synod, which together had about 80 students, and where all these and most of the teachers, too, lived in a building which according to our present standards was very much lacking and was far too small for so many inhabitants." *College Chips*, 131 (1896). See bibliographical note *f*.

4. *Maanedstidende*, 132, 173 (1858); Andreas Brandrud, in *Norsk biografisk leksikon*, 1:2–4 (Christiania, 1923). The Norwegian title of Aabel's grammar was *Det nye testamentes grammatik af Dr. G. B. Winer* (Christiania, 1852); and, of the outline, *Omrids af det christelige troesinhold* (Christiania, 1855). The grammar was translated from Winer's *Grammatik des neutestamentlichen Sprachidioms als sichere Grundlage der neutestamentlichen Exegese* (Leipzig, 1830).

5. *Maanedstidende*, 93 (1859); Karen Larsen, *Laur. Larsen: Pioneer College President*, 12, 19 (Northfield, Minnesota, 1936).

6. Karen Larsen, *Laur. Larsen*, 29.

7. *Maanedstidene*, 80 (1859).

8. *Maanedstidende*, 192 (1859), 30, 126 (1860).

9. *Maanedstidene,* 165–176, 192 (1858), 62 (1859).

10. *Maanedstidende,* 263, 285 (1860).

11. *Maanedstidende,* 352 (1860); P. E. Kretzmann, "The Development of Higher Education in the Missouri Synod," in Dau, ed., *Ebenezer,* 233.

12. *Maanedstidende,* 245, 255, 303 (1860).

13. Larsen, "Foredrag over de kirkelige forhold blandt de norske i Amerika," reprinted from *Morgenbladet* in *Maanedstidene,* 40–51 (1861), and "Beretning om min reise til Norge," in *Maanedstidene,* 67 (1861).

14. Larsen, in *Maanedstidende,* 68, 73 (1861), and Larsen, "Til redaktoren af norsk kirketidende i Christiania," in *Maanedstidende,* 201–206 (1861); Bothne, in Heggtveit's *Kirkehistorie,* 881.

15. Karen Larsen, *Laur. Larsen,* 124; for further comment, see Professor Fredrik W. Bugge's remarks in 1874 in *Nogle vidnesbyrd fra moderkirken,* 16 (Decorah, 1874).

16. Samuel F. Batchelder, *Bits of Harvard History,* 14 (Cambridge, Massachusetts, 1924). Holden Chapel (erected 1742–44 for £400) is said to be the only building "*ever* given by an English donor—the sole tangible, brick-and-mortar evidence of the mother country's goodwill to Harvard." Italics in the original.

17. Einar Molland, *Church Life in Norway 1800–1850,* 49–57, 91 (Minneapolis, 1957). The translation is by Harris Kaasa.

18. Molland, *Church Life in Norway,* 91–93.

19. Laur. Larsen, communication dated April 26, 1861, in *Emigranten,* May 6, 1861.

IV. HALFWAY CREEK TO DECORAH

1. *Maanedstidende,* 19, 291–294 (1860).

2. Bothne, *Luther College,* 36.

3. The land was bought from J. Gibbons, Quaker, for $1,500 in October 1860. *Maanedstidende,* 351 (1862).

4. Erwin L. Leuker, ed., *Lutheran Cyclopedia,* 609 (St. Louis, 1954). There was to have been a second Norwegian teacher, and Larsen was instructed to seek one in Norway. He found Fredrik W. Bugge; in 1861 the Synod granted Bugge a stipend of $700 for two years' study, stipulating only that he spend the second year "at an orthodox institution in America." Bugge regarded this condition as an aspersion on the mother church and declined the offer; Rohne, *Norwegian American Lutheranism,* 211; *Maanedstidene,* 52, 263 (1861); J. C. Jensson, *American Lutheran Biographies,* 693 (Milwaukee, 1890).

5. For the Synod meeting of June, 1861, see *Maanedstidene,* 225–272 (1861).

6. *Det kongelige Fredriks Universitet 1811–1911, festskrift,* 248 (Christiania, 1911).

7. Olaf M. Norlie, "Religious Aim and Character," in *Luther College through Sixty Years,* 24 (Minneapolis, 1922); Laur. Larsen, in *Kirketidende,* 1778–1781 (1912), 407 (1877). See bibliographical note g.

8. Laur. Larsen, "Nogle gamle minder," in *Symra,* 9:164 (1913);

Footnotes

Maanedstidende, 351 (1862). The expense figure is from the latter. See bibliographical note *h*.

9. Koren warned Larsen that if he came to Decorah he would have to do so with "diminutive expectations." His wife, Koren added, thought anything found there would be inadequate. "My wife is always right," he concluded; Karen Larsen, *Laur. Larsen*, 136. Koren, says Bothne, like the other university men, still used the "philologian's polyglot language." Koren's wife made him step down from the learned heights. "Do you think the farmers understood what you said today?" she asked dryly, when he had preached a sermon after the Christiania pattern. Bothne, in Heggtveit, *Illustreret kirkehistorie*, 858.

10. *Maanedstidende*, 277 (1861). The parsonage burned in 1865; Johan Th. Ylvisaker, in *Det norske Luther College*, 8 (Decorah, 1890). This 68-page history was also published in English in 1890. The site of the parsonage was the present Oscar R. Lee farm east of Holmen.

11. See *Maanedstidene*, 370 (1861), for the complete timetable and schedule of courses.

12. These details are from Protokol No. 1. See bibliographical note *i*.

13. Laur. Larsen, "Nogle gamle minder," in *Symra*, 9:166 (1913) quoted by Knut Gjerset in "Important Events," in *Luther College through Sixty Years*, 382. The succeeding sentences were translated by the author.

14. Bothne, *Luther College*, 41.

15. *Maanedstidende*, 369 (1861).

16. *Maanedstidende*, 258 (1860); Ole Paulson, *Erindringer*, 211 (Minneapolis, 1907); Brynjolf Hovde to Gullik M. Erdahl, September 21, 1861, ELC archives, Luther Theological Seminary, St. Paul.

17. Ylvisaker, *Luther College* (English edition), 10.

18. Karen Larsen, *Laur. Larsen*, 157; *Maanedstidende*, 330, 351 (1862). F. E. Peterson, in *Luther College through Sixty Years*, 143, states that the property was purchased from Nathaniel Otis; he calls it the Otis Building. It was of brick, 30 by 46 feet, with two stories, full basement, and attic. The lot was 53 by 119 feet; to the rear was a baking oven, besides a brick stable for five horses or cows. See *Maanedstidende*, 287 (1865).

19. Laur. Larsen, speech given in Minneapolis, October 14, 1896, in *Chips*, 131 (1896); *Maanedstidende*, 331 (1862).

20. A "seven-octave" piano was purchased by Professor Schmidt for $320 in Chicago, according to a receipt February 10, 1864; Bothne, *Luther College*, 391.

21. *Maanedstidende*, 287 (1863).

22. This brick structure, 24 by 32 feet, had two stories and a basement, on a lot 53 by 119 feet. There was also a small frame building on the premises; *Maanedstidende*, 287 (1865).

Linka (Mrs. H. A.) Preus quoted the nursery rhyme:

> Hututu, jeg fryser saa,
> Jeg fryser paa mine fødder.
>
> (Hututu, I am freezing so,
> My feet are simply freezing.)

See Christian K. Preus, "Minder fra Spring Prairie prestegaard," in *Symra*, 2:21 (1906).

23. *Maanedstidende,* 284 (1863). Billington immigrated with his father from Stenkjær near Trondhjem in 1853; he studied medicine and afterwards practiced at Black Earth, Wisconsin—later, for many years, at Decorah. See Karl E. Erickson, "The Emigrant Journey in the Fifties," edited by Albert O. Barton, in *Norwegian-American Studies and Records,* 8:85 (Northfield, Minnesota, 1934). See also Knut Gjerset and Ludvig Hektoen, "Health Conditions and the Practice of Medicine among the Early Norwegian Settlers, 1825–1865" in *Norwegian-American Studies and Records,* 1:54 (Northfield, Minnesota, 1926).

24. *Maanedstidende,* 6–8 (1862).

25. *Maanedstidende,* 259 (1864). For Koren's authorship, see Tingelstad and Norlie, *Christian Keyser Preus,* 309. Norlie ascribes this broadening of aim and purpose to Claus L. Clausen.

26. *Maanedstidende,* 249 (1862).

27. See *Maanedstidende,* 362–372 (1864), for a detailed account of the cornerstone ceremony.

V. THE FIRST MAIN BUILDING

1. *Luther College Bulletin* (December, 1936). See bibliographical note *j.*

2. For the above and other details about the building, from its earliest planning stages for its completion, see Laur. Larsen's careful account in *Beretning,* 70–80 (1886). See bibliographical note *j.*

3. Lyder Siewers in *Decorah-posten,* October 20, 1886, translated by Ylvisaker in *Luther College* (English edition) 22–24.

4. Synneve Lommen, Malene Trørvig, and Gjertrude Kristoffersen gave $32.55 to provide this flag. It is one of the first gifts made to the college by women; *Maanedstidende,* 93 (1866). Earlier gifts had been made by the women of First Lutheran Church, who about 1862 organized to sew garments which were sold to help pay for the first building. See Mrs. John C. Hexom, *History of the F. N. E. L. Church Ladies' Aid Society,* 22 (Decorah, 1926).

5. Lars S. Reque, '68, later professor at Luther, carried the Norwegian flag, and Newton Adams carried the American flag, according to an oral statement made to the author by Sigurd S. Reque, '03. On the seventy-fifth anniversary of the college, Helen Adams Bodensteiner, granddaughter of Newton Adams and instructor in dramatics and speech, and S. S. Reque carried flags in a procession re-enacting the earlier one of 1865.

6. The hymn was composed by Pastor Koren.

7. *Emigranten,* October 23, 1865.

8. See Bothne, *Luther College,* 88–110, for the quotations from Brandt, Preus, and Schmidt.

9. *Maanedstidende,* 65–69 (1866). Of Koren's remarks, Walther wrote, "I am almost inclined to envy our descendants, to whom the dear Koren presented the *prognostikon* that they would sometimes speak the same language as the Norwegian brethren and thus merge altogether." See C. F. W. Walther to J. A. Ottesen, St. Louis, January 5, 1866, in P. E. Kretz-

Footnotes

mann, tr., "Letters—Walther to Ottesen," in *Clergy Bulletin*, 94 (April, 1953). The *Clergy Bulletin* was published at Northwood, Iowa.

10. Reported in *Emigranten*, October 30, 1865.

11. *Emigranten*, October 23, 1865.

VI. REBELLION AND SLAVERY

1. For Anderson's account of the affair and of his days at Luther College, see *Life Story of Rasmus B. Anderson*, 34–70 (Madison, Wisconsin, 1915). A brief and quaint version is "A Student Rebellion at Luther College," in Einar Haugen, *The Norwegian Language in America*, 2:506–509 (Philadelphia, 1953). The student quoted was probably Reinhard T. Bentson, '64–70. He described Anderson's dismissal thus (in Haugen's translation):

"And then—well I stood there and saw it when Professor Sievers came dragging with him, chased him in front of him; I stood there looking up at it as he came dragging him along down the steps there, and drove him ahead, and said, 'Walk fast, walk fast!' And he shoved him so that he should hurry. Anderson wasn't in quite such a hurry, but he kept shoving so he would go—he mustn't stop and talk to anyone. And then he was chased down, down the stairs and out; Sievers followed him, he was chased like a dog.

"Then he stopped when he got outside the college, and looked back. 'Well,' said Sievers, 'go away,' he said, 'go away.' Then he had to go down and away."

See bibliographical note *k*.

2. *Beretning*, 87 (1866).

3. Claus L. Clausen, in *Gjenmæle*, 23 (Chicago, 1869), reports that Ottesen and Larsen maintained that the American Revolution was "an ungodly insurrection" and the Declaration of Independence "a product of the spirit of lies." See Ulrik Vilhelm Koren, *Samlede skrifter*, 3:40–43 (Decorah, 1911), for Koren's attitude toward the French Revolution and its ideas. See also the Church Council's statement to the theological faculty of Christiania University, that "the assertion of the absolute sinfulness of slavery is only one of the paragraphs of the anti-Christian program of the spirit of the times," involving temporal freedom as one of the "natural and inalienable rights of men: freedom, property, security, and opposition to oppression." The council also referred to the "ultra-abolitionist, even communistic ideas" of the spirit of the times; "its depraved confusion of spiritual and corporal freedom"; and calls it "the ungodly spirit" and "the anti-Christian spirit of the times." See Blegen, *Norwegian Migration: American Transition*, 444; and Johan A. Bergh, *Den norsk lutherske kirkes historie*, 165–171 (Minneapolis, 1914). The same theories may be found in Laur. Larsen, *Historisk fremstilling*, 4 (Madison, Wisconsin, 1868).

4. Haugen, *Norwegian Language*, 2:506–509.

5. Protokol No. 1, p. 77.

6. Protokol No. 1, p. 91.

7. Laur. Larsen Papers, 1864–68, Koren Library, Luther College.

8. Apparently Larsen found in the old Lutheranism espoused by Walther something he had missed during his theological training in Norway. Writing April 10, 1861, to the editor of *Norsk kirketidende* (Christiania), he stated his position clearly. On the question of whether he had not met other learned and amiable men than Walther, he said: "In Norway I followed no one; I rejected pietism, I rejected Grundtvigianism. I had given my heart to the doctrine of justification, but I found no theological tendency which exactly fitted it; in fact, there was no study of the symbols or of Luther or of the old fathers; but in an attempt to follow the progress (!?) *[sic]* of the times, men reached out as best they could for the crumbs of the newer theology. Over here, on the other hand, I was immediately directed to those good old sources, and it was not long before I saw clear as day that in these was found the truth. . . . Therefore, we are able to take our stand fearlessly and positively against any opposition because we know that our faith and doctrine are grounded in God's Word." When Larsen wrote these words, he was not yet 28; Walther was almost 50. See *Maanedstidende*, 204 (1861).

9. In the Peasants' War the peasants argued in their "Twelve Articles" that "it accords with the Scripture that we are free, and we desire to be free. Not that we are free without restriction, not that we would have no government—God does not teach us that." Melanchthon then said, "It is both a crime and an act of violence that they refuse to be serfs." Luther wrote, "This article is directly contrary to the Gospel and robberlike in character: for in this way each one would take away his body from his lord, whose property it is." These were unfortunate citations of unfortunate utterances made by the two reformers during a time of crisis. See *Maanedstidende*, 351 (1861); *Lehre und Wehre* (St. Louis), 225, 352 (August, November, 1856).

10. C. F. W. Walther to A. C. Preus, January 8, 1869, in L. Fürbringer, ed., *Briefe von C. F. W. Walther*, 1:124-130 (St. Louis, 1915, 1916). Fürbringer mistakenly dated the letter January 8, 1860. Gerhard L. Belgum noted the error in "The Old Norwegian Synod in America, 1853–1890," 362-366, a doctoral dissertation presented at Yale University in 1957; a copy is in the Koren Library. P. E. Kretzmann, in *Clergy Bulletin*, 115–118 (May-June, 1953), translated the letter of January 8, a postscript of January 9, and Walther's letter of January 9, 1869 to J. A. Ottesen. The internal evidence of the three documents is conclusive against the earlier date. Blegen, in *Norwegian Migration: American Transition*, 420–422, was misled by Fürbringer's erroneous dating. The letter, nevertheless, contains a good statement of Walther's position on the slavery question. A. C. Preus may have written him before publishing "Et mæglende ord i slaveristriden" (A Word of Conciliation in the Slavery Controversy), in *Emigranten*, March 4, 1869.

11. *Emigranten*, May 6, 1861.

12. Solberg's interesting attitude toward Larsen may be observed more fully in a later issue of *Emigranten*. Erik Ellefsen (Slen) had contributed an article to *Emigranten*, attacking the pastors' declaration of the Synod meeting of June 1861. In the January 20, 1862, issue, Larsen severely

criticized Ellefsen's article and likewise castigated *Emigranten* for printing it. In the same issue, Solberg, over his own signature, replied. He said that Larsen's article was confused; he defended Ellefsen's statement as proper and in order; he also asserted the right and duty of an editor to keep his columns open for expressions of opinion. He then went on to call Larsen's article "really amusing." He said: "There is a naiveté running through it which is refreshing after all the harsh things which today's events force the newspaper-reading public to digest. . . . The point is that the professor ought to clarify a little more his ideas of the function of a newspaper before he begins to sound off publicly about it."

13. Walther's prestige among the Synod leaders led them to attach great weight to his views, particularly since the opposition was led by nonuniversity, nontheologically-trained laymen. "There is no doubt at all that Larsen, Ottesen, Koren, and H. A. Preus received their ammunition throughout the conflict from Walther," says Belgum in "The Old Norwegian Synod," 364; of Walther's method, Belgum writes (p. 348), "In his conviction that he writes every word on the basis of God's Word, Walther's certainty of his position is complete. Kindliness and piety are blended with an assumption of virtual infallibility."

14. Nelson and Fevold in *The Lutheran Church*, 1:174, are in error in saying of the pastors that "unlike the laity, many were Democrats and supporters of states' rights." Apparently only Larsen was a Democrat. See U. V. Koren, "Hvorfor er der ingen kirkelig enighed mellem norske lutheranere i Amerika? Svar til Hr. M. Ulvestad og mange andre, 1905," in *Samlede skrifter*, 3:463.

15. *Maanedstidende*, 261 (1861).

16. *Emigranten*, July 29, October 7, 1861.

17. *Maanedstidende*, 262 (1861); the translation is Blegen's in *Norwegian Migration: American Transition*, 428.

18. Brynjolf J. Hovde, "Luther College and Its Secular Tradition," a Founders Day address given in 1941. *Luther College Bulletin*, October, 1941.

19. Hovde, in *Luther College Bulletin*, October, 1941.

20. A. C. Preus stated in *Emigranten* as early as May 4, 1858, that it was due to the efforts of the Scandinavian Press Association (which, founded in part by Synod pastors, published *Emigranten)* that the Norwegian electorate switched from Democratic to Republican and supported Lincoln. See Carl G. O. Hansen, "Pressen til borgerkrigens slutning," in Johannes B. Wist, *Norsk-amerikanernes festskrift 1914*, 31 (Decorah, 1914). Earlier Hansen says (p. 27): "From the opinions expressed in that paper during the ten years preceding the Civil War, it is very clearly evident that the abolition of slavery is one of the planks of its platform. It seems strange, therefore, that the leading ministers of a church organization which in its time has been accused of supporting slavery should have been the ones who gave direction to the Norwegian paper which, during the time that this great question was to the fore, was most zealous in behalf of this reform."

21. Bothne says that Clausen "was only a seminarian and did not under-

stand the original languages of the Bible, so it was easy to silence him. With so peaceful a disposition and so warm a heart as he had, he would surely in spite of all have remained within the church body which he had had a share in founding, if he had not been denied Holy Communion because he believed it was a sin to own slaves. But when, in their blind zeal, they [the Synod] placed him under church discipline and denied him admittance to the Lord's Table, he shook the dust from his feet and went out from them"; *Kirkehistorie,* 872. See also Nelson and Fevold, *The Lutheran Church,* 1:1:78. Clausen admitted the contradictions himself. "Let us assume that everything written against me is true; at best that would prove only that I was not the right man to defend the cause, but in no wise that the cause itself was not good"; Clausen, *Gjenmæle,* 6. For the Synod's action of 1869, see *Beretning,* 86 (1869).

22. Karen Larsen, *Laur. Larsen,* 178, 133; Nelson and Fevold, *The Lutheran Church,* 1:176, 178, 180. It has been said that Walther did not understand Norwegians, who were unlike the Germans he had to deal with, and there may be some truth in this. But at the very time he was encouraging the Synod leaders to stand for "the truth," for "the pure doctrine," he took pains to let no utterance of his among his own people provoke any such bitter controversy as had broken out among the Norwegians. His two sermons of 1861 and 1862, delivered on the days of penitence and prayer called for by President Lincoln, are notable for what they leave unsaid. They are rhetorical utterances, but they do not come from a full heart, stirred by the great issues of the day. See sermons by C. F. W. Walther, September 26, 1861, November 27, 1862, translated by N. Brandt, in *Maanedstidende,* 146 (1862), 129 (1863).

23. Walther to A. C. Preus, January 8-9, 1869, quoted in Belgum, "The Old Norwegian Synod," 363.

24. Blegen, *Norwegian Migration: American Transition,* 453. Dean Blegen's chapter, "Slavery and the Church," from which the passage is quoted, is an admirable analysis of this extraordinary controversy within a church group that had practically no direct contacts with the institution of slavery.

25. The words quoted are from August Weenaas, *Wisconsinisme belyst ved historiske kjendsbjerninger,* 127 (Chicago, 1875).

26. Jakob Aall Ottesen, *Kort uddrag af den norske synodes historie,* 25 (Decorah, 1893); *Beretning,* 68 (1866); Laur. Larsen Papers, 1864-68.

27. See Larsen's resumé of his talk to the students when school opened after the first Christmas holiday; Protokol No. 1, p. 8.

28. It is one of the ironies of the old Synod's history that its leaders, who had made outstanding records at the university and most of whom had taught in Nissen's school in Christiania, apparently did not grasp the progressiveness of Ole Hartvig Nissen's ideas nor follow their development. In 1859 his program for the common schools of Norway was adopted, and, similarly, in 1869 and 1871, his proposals for higher general education. To some extent he was the Horace Mann of Norway.

In this country Herman A. Preus, who was justified in criticizing the level of instruction in the public schools, became involved in a violent controversy over them instead of using his influence to improve them. In

Footnotes

part, no doubt, his attitude had its roots in the milieu of officialdom and the cultured classes that he had known in Norway. In families such as his, tutors were the rule, and the rule was adhered to in this country. No child of his, nor of Koren's, attended a public school. In part, also, this viewpoint was that of members of the educated class in Norway toward the crudities of frontier life and toward the "Yankees." Preus said in 1864, "If it were a matter of establishing a college on the American pattern, I would not advise giving one cent thereto, even if instruction in the secular subjects was much more thorough than it is as a rule"; *Maanedstidende,* 167 (1864). Earlier he had said, "So far as nationalities go, we stand much closer to the Germans than to the Yankees, who can scarcely be said to have any other nationality than the one Henrik Wergeland describes when he says that the Yankee's heart is a gold dollar"; *Maanedstidende,* 215 (1856). Such a statement clearly reflects the prejudices of the class to which Preus belonged in Norway and was perhaps prompted by the sharp practices which his countrymen often endured in America before they became acquainted with the language and laws of their new country. Later his views were considerably altered; when an uncle offered to have Preus's oldest son, Christian K., educated in Norway, he unhesitatingly declined, saying that he wanted his son trained for life and work in America and thought that it would be better accomplished here. See Christian K. Preus, "Minder fra Spring Prairie prestegaard," in *Symra,* 2:26 (1906).

Larsen exhibited similar early views. Writing his wife from Cleveland, Ohio, May 19, 1866, when he was staying with the German pastor Schwan during his inspection tour of American colleges and universities, he wrote, "I am glad that I shall be here over Pentecost; thus I shall escape spending a single Sunday among the Americans." On May 23 he wrote from Chicago of his visit to Oberlin, describing the college as the "very peak of Yankee humbug and pride, so that I was truly disgusted with it. . . . Today I am better and . . . light of heart, because at last I am all through with Yankee schools for this trip." Laur. Larsen Papers, 1864–68. Considering Larsen's views at this time, his reaction to Oberlin is understandable. Oberlin was coeducational, an early hotbed of abolitionism, a stronghold of Republicanism, and so advanced a foe of slavery that, before the Civil War, faculty and students, invoking the "higher law," had united to rescue runaway slaves from slavehunters and enforcement officers who were attempting to return them under the Fugitive Slave Law. Larsen could hardly have found this atmosphere to his taste. See Robert Samuel Fletcher, *A History of Oberlin College,* 205–426 (Oberlin, Ohio, 1943); Karen Larsen, *Laur. Larsen,* 186–188; Karen Larsen, ed., "A Newcomer Looks at American Colleges" in *Norwegian-American Studies and Records,* 10:107–126 (Northfield, 1938).

Of Koren, Bothne says that, regarding slavery, he "appeared slow to learn, but finally crammed his lesson after a fashion. So far as I know, he was the first, later on, to see that the lesson was wrong"; *Kirkehistorie,* 871. In 1862 Koren referred approvingly to Luther's reply to the peasants, and ascribed to the French Revolution what he considered the erroneous views that had grown up about slavery and the rights of man. See Koren,

Footnotes

Samlede skrifter, 3:40–44, an article reprinted from *Emigranten* of March 31, 1862. Koren himself actively supported the Union cause, and, as early as August 17, 1862, was elected vice president of a county-wide mass war meeting held in Decorah; *Decorah Republic*, August 21, 1862.

29. Ove J. Hjort to Larsen, April 6, 1867, Laur. Larsen Papers, 1864–68; Bothne, in *Kirkehistorie*, 871.

30. Interview with S. S. Reque, March 1960.

31. Reinhart T. Bentson to *Decorah-posten*, an undated communication filed in the Koren Library.

32. *Katalog*, 8 (1872).

VII. THE EMERGING AMERICAN COLLEGE

1. *Katalog*, 8, 17 (1872). See also H. A. Preus, *Syv foredrag*, 46 (Christiania, 1867).

2. Andrew A. Veblen, "At Luther College (1877–1881)," a hand-written account in the Andrew Veblen Papers, Minnesota Historical Society, St. Paul.

3. "What Became of Jens: A Study in Americanization Based on the Reminiscences of James C. M. Hanson," 43, 46, a typed manuscript written in 1943, deposited in the Koren Library; see also Robert Foss's account of the University of Wisconsin in *Encyclopedia Americana*, 29:424 (New York and Chicago, 1950).

4. Hanson, "What Became of Jens," 49.

5. Protokol No. 1, *attest* no. 61; Veblen, "At Luther College."

6. A. E. Strand, ed., *A History of the Norwegians of Illinois*, 223 (Chicago, 1905). Bjørn Edwards was a great-uncle of Professor C. N. Evanson of Luther College.

7. Later the "Chicken Coop" housed the museum; after that, it held a portion of the music department; and it continued in use until it was torn down in 1952, when the present Main Building was erected.

8. O. A. Solheim, "Luther College," in *Symra*, 6:225 (1910); O. A. Tingelstad, *History of the F. N. E. L. Church of Decorah*, 16 (Decorah, 1926).

9. Oscar Ludvig Olson, "A History of My Administration as President of Luther College, Decorah, Iowa, 1921–1932," 113. This is a manuscript record deposited in the president's office, Luther College.

10. *Maanedstidende*, 332 (1862).

11. Knut Bergh to Rasmus B. Anderson, Anderson Papers, State Historical Society of Wisconsin at Madison. This letter is quoted by Lloyd Hustvedt in chapter 1 of his doctoral thesis on Anderson, to be submitted at the University of Wisconsin. For a good description of the atmosphere of the college in the 1870's, see Peer Strømme's *Halvor*, translated and adapted by Inga B. Norstog and David T. Nelson (Decorah, 1960) from the original *Hvorledes Halvor blev prest* (Decorah, 1893).

12. Data on early students is in Protokol No. 1, as is the wording of the diploma (see *attest* no. 33).

Footnotes

13. *Chips,* November 30, 1927; O. A. Solheim, in *Symra,* 6:232 (1910); Protokol No. 2, p. 51.

14. William C. Benson, *High on Manitou,* 333–335 (Northfield, Minnesota, 1949); Protokol No. 2, p. 34.

15. Sven Oftedal and August Weenaas, "Aaben erklæring," in *Skandinaven* (Chicago), January 30, 1874; Weenaas, *Wisconsinisme,* 44; *Festtaler,* 27, 28 (Festival Address—Chicago, 1890).

16. Karen Larsen, *Laur. Larsen,* 288.

17. Peer Strømme, *Erindringer,* 52 (Minneapolis, 1923).

18. Blegen, *Norwegian Migration: American Transition,* 588; Wist, "Pressen efter borgerkrigen," in *Festskrift,* 78, 183. A complete file of *For hjemmet* is in the Koren Library.

19. H. E. Jacobs, *A History of the Evangelical Lutheran Church in the United States,* 501 (New York, 1893); Laur. Larsen, "Tale af Prof. Larsen," in *Mindeskrift over Jacob D. Jacobsen* (Decorah, 1881).

20. *Landsmaal* is a language developed in Norway in contrast to the official Dano-Norwegian used before Norway became independent in 1814. Peer Strømme relates that in Larsen's absence, Seippel, who was a bachelor, often assigned chapel hymns at random. Thus the students sometimes sang hymns that were intended to be sung at the churching of a woman after confinement. In Ove H. Guldberg's Norwegian hymnary, which was then in use, there was one number entitled "For the Confirmation of a Princess." When Seippel announced this hymn one morning, the students had a hard time keeping straight faces as they sang, "Lo, the king's daughter is kneeling!" *Erindringer,* 54.

21. "God preserve us, sit down and hide your shame!" See Hanson, "What Became of Jens," 49.

22. Veblen, "At Luther College."

23. Strømme, *Erindringer,* 66.

VIII. EARLY STUDENT LIFE

1. Material on campus societies is drawn chiefly from Carl W. Strom's chapter, "Student Organizations," in *Luther College through Sixty Years,* 309–327, besides student "Journals" and other papers that are preserved in the Koren Library.

2. From an unsigned article on Niffelheim in *Luther College Semi-Centennial 1861–1911* (Decorah, 1911). This was the first annual at Luther College, published by the class of 1912, with Enoch E. Peterson, '12, as editor-in-chief.

3. Veblen, "At Luther College."

4. Much of this material on music is drawn from Chellis N. Evanson's chapter, "Music," in *Luther College through Sixty Years,* 361–382. See also Ivar A. Thorson, '95, in *Chips,* 83, 149 (1895).

5. Unsigned article on "Music at Luther College," in *Luther College Semi-Centennial.*

6. Protokol No. 2, p. 9.

7. R. J. Wisnæs, *Erindringer,* 104 (Fargo, North Dakota, 1934).
8. Hanson, "What Became of Jens," 60.
9. Hanson, "What Became of Jens," 46.
10. Hanson, "What Became of Jens," 51–53.
11. Strømme, *Halvor,* 125.
12. Hanson, "What Became of Jens," 46.
13. *Pioneer,* 178 (Decorah, 1932). This is an "annual" published by the junior class; it appeared intermittently 1920–46, and since then has been issued annually, 1948 to the present. See bibliographical note *l.*
14. Veblen, "At Luther College."
15. Veblen, "At Luther College."
16. Strømme, *Erindringer,* 64.
17. Protokol No. 2, p. 46.
18. Protokol No. 2, p. 10.
19. Protokol No. 2, p. 77, 78, 83.
20. P. J. Eikeland, "Thrond Bothne som lærer," in *Symra,* 4:23 (1908).
21. Strømme, *Erindringer,* 61.
22. J. A. Blilie, in *Luther College Bulletin,* October, 1927.
23. *Chips,* 28 (1885).
24. Ylvisaker, *Luther College* (Norwegian edition), 50, 51.
25. Blilie, in *Luther College Bulletin,* October, 1927.
26. Katherine Hustvedt, "Luther Coeds of the 1870's," in *Decorah Public Opinion,* August 19, 1957.
27. Blilie, in *Luther College Bulletin,* October, 1927.
28. Strømme, *Halvor,* 167.

IX. CRISIS AND RECOVERY

1. Halvard G. Roalkvam, '74, left the college in February 1886 and joined the Anti-Missourians. Peter Rudolf Oscar Olsen, who resigned in 1885, went to Norway to study and returned to America in 1890 to join the United Norwegian Lutheran Church. On the church cleavage, see chapter 1 of this study, p. 15.
2. Two boys from the town of Decorah, the Coleman brothers, were badly burned when, in spite of warnings, they stayed in the building too long. One of them died soon afterwards. *Beretning* (Iowa District), 45 (1889). For another account, see Oscar Ludvig Olson and Mrs. Olson, "A Family Saga," 40. This is a manuscript volume deposited in the president's office, Luther College.
3. Bothne, *Luther College,* 405; Belgum, "The Old Norwegian Synod," 251n.
4. Gjerset, in *Luther College through Sixty Years,* 385.
5. *Kirketidende,* 342 (1891).
6. *Festtaler,* 23.
7. Protokol No. 6, May 9, 1913.
8. Ludvig Hektoen, "Dr. V. Koren," in *Chips,* 21 (1911). "Gamle Koren" means "Old Koren."

Footnotes

9. *State Journal* (Madison, Wisconsin), November 11, 1901; information furnished by the State Historical Society of Wisconsin through the courtesy of Reverend Max D. Gaebler, First Unitarian Society, Madison.

10. Protokol No. 3, p. 87.

11. *Beretning,* 54–56 (1902).

12. Protokol No. 3, p. 171.

13. Larsen's report, in *Beretning,* Bilæg (Appendix) XVIII (1887).

14. *Chips,* 42 (1886), 95 (1889), 11, 13, 50 (1890).

15. *Beretning,* 63 (1890); *Kirketidende,* 392 (1891). Lutheran Ladies Seminary opened its doors November 5, 1894. It is said that H. A. Preus was the first member of the Norwegian Synod to raise the question of the education of women and that he stated, during a meeting in Red Wing, "You ought to establish a school for women here." The seminary was incorporated in 1889; 16 acres were purchased for a site, but the burning of the Main Building at Luther College caused a postponement of plans. In July 1892 work was resumed and the cornerstone of the building was laid May 11, 1893. See H. Allen, report, in *Beretning,* 74–78 (1902).

16. *Beretning,* 46 (1881).

17. Larsen, in Beretning, Bilæg XVI (1887).

18. Protokol No. 3, p. 12–14, 28–30; *Catalog,* 31 (1889–90).

19. *Chips,* 18, 35 (1890).

20. *Catalog,* 16 (1882–83); Protokol No. 3, p. 219.

X. CLOSE OF AN ERA

1. Harold M. Tolo, "Ulrik Vilhelm Koren as a Norwegian-American Pioneer Minister on the Middle-west Frontier," 75. This is a typewritten thesis submitted for the Master of Arts degree at the University of Minnesota in 1926. A copy is in the Koren Library.

2. Protokol No. 2, p. 167–169. For a fuller discussion of the last years of Larsen's administration, see Karen Larsen, *Laur. Larsen,* chapter 15.

3. Protokol No. 2, p. 167.

4. Protokol No. 3, p. 42, 46.

5. For an enlightening discussion of the growth of Puritanism in pioneer communities, see Marcus L. Hansen, "Immigration and Puritanism," in *Norwegian-American Studies and Records,* 9:1–28 (Northfield, Minnesota, 1936). One paragraph (p. 21) may be quoted: "The process of Puritanization can be followed by anyone who studies the records of a congregation or the minutes of a synod. Discipline became more and more strict. One after the other, social pleasures that were brought from the Old World fell under the ban. Temperance and Sunday observance were early enforced. Then card playing and dancing were prohibited. Simplicity in dress and manner of living were praised as virtues. The children of the immigrants were the object of much concern. When they began to forget the language of their parents and absorb the culture of their American contemporaries an effort was made to prevent all mingling in surrounding society by decreeing the sinfulness of any pastime that tempted such association. By the last quarter of the nineteenth century the Protestant immigrant churches had adopted so much of the New England atmosphere

that clergymen who came from the European seminaries of the various denominations were strangers in theology and ecclesiastical practice."

6. Protokol No. 3, p. 205.

7. Protokol No. 3, p. 245–259.

8. Protokol No. 2, p. 17. Cf. Hansen, in *Studies and Records,* 9:1–28.

9. Protokol No. 3, p. 179; *Beretning,* 75 (1899).

10. *Pioneer,* 104 (1929).

11. Evanson, in *Luther College through Sixty Years,* 361–382.

12. Olson, "A Family Saga," 34.

13. Details of the story were furnished by S. S. Reque, who had it from one of the members of the team. For the box score, see the article on athletics in *Luther College Semi-Centennial.*

14. Protokol No. 3, p. 151, 152, 169.

15. Protokol No. 3, p. 262.

16. Information furnished by N. A. Larsen, '96, and S. S. Reque, '03.

17. Olson, "A Family Saga," 37.

18. Francis E. Peterson, "Presidents and Principals," in *Luther College through Sixty Years,*" 70, 71.

19. Ole J. Kvale, '90, *The Soul of Luther College,* an address presented at commencement exercises, June 2, 1925 (Minneapolis, n.d.) A copy is filed in the Koren Library.

XI. EXPANSION AND GROWTH

1. Olaf M. Norlie, ed., *Norsk lutherske prester i Amerika 1843–1915,* 76 (Minneapolis, 1915).

2. *The Union Documents of the Evangelical Lutheran Church,* 67 (Minneapolis, 1948). A member of the class of 1917 wrote: "I saw Preus immediately after the memorable Austin Conference, and his evident happiness at the prospect of being able to join the new church body revealed to me as nothing else could his true position in regard to the church controversies." Quoted in Tingelstad and Norlie, *Christian Keyser Preus,* 181.

3. The story, with supporting documents, is found in J. C. K. Preus, *The Union Movement and the "Minority," 1917* (Privately printed, [Minneapolis, 1958]). See p. 12–14 for Graebner's acknowledgment of the interpretation of Preus and Torrison as correct.

4. *Beretning,* 320 (1918).

5. *Beretning,* 14 (1908).

6. *Beretning,* 13–17 (1907), 15 (1908), 216–218 (1914). The architects were Buechner and Orth, St. Paul, Minnesota; and the contractor was O. H. Olson, Stillwater, Minnesota.

7. *Chips,* 171–175 (1907).

8. Trustees Minutes, 32–38 (August 8, 1905). See bibliographical note *m*.

9. H. M. Tolo, "Ulrik Vilhelm Koren," 110.

10. Protokol No. 7, December 20, 1915; *Beretning,* 185 (1917).

11. Trustees Minutes, 49 (June 17, 1909); *Beretning,* 13 (1909).

12. The architects were Magney and Tusler of Minneapolis; James C. M. Hanson, '82, was consultant on library planning. The general contract was

Footnotes

let to A. R. Coffeen, and the plumbing and heating contract to Peter
Johnson and Sons, both of Decorah.

13. Olson, "My Administration," 27, quoting Professor Hardin Craig.

14. *Beretning,* 273 (1921).

15. *Beretning,* 96, 132 (1915); Trustees Minutes, April 25, 1918.

16. *Beretning,* 184, 192 (1917); Luther College Faculty, Minutes, October 9, 1919, March 12, October 7, November 29, 1920. These will be
cited henceforth as Faculty Minutes. See bibliographical note *i* on Protokol.

17. Protokol No. 4, p. 19, 31.

18. Faculty Minutes, January 23, 1918.

19. Faculty Minutes, February 6, 9, September 18, 1918, May 8, 1919.

20. For the struggle in England, see Matthew Arnold, "Literature and
Science," and Thomas Henry Huxley, "Science and Culture," in Paul Robert
Lieder, Robert Morss Lovett, and Robert Kilburn Root, *British Poetry and
Prose,* 2:709–719, 748–756 (Boston, 1938).

21. Knut Gjerset, "Important Events," in *Luther College through Sixty
Years,* 391.

22. *Beretning,* 65 (1911); Trustees Minutes, October 16, 1911, May 12,
1912.

XII. THE PIONEER PASSES

1. Faculty Minutes, May 19, 1921.

2. *Chips,* 383, 443 (1913); Faculty Minutes, November 4, 1920.

3. *Beretning,* 53 (1905).

4. Protokol No. 3, p. 287, No. 4, p. 14, 15.

5. Protokol No. 6, October 5, 1914.

6. Faculty Minutes, April 5, 1919.

7. Tingelstad and Norlie, *Christian Keyser Preus,* 133. The nickname was
derived from Nick Carter, the famous dime-novel detective.

8. *Beretning,* II, 11 (1904); *Catalog,* 35 (1904); Gerald Jenny, *The Young
People's Movement in the American Lutheran Church,* 94 (Minneapolis,
1928); Olson, "A Family Saga," 52, 84.

9. *Pioneer,* 95–100 (1920); *Chips,* 36 (1903).

10. *Pioneer,* 101–104 (1920).

11. *Den norske studentersangforenings koncerttourné gjennem det norske
Amerika,* 182 (Christiania, 1903); Oscar A. Tingelstad and Johan C. K.
Preus, *Norgesfærden,* 34 (Decorah, 1914). The career of Elizabeth Fedde,
founder of the first Norwegian-American deaconess mother house in Brooklyn, New York, is sketched in Beulah Folkedahl, "Elizabeth Fedde's Diary,
1883–88," in *Norwegian-American Studies and Records,* 20:170–193 (Northfield, Minnesota, 1959).

12. Full details of the tour are found in Tingelstad and Preus, *Norgesfærden.* Unfortunately for the average reader, the account is written in Norwegian, but there are hundreds of illustrations.

13. "St. Olson" refers to Oscar L. Olson, to whom Preus had assigned

the task of ferreting out the names of those who had played ball in Calmar on Sunday.

14. Protokol No. 7, January 18, 1916.

15. *Pioneer*, 143 (1920).

XIII. MODERNIZING THE COLLEGE

1. J. A. O. Stub, address at the Diamond Jubilee celebration, in *Bulletin*, December, 1936.

2. Details of Olson's background and early life are based on "A Family Saga."

3. Olson, "A Family Saga," 22.

4. Olson, "A Family Saga," 58, 86.

5. Olson, "A Family Saga," 68.

6. Trustees Minutes, April 21, 1923, January 17, 1924; Olson, "My Administration," 87, 88.

7. Carlo A. Sperati, "Sixtieth Anniversary," in *Luther College through Sixty Years*, 403.

8. On April 13, 1926, the contract for construction was let to A. R. Coffeen, for plumbing and heating to Peter Johnson and Sons, and for electrical work to the Electric Service Company; all three were Decorah firms.

9. The consideration was $8,134. Luther College Corporation, Minutes, May 23, 1930; Trustees Minutes, October 1, 1930; Olson, "My Administration," 112. The Luther Corporation (college farm) of the preceding paragraph was dissolved in 1952. Trustees Minutes, October 10, 1952.

10. *Chips*, February 16, 1927.

11. Olson, "My Administration," 2, 21.

12. J. C. M. Hanson, quoted in Olson, "My Administration," 32.

13. Trustees Minutes, October 15, 1925.

14. *Chips*, December 1, 1926, April 27, 1927; Knut Gjerset, "The Norwegian-American Historical Museum," in *Norwegian-American Studies and Records*, 6:154–156 (Northfield, Minnesota, 1931).

15. Trustees Minutes, October 14, 1932. The college acquired title to the building in 1945; Trustees Minutes, April 23, 1945.

16. *Chips*, June 3, 1931.

17. *Chips*, February 5, March 5, 1930.

18. The amount of the gift was announced as $72,136.04 in cash and pledges; *Chips*, October 21, 1931. The realized amount was $47,507.37. See *Catalog*, 37 (1932); Oscar Ludvig Olson, "Addresses and Other Compositions," 109. The latter is a typed manuscript filed in the Koren Library.

19. *Chips*, October 15, 1931.

XIV. THE GATHERING STORM

1. Olson, in *Luther College through Sixty Years*, 474, 482.

2. Olson, in *Luther College through Sixty Years*, 474, 479–480.

3. *Pioneer*, 72 (1929).

4. Olson, "My Administration," 65.

Footnotes

5. Faculty Minutes, January 16, 1924.
6. *Catalog*, 27, 28 (1923); *Pioneer*, 110 (1932).
7. Olson, "My Administration," 85.
8. *Chips*, November 17, December 8, 1926.
9. Faculty Minutes, March 13, June 16, 17, December 16, 1926, January 4, 5, 7, 1927.
10. Faculty Minutes, October 8, 1924, September 5, 1927, February 1, November 11, December 5, 1929, May 5, 1931; *Catalog*, 39 (1924), 40 (1925).
11. *Catalog*, 36–38 (1931–32); Olson, "My Administration," 105–109; Faculty Minutes, November 8, 1923; Trustees Minutes, April 21, 1923.
12. Olson, "My Administration," 102; Trustees Minutes, June 25, 1929, October 2, 1930; the latter reference shows that bank loans amounted to $109,000.
13. Olson, "My Administration," 126, 127.
14. Olson, "My Administration," 102.
15. For Stub's statement, see chapter 7 of this history. J. Magnus Rohne, in "The Lutheran Church and Higher Education," in *Lutheran Herald*, 15:1128–1131 (1931), had pointed out that Lutherans in this country had followed three types of higher education: (1) The Missouri type, restricted to training for the ministry and therefore limited to men; (2) A moderately restricted type, aiming particularly at preparing men for the ministry, but preparing also for other professions, and admitting women; (3) A type of popular education, unrestricted, open to both men and women, which has proved very successful.

Knut Gjerset, in "The Historical Background of Norwegian American Lutheranism," in *Lutheran Herald*, 16:683 (1932), argued that the changes which had taken place in church life made it necessary to maintain "educational institutions sufficiently broad in scope and character to develop well trained lay leaders and church workers," because in the future "what the men in the pews are thinking will be no less important than what the preacher in the pulpit is preaching."

16. Faculty Minutes, January 16, 1932; minutes of the Board of Education, Norwegian Lutheran Church of America, December 16, 1931.
17. Faculty Minutes, January 7, 1932; the typed, signed statements are found in the Koren Library. Committee members were Knut Gjerset, Knute O. Eittreim, Carl W. Strom, '19, David T. Nelson, '12, and Chellis N. Evanson, '18.
18. Olson, "My Administration," 102; Trustees Minutes, February 20, 1932; Board of Education Minutes, February 26, 1932.
19. Report of the Tenth General Convention of the Norwegian Lutheran Church of America, 240 (Minneapolis, 1932). See bibliographical note *d*.
20. *Report*, 217 (1932); the deficit in 1932–33 was $5,700, according to the audited accounts of the college.
21. Olson, "My Administration," 65; *Chips*, May 31, 1932.

XV. STRUGGLE FOR SURVIVAL

1. *Luther Alumnus*, May 1948. Volume 1, number 1, appeared in January 1932; it is published monthly except during July, October, and December.

2. From Preus's statement of acceptance in *Report,* 131 (1932).

3. Olson, "My Administration," 135n.

4. Trustees Minutes, February 26, 1932; report of the Luther College Corporation in *Report,* 247 (1932).

5. Luther College Alumni Association, Minutes, August 13, 1934, filed in the alumni office, Luther College.

6. Trustees Minutes, July 26, 1933.

7. Figure furnished by W. O. Kalsow, college treasurer, from the official audit.

8. Trustees Minutes, February 1–2, December 3, 1934.

9. Trustees Minutes, June 17, 1932.

10. Norwegian Lutheran Church of America, Board of Education, Minutes, July 6, 1932; these are filed in the office of the executive secretary, Board of Education, American Lutheran Church, Minneapolis.

11. For material regarding Decorah College for Women, the author is indebted to the detailed account in Olson, "My Administration," 146–157.

12. Trustees Minutes, October 14, 1932.

13. Trustees Minutes, July 26–27, 1933.

14. *Lutheran Herald,* 247–248 (March 13, 1934); Board of Education, Minutes, February 1, 1934. For the resolution, see *Lutheran Herald,* 166 (February 13, 1934).

15. Board of Education, Minutes, April 11, 1934. Members of the Executive Committee at this time were J. A. Aasgaard, J. C. K. Preus, and Joseph Norby.

16. *Report,* 36 (1934).

17. Henry O. Talle, '17, in a letter to the author of June 24, 1960, confirms this account.

18. D. G. Ristad, in *Skandinaven,* March 28, 1933, an article purporting to set forth L. W. Boe's views on overhauling the organization and machinery of the church body. Knut Gjerset discussed the proposal in *Decorahposten,* April 18, 1933.

19. *Report,* 307–317 (1934).

20. C. N. Evanson, '18, in *Luther Alumnus,* June–July, 1934.

21. Luther College Alumni Association, Minutes, August 13, 1934; *Luther Alumnus,* November 1934.

22. M. O. Grangaard, address to the Twin City Luther College Club, February 22, 1935, in Luther *Alumnus,* March 1935.

23. *Luther Alumnus,* March 1933.

24. *Luther Alumnus,* January 1935.

25. *Chips,* May 15, 1935; *Luther Alumnus,* August 1935.

26. Talle to the author, June 24, 1960.

27. *Luther Alumnus,* June 1935.

28. *Chips,* February 14, 1934.

29. Board of Education, Minutes, June 26, 27, 1934.

30. From manuscript material in the possession of the author, including letters of May 13 and October 28, 1935, from M. O. Grangaard. Committee members were John Nystul of Concordia College, Martin Cole of Augustana College, P. O. Holland of St. Olaf College, and David T. Nelson of Luther College.

Footnotes

31. Board of Education, Minutes, February 14, 1936. See also *Lutheran Herald,* March 4, 1936.

32. Luther College Alumni Association, Minutes, February 22, 1932, June 4, 1935. Committee members were David T. Nelson, '12, Edwin R. Selnes, '16, and Wilford A. Johnson, '99. The spade work was done by the first member of the committee and submitted to the two other members. Thereupon the draft of the new articles was submitted by Professor Nelson in January 1936 to the Executive Committee of the Board of Trustees at the Curtis Hotel at Minneapolis, where two or three minor changes were made.

33. N. B. Hanson, '99, address at Homecoming, October 14, 1944, quoted by Olson, "My Administration," 143.

XVI. THE TRIUMPH OF COEDUCATION

1. *Luther Alumnus,* November 1936; *Bulletin,* December 1936.

2. *Bulletin,* December 1936.

3. *Chips,* March 22, 1939, January 29, 1941; *Bulletin,* December 1939, March 1940; *Report,* 402 (1940); *Luther Alumnus,* June 1942.

4. Trustees Minutes, June 11, 1937, February 27, 1945, July 9, 1946. Committee members were Karl Hanson, '08; Chellis N. Evanson, '18; Henry O. Talle, '17; David T. Nelson, '12; and Herman E. Ellingson, '24.

5. *Bulletin,* December 1937; Faculty Minutes, October 12, 1936, March 15, 1937, May 18, 1939, September 25, 1940, March 18, 1941; *Catalog,* 1936–37, p. 87.

6. *Chips,* September 18, 1940.

7. *Chips,* November 2, 1938; Trustees Minutes, October 9, 1940, August 29, 1951, December 6, 1946; *Bulletin,* February 1943, and subsequent annual issues of the *Bulletin* dealing with KWLC. (One issue a year is devoted to the radio station.)

8. Faculty Minutes, May 31, 1942.

9. *Report,* 414–415 (1942); Faculty Minutes, May 31, June 4, 1942; *Bulletin,* July 1942.

10. *Luther College through Sixty Years,* 396, gives the figure for World War I as 356, but no verification has been found for this.

11. *Bulletin,* December 1938.

12. Luther College Alumni Association, Minutes, October 12, 1935; Trustees Minutes, January 31, 1936, June 11, 1937, September 17, 1943, October 15, 1943, December 7, 1944, August 13, 1945, May 13, 1946, August 24, 29, 1946.

XVII. POSTWAR ADJUSTMENTS

1. Trustees Minutes, May 18, 1942.

2. *Bulletin,* January 1942, December 1946.

3. Architect, Charles Altfillisch, Decorah; general contract, $40,445, Rye and Hinkel, Mason City, Iowa; heating equipment, $72,650, Grudem Brothers, St. Paul; tunnels, $22,763, A. R. Coffeen Company, Decorah.

4. President Preus's report, in *Report,* 95 (1947); *Luther Alumnus,* May 1946, January 1947.

Footnotes

5. *Chips,* May 14, 1946, May 13, 1947; *Bulletin,* December 1946.

6. Preus, in *Report,* 95 (1947); Trustees Minutes, April 22, 1946, June 2, August 18, October 10, 1947; *Bulletin,* December 1946.

7. *Luther Alumnus,* August 1944, June 1955. Copies of *Catiline* are in the Library of Congress and the University of Illinois library.

8. *Catalog,* 1936, p. 9; Faculty Minutes, September 20, 1936; Trustees Minutes, May 27, 1946.

9. Faculty Minutes, September 5, 1941, October 14, 1942, October 27, November 10, 1943; *Catalog,* 1945. Members of the postwar planning committee were Nelson, chairman, Hoslett, Qualley, Frank, Fadness, and Paulson.

10. Faculty Minutes, November 14, December 12, 1945, February 27, March 27, May 15, 1946.

11. Faculty Minutes, September 14, 1945, February 27, March 13, 1946; Trustees Minutes, May 27, 1946.

12. Faculty Minutes, March 3, 1948. For the full statement see Appendix, p. 347.

13. Janet Campbell, "Seventy-Seven Years with the Luther College Concert Band," 24-31 (1955). This is a typewritten history filed in Koren Library.

14. *Bulletin,* August 1942.

15. *Luther Alumnus,* April 1948; *Pioneer 1948,* 22–23.

16. *Luther Alumnus,* June 1960.

17. It is difficult at best, if not hazardous, to single out alumni among graduates who are still so definitely contemporary. Nevertheless, without prejudice to those not mentioned, some from this period not elsewhere discussed may be noted as representative: John Breiland, '33, assistant professor of physics and meteorology, University of New Mexico; Ruben H. Huenemann, '33, pastor of Grace Church, Milwaukee, president of the California Synod, Evangelical and Reformed Church, 1950–54, and moderator of the General Synod, Tiffin, Ohio, 1953; Lauren B. Nesset, '33, physician and surgeon, Minneapolis; Carroll B. Hanson, '34, director of publicity, United States Department of Health, Education, and Welfare; Gerhard B. Naeseth, '34, associate director of the University of Wisconsin Library; Marvin S. Thostenson, '34, assistant professor of music, the State University of Iowa; Sam Legvold, '35, professor of physics, Iowa State University, Ames; Norman C. J. Owen, '35, vice president, Scott Atwater Company, Minneapolis; Gerhard H. Jacobsen, '35, administrative specialist of cost improvement division, Missile and Space Vehicle Department, General Electric Company, Philadelphia; Christian L. Strom, '35, associate actuary, Continental Assurance Company, Chicago; Edward Struxness, '35, assistant director of health, Physics National Laboratory, Oak Ridge, Tennessee; Karl M. Torgerson, '36, chief auditor, Iowa Power and Light Company, Des Moines, and since March 1, 1961, director of development, Luther College; Paul C. Preus, '36, assistant dean, Julliard School of Music, New York City; Kenneth H. Fagerhaugh, '36, librarian and associate professor of library science, Carnegie Institute of Technology, Pittsburgh; John O. Hjelle, '36, editor of the *Bismarck* (North Dakota) *Tribune;* Russel O. Saxvik, '36, superintendent, State Mental Hospital, Jamestown, North Dakota; Donald O. Rod, '38, librarian and head of the department of library

397

Footnotes

science, Iowa State Teachers College, Cedar Falls; Clifton M. Weihe, '38, chairman of the Lutheran Evangelism Council and pastor in the United Lutheran Church in America; Laurel O. Johnson, '40, missionary, Fort Dauphin, Madagascar; Frank R. Barth, '40, vice president, Pettibone Mullikan Corporation, Chicago; L. Reuben Lerud, '40, auditor, American Lutheran Church, Minneapolis; Adrian Helgeson, '41, partner, Boulay, Anderson, Waldo, and Company, Minneapolis; Frederick W. Moen, '41, editor, the Associated Press, Kansas City, Missouri; J. A. O. Preus, Jr., '41, professor, Concordia Seminary, Springfield, Illinois; Wesley L. Nyborg, '41, professor of physics, University of Vermont, Burlington; Robert E. A. Lee, '42, executive secretary, Lutheran Church Productions, New York City; Theodor L. Jacobsen, '42, executive director, Lutheran Deaconess and Lutheran General Hospital, Chicago; John V. Halvorson, '43, professor, Luther Theological Seminary, St. Paul, Minnesota; Fridtjof C. M. Schroder, '43, assistant professor of art, University of Cincinnati; Robert D. Preus, '44, professor, Concordia Seminary, St. Louis; Mildred Knapcik, '47, missionary, Entumeni, South Africa; R. Kermit Vanderbilt, '47, assistant professor of English, University of Washington, Seattle; and Robert M. Josephson, '47, manager, Arthur Andersen and Company, Chicago.

18. "A Message From Dr. O. J. H. Preus," in *Luther Alumnus*, February 1947.

19. The general contract on a cost-plus basis went to A. R. Coffeen Company, Decorah; the plumbing contract to Grudem Brothers, St. Paul; and the electrical contract to Dudley Larson, Decorah.

20. *Bulletin*, December 1932.

XVIII. PLANNING FOR GROWTH

1. *Luther Alumnus*, December 1947; Luther College Alumni Association, Minutes, June 2, October 11, 1947.

2. *Luther Alumnus*, March 1959.

3. The bonds were issued by the B. C. Ziegler Company, West Bend, Wisconsin. Trustees Minutes, July 22, 1948.

4. Architect, Charles Altfillisch of Decorah. General contract, $382,500, Johnson Construction Company, Winona, Minnesota; electrical, $23,113, Brayton Electric Company, Waverly, Iowa; mechanical, $49,959, Flom and Forsyth, Houston, Minnesota; trunk elevator, $12,759, the R. and O. Elevator Company, Minneapolis; *Luther Alumnus*, March 1957.

5. Architect, Charles Altfillisch of Decorah. General contract, $435,000, Johnson Construction Company, Winona; plumbing and heating, $78,105, Grudem Brothers, St. Paul; electrical, $21,260, Dudley Larson, Decorah; elevator, $15,553, Northwestern Elevator Company, Milwaukee.

6. Architects, Charles Altfillisch of Decorah. General contract, $398,144, Johnson Construction Company, Winona; heating and plumbing, $68,682, Vick's Heating and Plumbing, Decorah; electrical, $26,600, Dewey Electric Company, Ventura, Iowa.

7. Architects, Altfillisch, Gray, Olson, and Thompson of Decorah. General contract, $638,950, Johnson Construction Company, Winona; plumbing and heating, $276,560, Kirckhoff Heating and Plumbing, Rochester, Minnesota; electrical, $156,477, Dewey Electric, Inc., Ventura, Iowa.

8. Architects, Altfillisch, Gray, Olson, and Thompson of Decorah. General contract $790,000, Johnson Construction Company, Winona; mechanical, $147,570, Carstens Plumbing and Heating, Ackley, Iowa; electrical, $73,657, Brown Electric, Decorah; temperature controls $9,750, Honeywell Company, Minneapolis; refrigeration, $16,362, United Cork Companies, Rock Island, Illinois; kitchen, $76,276, Hockenberg Fixture and Supply Company, Des Moines; freight elevator, $14,994, Otis Elevator Company, Des Moines.

9. Algo D. Henderson, "Report on Luther College to the Gardner Cowles Foundation," February 13, 1956. A copy was furnished to President Ylvisaker by Gardner Cowles and is on file in the former's office.

10. Mars A. Dale, report, in *Report*, 104 (1951); J. A. Aasgaard, "President's Message," in *Report*, 12 (1952).

11. *Luther Alumnus*, March 1955.

12. Letters dated Mansfield, Ohio, June 23, and August 28, 1952, from Louis W. Olson to G. A. Sundby, now on file in the president's office, Luther College; memorandum from Mrs. G. A. Sundby dated Decorah, Iowa, July 7, 1959, in the possession of the author; *Luther Alumnus*, September 1955.

13. Trustees Minutes, September 20, 1955; Regents Minutes, February 26, 1960. Under a revision of the Articles of Incorporation of October 28, 1958, the Board of Trustees became the Board of Regents. Minutes of this board will be referred to henceforth as Regents Minutes.

14. Luther College Alumni Association, Minutes, October 21, 1950; *Luther Alumnus*, December 1952.

15. *Luther Alumnus*, December 1953; Luther College Alumni Association, Minutes, August 30, 1954.

16. *Luther Alumnus*, March, August, 1956; Trustees Minutes, February 21, 1958.

17. *Luther Alumnus*, June 1959.

18. *Luther Alumnus*, June, November 1958.

19. *Luther Alumnus*, March 1957, September 1960.

20. *Luther College: The President's Report, 1958–59* (Decorah, 1959). This report has been printed annually since 1954–55.

21. *Luther Alumnus*, March 1959.

XIX. RAISING STANDARDS

1. Trustees Minutes, August 17, 1950, October 14, 1955, February 17, 1956.

2. The handbook was compiled by the faculty affairs committee, consisting of Sherman A. Hoslett, '30, George E. Knudson, David T. Nelson, '12, Clara J. Paulson, and Oivind M. Hovde, '32.

3. Trustees Minutes, May 30, 1949.

4. *Luther Alumnus*, August 1959; dean's report, in Regents Minutes, October 9, 1959.

5. J. C. K. Preus, "Introductory Remarks," in Karl T. Jacobsen, comp., *Library of Congress Classification Schedules for the Lutheran Church, Modified and Expanded* (Department of Christian Education, Evangelical Lutheran Church, *Monograph Series*, vol. 2, no. 3—Minneapolis, 1953).

Footnotes

6. Knute Lee, *Plain Talk in an Arctic Chapel* (Minneapolis, 1954), 182 p.; Gerhard E. Frost and Gerhard L. Belgum, *Chapel Time* (Minneapolis, 1956), 149 p.; *The Diary of Elizabeth Koren*, translated from the Norwegian and edited by David T. Nelson (Northfield, Minnesota, 1955), 381 p.; *Halvor*, translated from the Norwegian and adapted by Inga B. Norstog and David T. Nelson (Decorah, 1960), 235 p.

7. *Luther Alumnus*, June 1953.

8. *Money and Banking*, by the Committee on Money and Banking, a collaborative writing group of money and banking professors (Pitman Publishing Corporation, New York, 1957); *Public Finance*, by the Committee on Public Finance, a collaborative writing group of public finance professors (Pitman Publishing Corporation, New York, 1959); *Principles of Accounting*, by the Committee on Accounting, a collaborative writing group of college accounting professors (Pitman Publishing Corporation, New York, 1959).

9. The four books of studies, all edited by Nilo W. Hovey and published by Belwin, Inc., New York, are *First Book of Practical Studies for Cornet and Trumpet* (1948); *Second Book of Practical Studies for Cornet and Trumpet* (1948); *First Book of Practical Studies for Tuba* (1955); *Second Book of Practical Studies for Tuba* (1955). Getchell has also written a *Teachers' Guide to the Brass Instruments* (Elkhart, Indiana, 1959).

10. Roland H. Bainton, Warren A. Quanbeck, and E. Gordon Rupp, *Luther Today*, vi (*Martin Luther Lectures*, vol. 1—Decorah, 1957).

11. The first volume is given in note 10 above. The other four are: Regin Prenter, Jaroslav J. Pelikan, and Herman E. Preus, *More about Luther*; Theodore G. Tappert, Lowell C. Green, and Willem J. Kooiman, *The Mature Luther*; George W. Forell, Harold J. Grimm, and Theodo Hoelty-Nickel, *Luther and Culture*; D. Peter Brunner and Bernard J. Holm, *Luther in the Twentieth Century* (*Martin Luther Lectures*, vols. 2–5—Decorah, 1958–61).

12. *Luther Alumnus*, December 1954.

13. *Luther Alumnus*, June 1954; dean's report, in Trustees Minutes, October 18, 1957, October 17, 1958.

14. *Bulletin*, September 1950.

15. Report to the Gardner Cowles Foundation, February 13, 1956; a copy is in the president's office.

16. *Luther Alumnus*, August 1958.

17. Dean's report, in Regents Minutes, August 28, 1959.

18. *Luther Alumnus*, May, 1960; "Report to National Council for Accreditation of Teacher Education on Luther College, Decorah, Iowa." A copy of the latter is on file in the registrar's office.

19. *Luther Alumnus*, June 1952.

20. Ellen Knudson Mather was born April 3, 1853 at Willow Farm and was christened by Elling Eielsen (Sunve). When her mother died, Laur. Larsen and P. A. Rasmussen officiated at the funeral. Ellen often heard her father and Laur. Larsen discuss the problems of the education of Norwegian Americans. In 1868, when she was 14 years old, she began to teach school, receiving $16 a month and board. Each month, from her first pay check and from every succeeding pay check throughout her teaching years, she sent a contribution to Luther College. She married Samuel Mather (of Quaker stock) January 26, 1878. They lived in Springdale, Iowa, 14 miles east of Iowa City. Her daughter Lydia Jeannette married Frederic P. Lord,

for some years a member of the faculty of the State University of Iowa and later of Dartmouth College.

21. *Luther Alumnus,* March 1952.

22. *Luther Alumnus,* September 1952. The recordings are available through the college business office.

23. *Luther Alumnus,* March 1952.

24. *Luther Alumnus,* November 1954; Henderson, "Report on Luther College," to the Cowles Foundation, February 13, 1956. A copy of the latter is on file in the office of the dean of the college.

25. *Luther Alumnus,* February 1952; March 1953.

XX. A LAST WORD

1. From a "Letter to Alumni," by N. B. Hanson, '95, L. P. Lund, '04, B. K. Savre, '96, and George A. Torrison, '85, in *Chips,* February 18, 1931.

2. Data based on individuals listed in *Who's Who.* Arthur E. Nealy, educational director of Marquis-Who's Who, Inc., to Irene Langlie, assistant director of public services, Luther College, June 20, 1960. The letter is filed in the office of public services.

3. N. N. Ronning, in "Glimpses of Luther College," *Bulletin,* September 1947.

Index

For the convenience of readers the Norwegian characters æ and ø are alphabeted respectively as ae and o.

Aabel, Oluf Andreas, 35
Aabel, Peter Pavels, 35
Aaberg Academy (Devil's Lake, N. D.), 144
Aadnesen, Mrs. ———, 141
Aaker, Adolph O., 217
Aaker, Jack, 297
Aase, Gil, 236
Aasen, Halvor A., 82
Aasgaard, Johan A., 229, 246, 247, 261, 281, 395
Abolitionists, 81, 386
Academy Conference, 233
Adams, Newton, 381
Adams, Mrs. Walter C., 200
Addison, student society, 115, 155
Adolf Gundersen Lecture Fund, 324
Adolf Gundersen Medical Foundation, 324
Ahl, Hildegard D., 358
Aid Association for Lutherans, 240
Aim, 17, 56, 88, 96, 101, 112, 130, 143, 179–185, 231, 239, 244, 270, 289, 290, 291, 318, 343, 349
Algyer, Durwin D., 238, 313
Algyer, Ray, 218, 276
Allison, Mary Clara, 358
Almlie, Magdalene M., 358
Alsaker, Leona, 326, 358
Altfillisch, Charles H., 217, 256, 396, 398
Altfillisch, Gray, Olson, and Thompson (Decorah), 398, 399
Alumni Directory (Decorah), 277
Alumni Fund, 314

Ambuel, J. Philip, 358
Ambuel, Louise, 358
American Alumni Council, 315
American Association of University Women, 329
American Legion, 283
American Lutheran Church, 16, 309, 310, 318
Americanization, 16, 18; of Luther College, 1, 4, 48, 90, 91, 92, 93, 214, 235, 239, 270; of Norwegians, 10, 386, 390. See also English language
Amland, Harold J., 358
Ammondsen, Clayton J., 358
Amphictyonic Literary Society, 155, 199, 234
Amundson, Dr. Albert C., 112
Andersen, Arthur, 264
Andersen, Esther, 358
Andersen, Gordon W., 358
Anderson, Amund, 12
Anderson, Carrie M., 358, 371
Anderson, Gerald S., 358
Anderson, Henry O., 358
Anderson, Isaac, 163
Anderson, John, 87
Anderson, Paul, 8, 9
Anderson, Rasmus B., 89, 97, 98, 147; leads student rebellion, 76–78, 382; sketch, 111
Anderson, Roger W., 358
Andrewson, Ole, 8
Anti-Missourian Brotherhood, 15, 132, 167, 389

403

Index

Anundsen, B. B., 256
Arlington Hotel (Decorah), 134
Arneson, Theresa, 328
Articles of Incorporation, 60, 102, 103, 239, 246, 254, 260, 268, 269, 271, 318, 399
Arveson, Mr. and Mrs. Adolph, 278
Asbjørnsen, Sigvald, 228, 331
Aslagsen, Isak, 82
Aslaksen, Knut W., 41, 49, 97
Asmus, Dorley M., 358
Aspenson, Mrs. Oscar, 362
Asperheim, O., 131
Associated College Press, 333
Astrup, Ingeborg, 104
Astrup, Johannes, 163
Astrup, Nikolai, 104
Athenian, student society, 155
Athletics and sports, 93, 95, 119, 145, 156–160, 203–207, 223, 235–238, 290, 298, 299, 336–339
Attendance, 49, 55, 56, 74, 89, 90, 132, 171, 215, 219, 231, 232, 233, 243, 249, 255, 266, 282, 284, 308, 309, 316, 340, 341, 355
Augsburg College and Seminary (Marshall, Wis., and Minneapolis), 9, 10, 15, 90, 140, 167, 184
Augsburg Confession, 7, 21, 22, 59, 107, 228
Augsburg Publishing House, 227
Augustana College (Sioux Falls, S.D.), 10, 191, 251, 252, 376, 395
Augustana College and Seminary (Chicago, Paxton, and Rock Island, Ill.), 9, 52, 184, 251, 252
Augustana Evangelical Lutheran Church, 9, 184
"Austin Agreement," 168, 391
Austvold, Edwin B., 173

Baccarini, Mrs. John, 360
Bache, Søren, 11
Bache, Tollef, 11
Bagley, Viola E., 266
Bahe, Barbara, 294, 358
Bahr, Vernon H., 358
Bailey, A. K., 136
Bainton, Roland H., 324
Baker, Barbara, 296

Baker, George A., 314
Baker, Jean, 296
Bakke, Nils J., 111, 118
Bale, Christian E., 207
Bale, John C., 326, 359
Band Music Festival, 336
Bang, A. C., 193
Barber, Mrs. Robert, 368
Barns, Shirley, 359
Barnum, P. T., 377
Barsness, Martha, 333
Barth, Frank R., 293, 359, 398
Barth, Margaret, 334
Barth, Ruth, 296
Baseball, 93, 119, 139, 149, 156–159, 170, 174, 190, 203, 213, 218, 223, 236, 251, 298, 337, 338
Basketball, 193, 205, 206, 223, 237, 298, 338
Bassøe, Peter Frederik, 37
Bear, Ben, 256, 274, 276
Beaver, Lyle B., 359
Beaver, Nellie, 146
Beaver Creek settlement (Iroquois County, Ill.), 2
Behrens Quartet, 118
Belding, Adolph L., 298
Belgum, Gerhard L., 322, 323, 324, 326, 338, 359
Belgum, Henrik O., 237
Benson, George, 311
Benson, Gordon M., 359
Bentson, Reinhard T., 120, 382
Berg, J. A., 357
Berg, Warren G., 322, 326, 359, 371
Bergan, Kenneth N., 359
Bergan, Martin, 299
Berger, Arne, 228
Berger, Kenneth L., 293, 296, 325, 359, 371
Berger, Marion, 359
Bergh, Johannes E., 49
Bergh, Knut E., 41, 49, 53, 97, 98, 105, 106, 108
Bergland, Allan, 359
Bergsaker, A. J., 281, 282
Bergstrom, Richard, 359, 371
Bernatz, George, Sons (Decorah) grocery, 134
Berntsen, Maxine, 359
Berven, Luther H., 359

Bestul, Valborg E., 359
Bickle, Junior, 288
Biermann, Fred, 204
Biewend, Adolph F. T., 28
Big Canoe (Iowa), Norwegian settlement, 25, 41, 49, 81, 87, 99
Billington, Dr. John T., 56, 381
Birkestrand, Harold O. S., 359, 371
Bishop, A. C., 256, 258, 275
Bjarnason, Jon, 107
Bjerkness, Odell, 359
Bjørgo, K., 117
Bjorkquist, James, 359
Bjornstad, William, 160
Black Earth (Dane County, Wis.), 40, 378, 381
Blegen, Theodore C., 85
Bleken, Martinus K., 194
Blilie, J. A., 126
Bloomfield, Mrs. Julia, 300
Board of Education, NLCA, 103, 181, 183, 214, 238, 243, 244, 246, 247, 248, 253, 254, 256, 257, 260, 262, 267, 268; ELC, 269, 307
Board of Professors, 103
Board of Regents, 187, 318, 319, 332, 356–358, 374, 399. *See also* Board of Trustees
Board of Trustees, 103, 141, 148, 176, 177, 187, 189, 226, 228, 243, 244, 245, 246, 247, 248, 253, 254, 256, 258, 260, 268, 274, 275, 281, 286, 288, 289, 300, 301, 304, 314, 315, 318, 319, 320, 356–358, 374, 399. *See also* Board of Regents
Bode (Iowa) Academy, 143
Bodensteiner, Helen Adams, 294, 334, 359, 381
Boe, Lars W., 168, 229, 281, 395
Boe, Nils N., 162
Boice, Vera L., 200
Borge, Michael O., 177
Borge, Paul D., 359, 371
Bothne, Erling A., 120
Bothne, Gisle C. J., 112, 141, 142, 144, 145, 146, 148
Bothne, Johannes, 141
Bothne, Thrond, 91, 93, 108, 123, 137
Braafladt, Louis H., 207, 296
Braafladt-Brevig Mission Society, 296
Braaten, Lila M., 359

Brandt, Christian, 121
Brandt, Margrethe, 127
Brandt, Nils O., pioneer preacher, 13, 25, 32, 69, 70, 99; scouting trip, 26–30; college pastor, 93, 106, 125
Brandt, Mrs. Nils O. (Diderikke), 127; sketch, 124–126
Brandt, Olaf E., 111, 125, 175, 216
Brandt, Realf O., 111, 141
Brandt, Mrs. Realf O., 229
Brandt Hall, 276, 304, 305, 316, 340
Branstad, Mrs. Elizabeth, 319, 357
Bratlie, Otto M., 359
Brattland, Shirley, 359
Brauer, Earnest A., 68, 69
Brayton Electric Co. (Waverly, Iowa), 398
Breckenridge's School (Decorah), 91
Breda, Olaus J., 123, 153
Bredesen, Adolph, 109, 117
Bredeson, Lewis B., 359
Breidablik, student society, 115
Breiland, John, 359, 397
Breivik, Mons, 228
Brekke, Arne, 359
Bremmer, Mrs. Lawrence, 362
Bremness, Gladys Glesne, 359
Brendsel, Thomas A., 359
Brevig, Tollef L., 296
Brevik, Olaf Christian O., 311
Brevik, Mrs. Olaf Christian O. (Beatrice), 311
Brodahl, Peter M., 14
Brogger, A. W., 226
Bronstad, Alvin L., 207
Brorby, Joseph, 153
Broward, Mrs. Robert, 361
Brown, Mrs. F. Q., 200
Brown, John N., 229
Brown Electric (Decorah), 399
Brudos, Alan R., 359
Bruemmer, John W., 326, 359
Bruflat Academy (Portland, N. D.), 144
Bruland, Mrs. Christian, 358
Brunner, D. Peter, 324
Brunsdale, C. Norman, 207, 263
Brunsdale, K. Edward, 207
Brunsdale family, 288
Brunsvold, Jørgen, 46
Brunsvold, P. O., 358

405

Index

Bruun, Anders H. J., 36
Brye, Martha, 288
Buechner and Orth (St. Paul), architects, 391
Buffalo Synod, 9, 21, 26, 28, 29, 30, 34
Bugenhagen, Johann, 72
Bugge, Fredrik W., 379
Building Committee of *1861*, 46, 56, 57, 58, 59, 61, 68
Buildings, 48, 50, 53, 55, 61–74, 75, 86, 93, 104, 133–135, 137, 173, 174–178, 215–218, 276, 283, 284, 286, 295, 301, 304, 305–308, 309, 316, 341. *See also* individual college buildings
Bull, Ole, 118
Bunge, Eldo F., 240
Bunge, Wilfred F., 359
Bungum, Robert M., 337, 359
Burling, J. P., 257
Burstrom, Warren F., 359
Butler, Bartlett R., 326, 335, 359
Butts, Porter, 307
Butts, Mrs. Virgil, 365

C. K. Preus Gymnasium, 137, 139, 145, 217, 221, 235, 237, 242, 243, 248, 277, 278, 279, 281, 286, 287, 331, 333, 336
Calmar (Iowa), ball game, 204, 393; tornado, 209
Campus House, 93, 125, 128, 138, 176, 283
Campus News (Decorah), 234
Campus Planning Committee, 308
Campus Players, 271, 334
Capital University (Columbus, Ohio), 20, 21, 22, 23, 28, 30, 34, 376, 377
Cappon, Franklin C., 223, 236, 359
Carey, DeVere, 359
Carlson, F. Hjalmar, 239, 314
Carlson, Roy E., 239, 358
Carlson, Ruth M., 359
Carstens Plumbing and Heating (Ackley, Iowa), 399
Carter, Nick, 392
Caspari, Carl Paul, 37
Catalog, 113, 142, 147, 172, 221, 239, 373
Catiline, Ibsen play, 288

Centennial Development Fund, 315
Century of Progress Exposition (Chicago), 264, 265, 294
Chandler residence, college building, 284
Chapel, 95, 152, 163, 172, 232, 233, 250, 260, 265, 279, 288, 332, 335, 340, 388
Chicago, Norwegian colony, 3; Century of Progress Exposition, 264, 265, 294
"Chicken Coop," college building, 64, 94, 115, 134, 143, 194, 225, 283, 305, 387
Chips, see *College Chips*
Choral Music Festival, 336
Christensen, Nehemias, 99, 117
Christenson (Kjores), Lars, 194
Christiania (Norway), 373
Christiansen, Karl, 323, 359
Christmas, 125, 126, 151, 340
Christy, Blanche, 310
Church Council of the Norwegian Synod, 23, 24, 26, 27, 28, 29, 30, 33, 35, 36, 38, 40, 48, 59, 61, 68, 85, 102, 103, 134, 139, 159, 187, 195, 198
Church Investment Committee, 242
Church School Cost of Living Appeal, 310
Ciardi, John, 325
Civil Aeronautics Authority, 280
Civil War, 45, 61, 83, 87, 89, 166, 186, 384; effect on Concordia College, 39, 44, 79, 80; Norwegians in, 75; Luther students in, 97, 99, 121
Classical Club, 271
Clausen, Claus L., 13, 14, 17, 291, 373, 381; in slavery controversy, 10, 15, 83, 84, 87, 131, 384; sketch, 11; promotes theological training, 20, 21, 22, 25, 46, 56; biography, 193
Claussen, Fredrik C., 14
Cleys, Mrs. Theodore, 366
Clio, student society, 114
Coeducation, 127, 143–145, 180, 223, 238, 244–248, 253, 254, 256–269, 270, 276, 280, 282, 284, 285, 291, 301, 319, 329, 330, 336, 390, 394

Coffeen, A. R., Co. (Decorah), 392, 393, 396, 398
Colby, Betty, 296
Cole, Martin, 395
Coleman brothers, 389
College Chips (Decorah), 144, 150, 157, 199, 231, 259, 266; history, 141, 142, 153–155, 197, 234, 282, 297, 333, 337, 374
College Retirement Equities Fund (CREF), 320
College Sports Information Directors of America, 325
College Union, 305, 307, 316, 332
Comisrud, Mildred, 296
Comitia Dumriana, 127
Commencement, 221, 259, 265, 346
Committee on Curriculum and Scholarship, 290
Committee on Educational Research, 289
Committee on Lectures and Entertainments, 290
Committee on Schools, 155
Concordia, student society, 155
Concordia College (Moorhead, Minn.), 376, 395
Concordia College and Seminary (Fort Wayne, Ind.), 28, 30, 33, 35, 39, 68, 69, 98, 378
Concordia College and Seminary (St. Louis), 28, 30, 35, 68, 69, 168, 170, 292, 378; affiliation with Norwegian Synod, 29, 33, 34, 38, 39, 44, 45, 46, 49, 80, 97, 105, 107, 137; use of German, 29, 39, 101, 131, 137; model for Luther College, 51, 52, 57, 58, 73, 90, 91, 95; during Civil War, 39, 44, 79, 80; in slavery controversy, 79, 80, 81, 84. *See also* Missouri Synod
Concordia Seminary (Springfield, Ill.), 376
Conference for the Norwegian-Danish Evangelical Lutheran Church in America (the Conference), 10, 15, 90, 167
Coon Prairie settlement (Vernon County, Wis.), Norwegian colony, 38, 40, 45
Cowles, Gardner, 399

Craemer, Friedrich A., 59, 84
Crøger, Mr. and Mrs. J. T., 109
Crown, Keith A., 360
Curriculum, 48, 51, 91, 102, 145, 146, 150, 163, 180–185, 195, 219, 238, 243, 244, 245, 249, 289, 290, 309, 317, 328, 341

Dahl, A. H., 356
Dahl, Constance E., 326
Dahl, Olaus, 162
Dahl, Orville, 308
Dahlberg, Lida, 360
Dahlquist, Dr. Ralph M., 293, 301, 370
Dain, Roland, 297
Dakotas, Norwegian settlements, 3, 129, 130
Dale, Herman F., 258
Dalemo, Ole P., 109
Dale's Hall (Decorah), 55
Dana College (Blair, Neb.), 376
Dane County (Wis.), Norwegian settlements, 3, 12, 26, 27, 30, 49
Danforth fellowships, 327
Daniels, Perry C., 360
Daniels, Phyllis McFarland, 360
Dau, W. H. T., 168
Davick, Albert O., 160
Davidson, Arthur O., 293, 308, 312, 314, 360, 369, 372
Davidson, L. E., 134
Dean of men, 332, 370
Dean of the college, 288, 369
Dean of women, 288, 332, 371
Decorah (Iowa), 118, 127, 172, 179, 187, 199, 226, 243, 267, 280, 318, 387; site of Luther College, 45, 46, 47, 48, 53, 98, 99, 102, 113, 134, 135, 137, 272; described, 46, 66, 135; map, 63; churches, 88, 95, 104, 105, 106, 126, 132, 136, 152, 219, 232, 311; schools, 91, 238; sidewalks, 94, 124, 209; sports events, 119, 120, 156, 204; relation to college, 122, 124, 136, 138, 151, 152, 195, 196, 202, 209, 218, 263, 264, 273, 274, 276, 279, 287, 310, 314, 316; civic improvements, 135, 136, 138, 174, 176; expansion, 173; flood, 209; streets and highways, 216, 228;

bank failures, 255; supports women's college, 256–258; swimming pool, 271, 283, 284. *See also* First Lutheran Church, Luther College, Norwegian-American Historical Museum

Decorah Chamber of Commerce, 218, 256

Decorah Choral Union and Orchestra, 175, 190, 202, 229

Decorah College for Women, 223, 265, 266, 268, 355

Decorah Concert Series, 277

Decorah Journal, 204, 258

Decorah Junior College for Girls, 257–259, 265

Decorah Lutheran Church, 229. *See also* Decorah

Decorah-posten, 106, 108, 226, 258, 279

Decorah Public Opinion, 258, 275

Decorah School of Music, 146

Decorah State Bank, 255

De Forest (Wis.), Norwegian Lutheran church, 171, 251

Delphian Sister Society, 266

Demosthenian, student society, 155

Dennis, John R., 360

Det Norske Selskab, student society, 115

Dewey Electric Co. (Ventura, Iowa), 398

Diamond Jubilee Chest, 263, 264, 271, 273

Diamond Jubilee Year, 263, 271–273, 294, 393

Dieseth, John, 310, 358

Dieseth, Mrs. John, 310

Dietrichson, Gustav F., 13, 25, 26, 32, 377

Dietrichson, J. W. C., pioneer pastor, 13, 14, 20; sketches, 11, 12

Dirksen, George, 299

Docken, Adrian M., 293, 360

Docken, Orene Madson, 360

Doctrine of absolution, 80

Dorian Society, 336

Dorrum, Ingebret, 221, 222, 272, 325, 360, 371

Doseff, Ivan, 223, 236, 360

Dotseth, Gregory M., 338

Downie, Mrs. Ruth, 200

Dramatics Club, 271

Drawing Club, 155

Driggs residence, 135, 176

Dubuque (Iowa) *Telegraph Herald,* 278

Duus, Olaus F., 14, 32

Eastvold, Seth C., 262

Economic crises, *1873,* 89, 90; *1890's,* 166; *1921,* 210; *1929,* 219; *1930's,* 243, 249, 253, 255, 258, 271, 274, 279, 298, 301, 304

Economics Club, 235

Edda, student society, 114, 115, 117

Education, 394, 400; Norway, 35, 36, 47, 90, 91, 385; school controversy, 89, 385; Decorah, 91; early scholastic levels, 92, 145. *See also* "University men," various educational institutions

Edwards (Haatvedt), Bjørn, 94, 387

Egge, Albert, 141

Egge, Erik, 194

Eggen, Peter, 299

Eggen, Thore, 111

Ehrich, Mr. and Mrs. Louis W., 313

Eid, Elmer S., 198

Eide, Knud Olsen, 2

Eide, Nils J., 41, 49, 97, 99

Eielsen (Sunve), Elling, 6, 7, 11, 13, 400

Eielsen Seminary (Cambridge, Wis.), 8

Eielsen Synod, 8, 9, 10, 14, 16, 81

Eitel, Eleonore, 360

Eittreim, Curt, 296

Eittreim, Knute O., 192, 292, 294, 360, 370, 372, 394

Eittreim, Oliver M., 193, 325, 360, 371

Eitzen, Leroy V., 360, 371

Eitzen, Leslie Mong, 360

Ekern, Sallie R., 360

Election controversy, 15, 131–133

Electric Service Co. (Decorah), 393

Eliason, Norman E., 234, 240, 360

Eliot, Charles William, 182, 183

Ellefsen (Slen), Erik, 25, 81, 82, 383

Ellefson, C. Ashley, 360

Ellefson, Elmer O., 360

Ellefson, Lou, 288, 311
Ellestad, Anders, 99
Ellestad, Nils J., 117, 118
Ellickson, Frank, 160
Ellingsen, Daniel J., 360
Ellingson, Birgit, 141
Ellingson, Clifford T., 360
Ellingson, Herman E., 222, 360, 370, 396
Ellis, Dr. Arlene Kalsow, 330
Elmore, Mrs. George P., 362
Elstad, Martin K., 273
Elstad, Mrs. Martin K., 364
Elvestrom, Victor A., 360
Emergency Appeal, 274, 281
Emigranten (Inmansville and Madison, Wis.), 21, 25, 26, 32, 49, 59, 65–70, 79, 80, 81, 89, 376, 383, 384
Endowment funds, 174, 175, 178, 218, 240, 242, 243, 248, 253, 255, 256, 274, 275
Engebretson-Gjerset lots, 307
Engelstad, Paul, 360
English language, 376, 377, 386; use by church, 18, 373; at Concordia, 29; at Luther College, 47, 91, 92, 93, 99, 100, 115, 136, 137, 141, 142, 143, 144, 145, 154, 172, 209, 214, 373, 374
Erdahl, Gullik M., 98
Erdman, Lowell P., 360
Erdman, Mrs. Lowell P., 368
Erickson, Doris A., 265
Erickson, Nora Otilia, 251
Erikson, Leif, 1
Ervingen (Decorah), 197
Esbjörn, Lars P., 8, 9
Espelie, Ernest M., 240
Estenson, Emil, 357
Estrem, Andrew O., 150
Estrem, Carl, 357
Evangelical Lutheran Church, 16, 307, 312, 313, 318, 373, 391
Evangelical Lutheran Church of America, *see* Eielsen Synod
Evangelical Lutheran Synod of Northern Illinois, *see* Synod of Northern Illinois
Evangelisk luthersk kirketidene (Racine, Wis.), 104, 113, 149, 161, 373
Evanson, Chellis N., 193, 220, 280, 282, 283, 297, 325, 360, 370, 371, 387, 394, 396
Evanson, Chellis N., Jr., 296
Evenson, G. A., 149
Evenson, Johannes, 32
Everson, Norman, 299
Executive Committee of the Board of Education, 260, 395

Faculty and staff, 68, 99, 104, 123, 127, 136, 137, 139, 151, 152, 154, 159, 172, 180, 184, 187, 204, 214, 215, 231, 232, 233, 238, 239, 243, 244, 247, 253, 257, 264, 268, 271, 279, 281, 289, 290, 307, 316, 317, 318, 319, 321, 329, 332, 336, 340, 341, 374, 399; members, 47, 49, 65, 69, 91, 94, 103, 105–110, 133, 145, 147, 148–150, 153, 179, 181, 182, 185, 186, 189–193, 194, 197, 206, 221–225, 242, 287, 288, 292–294, 295, 298, 299, 301, 308, 310, 314, 322, 323, 325, 327, 334, 335, 337, 338, 339, 358–372; characterized, 110, 141, 228; welfare, 140, 142, 276, 320; favors coeducation, 254, 260, 261; includes women, 291
"Faculty Follies," 326
Faculty Handbook, 320
Fadness, N. Lewis, 293, 360, 371, 397
Fadness, Signe Adolphson, 360
Fagerhaugh, Kenneth H., 360, 397
Fardal, A. N., 287
Fedde, Elizabeth, 201, 392
Felland, Alfred T., 200
Fellowship Forum, 296
Field, Laurence N., 281, 293, 360, 370
Fifteenth Wisconsin Regiment, 83
Finances, 20, 21, 25, 26, 27, 32, 38, 45, 46, 47, 61, 78, 86, 96, 103, 133, 137, 142, 177, 178, 218, 219, 240–249, 253–256, 262, 267, 270, 273–275, 281, 287, 301, 304, 305, 309–316, 340, 341, 394. *See also* various gifts and funds
Finanger, Kenton E., 360
First Lutheran Church (Decorah), 94, 134, 136, 148, 151, 219, 229, 243, 257, 279, 292, 381. *See also* Decorah

Index

First National Bank (Minneapolis), 255, 256
Fisher, Harold H., 185, 186
Fiskerbeck, Victor A., 360
Fjeldstad, O. G., 357
Fjelstad, Mrs. Marie, 300
Fjelstad, Ruth N., 326, 360
Flaten, Nils, 92
Fleischer, Jacob F., 41
Fleischer, John A., 41
Fleischer, Knud J., 26, 32
Fletty, Valborg O., 360, 371
Flickinger, Lois L., 300
Flom and Forsyth (Houston, Minn.), 398
"Fluen," student publication, 117
Folkestad, Knut, 97
Folkestad, Lars E., 41, 49
Football, 120, 159, 193, 206, 223, 235, 236, 298, 337
For hjemmet (Decorah), 106
Ford Foundation, 320
Forde, Amanda Magdalene, 251
Forde, Bernice G., 300, 370, 372
Forde, Betty Mae, 360
Forde, Janet Jerdee, 360
Førde, Nils A., 117, 118, 251
Førde, Mrs. Nils A., 174, 251
Foreign Service, 108, 111, 162, 208, 292, 293, 345
Forell, George W., 324
Formula of Concord, 167
Fort Wayne (Ind.), *see* Concordia College and Seminary (Fort Wayne, Ind.)
Fortun, Oscar, 160
Fosmark, John, 377
Foss, Merle, 339, 360
Founders Day, 39, 65, 67, 75, 120, 193, 245, 271. *See also* Homecoming
Fox River settlement (La Salle County, Ill.), 2, 3, 6, 7
Franckean Synod of the Evangelical Lutheran Church in the State of New York, 8
Frank, Emily, 288, 292, 360, 371, 397
Franklin, student society, 114
Fremming, Eivind, 160
"Freshman Days," 277
Fretheim, Martin E., 199
Frich, B. J., 53

Fried, Madeleine, 339, 361
Frings, Hubert W., 361
Fritchen, Marjette, 296
Fritz, Rev. and Mrs. C. A., 288
Fritz, Luther E., 361
Frost, Gerhard E., 240, 293, 322, 323, 361, 370
Fryslie, B., 109
Fugitive Slave Law, 386
Fuglei, Ole K., 154
Fulbright fellowships, 327
Furst, Mrs. Edward J., 367

Gaalswyk, Arie, 361
Gaebler, Max D., 390
Gale College (Galesville, Wis.), 273
Gamelin, Francis E., 361
Gardner Cowles Foundation, 274, 308, 329
Gattiker, Godfrey, 361
Gattiker, Irene, 361
Gauger, A. F., 135
Gausta, Herbjørn N., 107, 112, 126, 150, 228, 328
Gedstad, Vilera, 361
General Synod of the Evangelical Lutheran Church in the United States of America, 8, 377
German language, 29, 39, 101, 131, 137, 149, 376, 377
Germans, *see* Missouri Synod
Germany, surrender, 300
Getchell, Robert W., 322, 377
Gettysburg (Pa.) College, 377
Giere, Frederic A., 294, 322, 361
Giere, Nils O., 288
Gifts and legacies, 140, 142, 174, 178, 229, 242, 263, 264, 273, 278, 281, 287, 306, 328. *See also* Finances
Gilbertson, Mathilda, 311
Gimbel, John, 325, 361
"Gjallarhorn," student publiation, 117
Gjems, Lina, 215
Gjerdrum, Donald W., 361
Gjerjord, Halvor Olson, 141
Gjerset, Knut, 181, 182, 187, 190, 193, 197, 198, 199, 225, 227, 242, 244, 292, 294, 361, 370, 394
Gjerset, Oluf, 274
Glambek, Finn, 326, 361
Glasoe, Oluf, 146, 156

410

Glenwood Lutheran Church (Decorah), 311
Glesne, Ole, 370
Goddard, Lorene J., 361
Goelberg, Ida, 310
Goellner, Karl E., 361
Gornitzka, A. Reuben, 357
Goulson, Hilton, 361
Grabau, J. A. A., 21, 22, 29, 34, 377
Graber, Paul A., 361
Graduates, 97, 98, 100, 111, 124, 128, 129, 130, 162, 170, 213, 233, 239, 250, 272, 330, 344, 345
Graeber, Ruth A., 266
Graebner, Theodore, 168, 391
Grangaard, Arthur M. (Beech), 299
Grangaard, Henry O., 205
Grangaard, M. O., 251, 256, 263, 267, 275, 309, 357
Granrud, Carl F., 256, 261
Granrud, John E., 147, 150, 181, 182, 244
Grant, Lane, 361
Green, Joseph M., 357
Green, Lowell C., 324
Gregerson, Harry R., 240
Griese, C. H., 56, 68
Griese and Weile, architects, 58
Grimes, Marjorie Ann, 361
Grimm, Harold J., 324
Grinager, Alex, 228
Griswold residence, 54, 134
Grudem Brothers (St. Paul), 396, 398
Grue, Charlotte B. Schilling, 294, 361, 370
Grundesen, Grunde H., 194
Grundtvig, N. F. S., 13, 291, 376
Grundtvigianism, 12, 13, 383
Grundy, Allen C., 185
Gulbrandsen, Gilbert, 141, 376
Guldberg, Ove H., 388
Gullickson, Gerald L., 361
Gullickson, Mrs. Gerald L., 368
Gullixson, Andrew, 174
Gullixson, Clara, 213
Gullixson, George A., 144
Gullixson, Thaddeus F., 207, 218, 273
Gulsvig, Elmo L., 361
Gundersen, Knut T., 361
Gunderson, Helga, 311
Gunderson, Sigurd, 357

Gunness, Mrs. Wayne, 361
Gunsolus, Victoria L., 361

Haatvedt, Bjørn, 94
Haatvedt, Rolfe A., 288, 293, 361, 370, 371, 372
Haatvedt, Mrs. Rolfe A., 372
Haeussler, Helmut H., 361
Hagerup, N., 228
Hagestad, Ole J., 41
Haines, Eleanor Dorrum, 361
Halbakken, David S., 361
Haldorson, Erwin L., 237
Halfway Creek (Wis.), early site of Luther College, 47–53, 104, 229
Halland, John G., 149
Hallen, Lois J., 361
Halverson, Paul M., 361
Halverson, R. Julian (Hoovey), 236
Halvorson, Aneken, 288
Halvorson, Hazel I., 358
Halvorson, Jeanne, 361
Halvorson, John V., 398
Halvorson, Mrs. John V., 362
Halvorson, Olaf, 274, 288
Halvorson, Ruth E., 361
Hamill, student society, 155
Hammond, J. C., 258
Hammond, Justin, 296
Hamran, Hans, 264
Hamran, Harald, 264
Hamre, James S., 361
Hansen, Clifford (Cliff), 236, 298, 361
Hansen, Erling M., 361
Hansen, Thomas, 109, 110
Hanson, A. E., 357
Hanson, Carroll B., 397
Hanson, Mrs. E. Kathinka, 258
Hanson, Esther M., 265
Hanson, Eugene Carl, 161
Hanson, Haldor, 143, 146, 148, 153, 155, 156, 159, 181, 194, 200, 202
Hanson, James C. M., 92, 120, 162, 193, 216, 288, 356, 391
Hanson, Karl, 223, 224, 242, 275, 292, 300, 361, 372, 396
Hanson, Lavern R., 358
Hanson, N. B., 253, 270
Hanson, Sarah V., 362
Hanson, Thore O., 175

411

Index

Harold Fardal Student Loan Fund, 274
Harris, Mrs. O. W., 368
Harrisville, Roy A., 357
Harrisville, Sigrid R., 326
Harstad, Bjug J., 111
Harvard University, 379
Harvey, Margaret, 362
Hass, Mrs. Arthur, 362
Hassel, Nicolai Severin, 106
Hasselquist, Tuve N., 52
Hasvold, Paul M., 362
Haugan, Hauman G., 193
Hauge, Hans Nielsen, 5, 6, 7, 8, 11
Haugeanism, 13, 43, 90
Hauge's Synod (Hauge's Norwegian Evangelical Lutheran Synod), 8, 16, 167
Haugen, G. N., 175
Haugen, Nils P., 112
Haugen, P. E., 146
Haukanes, Lars, 228
Heg, Even, 11
Heg, Hans C., 87
Heggen, Alan T., 338
Hegland, Margaret Naeseth, 370
Heitmann, Mrs. Borghild, 331
Hektoen, Ludvig, 162, 175, 193
Helgeson, Adrian, 398
Helgeson (Overn), Charles T., 161
Helgeson, Thor, 378
Helle, Mrs. Nils N., 127
Hellen, Selmer A., 266
Helms, John, 362
Helms, Mrs. John, 365
Henderson, Algo D., 308, 329
Henderson, Ida Marie, 311
Hendrickson, Edwin H., 362
Hendrickson, Kermit T., 362
Hennings, Ralph Waldo, 362
Henningsgaard, Loyes M., 370
Henriksen, Christian, 377
Henriksen, George C., 220, 234, 362
Henryson, Mrs. Carrie O., 288
Henzler, Mrs. Paul F., 367
Hervig, Richard B., 362
Herwig, Lloyd O., 362
Heskin, Oscar E., 239
Hetaeria, student society, 114
Highby, Leo I., 222, 362
Highby, Paul R., 277, 362

Hill, James J., 174
Hill, Ordelle, 362
Hill Street (Decorah), 216
Hilleboe, Hans S., 190
Hiller, Philip C., 362
Hjelle, Albert E., 362, 372
Hjelle, John O., 397
Hjelle, Lester C., 362
Hjort, Louise Augusta, 127, 170
Hjort, Ove J., 87, 170
Hjort, Mrs. Ove J., 125
Hobart, Richard M., 362
Hockenburg Fixture and Supply Co. (Des Moines), 399
Hodges, Lucianne, 362
Hoegh, Mr. and Mrs. Simon, 278
Hoelty-Nickel, see Nickel
Hof, Lawrence, 362
Hoff, Harold E., 362
Hoff, Helen M., 266, 372
Hoff, Thoralf A., 113, 200, 222, 257, 258, 279, 357, 362, 370
Hofland, Sigvart A., 293, 294, 325, 334, 362
Holden (Minn.), 57
Holden (Minn.), Academy, 100
Holden Chapel (Harvard University), 379
Holey, James M., 362
Holland, P. O., 395
Holm, Bernard J., 324
Homecoming, 221, 249, 264, 297, 335, 346, 396. See also Founders Day
Homme, Even J., 111
Homme, Thorleif, 149
Hommen, Donovan L., 362
Honeywell Co. (Minneapolis), 399
Hoover, Herbert, 211, 229
Hoslett, Sherman A., 292, 362, 397, 399
Hoslett, Mrs. Sherman A., 362, 370
Hovde, Brynjolf, 41, 49, 52, 97, 107
Hovde, Brynjolf J., 179, 192, 328, 362
Hovde, Mrs. Brynjolf J., 328
Hovde, Oivind M., 292, 362, 369, 399
Hovden, Ed, 236
Hove, Einar W., 238
Hove, Elling O., 149, 154
Hove, O. Hjalmar, 240
Hoyme, Gjermund, 15

Hoyt, Clara Maude, 293, 295, 325, 362
Huenemann, Ruben H., 397
Hurster, Mrs. William, 361
Hustad, Alice M., 362
Hustad, Brad K., 337
Hustad, Mrs. Jack, 366
Hustvedt, Halvor B., 111, 150
Hustvedt, Mrs. Halvor B., 128
Hustvedt, Katherine S., 201
Hustvedt, Lloyd M., 362
Hustvedt, Olaf M., 207
Hustvedt, Sigurd B., 153, 163
"Hututu," college building, 55, 96, 380

Ibsen, Henrik, 288
Icelandic Lutheran Synod, 107
Idun, student society, 199
Idun Quartette, 118, 119
Illinois, Norwegian settlements, 2, 3, 4
Illinois State University (Springfield), 375, 377
Illinois Synod (Synod of Illinois and Adjacent States), 89
Immigration from Norway, 1–5, 6, 12, 18, 20, 30, 40, 89, 97, 110, 128, 342, 343
Ingebretson, Iver, 377
Ingebrigtson, Carl B., 173
Ingvoldstad, W. B., 263, 287
Ingvoldstad, Mrs. W. B., 287
Inman, Bob, 296
Inmansville (Rock County, Wis.), 373
Inner Mission, 43
Intercollegiate Debating Association, 200, 234
Investment Committee, 274
Iowa, 3, 4. *See also* Decorah
Iowa Board of Educational Examiners, 329
Iowa College Conference, 327
Iowa College Foundation, 313
Iowa Daily Citizen (Iowa City), 157
Iowa Forensic Association, 334
Iowa State Board of Examiners, 259
Iowa State Oratorical Association, 200
Iowa State Peace Oratorical Association, 200
Irgens, Le Roy, 237
Irving, John, 146

Irving Literary Society, 115, 155, 160, 199, 234, 266
Isenberger, Eleanor G., 266
Isenberger, R. G., 258
Iversen, Iver, 362
Iverson, Hazel L., 362, 372
Iverson, Lloyd A., 362
Iverson, Ralph G., 362

J. A. O. Preus Award, 325
Jacobsen, Anna, 362
Jacobsen, Gerhard H., 397
Jacobsen, Glenn D., 363
Jacobsen (Ballestad), Jacob D., 39, 41, 94, 99, 107, 108, 116, 118, 128, 140, 192
Jacobsen, Karl T., 107, 185, 192, 221, 225, 293, 321, 363, 369
Jacobsen, Mrs. Karl T., 258, 264
Jacobsen, Robert S., 107, 192, 293, 363
Jacobsen, Mrs. Robert S., 364, 371
Jacobsen, Theodor L. (Ted), 296, 398
Jacobson, Abraham, 9
Jacobson, Angeline, 326, 363
Jacobson, Dorcas V., 266
Jacobson, P., 377
Jacobson, Paul B., 239
Jacobson, Reuben I., 240, 358
Jaer, Lars, 82
Jahr, Torstein, 153
James, Ronald G., 338
Janesville (Wis.), 45, 46
Janson, William K., 237, 338, 363
Japan, surrender, 300
Jefferson Prairie settlement (Rock County, Wis.), 3, 9, 27
Jensen, Dinniemaud V., 363
Jensen, Jens, 174
Jensen, Nils E. S., 14
Jensen, Olive M., 363
Jenson, Martin, 357
Jenson, Robert W., 326, 334, 363
Jensvold, Christopher, 161
Jerdee, Joseph C., 363
Jesme, Tosten, 100
Jessen, Carl A., 207
Jewell, Frank, 218
Jewell, Walter, 206
Johanneson, Johannes, 11, 376

413

Johansen, David Monrad, 272
Johnson, Alfred O., 151, 156
Johnson, Armin M., 234
Johnson, Bernhard A., 208
Johnson, Christine E., 311
Johnson, Clare I., 363
Johnson, Mrs. Dagny, 370
Johnson, David C., 363
Johnson, Einar O., 363, 371
Johnson, Erling, 357
Johnson, George W., 263, 275, 357
Johnson, Georgiann, 296, 297, 299, 363
Johnson, Gisle, 37, 43
Johnson, Guy C., 363
Johnson, Herbert G., 234, 240
Johnson, John A., 139
Johnson, Laurel O., 398
Johnson, Mae, 288
Johnson, Miles B., 363
Johnson, O. C., 274
Johnson, Peter, and Sons (Decorah), 392, 393
Johnson, Mrs. Rachel, 274
Johnson, Theodore, 363
Johnson, Thomas, 41
Johnson, W. C., 363
Johnson, Wallace T., 337, 339, 363
Johnson, Wilford A., 396
Johnson, William N., 314
Johnson Construction Co. (Winona, Minn.), 398, 399
Johnsrud, Torkel Gulbrandson, 82
Johnston, Gladys C., 363
Johnston, Stanley L., 363, 372
Joint Synod of Ohio, 20, 21, 22, 23, 28, 29, 30, 34, 89, 376, 377
Joint Union Committee, 167, 168
Jonas, Abner, 323, 363
Jones, T. H., 280
Jordahl, Leigh D., 363
Jordahl, Olaf M., 222, 363
Jordahl, V. Trygve, 239, 305, 358
Josephson, Robert M., 363, 398
Judd, Walter H., 324
Julsrud, Ingrid, 363
Juul, Ole, 41
Juve, Tarje O., 98

KDEC (Decorah), radio station, 278

KDTH (Dubuque, Iowa), radio station, 278
KFUO (St. Louis), radio station, 292
KGLO (Mason City, Iowa), radio station, 278
KWLC (Decorah), college radio station, 193, 200, 278, 279, 297, 325, 371, 396
Kaasa, Harris E., 363
Kaasa, Olaf J., 237
Kalheim, Ole M., 144
Kalnes, Ruth, 297
Kalsow, Wilbert O., 310, 326, 372
Karlton, Jerry, 297
Kasberg, Karl A., 146, 156
Kendall settlement (Orleans County, N. Y.), 2
Kendrick, Mary F., 266
Kessel, Dr. George, 288
Keyser, Caroline Dorthea Margrethe, 170
Keyser, Christian N., 170
Kildahl, John N., 100, 111, 168
Kirckoff Heating and Plumbing (Rochester, Minn.), 398
Kirk, Russell, 324
Kirkelig maanedstidende (Inmansville and Madison, Wis., and Decorah, Iowa), 38, 104, 373
Kirketidende (Racine, Wis.), 104, 113, 149, 161, 373
Kjorlaug, Eunice, 363
Klaeber, Friedrich, 213
Klemme, W. H., 274
Kleppen, Andrew, 161
Kloster, Clair G., 294, 363, 371, 372
Knapcik, Mildred, 398
Knapp, Mrs. Cliff, 297
Knepple, Beth Evanson, 363
Knispel, John, 363
Knudson, Ellen, 331, 400
Knudson, George E., 294, 322, 363, 399
Knudson, Gilbert, 356
Knudson, O., 377
Knudtson, Glenn W., 363
Knute Preus Stalland Memorial Fund, 324
Knutson, Erling K., 300, 372
Koefod, Magnus M., 117, 118
Kohn, James D., 363

Kolstad, Gertrude M., 363
Kooiman, Willem J., 324
Kopang, John P., 118
Kopperdal, Hans J., 120
Korean War, 308
Koren, Caroline, 127
Koren, Henriette, 127
Koren, John, 141, 175
Koren, Paul, 175, 177
Koren, Ulrik Vilhelm, pioneer pastor, 25, 42, 58, 84, 90, 131, 150, 375, 380, 381, 384, 386; arrival in America, 14; at Washington Prairie, 30, 127, 194; age, 32; fund-raising activities, 45, 46; relations with Luther College, 54, 56, 57, 69, 72, 108, 118, 161, 173, 174; sketch, 137; Synod president, 139, 161, 173, 181, 183; death, 169; memorial library, 177, 216, *see also* Koren Library; nickname, 389
Koren, Mrs. Ulrik Vilhelm (Elisabeth), 194, 322, 380
Koren, William, 147, 149
Koren Library, 171, 177, 216, 225, 242, 264, 265, 277, 287, 288, 328
Korsrud, August O., 299
Korsrud, Ole L., 287, 299, 372
Korsrud, Walter W., 238
Korsrud, Mrs. Walter W., 368
Korsrud Heating Plant, 277, 278, 284, 286, 287, 305, 307
Koshkonong settlement (Dane County, Wis.), 3, 12, 26, 27, 30, 49
Kraabel, Alf M., 357
Kraabel, T. Oswald, 208
Kresge Foundation, 315
Kristoffersen, Gjertrude, 381
Krogh, Hans J. G., 149
Krogstad, Guroe Larsen, 211
Krohn, Eugene, 146, 156
Kruse, Elouise, 363
Kuhl, Paul, 363
Kvale, Ole J., 163, 181, 219, 318
Kvale, Paul J., 208
Kvamme, Kristen, 150
Kvammen, Alfred G., 363
Kyler, Rudolf H., 293, 363

"L" Club, 207
La Crosse (Wis.), 45, 46, 134

La Follette, Robert M., 252
Landmark, Gabriel H., 106, 128
Landsmaal, defined, 388
Landsrud, Ingrid, 311
Landsverk, J., 377
Landsverk, Tarkjel, 264, 272
Lane, Gerhard A., 284
Lane Court, college building, 284
Lange, C. H. R., 68, 69
Langeland, Knud, 32, 86
Langhammer, Franz, 364
Langlie, Irene J., 326, 372
Language problem, in the church, 18, 47, 101, 131; at Luther College, 91, 92, 93, 141, 145, 154, 172, 209, 214, 381
Larsen, Emma, 127
Larsen, Henning, 206, 207
Larsen, Mr. and Mrs. Herman, 36
Larsen, Iver, 41, 49, 97
Larsen (Lawson), Iver, 87
Larsen, Jacob A. O., 207
Larsen, Karen, 84, 271
Larsen, Laur. (Peter Laurentius), 47, 175, 184, 271, 291, 374, 378, 380, 382, 383, 384, 400; quoted, 14, 45, 50, 73, 75, 77, 92, 95, 272, 386; sketch, 36–38; pastor, 36, 38, 104, 105; at Concordia Seminary, 38, 39, 44, 79; trip to Norway, 40, 42; characterized, 43, 76, 78, 87, 88, 114, 123, 162, 163–165, 212; at Halfway Creek, 48–53; president of Luther College, 53–165; in slavery controversy, 79–81, 84, 86, 87, 384; functions, 104, 106, 113, 143, 148, 161; resigns presidency, 161; death, 162; memorials, 264
Larsen, Mrs. Laur. (the first), 37, 104, 124
Larsen, Mrs. Laur. (the second), 104, 126
Larsen, Lauritz, 163
Larsen, Lauritz A., 136, 146, 156
Larsen, Marie Weltzin, 364
Larsen, Myron W., 207
Larsen, N. Astrup, 163
Larsen, Ole A., 109
Larsen, Thora, 127
Larsen Hall, 173, 178, 246, 281, 286, 306, 307

415

Larson, Donald J., 293, 364
Larson, Dudley, 398
Larson, Einar R., 357
Larson, Grayce A., 300
Larson, L. Arthur, 324
Larson, Olaf, 120
Latin school, 35, 47, 90, 91, 183
Laudell, Arthur, 205
Laur. Larsen Memorial, 264
Laur. Larsen Student Loan Fund, 264
Laymen, church activities, 19, 25, 32, 34, 43, 45, 102, 131; in slavery controversy, 81, 82, 83, 86; education of, 56, 96, 130, 143, 180, 181, 182, 184, 231, 244, 270, 290, 291, 384
Lee, Allen V., 240
Lee, Atle J., 120
Lee, Gustav T., 162
Lee, Jens L., 121
Lee, Johannes C., 82
Lee, Dr. Joyce Everson, 330
Lee, Knute W. D., 322, 326, 364
Lee, Milo E., 364
Lee, Norlan J., 364
Lee, Oscar R., 380
Lee, Robert E. A., 398
Lee, Ronald S., 307
Lee County (Ill.), Norwegian settlement, 87
Legvold, Sam, 364, 397
Lehmann, William F., 35, 376
Leidal, Floyd L., 364
Leikvold, Clarence W. (Colonel), 300, 372
Leitch, Rosemary, 296
Leiv Eiriksson Drive (Decorah), 216, 307
Leland, Earl J., 364
Leraas, Harold J., 237, 364
Lerud, L. Reuben, 364, 372, 398
Lerud, Mrs. L. Reuben, 358
Lester, William L., 333
Lewison, Eli, 151
Lewison, Nora V., 364
Ley, Willy, 324
Library, 47, 106, 107, 113, 116, 134, 135, 140, 152, 153, 173, 185, 193, 199. See also Koren Library
Lie, Lars J., 377, 378
Lien, Beth, 333, 334

Lien, Jacob O. (Jack), 296, 364, 372
Limburg, Mrs. James, 303
Lincoln, Abraham, 49, 56, 88, 161, 174, 203, 220, 385
Lind, Jenny, 20, 21, 29, 377
Linde, Andrew A., 311
Lindemann, Friederich, 108
Linné Society, 266
Linnevold, Johan, 146, 156
Lionberger, Mrs. Anna, 300
Lionberger, Justine Holum, 364
Lionberger, Paul H., 307, 326, 364, 371
Liquor, 152, 196, 211, 390
Lisbon (Ill.) Seminary, 8
"Little Synod," 16, 169
Livdahl, Gustav, 175
Locks, Joyce O., 364
Lokken, Olin, 357
Lomen, Gilbert J., 112
Lomen, Gulbrand, 109
Lomen, Mrs. Gulbrand (Elisabeth), 109
Lomen, Oscar M., 364, 370
Lommen, Synneve, 381
Lono, Mikkel, 175
Lord, Frederic P., 400
Lord, Mrs. Frederic P., 331, 400
Lore, Marv, 296
Losna, student society, 115
Lowell, student society, 155
Loyalty Hall, 175, 196
Lund, John H., 162
Lunden, Laurence R., 357
Luren Singing Society, 136
Luther, August A. (Augie), 298, 338
Luther, Martin, 20, 34, 79, 166, 174, 323, 383
Luther Academy (Albert Lea, Minn.), 144, 273
Luther Alumnus (Decorah), 221, 263
Luther College, Norwegian background, 1, 4; founders, 6, 7, 10, 14, 33; relationship with church, 16, 166–169, 172, 219, 344; students, 39, 41, 49, 50, 265, 295, 298; proposed sites, 46, 134; names, 47, 57, 60, 90, 130, 172, 377, 378; at Halfway Creek, 47–53, 104, 229; moved to Decorah, 53–60; student life, 54,

76–78, 113–129, 150, 289, 295–297, 326, 331, 334, 339; tuition, 57, 96, 139, 178, 220; admission policies, 58, 96, 103, 239, 317, 327, 329; utilities, 64, 94, 135, 136, 138, 139, 142, 156, 173, 176, 286, 305; mottoes, 65, 99, 107, 165, 216, 334, 336, 346; in slavery controversy, 75–88, 118; established, 82, 83, early development, 89–112; bells, 94, 139, 187; land area, 94, 215, 218, 283, 307, 309, 329; sidewalks, 94, 124, 209; seal, 99; teachers' training program, 100, 271, 328, 330; Board of Visitors, 102, 103; incorporated, 102, 140, 187; student organizations, 114–116, 155, 271, 294, 296, 299, 332, 336; student publications, 116, 150, 153–155, 197, 198, 333, 374, 388; military training at, 120, 185; democratic aspect, 123; in election controversy, 130–133; special degrees, 147, 215, 227, 238, 249, 279; histories, 148, 150, 198, 221; gymnasium, 159, 172, *see also* C. K. Preus Gymnasium; colors, 160; songs, 160, 217, 351; semicentennial, 174; in World War I, 186; speech department, 199, 296, 297, 334, 344; modern era, 210–229; seventieth anniversary, 228–230, 242, 243, 245; student self-government, 233, 295, 332; affiliation with Decorah College for Women, 258, 265, 266, 268; summer school, 259, 266, 288, 308, 355, 371; Diamond Jubilee, 263, 271–273, 393; in World War II, 280, 282, 285, 295, 301, 304, 317; student veterans, 284, 295; carillon, 288, 331; dean of women, 288, 332, 371; dean of college, 288, 369; standards, 309, 317, 318, 321, 327, 328, 340, 341; lecture series, 323–325; evaluated, 329, 344, 345, 346; dean of men, 332, 370; fine arts festival, 332. *See also* Aim, Americanization, Articles of Incorporation, Athletics and sports, Attendance, Buildings, Catalog, Chapel, Coeducation, Curriculum, Faculty and staff, Finances, Founders Day, Gifts and legacies, Graduates, Homecoming, individual presidents, KWLC, Language problem, Library, Medical facilities, Museum, Music, Preparatory department, Rules and Regulations

Luther College Alumni Association, 107, 129, 138, 141, 174, 176, 178, 179, 193, 194, 221, 241, 245, 253, 254, 263, 268, 271, 273, 276, 289, 301, 303, 304, 315, 319

Luther College Alumni Forening, 141

Luther College Athletic Association, 160, 207, 218, 238

Luther College Boarding Club, 140, 225

Luther College Bookshop, 278, 332

Luther College Bulletin (Decorah), 179, 220, 282, 374

Luther College Cadet Corps, 186

Luther College Catalog (Decorah), 221, 239, 374. *See also* Catalog

Luther College Chapel Choir, 335

Luther College Choir, 295, 335

Luther College Chorus, 229, 235

Luther College Clubs, 178, 179

Luther College Concert Band, 119, 133, 190, 201, 202, 217, 235, 251, 265, 271, 273, 279, 294, 335

Luther College Corporation, 187, 214, 253, 256, 268, 318

Luther College Entertainers, 235

Luther College Forensic Association, 234

Luther College Musical Union, 156

Luther College News Service, 220

Luther College Oratorical Association, 200, 234

Luther College Pep Band, 335

"Luther College Phalanx," 121

Luther College Press, 324

Luther College Semi-Centennial 1861–1911 (Decorah), 198

Luther College Sunday Association, 198, 232

Luther College through Sixty Years (Minneapolis), 221, 374

Luther College Varsity Band, 335

Luther College Woman's Clubs, 218, 264, 305, 310, 311

Index

Luther College Women's Chorus, 295, 325, 335

Luther Corporation (college farm), 219, 247, 253, 256, 307, 393

"Luther Field Song," 217, 351

Luther League, 199

Luther Memorial Fund, 240

Luther-St. Olaf Endowment Appeal, 221, 242, 309

Luther Seminary (Madison, Wis., Robbinsdale, St. Paul, Minn.), 101, 131, 132, 133, 166, 174, 251. *See also* Luther Theological Seminary

Luther Theological Seminary (St. Paul), 111, 167, 207, 208, 232, 233, 240, 250, 273, 293, 294, 303, 321, 324, 325

Luther Valley settlement (Rock County, Wis.), 3, 13, 25, 26, 27, 30, 46, 48, 80, 87, 373

Lutheran Alumni Mobilization Plan (LAMP), 315

Lutheran Brethren, 16

Lutheran Brotherhood Life Insurance Society, 111, 163, 196, 207, 240, 323, 325

Lutheran Church, 72, 209, 303, 343; educational program, 4, 7, 10, 20, 105, 394; Norway, 5, 6, 7, 13, 17, 35, 36, 40, 43, 342, 383; union movement, 8, 9, 10, 15; hymns, 117. *See also* various synods

Lutheran Common Service, 290

Lutheran Daughters of the Reformation, 296

Lutheran Free Church, 15, 16, 167

Lutheran Herald (Minneapolis), 111, 208

Lutheran Ladies Seminary (Red Wing, Minn.), 144, 273, 390

Lutheran Normal School (Sioux Falls, S. D.), 10, 100, 134

Lutheran Publishing House (Decorah), 104, 134, 227

Lutheran Students Association, 296

Lutheran Students Union, 233, 296

Lutheran Synod of Buffalo, *see* Buffalo Synod

Lutheran Watchman (Decorah), 104

Lutheraneren (Minneapolis), 373

Lyon, William M. (Clay), 338

Maakestad, Norvald G., 217, 351

Maanedstidende (Racine and Inmansville, Wis.), 20, 21, 22, 25, 45, 57, 149, 373

McDowell, Donald R. (Rufe), 299

Madison (Wis.), 46, 48

Madison Agreement, 167, 168

Madson, Martin, 141

Madson, Norman A., 207

Magelssen, Claus F., 14

Magelssen, H. Gynther, 229, 242, 273

Magelssen, J. C., 307

Magelssen, Mrs. J. W., 127

Magelssen, Jacob A., 161

Magelssen, Nils S., 263

Magelssen, Willie, 151

Magney and Tusler (Minneapolis), architects, 391

Main Building (first), 96, 99, 113, 116, 156, 171, 173, 174, 175, 178, 185, 195, 197, 216, 265, 381; cornerstone, 4, 57; erected and dedicated, 61–74, 95; described, 62, 67, 135, 136; enlarged, 78, 93; fires, 94, 133, 142, 153, 174, 276, 280, 283, 285, 286, 296, 301, 389, 390; living quarters, 104, 124, 125; rebuilt, 135

Main Building (new, *1950–52*), 58, 282, 284, 287, 296, 306, 331, 346, 387; honor roll memorial, 283; built, 305, 314

Major, Mrs. Thomas H., 364

Malli, Alma, 300

Malmin, Gunnar J., 239

Malmin, Olaf G., 208, 364

"Mamalandet," student publication, 117

Mandt, Gunder, 25

Mann, Horace, 385

Mansfield (Ohio), 312

Markhus, George, 98, 149, 153, 194

Marsh, J. J., 258

Marsh, Mrs. Jessie Ervin, 201

Marshall (Wis.), Academy, 9, 10

Märtha, crown princess of Norway, 279

Martin Luther College (Buffalo, N. Y.), 29, 30

Martin Luther Lectures, 323

Mathees, Arnold J., 364

Mather, Lydia Jeannette, 400

Mather, Samuel, 400
Mather, Mrs. Samuel, 331, 400
Matthews, James T., 364
Mattson, Martha M., 364
May *17*, 56, 157, 202, 204, 340
Medical facilities, 55, 56, 138, 150, 176, 196, 277, 288, 293, 310, 370
Megorden, C. H., 357
Megorden, Tennis H., 229
Melaas, Ira J., 338, 364
Melanchthon, Philipp, 79, 383
Mellby, Carl A., 163
Mellem, Edwin G., 156
Melody Manor, college building, 284
"Men for the Ministry" conference, 333
Menighedsfakultetet, theological group, 43
Men's Senate, 295
"Messiah," 202, 335
Michigan, Norwegian settlements, 3
Mickelson, Harlan, 364
Middle West, 203; population increase, 130; prosperity, 166; Norwegian settlements, 194, 241, 342; in depression, 210
Mikkelsen, Amund, 41
Mikkelsen, Anna S., 364
Mikkelsen, Michael A., 162
Miller, Emil C., 280, 293, 322, 364
Miller, Frank R., 301, 319, 357, 364
Mimer, student society, 113, 116, 123
Minde, student society, 114
Minerva, student society, 155
Minge, Margaret, 364
Minneapolis Luther College Club, 142
Minnesota, Norwegian settlements, 3, 4, 38, 129, 130
Minnesota Synod, 89
Mission Society, 232, 235, 296
Missouri Synod, 9, 29, 30, 35, 37, 47, 89, 101, 376, 394; relations with Norwegian Synod, 15, 28, 31–33, 34, 42, 68, 72, 79, 131, 137, 168, 378; in slavery controversy, 81, 131, 385. *See also* Concordia College and Seminary (Fort Wayne), Concordia College and Seminary (St. Louis)
Mjølner, student society, 199
"Moderlandet," student publication, 116

Moe, Mrs. Caroline Jacobson, 200, 201
Moe, Leonard A., 193, 364, 370
Moe, Lois, 364, 371
Moen, Frederick W., 398
Moen, Lars, 135
Moen, Mrs. Norman W., 368
Moen, Wallace A., 240, 358
Mohn, Thorbjørn N., 100, 111
Mohr, George C., 327, 364
Mohr, Martin A., 326, 364
Moldstad, John A., 203
Møller, Tønnes, 99
Monhardt, Maurice, 364
Monona Academy (Madison, Wis.), 143
Monrad, R. M. J., 149
Monson, Ingvard G., 120
Monson, Laura M., 266, 364
Monson, Paul H., 364
Monson, Mrs. Paul H., 366
Montgomery, Mrs. Sarah Richardson, 146
Moore, Henry W., 156
Moore, Mattie, 307
Morrell and Nichols, architects, 286
Morris, Eloise M., 364
Mostrom, Ruth, 326, 330, 364, 370, 371
Movold, Ralph, 206
Munch, Johan Storm, 14, 32, 378
Munk, Jens, 1
Museum, 113, 143, 149, 153, 173, 176, 190, 194, 225, 387. *See also* Norwegian-American Historical Museum
Music, 91, 95, 117–119, 137, 146, 148, 155, 173, 190, 194, 200–203, 223, 235, 250, 283, 287, 290, 322, 336, 380
Muskego (Wis.), Norwegian settlement, 2, 3, 11, 13, 30, 87
Muspelheim, student society, 116, 155, 199
Muus, Bernt J. I., 14, 42, 46, 100
Myhre, Gudbrand, 82, 377, 378

Naeset, Jens J., 46, 93
Naeseth, Adolph O., 205
Naeseth, Mrs. Carelius G., 229
Naeseth, Christen A., 142, 146, 148, 153, 173, 189

419

Index

Naeseth, Mrs. Christen A., 127
Naeseth, Erling O., 322, 326, 364
Naeseth, Gerhard B., 397
Narveson, Cornelius, 94, 108, 140
Nasby, Helge, 364
National Council for Accreditation of Teacher Education, 330
National Defense Fellowships, 327
National Scholastic Press Association, 234, 333
Nattestad, Ole, 2
Natvig, Alvin J., 206
Nelson, A. Alvon, 307
Nelson, Allen E., 365
Nelson, Andrew O., 112
Nelson, Anita Pleuss, 357, 365
Nelson, David T., 222, 223, 229, 234, 237, 260, 263, 277, 283, 300, 301, 322, 365, 372, 394, 395, 396, 397, 399
Nelson, Mrs. David T., 264
Nelson, David Torrison, 326, 365
Nelson, Jacob A., 248, 257, 258
Nelson, Lawrence G., 238
Nelson, Lily B., 266
Nelson, Louise Helen, 297
Nelson, Marjorie Moore, 365
Nelson, Martin J., 208
Nelson, Thomas O., 287
Nelson, Wendell A., 365
Nelson, Mr. and Mrs. William, 288
Nesheim, Obed J., 365
Ness, Dr. Hildus A., 287
Ness, Jens A., 150
Nesset, Arla Gredvig, 371
Nesset, Eldred J., 372
Nesset, Lauren B., 237, 298, 397
Neste, Knut K., Jr., 141
Neuberg, Karen, 37, 104
New Impressions (Decorah), 333
New Main, see Main Building (new)
New York, Norwegians in, 1
Newspapers, Norwegian-American, 235, 287, 328. See also individual newspapers
Ney, Nancy, 297
Nickel, Theodore C. F. W. H., 222, 229, 235, 265, 272, 292, 294, 324, 362
Nickoley, C., 299
Nielson, Wilbur A., 220

Niffelheim, student society, 94, 115, 117, 155
"Nightingale," flageolet sextet, 156
Nilsen, Mr. and Mrs. Christian, 49, 50
Nilssen, Morton O., 292, 365, 371
Nilsson, Thomas, 144
Nissen, Hartvig, 35, 36, 385
Noble, Weston H., 322, 365
Norby, Charles H., 234, 284, 288, 365
Norby, Joseph, 395
Norby Court, college building, 284, 336
Nordby, Mrs. E. J., 363
Nordby, Jørgen, 117, 118
Nordby, Mrs. Jørgen, 127
Nordgaard, Karl H., 278, 293, 372
Nordgaard, Knut E., 117
Nordic Cathedral Choir, 295
Nordsieck, Henriette, 365
Nordstierna, student society, 115
Norlie, Olaf Morgan, 191, 221, 224, 277, 292, 365, 371
Normann, Halvor M., 179, 218
Normann, Olaus A., 49, 51, 98
Normannalaget, student society, 115, 155, 199
Norrøna, student society, 199
Norse-American Centennial, 216, 221, 225, 227
Norstog, Mrs. Inga Bredesen, 271, 294, 322, 325, 331, 365, 370
Norstog, Knut J., 365
Norswing, Knut, 309
Norswing Foundation, 309
North Central Association of Colleges and Secondary Schools, 185, 238, 240, 265, 288, 327, 330
Northwestern Elevator Co. (Milwaukee), 398
Northwestern University, 297
Norway, 203, 226, 280, 386; state church, 5, 6, 7, 13, 17, 35, 40, 42, 342, 383; independence day, 56, 157, 202, 204, 340; schools, 35, 36, 47, 90, 91, 385. See also Immigration from Norway
Norway Grove (Wis.), 171, 251
Norwegian-America Line, 265
Norwegian-American Historical Association, 226, 227

Norwegian-American Historical Museum, 134, 190, 225–227, 239, 242, 279, 294, 311, 325, 331, 370. *See also* Museum

Norwegian Augustana Synod, 10, 15, 81, 89, 167

Norwegian-Danish Evangelical Lutheran Augustana Synod, 9, 10

Norwegian Evangelical Church in America, *see* Norwegian Synod

Norwegian language, 18, 24, 91, 92, 101, 114, 115, 131, 141, 143, 144, 145, 154, 172, 197, 208, 209, 212, 214, 239, 289, 373, 374, 390

Norwegian Lutheran Church of America, 8, 111, 169; founded, 16, 268, 373; name, 16, 318; educational program, 233, 242, 261, 262, 267, 269, 281; Board of Trustees, 248, 253, 262, 267; finances, 246, 275

Norwegian Student Singers, 202, 227

Norwegian Synod, 38, 45, 46, 47, 48, 57, 58, 60, 61, 69, 76, 80, 84, 95, 128, 140, 148, 161, 169, 170, 174, 177, 178, 179, 181, 183, 184, 187, 198, 203, 379, 384; educational program, 7, 19, 21, 25–33, 35–38, 45, 47, 48, 96, 100, 101, 103, 113, 134, 143, 166, 172, 180, 187; founded, 9, 10, 13, 14, 17, 20, 23, 169; in slavery controversy, 10, 42, 75, 79–88, 89, 123, 131, 132, 383, 385; growth, 15, 17, 89, 90, 166; in election controversy, 15, 131–133; relations with Missouri Synod, 15, 28, 31–33, 34, 37, 42, 45, 68, 72, 79, 131, 137, 168; joins NLCA, 16; organization problems, 17, 43; language problem, 18, 47, 93, 101, 131; need for pastors, 18, 20, 30, 35, 40, 44, 48, 97, 111, 129, 130, 270; union movement, 22, 35, 167, 168, 177; Golden Jubilee, 172; reports, 373

Norwegian Synod of the American Evangelical Lutheran Church ("Little Synod"), 16, 169

Norwegians, 400; settlements, 1, 2, 3, 4, 12, 30, 38, 40, 129, 130, 194, 241, 342; in Civil War, 75; Puritanism, 390. *See also* Immigration from Norway, individual settlements, Laymen, Lutheran Church

Nustad, Nordahl, 215, 274, 275, 357

Nustad Field, 215, 229, 235, 284, 287, 307, 337

Nybakken, Oscar E., 240, 365

Nyborg, Wesley L., 398

Nystul, John, 395

Oberlin (Ohio) College, 386

Ode, Sigurd J., 240

Ofstedal, E. Dorothea, 365

Ofstedal, Rudolph A., 178

Oftedahl, Ellen Else Marie, 36

Oftedal, Sven, 90

Ohio Synod, *see* Joint Synod of Ohio

Oien, Arthur, 365

Olav, crown prince of Norway, 279

Old Main, *see* Main Building (first)

Ollis, John, 140

Olsen, A. Loran, 365

Olsen, Ellef, 98

Olsen, Jervis D., 365

Olsen, Martin I., 163

Olsen, Nils A., 207

Olsen, O. Bernhard (Tex), 236

Olsen, Ole N., 55

Olsen, Peter Rudolf Oscar, 149, 389

Olsen, Theodore L., 365

Olson, Alvin (Avy), 236

Olson, Andrew B., 211

Olson, Arthur R. (Art), 236

Olson, Clifford O. (Cliff), 236, 240

Olson, Della, 211

Olson, Doris M., 365

Olson, Ernest W. (Ernie), 236

Olson, Esther J., 325, 334, 365, 371

Olson, Henry A., 357

Olson, Knud, 311

Olson, Mrs. Knud (Gjertrud), 311

Olson, Leonard A. (Lefty), 236, 240

Olson, Louis W., 306, 311, 331

Olson, Mrs. Louis W., 306, 311, 312, 331

Olson, Louise N., 365

Olson, Marvin C. (Marv), 236

Olson, O. H., 391

Olson, O. Rolf, 365

Olson, Mrs. O. Rolf, 363

Olson, Oscar L., 160, 194, 301, 356, 369; administration, 103, 210–250;

faculty member, 150, 172, 179, 181, 198, 249, 365, 392; sketches, 189, 211–213; speaker, 214; policies, 231, 244–246, 249; resigns presidency, 247; death, 250
Olson, Mrs. Oscar L., 213, 228
Olson, Paul F., 213, 238
Olson, Ralph M., 300, 372
Olson, Mrs. Ralph M., 370
Olson, Roger M., 365
Olson, Walter A., 213, 238
Olson, William (Bill), 236
Omlie, Oscar K., 156
Oneota Valley, 174
Opdahl, Einar E., 161
Opsahl, Alert M., 365
Opsahl, Theodor G., 120
Opstad, Iver A., 365
Ordal, Zakarias J., 150, 194, 357
Orton, Lambert S., 365
Orwold, Oswald (Ossie), 236
Orwoll, Harold S., 365
Orwoll, Styrk, 297
Osborne, Charles A., 300
Oscar L. Olson Hall, 306, 307, 310, 316
Oslo (Norway), 373
Osseo, student society, 115
Osterkamp, Daryl, 365
Ostrem, Mrs. C. H. (Lena), 310
Otis, Nathaniel, 380
Otis Building (Decorah), 380
Otis Elevator Co. (Des Moines), 399
Otte, Carl N. H., 239, 365
Otte, Heinrich, 163, 232
Ottesen, Diderikke, 125
Ottesen, Jakob Aall, pioneer pastor, 13, 32, 42, 69, 84, 125, 136, 382, 384; scouting trip, 26–30
Ottesen (Lunde), Jacob, 99
Ottun, Niels, 49
Our Saviour's Lutheran Church (Minneapolis), 229, 303
Overn, Oswald B., 185, 186
Owen, Christine H., 365
Owen, Ernest M., 365
Owen, Marguerite, 365
Owen, Norman C. J., 397
Oyloe, Helge, 171

P. A. Munch Historical Society, 199

Pacific coast, Norwegian settlements, 4
Pacific Lutheran University (Tacoma, Wash.), 111, 191, 222, 224, 239, 240, 277, 310, 325, 376
Pannkoke, O. H., 241
Park Region Luther College (Fergus Falls, Minn.), 144
Parkersburg (W. Va.) *News,* 236
Pastors, need for, 18, 20, 30, 40, 44, 97, 111, 129, 130, 233, 270; political affiliations, 81, 88, 252, 384
Pastors' Declaration, 81, 82, 83, 383
Paulsen, Fayetta, 307, 326, 330, 365, 371
Paulson, Arthur C., 234, 239
Paulson, Clara J., 293, 329, 365, 371, 397, 399
Paulson, Donald C., 338
Paulson, Keith W., 338
Peasants' War, 383
Pederson, Martin, 141
Pederson, Pernie C., 365
Peerson, Cleng, 2
Peik, W. E., 290
Pelikan, Jaroslav J., 324
Pennsylvania College (Gettysburg, Pa.), 377
Peters, Mrs. Jack V., 361
Petersen, Emil J., 149, 153
Peterson, Agnes, 366
Peterson, Cecil H., 372
Peterson, Enoch E., 191, 192, 198, 366, 388
Peterson, Francis E., 222, 223, 237, 366
Peterson, Hamlet E., 223, 237, 298, 299, 301, 366
Peterson, Helen L., 366
Peterson, Henry C., 366
Peterson, John R., 163
Peterson, Mrs. John R., 264
Peterson, Olivia, 176
Peterson, P. D., 227
Peterson, Mrs. Peter, 358
Peterson, Samuel, 161
Peterson, Vivian A., 325, 366
Pfabel, Wolfgang, Jr., 366
Phelps, Betty Lou, 366
Phelps, George, 133
Phi Theta Theta, 299

Philomathean, student society, 155
Physical education, *see* Athletics and sports
Pi Kappa Delta, 271
Pi Kappa Tau, 299
Piano and Organ Festival, 336
Pieper, F., 168
Pierson, Mrs. Stuart, 365
Pilgrim, Donald, 326, 366
Pioneer (Decorah), Luther College annual, 198, 234, 297, 333, 389
Pioneer Memorial, 271, 274
Piper, Arthur R., 338
Plasse, George, 331
Platonian, student society, 155
Pontoppidan, Erik, 132, 167
Population Bureau (Washington, D. C.), 330
Posson, Shirley A. M., 366
Prenter, Regin, 324
Preparatory department, 92, 96, 139, 145, 180, 195, 199, 215, 223, 231, 233, 355
Prestgaard, Kristian, 226
Preus, Adolph C., pioneer pastor, 13, 26, 27, 32, 376, 377, 383; Synod president, 14, 22; in slavery controversy, 84, 87
Preus, Anthony A., 327
Preus, Christian Keyser, 251, 391, 392; student, 117, 118, 386; faculty member, 150; administration, 161, 166–209, 244; sketches, 170, 196, 197, 208; nickname, 171; policies, 180, 192, 195, 196, 224; quoted, 189; biography, 191; museum curator, 194; memorial, 218; death, 177, 194, 208
Preus, Mrs. Christian K., 127, 170
Preus, David W., 296, 299
Preus, Herman Amberg, pioneer pastor, 13, 23, 26, 29, 30, 32, 46, 228, 252, 377, 385, 390; quoted, 59, 69, 71, 86; Synod president, 60, 61, 89, 90, 100, 139, 170, 183; in slavery controversy, 84, 384; death, 171
Preus, Mrs. Herman Amberg (Linka), 170, 380
Preus, Herman Amberg, theological professor, 208, 324

Preus, Jacob A. O., 207, 216, 217, 245, 356
Preus, Jacob A. O., Jr., 398
Preus, Johan C. K., 163, 177, 203, 247, 311, 395
Preus, Mrs. Johan C. K., 311
Preus, Nelson F., 366
Preus, Ove J. H., 177, 217, 218, 229, 305, 312, 357, 366, 369; administration, 251–302; sketch, 251–253; financial problems, 254, 264, 275, 282; attitude on coeducation, 257, 260; death, 301; evaluated, 301; quoted, 302
Preus, Mrs. Ove J. H., 174, 251
Preus, Ove J. H., Jr., 366
Preus, Paul C., 397
Preus, Robert D., 398
Preus, Rosine, 127
Prima, student society, 299
Proceedo, student society, 155
Protokol, 374

Quakers, 6, 400
Qualley, Orlando W., 193, 223, 281, 288, 290, 298, 301, 325, 330, 366, 369, 370, 371, 397
Quanbeck, Warren A., 324
Quarta, student society, 299
Quintets, student group, 235

R. and O. Elevator Co. (Minneapolis), 398
Radzin, Hilda, 366
Ramsland, Dorothy E. A., 366
Ramstad, Ola, 141, 149
Rand, Sidney A., 307
Raridon, Wade, 335, 366
Rasdal, Sverre, 326, 366
Rasmussen, Peter A., 8, 15, 400
Rausch, E. H., 229
Ravndal, Christian M., 208
Ravndal, Eric, 238, 366
Ravndal, Olaf, 208
Rebassoo, Herbert J., 326, 366
"Reed's Castle" (Decorah), 48
Reformed church, 9, 22
Reishus, Harald T., 239
Reishus, Olaf S., 99
Reiso, Curtis, 326, 372

Index

Relf, Janice W., 266
Religious Emphasis Week, 331
Rem, Oscar E., 234
Remmen, Mrs. Inga, 288
Remmen, Dr. Nils E., 288
Reque, David, 366
Reque, Lars S., 94, 98, 101, 108, 118, 136, 139, 140, 141, 142, 146, 148, 189, 190, 381
Reque, Mrs. Lars S., 127
Reque, Marie, 128
Reque, Peter R., 366
Reque, Peter S., 99, 121
Reque, Sigurd Styrk, 176, 190, 205, 217, 220, 223, 236, 272, 294, 298, 299, 301, 366, 370, 381
Reque, Styrk S., 41
Reserve Officers Training Corps, 186
"Restoration," sloop, 2
Reuter, Fritz, 229
Reynolds, William M., 20, 35, 377
Rhodes scholarships, 222, 327
"Ridderen uden frygt og dadel," student publication, 117
Rietschel, E. F. A., 174
Risvold, Gilbert, 228
Ritland, Lloyd O., 366
Roalkvam, Halvard G., 109, 123, 141, 153, 389
Rober, Norlin A., 366
Roberts, Hall, 281
Roberts, Mary Margaret, 299, 366
Roberts, T. R., 258
Rock County (Wis.), Norwegian settlements, 9, 12
Rock Prairie settlement (Rock County, Wis.), 3, 38. See also Luther Valley
Rod, Donald O., 293, 366, 397
Rod, Herbert L., 366
Roe, K. S. N., 366
Rogstad, Thilman M. (Tex), 236
Rohne, J. Magnus, 148, 221, 222, 366, 370
Rollefson, Arthur M., 366
Rollins, Dean B., 366
Rølvaag, Ella V., 366
Rølvaag, Ole E., 226
Romig, Mary R., 366
Ronan, Fred W., 238
Ronning, Sharon F., 366
Rood, Phyllis, 366

Roosevelt, Franklin D., 280
Rosholt, Karlton J. (Jerry), 296, 297, 366
Rosholt, Mr. and Mrs. Robert L., 367
Rossing, T. A., 174
Rossing, Thomas D., 367
Rossing, Torstein S., 282
Rotto, Curtis A., 307
Rousseau, Eugene E., 367
Rovelstad, Adolph M., 182, 191, 217, 224, 367
Rowe, Helen, 367
Royal Fredrik University (Christiania, Norway), 12, 21, 35, 37, 48, 84, 92, 118, 147, 202, 382, 385
Rude, Leslie G., 367, 371
Rugland, Sigvart L., 367
Rugland, Walter L., 240
Ruid, Lloyd W., 367
Rules and regulations, 52, 56, 77, 103, 114, 121–124, 151, 195–197, 204, 352–355
Rundle, Richard R., 337
Running, Adolph, 299
Running, Mrs. Cyrus, 368
Running, Orville M., 294, 323, 367
Rupp, E. Gordon, 324
Rush River (Wis.), Norwegian settlement, 36, 38
Rustad, Gulbrand O., 46
Rustad, Ole Arnesen, 99
Ruste, Ole A., 82
Rydning (Swenson), Lars, 99
Rye and Hinkel (Mason City, Iowa), 396
Rygh, George Taylor, 149
Rynning, Ole, 2

Saga, student society, 114
Sagen, Lyder, 35
Sagen, Oswald K., 240, 367
Sagvold, Enid Erickson, 367
St. Ansgar (Iowa), settlement, 87
St. Cloud Hotel (Decorah), 54, 55
St. Louis, 46. See also Concordia College and Seminary (St. Louis)
St. Olaf College (Northfield, Minn.), 57, 100, 111, 143, 144, 167, 169, 187, 226, 233, 240, 241, 260, 261, 268, 269, 275, 281, 292, 309, 310, 311, 376, 395

424

St. Olaf's School (Northfield, Minn.),
    see St. Olaf College
St. Paul, 134
Salaverria, Helena C., 367
Samsonen (Fosse), Lars, 39, 41
Sandbach, O., 257, 258
Sander, Anton B., 99, 109
Sandvig, Anders, 226
Sauer, Theodore C., 367
Savre, Bertinius K., 150, 179, 182,
    203, 357
Saxons, found Concordia Seminary,
    378
Saxvik, Russel O., 397
Scandinavian Evangelical Lutheran
    Augustana Synod of North America,
    9
Scandinavian Press Association, 32,
    384
Scarvie, Walter B., 367, 370
Scenic Broadcasting Co., 278
Schesvold, Thore P., 99
Schilling, Elsa E., 167
Schink, Hans R., 338
Schmidt, Friedrich A., 47, 49, 50, 51,
    53, 54, 69, 72, 78, 84, 95, 99, 105,
    131, 132, 380
Schmidt, O. E., 356
"Schmidt's Hall," 134
Schola Cantorum, 223, 235, 265, 294,
    335
School controversy, 87, 89, 385
Schreuder, H. P. S., 13
Schroder, Fridtjof C. M., 367, 398
Schroeder, Paul C., 367
Schutz, Howard, 339, 367
Schwan, Heinrich Christian, 386
Schweizer, Edsel K., 326, 337, 367,
    371
Schweizer, Helen Pearson, 367
Schwidder, Ernest C., 323, 367
Science Hall and Centennial Fund,
    316
Scriptures, as authority, 81, 82, 84,
    85, 87, 168, 383, 384
Scuttlebutt (Decorah), news sheet,
    282
Secunda, student society, 299
Seegmiller, Bob, 296
Seehus, Knut, 120
Seippel, A., 107, 388

Selbo, Gordon A., 307, 332, 367, 370
Selbo, Warren K., 367
Selnes, Edwin R., 396
Selness, Martha E., 367
Sevareid, Alfred, 205
Seventieth anniversary gift, 229, 242,
    243
Severtson, S. E., 357
Sextonian, student society, 155
Shafland, Sanford O., 237
Shakespearean Club, 155
Sheel, Herman W., 145, 149, 192, 194,
    367
Siewers, Lyder, 64, 99, 105, 106, 107,
    128, 382
Siewers Springs (Iowa), 106
Sigma Alpha Delta, 299
Sigma Alpha Phi, 299
Sihler, William P., 84, 149, 153, 155,
    159, 265, 367
Simmons, O. K., 135
Simonson, Laura, 367
Skandinaven (Chicago), 87, 89, 107,
    108, 114
Skarshaug, Emry C., 367
Skipsnaes, Jens Johnson, 377
Skirbeck, Thora, 367
Skoglund, H. P., 357
Skogsmark, Helen A., 367
Skramstad, Marie O., 367
Slavery controversy, in Norwegian
    Synod, 10, 42, 75, 79–88, 89, 123,
    131, 132, 161, 382, 384, 385, 386
Sloopers, 2, 6
Smaby, Arthur J., 357
Smale, Charlotte, 367
Smeby, Hartwick, 230
Smedsrud, C., 82
Smedsrud, C. N., 274
Smith, Dr. Axel C., 150
Smith, Leonard S., 367
Smith, Mrs. Leonard S., 366
Snow, Ruth Gordon, 367
Social Security, 320
Solberg, Carl F., 33, 79, 80, 383, 384
Solem, Oscar M., 206
Solem, T. B., 357
Solheim, Ola A., 119, 146, 149, 155
Sønnichsen, Yngvar, 228
Sørenson, Dr. Alfred R., 163, 331
Sorenson, Garfield O., 237

Sørenson, P., 12
Sorenson, Sigurd T., 257, 357
"Sørlandet," training schooner, 264
Sorlien brothers, 205
Southern Wisconsin Luther College Club, 200
Sovik, Gertrude S., 367
Spanish-American War, 160, 166, 186
Sparhawk, Ruth M., 367
Speed, Robert C., 338
Sperati, Carlo A., 133, 146, 156, 159, 175, 190, 201, 235, 265, 271, 292, 294, 367
Sperati (Olaf Angelo) Memorial Organ, 271
Sperati, Vittorio, 237
Sperati Point (N. D.), 190
Spielmann, Christian, 35
Spring Prairie (Columbia County, Wis.), church, 24, 30, 170, 171
Stabo, Dr. Trond, 217, 288, 356, 370
Stadsvold, Lillian R., 297
Stagg, Alonzo A., 223
Stalland, Knute D., 208, 256, 257, 324
Stalland, Mrs. Knute D., 324
Stalland, Knute Preus, 288
Stansberry, Lucile, 367
State University of Iowa, 330, 401
Stavig, David, 368
Stearns, Gretchen Woldt, 368
Steele, Evelyn, 368
Steen, Mr. and Mrs. Olai, 311
Steen, Margery Mayer, 368
Steen, Sigvart J., 239, 293, 294, 295, 368
Steen, Theron, 161
Steensland, Halvor, 82
Steinau, Stanley, 368
Stephenson, Audrey, 368
Stephenson, Marie A., 193
Stoen, Charles G., 255
Stoen, Helen E., 297
Stokke, Myrtle G., 368
Stolfa, Anton J. (Butch), 298
Storaasli, Gynther, 205
Stortz, Ben, 258
Storvick, A. O., 357
Storvick, Roy O., 357
Stoughton (Wis.) Academy, 143
Strand, Helen A., 326, 368

Strand, Henrik J., 118
Strandjord, Eunice, 370
Strandjord, Nels M., 296, 368
Strandvold, Georg, 258, 279
Strom, Carl W., 179, 208, 260, 292, 368, 369, 372, 394
Strom, Christian L., 397
Strom, Christine R., 370
Strom, Solva J., 311
Strømme, Peer, 109, 112, 127, 128, 271, 322
Strunk, William L., 222, 292, 368
Struxness, David F., 368
Struxness, Edward, 397
Struxness, Erling B., 368
Stub, Hans A., pioneer minister, 13, 32, 42, 376, 378
Stub, Hans A., the younger, 163
Stub, Hans Gerhard, 137, 173, 175, 180, 244, 291; student, 98, 117; sketch, 101; church president, 111, 149, 169, 177, 203, 229; honorary degree, 227
Stub, Jacob A. O., 163, 218, 273, 286
Stub, Mathilda, 128
Stub, Olaf T. A., 107
Students Army Training Corps, 185, 206
Students Union, 115, 155
Suckow, Kristofer, 100
Summerside, Mrs. Frank, 359
Sundby, Gustave A., 312, 368
Sundby, Mrs. Gustave A., 229
Sundby, Martha, 362, 370
Sunnyside, college building, 171, 226, 283, 336
Svanoe, Harold C., 334, 368, 371
Svebakken, Dr. Otto, 265
"Svein uræd," student publication, 117
Svendsen, Reinert N., 301
Swansen, H. Fred, 186, 192, 222, 368
Swaren, Dorothy A., 266
Swenson, Laurits S., 162, 175, 193, 272, 356
Symra (Decorah), 374
Symra Literary Society, 374
Synod, the, *see* Norwegian Synod
Synod of Northern Illinois, 8, 9, 14, 375

Synodical Conference, 34, 89, 101, 132, 161

Talle, Henry O., 208, 221, 234, 260, 262, 265, 292, 368, 372, 396
Tappert, Theodore G., 324
Tatley, Helen, 368
Tatley, Melvin N., 237
Tawzer, Hannah Stevenson, 368
Teachers Insurance and Annuity Association (TIAA), 276, 320
Teisberg, A. K., 108
Tennis, 159, 206, 207, 237, 298, 307, 338
Tertia, student society, 299
Texas Lutheran College, 376
Thayer, Jean M., 368
Thistedahl, Christian, 36, 37
Thomas, Mrs. C. V., 361
Thomas, Joseph, 300
Thomas, Shirley Mortenson, 368
Thompson, Florence A., 299
Thompson, Ted R., 368
Thompson, Theodore E., 173
Thompson, Thomas A., 92
Thompson, Vera Bucknell, 293, 368
Thomte, Reidar, 368
Thorgrimsen, Hans B., 95, 118, 120, 257
Thorgrimsen, Mrs. Hans B., 128
Thorlaksson, Nils S., 162
Thorpe, Eldrid M., 277, 368
Thorsgaard, Karl L., 158
Thorsgaard, Lars J., 161
Thorsnaes, Karl, 100
Thorson, Ivar A., 156, 356
Thorstenson, Mabel, 273
Thostenson, Marvin S., 397
Throndsen, Knud, 65–70, 106
Tinderholt, Victor, 296
Tingelstad, Edvin, 277, 368
Tingelstad, Gertrude B., 368
Tingelstad, John O., 146, 150, 155
Tingelstad, Oscar A., 182, 191, 197, 203, 221, 224, 232, 292, 325, 356, 368, 369, 371
Tinglum, Ottar, 223, 258, 265, 368
Tjernagel, Helge M., 156
"To Luther," song, 160, 351
Tolo, Arthur J., 217, 351, 368
Tolo, Harold M., 368

Tolo, T. O., 144
Tonning, Ole, 368
Tønsberg, Nels, 117
Topness, Mrs. Sibert M., 229
Torgerson, Mrs. J. A. C., 211
Torgerson, Karl M., 358, 372, 397
Torgerson, Lucille, 303
Torgerson, Torger A., 39, 41, 137
Torgrim, Marie Hjelle, 368
Torrison, Aaron, 158
Torrison, George A., 162
Torrison, Isaac B., 120, 167, 168, 169, 176, 195, 198, 368, 370, 391
Torrison, John W., 240, 358
Torrison, Oscar M., 162
Torrison, Osul, 134, 228
Torrison, Thomas E., 120
Torrison brothers, 205, 228
Townsend, Lloyd, 296
Track, 139, 160, 206, 223, 237, 298, 338
"Trade Wind," sailboat, 264
Treat, Ella, 146
Trilhus, Helen, 296, 297
Trøvig, Malene, 381
Trytten, Clarysse E., 266
Trytten, Merriam H., 192, 358, 368
Tulane University, 297
Turmo, Mrs. Stener, 229
Turning, 159, 206, 223, 237, 298, 338
Tweit, Mrs. Thorliff, 366
Tweten, J. O., 357
Tweten, Mrs. J. O., 229

Ulvilden, George J., 263, 358
Ulvilden, Kathryn M., 294, 368
Union, 75, 99, 161, 387
Union Hotel (Decorah), 54
Unit, student society, 114
United Christian Education Appeal, 310
United Church Seminary (St. Paul), 167
United Evangelical Lutheran Church, 16, 318
United Norwegian Lutheran Church in America, 15, 16, 167, 187, 389
United States Naval Reserve, 280
United States Office of Education, 309
United States Public Health Service, 315

427

Index

University Fund, 45, 48, 86, 378
"University men," 12, 13, 14, 15, 18, 35, 77, 84, 92, 105, 106, 377, 380, 385
University of Christiania, *see* Royal Fredrik University
University of Michigan, 191, 329
University of Minnesota, 112, 289, 290, 328
University of Wisconsin, 24, 92, 98, 112, 307, 311, 330
Upper Iowa River, 66

Valder, Charles H., 150
Valder Business College (Decorah), 92, 150
Valders (Norway), 306
Valders (Wis.), 306
Valders Memorial Hall of Science, 278, 305, 306, 312, 315, 332
Vanaheim, college building, 284
Vanderbilt, R. Kermit, 398
Vangsness, Ole P., 118
Veblen, A. A., 91, 93, 96, 99, 109, 121
Veglahn, Arnold (Judge), 299, 338
Veterans of Foreign Wars, 283
Vetlesen, Georg Unger, 331
Vick's Heating and Plumbing (Decorah), 398
Viker, Joe H., 237
Vinger, Torgeir, 376
Vinje, John, 1
Vischer, Christine D., 368
Voldeng, M. Nelson, 162
Volk, Leonard W., 174

Wagner, Beulah O., 369
Wagner, Roger, 323
Waldeland, Conrad R., 289, 293, 369
Walhus, Nora, 370
Waller, Martinus C., 369
Walstad, Orlow M., 369
Walther, C. F. W., president of Concordia Seminary, 35, 59, 131, 378; in slavery controversy, 79, 81, 84, 85, 86, 384, 385
Wanberg, Larrie D., 369
Warbington, Mrs. A. Lee, 365
Wartburg College (Waverly, Iowa), 376

Washington, George, 2, 215
Washington Prairie (Iowa), Norwegian settlement, 30, 36, 127, 194
Waters, Alfred, 333
Webster, student society, 155
Weenaas, August, 10, 90
Weihe, Clifton M., 398
Weinkauf, Ferneva F., 299
Weiser, Charles J., 175, 258
Weiser residence, college building, 258
Wergeland, Henrik, 386
Werthwein, Pearl, 200
West Decorah (Iowa), 173, 209
Westly, Malcolm K., 369
Wheaton, Harold, 296
Whistler, James A. McNeill, 288
White, Bertha S., 311
White, Nell W., 312
Wiener, Elaine, 369
Wiese, Markus F., 193
Wik, Esther L., 369
Wiley Piano Co. (Minneapolis), 311
Williams, Mrs. Clarence E., 367
Williams, Norman, 334
Willmar (Minn.) Seminary, 143, 274
Wilson, George A., 279
Wilson, Harlan D., 338
Winneshiek County (Iowa), courthouse, 172; roads, 228. *See also* Decorah
Winneshiek County Farm Bureau, 48
Winneshiek County State Bank (Decorah), 175, 255
Winneshiek Hotel (Decorah), 151, 279
Winona (Minn.) *Herald*, 237
Winterlin, DeWayne E., 369
Wisconsin, Norwegian settlements, 2, 3, 4, 12, 38, 129
Wisconsin Synod, 89
Wittman, Thalia, 333
Wold, Elliot R., 326, 369
Wold, Erling H., 369, 372
Wold, Mrs. Erling H., 334
Wold, Margaret Barth, 369
Wold, Ruth G., 333
Wollan, G. B., 160, 351
Wollan, Pernille L., 369
Woolery, Arlo D., 369
Women's Recreation Association, 299

428

Women's Self-Governing Association, 295, 332
Woodwood Wilson fellowships, 327
Woods Charitable Fund, 315
Works, George A., 265
World War I, 171, 179, 185–187, 198, 202, 206, 209, 210, 249, 276, 280, 283, 396
World War II, 271, 279, 282, 283, 285, 295, 301, 304, 309, 317, 331
Wraalstad, Jørgen Olsen, 82
Wraalstad, Ole Olsen, 82
Wrestling, 339
Wulfsberg, Einar, 369
Wyneken, Henry C., 137

Ygdrasil, student society, 114, 115
Ylvisaker, Carl B., 208
Ylvisaker, Ivar D., 146, 156, 163, 211
Ylvisaker, J. Wilhelm, 357, 369; administration, 303–341; quoted, 303, 323; sketch, 303; policies, 304, 340; characterized, 304; building program, 305–308; president of Iowa College Foundation, 313

Ylvisaker, Mrs. J. Wilhelm, 303
Ylvisaker, James William, 303
Ylvisaker, Johan Th., 136, 150
Ylvisaker, Johannes Th., 111, 175, 303
Ylvisaker, Lauritz S., 206, 207
Ylvisaker, Martha Elizabeth, 303
Ylvisaker, Nils M., 163, 357
Ylvisaker, Sigurd C., 186, 191, 207
Ylvisaker, Skak J. N., 222, 229, 242, 356
Ylvisaker family, 303
Young, Frisbie L., 220, 273
Young People's Association of the Norwegian Synod, 199
Youngberg, Karin, 369

Zaiser, Carl Freshwater, 369
Zastrow, Joyce R., 369
Ziegler, B. C., Co. (West Bend, Wis.), 398
Zorn, Anders L., 288
Zumbrota (Minn.), church, 274